KU-488-639

HIGHWAYS AND BYWAYS

IN

SOMERSET

MACMILLAN AND CO., LIMITED
LONDON . BOMBAY . CALCUTTA
MELBOURNE

THE MACMILLAN COMPANY
NEW YORK . BOSTON . CHICAGO
DALLAS . SAN FRANCISCO

THE MACMILLAN CO. OF CANADA, LTD.
TORONTO

Wells Cathedral. The North-west Tower and North Porch.

Highways and Byways

IN

Somerset

BY

EDWARD HUTTON

WITH ILLUSTRATIONS BY

NELLY ERICHSEN

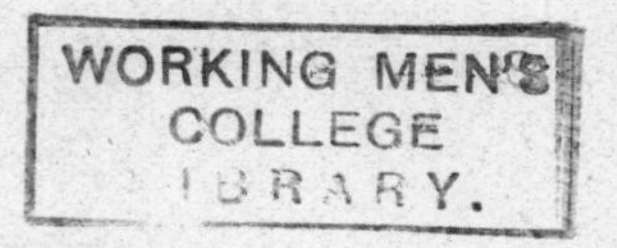

MACMILLAN AND CO., LIMITED
ST. MARTIN'S STREET, LONDON
1912

RICHARD CLAY AND SONS, LIMITED,
BRUNSWICK STREET, STAMFORD STREET, S.E.
AND BUNGAY, SUFFOLK

INTRODUCTION

THE traveller who on his way southward from Bath leaves that ancient city at dawn, as it were out of the old South Gate, by Southgate Street, and, crossing the Avon, takes the Holloway up Beechen Cliff and so follows the Fosse Way as well as he can through Radstock and Stratton, up hill and down dale, will come at evening on the crest of Mendip, which is there called Beacon Hill, upon one of the most astonishing views in all Southern England. For suddenly and without warning, from that great height he will see spread out beneath him a vast and mysterious plain, blue and grey and gold in the setting sun, and beyond, far and far away, the great broken hills of the West Country. To one returning after long absence that view must always be the most beautiful and the most consoling in the world, for it gives him at a glance all his childhood and his home.

Much else doubtless he may see as he lingers there: the boundaries of his beloved kingdom, the chalk hills of Wiltshire in the east, the shining Channel to the west, to the south the dark highlands of Dorset and Devon, and to the north the spurs of the Cotswolds; but this chiefly—his home, the whole county of Somerset from Bath and Bristol to Dunkery Beacon, from Penselwood and the Blackdown Hills to the Severn Sea.

Such a prospect as that, common enough in Italy, is rare in England. So in Tuscany one coming out of the Forest at sunset on Mont' Amiata suddenly beholds the Patrimony; so one coming out of the Roman gate of Siena on the Via

Francigena is suddenly king of all that country; so one coming over the shoulder of Monte Cimino from Viterbo suddenly sees beneath him the City, the Campagna, and the Latin Plain. In Southern England, however, I know but two sights that for admiration may be compared with these. I mean the first sudden breathless view of the Weald and the South Downs to be had from Leith Hill in Surrey; and the equally sudden wonder of Salisbury spire, a thing to stop the heart, as one comes weary at evening round a corner of the Downs near Figsbury Ring. Yet fine as these two prospects are they have neither the mystery nor the enchantment of the wide land of mere and fen, with its isolated hills and enclosed valleys, its great far-stretched uplands, and its sea, which Beacon Hill still gives us from Mendip.

I remember very well the first time I stood there on that old Roman road on Mendip, and, with all the faith and astonishment of a child, believed I saw the world spread out beneath me with its cities: Bristol there in the north trailing banners of smoke, wind-blown, the port of the sea; Bath, radiant and beautiful, upon the hills; Wells under my feet, mysteriously quiet, half hidden in a secret valley, a city out of a Missal; Taunton with shining, wind-vaned towers. . . . I remember all the places of the world were there, I counted them all. Here on the hill-top the Legion halted ere it went singing down the Way—to Rome. There, mysteriously alone, islanded in the evening mist, rose Avalon where St. Joseph hid the Grail. Beyond loomed Camelot, very dark and strong, that was King Arthur's, that had seen Guinevere go by, and heard the tumult and the shouting. Yonder in the marsh lay Athelney that hid King Alfred, and Wedmore, where he curbed the Danes. Somewhere on that long and melancholy coast Earl Harold hailed from Ireland. . . . It is a glory that cannot pass away.

And now when half my life is spent, as I wait on Beacon Hill in these September evenings for the sunset to transfigure the vast, low, empty moors and to discover to me the sea, I ask myself what it means to me, this my home, now that between it and me there shines all the gold of Italy. And it seems to me that I think of it as perhaps the last stronghold of English life, of English poetry and legend. It keeps alive for me and in me the ideal England of my heart. It actually embodies a life that never perhaps really existed, but is the only true life nevertheless. And the noble architecture both of manor and cottage, village church and cathedral, set as it is in natural surroundings often of rare beauty and always of great peace, seems to me the expression of something that is perhaps no longer to be found in the world, or is there in no satisfying quantity.

Indeed, what remains in my mind most deeply, coming home as it were, as I have done, after a long absence, is a curiously solemn sense of having witnessed the passing of the old order, the crumbling of the old system, feudal still and with much that we shall regret.

And I ask myself as I wait on Beacon Hill, the old Roman road dim in the twilight before me, what is to take the place of all that I have known and loved and thought good? And I ask myself, what is about to befall my home?

E. H.

September, 1912.

NOTE

I MUST express my gratitude and thanks to all those who have helped me in so many ways in the writing of this book and especially to my brother, Walter Hutton, for his notes upon stag hunting. My indebtedness to former writers upon Somersetshire History and Archaeology is, of course, very great, and I would especially acknowledge my debt to the contributors to the *Proceedings of the Somersetshire Archaeological Society* and to the various writers of the *Victoria County History of Somerset*, vols. 1 and 2.

E. H.

CONTENTS

CHAPTER XVII

CHAPTER XVIII

CHAPTER XIX

CHAPTER XX

CHAPTER XXI

CHAPTER XXII

LIST OF ILLUSTRATIONS

HIGHWAYS AND BYWAYS

IN

SOMERSET

HIGHWAYS AND BYWAYS

IN

SOMERSET

CHAPTER I

BATH

As you discern the long lines of her terraces, so orderly for England, about the vast amphitheatre of her hills, you might think Bath, even from the railway, the capital of some Italian province, a Latin city, full of Roman traditions and memories of the south.

Florence in England you might say indeed, with Landor, as you make your way about those beautiful hill-sides that everywhere look down upon the city, through which, not the tawny Arno, but the crystal Avon flows; and more especially perhaps if you come to her first along the road from London or through Widcombe from that truly Italian palace Prior Park, under Combe Down, or, better still, from Charlcombe on the shoulder of Lansdown between white villas and garden-walls hung with stone-crop and geraniums and battlemented with roses as though Charlcombe were Settignano.

Nevertheless on a nearer view something pleasantly and even characteristically English in those sober streets and quiet crescents obscures your first impression until you are ready to discern, and above all in the grey towers and pinnacles, the lean buttresses and traceried windows of the

Bath. West Front of the Abbey with the Pump Room.

great church of the place something peculiarly your own. And yet little by little, even there too you seem to find something —how shall I say?—alien, strange. That great church you note, stands not in any green close as you might expect, but in a paved piazza in the very midst of the city ; while the street which was at first sight most unmistakeably English, proves on closer acquaintance to be in truth a way older far than any English town.

And so at evening in the twilight as you loiter perhaps on Beechen Cliff for the sake of the view, or pass down one of those great silent terraces on Lansdown, or linger in the windy piazza by the Church, your first impression returns to you, and you remember the Roman city that lies buried at the roots of that you now see; and in a moment you understand that this alone of all English cities has by some fortune or some miracle remembered her origins, that those ruins on which she stands have in a very real way passed into her life, involved her in their beauty, and given her, as a free gift, something of their nobility ; that indeed they have attained to this much immortality, that they live again in her.

That Roman note which so many have found in Bath becomes ever more dominant as you linger with her; nor is it only to be explained by the fact that the Latin ruins upon which she stands are so considerable and so haunting in their fascination and interest. Bath, in fact, mainly, as we see her, a creation of the eighteenth century, added to and modified but not altogether spoilt in the nineteenth century, seems, if we compare her with her rivals in the South of England, Canterbury and Winchester for instance, scarcely English at all, to be, as we might think, out of our tradition.

Those cities of rosy brick, lovelier by far than Bath with the loveliness of that Middle Age of which they are full, and as English as the meadows in which they stand, fill with their fame the history of our country; but Bath has almost no memories of the Dark Age which brought St. Austin to Canterbury and established Winchester as the capital of England, and but few of mediaeval times. Founded by the Romans for the sake of her hot springs, she was ruined by the fall of the Empire and for over a thousand years she remained little more than a village clustered about a monastery, Roman still in this if you will, that the Church held what the Empire had abandoned, but of little or no national importance till her marvellous resurrection in that great classical period of English life, the eighteenth century, when once more, as in Roman times, and for the same reason, the city became the focus of fashionable life, and the Baths, after how much more than a millennium, were rediscovered and rebuilt; and for a brief hundred years, from the visit of Queen Anne in 1702, this city of western England became as it were the epitome of English social life, the school of manners of a new civilisation, the home and perhaps the inspiration of a new art which we regard as classical and look back upon, amid all the confusion of to-day, with reverence and regret.

Thus Bath, which had had almost no part, certainly no great part, in the history of England till then, suddenly in the eighteenth century comes to fill a great *rôle*, and what we see inevitably is not the creation of anything new, but the resurrection of the old Roman city with its beautiful classical buildings, its temples, as one might think, its palaces certainly, and its Thermae, so strange and so delightful in England, which give the city a unique splendour, built as they are of enduring stone and in so fortunate a moment.

That stately eighteenth century city, shining upon the western hills, full of a beautiful dignity that seems to draw its life, as it certainly does its beauty, from something older and greater than England, is the gate of Somerset; and since all western England, with its isolated hills and enclosed valleys, has everywhere something Roman about it, it is well that it should be held by so noble and so Roman a port as this.

I.

The origin of Bath, upon an unnavigable river, in a deep valley far from the centres of population and difficult of approach, is revealed by her name. Ptolemy, the geographer, calls the place Ὕδατα Θερμά, and the Roman Itinerary, Aquae Sulis; but it is doubtful whether the Romans were the first discoverers of the Springs which under them were to make Bath famous throughout Britain.

At any rate we have a legend recorded by Geoffrey of Monmouth which asserts that the healing qualities of the Bath waters were known to the Britons or ever the Romans came, and we should like to believe it if we might, for it connects Bath with the father of King Lear.

According to Geoffrey, Bladud, eighth in succession from Brutus the great-grandson of Venus, son and successor of the British King Hudibras, was a magician and in league with the Devil. He made the Bath by his magic skill, laying a "cunning stone" as big as a tree in the spring which made the water hot and healed the sick; and there he built a Temple in honour of that goddess whom Geoffrey calls Minerva. Bladud,

Bath. Pulteney Bridge.

according to Geoffrey, was also the first aviator, for desiring to fly like a bird, as many have done, he had wings made and mounted into the air by their aid in a bold flight, but presently meeting with contrary winds his strength failed and down he fell to be dashed to pieces upon the roof of the Temple of "Apollo." He had then reigned twenty years, and his son Lear, who had no son, but three daughters, Goneril, Regan and Cordelia, reigned after him.

Another and perhaps a later myth is recorded by Wood, who not only built the Bath we know but wrote an "Essay towards a Description of Bath," an amazing and interesting book. Here Bladud appears too, but as a leper dismissed from his father's court and employed as a swineherd at Keynsham. The pigs he breeds, however, are soon afflicted with his malady, and dreading the anger of his master he drives them across Avon at a place thereafter to be called Swineford, on the pretext that the acorns are finer on the northern side of the stream. Thence the swine rush violently downhill and plunge into the muddy morass below. Presently Bladud discovers that they are healed, bathes himself, and, driving the pigs back to their owner, returns to court and erects baths, and even builds a city, upon the place of his healing, living and reigning there for many years, till indeed he attempts to fly and is killed as recorded in the former story.[1]

These legends, though certainly false in their details, would seem to bear witness to the probable fact that the hot springs were known to the Britons before the advent of the Romans, who thus only turned to the account of civilisation what barbarism had but vaguely known how to employ.

However this may be, the place was occupied at the beginning of the Romano-British period, probably in the reign of the Emperor Claudius and certainly in that of Nero; and before the end of the first century the Roman civilisation had reached there a considerable development.

What the Romans built and continued there was in fact very much what Bath again became in the eighteenth century, though the Roman town was of course very much smaller than the eighteenth century city, occupying indeed but twenty-three acres; it was a mere watering place, a British Baia.

Let us put out of our heads once and for all, if we are to get any real ideal of Roman Bath, the picture of a fortress or even of a military post. Bath was never that either in the early days of the Conquest or in later times. Nor was it a great

[1] An amusing variation is supplied by a modern, and, I think, a local poet:

> . . . Vex'd at the brutes alone possessing
> What ought to be a common blessing;
> He drove them thence in mighty wrath
> And built the stately town of Bath.
> The hogs thus banished by the prince
> Have lived in Bristol ever since.

municipality like Verulam or a colonia like Colchester, Lincoln, York, and Gloucester. It had no town council, nor a basilica, such as Silchester and Cirencester had; it was a small place, consisting of the Thermae, the Temple of the presiding Deity Sul, Sulis—the Romano-British Minerva,—and a number of houses; the whole surrounded probably by a wall or *vallum*. Solinus, writing in the third century of our era, thus describes it:—"In Britain are hot springs furnished luxuriously for human use; over these springs Minerva presides, and in her Temple the perpetual fire never whitens into ash, but as the flame fades, turns into rocky balls."

Roman Bath, which thus appears meagre enough, a place of far less importance than York or Colchester or Lincoln, than Silchester or Verulam, has yet yielded more Roman remains than all these put together and is in her ruin one of the most important Roman relics in the western provinces of the Empire. This is to be accounted for easily enough I think, by the fact of the geographical position of Bath, far from the centres of population, and of the enduring stone of which, unlike other Roman towns in Britain, she was then built as she is to-day.

I have said the Roman town consisted but of twenty-three acres. The centre of this area would have been found where the Abbey Church-yard is now; and the boundary walls, for the town was probably walled completely, and certainly on the north, where remains have been found, ran, as is thought, along the line occupied later by the walls of the mediæval city; that is to say on the north along what we call Upper Borough Walls, on the west along Westgate Buildings, on the south along the Lower Borough Walls, and on the east, more doubtfully, just outside the Weymouth House school and Orange Grove. As to the date of these walls we know nothing; if we are to apply to them the general rule of the Western Provinces we should have to consider them as late, as belonging indeed to the last years of the Roman civilisation in Britain.

We are equally ignorant of the site of the gates, for no remains of them have been discovered, nor have we any clue as to the certain direction of the streets within the town; no pavement, no building frontage have been found in Bath, and the two streets of the modern city, Union Street and Stall

Street, which are supposed to represent the Fosse Way within the Roman town, through which it certainly passed, are later than Roman times; for Roman Thermae underlie Stall Street, and Union Street is absolutely modern.[1]

There remain to be discussed the buildings of Aquae Sulis; these so far as we have any evidence consisted of the Thermae, a Temple of Sul-Minerva and the dwelling houses of the inhabitants.

It has always been known that there were Roman baths at Bath, but we knew nothing definite concerning them till a century and a half ago, and it is only with the last twenty-five years that our knowledge can be called systematic. To this day we do not know who built and owned the baths, nor whether they were in public or in private hands. Tomb-stones and inscriptions have told us something of the bathers, the visitors to Aquae Sulis. Many of these were legionaries. Three came from the Sixth Legion at York, three from the Twentieth at Chester, and one from the Second Augusta at Caerleon. Others were Romano-British civilians, and we know of a town councillor from Gloucester and a sculptor from Cirencester. Others again were what we should call foreigners and came for the sake of the waters from Northern Gaul, from so far as Metz and Chartres, but not from south of the Alps. The dates of these visits begin early and continue right through the Roman years, and we learn from coins that Bath was still inhabited at least till the year 400.

All this is little enough; but even this we should probably not know if early in the eighteenth century Bath had not suddenly become popular as a watering place among the wealthier classes. The first discovery of Roman remains was made in 1727; exactly what was then found we do not know, though we possess the gilt bronze head of Minerva about life size and of excellent workmanship, which was then recovered and is now in the Pump Room. In 1755, in the course of pulling down a house to make room for the Duke of Kingston's baths, a large swimming basin was found, and traces of the Great Bath were discovered; but little more was done

[1] *Cf. Victoria County History of Somerset* (Constable, n. d.), vol. i, p. 228. I am very deeply indebted to Professor Haverfield's articles both here in my account of Roman Bath and elsewhere in my account of Roman things within the county.

till, in 1878, the Corporation of Bath employed the late Major Davis, then the city architect, to conduct extensive excavations, with the result that between 1880 and 1896 the Great Bath was wholly uncovered, the Circular Bath was brought to light, the bath west of this explored, and, together with a vast number of smaller details, the large rectangular bath under Stall Street was excavated (1896). These discoveries cover about an acre of ground; the original extent of the bath was somewhat greater.[1]

One comes into the ruins to-day from the north out of the Abbey Church-yard. To the north-west lie the hot springs, under the King's Bath, rising directly into a Roman reservoir, with walls some six feet high and three feet thick, which still supplies the baths. This wonderful piece of construction unhappily cannot now be seen. The main building, in the ruin of which one stands, contains the Great Bath, seventy-three by twenty-nine feet, a really splendid Roman construction, the floor covered with lead, forty pounds to the foot, which the Romans obtained from their mines in the Mendips. It was surrounded by pavements fourteen feet wide, upon which, close to the waters, to the north and south of the great Bath, stand the ruins of the twelve great piers that upheld whatever roof covered the building, which in its full extent measured some sixty-eight by one hundred and ten feet. Its walls to the north and to the south contain recesses; a rectangular recess in the midst flanked by two of semicircular shape, each about eighteen feet wide.

To the west of the Great Bath, and directly south of the Reservoir under the King's Bath, stands the great Circular Bath, and to the west of this, and to the east of the Great Bath, are several large basins of various shapes. Beyond these on the east and on the south-west were the hot-air baths, great rooms filled with hypocausts. Nor was the drinker of the waters forgotten, a small Dipping Well has been found to the east of the Reservoir.

In workmanship, Professor Haverfield tells us the baths reached a high level, and they are the only Roman Thermal

[1] The best guide to the Roman Baths is that of Alfred J. Taylor, M.S A., published by the authority of the Corporation of Bath, price sixpence. It has an excellent plan.

Bath. Abbey and the Roman Baths.

baths in which any provision has been discovered for drinking the waters.

At the north-western corner of the Baths, close to the hot

spring, stood, as is supposed, the Temple of Sul-Minerva of which Solinus speaks. The remains were discovered in 1790, and consist of part of a wall, a pavement of large square slabs of freestone, some steps, and a mass of architectural fragments; among them parts of a remarkable tympanum, twenty-six feet by eight, consisting of twelve slabs in all, of which we possess six, the central panel being in the most excellent preservation. It is generally admitted that hardly another site north of the Alps can show the remains of a sculptured pediment, and none perhaps so striking an example as this. Though not designed upon a strictly classical model, in the main it follows good Roman precedent. Its decoration is a little excessive, perhaps a little awkward, but it is so full of life that we may well think we see here the work of some native genius. In the centre is a round shield upheld upon either side by Victories. Of the figures of the Victories only two small fragments are preserved, but the central carving of the shield and round boss, thirty inches in diameter, carved in low relief, is little short of amazing. There we see the face of the Gorgon Medusa which frequently appears upon Minerva's shield. This is shown in full face like a rising sun surrounded by locks of hair like tongues of fire, with beard and moustache too, a puzzled provincialism, perhaps, and frightening eyes under a scarred forehead. In its vigour and astonishing individuality this head is perhaps the most remarkable work of art not of Roman manufacture yet found in the western provinces. It has no trace of conventionality, but strikes one as an original work of native genius, which gives us a very noble conception of the work that Roman civilisation had accomplished in this island.

That the Temple of Sul Minerva and the Thermae were the chief buildings of Aquae Sulis would seem to be certain, but they obviously did not stand alone. About them must have stood the houses of the inhabitants and of these we have many traces within the circuit of the walls, though of course no complete house. Most of them seem to have stood in the north-west corner of the place, on the site now occupied by the Bluecoat School and the Mineral Water Hospital. The chief finds, made in 1738, in 1859, in 1884 and in 1897 consist of mosaics, wall tiles, and miscellaneous coins covering a vast period of time, with ornaments, and bone pins, pewter vessels, and a bag of exquisite gems, yet all save the last curious rather than beautiful, but assuring us, in their humble way, as surely as Hadrian's Wall can do, of our part in that great civilisation; of the fact that we too are heirs of the Empire.

And seeing that Bath was a health resort we should naturally expect to find beside the Baths, the Temple, and the houses, a cemetery. This, as in every Roman town, lay outside the walls along the great road, and here in Aquae Sulis we find it upon the Fosse Way in the level space between Lansdown and the Avon.

All these, and especially the perfection of the Thermae, their size and beauty, give us perhaps a better and a firmer idea of what the Romanisation of Britain was, than anything we can see elsewhere; yet when we consider the long continuance here of Latin civilisation—more than three hundred and fifty years—we cannot but be astonished at the poverty of its remains, above all of its Christian remains. The Thermae here in Bath, the Wall in the North, give us an impression of an advanced and permanent civilisation; but the monumental remains generally are so few as to seem to cast a doubt upon it.

Yet even to-day from Odd Down, or better from the top of Mendip, we are spectators of one of the most astonishing, enduring, and splendid achievements of Rome to be found anywhere within the Empire—I mean that dauntless road, the Fosse Way, which the Romans drove over hill, over dale, through forest and through marsh, straight as a javelin thrust from Bath to Chard and Axminster and beyond. Even to-day as we look on it from Beacon Hill it is a wonder evoking all our past; what must it have seemed to the Celtic barbarians that presently under Roman influence were to call themselves *Romani*, to write and speak in Latin, and to be not altogether unworthy of the Roman name? It can have seemed nothing less than the symbol of an everlasting government and order in the world. For consider the physical condition of Somerset: those broken hills to the south-west that the Fosse skirted but did not cross, those wide mysterious marshes scarcely inhabited till then, that tremendous rampart of the Mendips that the Fosse took as an arrow flies, and all the broken country between the crest of those hills and Bath. What did the Briton know of roads? He had but his track ways upon the hills.

The Fosse Way gives us the key to "Roman Somerset." It is the one great Roman road within the borders of our county which made a part of the main Roman road system of Britain. Yet though we call the great series of Roman roads that stretches from Exeter through Bath to Lincoln the Fosse Way, it is doubtful whether the Romans regarded it as one road, whether indeed the road which continues the Fosse from Bath to Cirencester was any more a part of the road from Exeter to Bath than was the road from Bath to London. Nevertheless we may regard the Fosse as one throughout its length, as one of the main Roman roads of the country and the only one that was not based on London.

Its route through Bath, which it certainly entered on the south and left on the north, can no longer be traced. But it ran from Bath south-west by Camerton,[1] Shepton Mallet, and Ilchester, then a little to the east of Chard to Axminster. It is as I have said the key to "Roman Somerset." For though Somerset is comparatively rich in Roman remains other than military, they are very partially distributed. Roughly it may be said that those regions of the county not served by the great road have yielded but few if any signs of Roman habitation. Thus all West Somerset, the great region of Exmoor and the Quantocks, the pleasant vale of Taunton Deane then undrained, and the impassable wide marshes of the Brue and the Parret, between Somerton and the sea, seem never to have known the civilisation of Rome, which we find almost entirely grouped along the Fosse Way and upon the two minor roads which served it.

For there were other Roman roads in Somerset, the chief being that which might seem to continue the road from London to Bath which runs west by north out of that city to Avonmouth and the Severn crossing. After leaving Bath it soon passes out of Somerset, however, and leaving Bristol a little to the south never touches our county again. Another road certainly of Roman origin is that which leaves the Fosse on Mendip top and runs due west along the crest. It served the Mendip lead mines. Yet another left the Fosse at Ilchester and made for Dorchester; and it is supposed by some archaeologists that a Roman road was built upon the old

[1] The Fosse has been excavated at Radstock. See *Proc. Som. Arch. Soc.*, vols. xxx and l, p. 108.

British trackway that may still be traced from Beacon Hill through Maiden Bradley to Old Sarum.

We may well ask here what we mean by Roman civilisation in Somerset. Materially in Britain as in most of the other provinces of the Empire, but especially in Gaul, we may distinguish it in two forms: in the town and in the villa. There were many towns in Britain, but they were for the most part small. The great *municipia* and *coloniae* of the greater and older provinces, the highest form of ordered and civilised life known to the Romans, are rare in Britain, which can boast indeed of but five examples, and none of them in Somerset; the *coloniae* of Colchester, Lincoln, York and Gloucester, and the *municipium* of Verulam. Yet though Somerset possessed nothing like these, in Bath she had a real Roman town. Aquae Sulis was, indeed, not only the largest town within the borders of the county, but it was a town as we have seen of a peculiar sort not to be matched elsewhere within the Province of Britain.

The only other places in Somerset that can make any claim to have been Roman towns or villages are Ilchester and perhaps Camerton. Both are upon the Fosse Way and both would appear to have been small.

The other material witness to Roman civilisation in Britain was the villa, and these as we might expect were common in Somerset, though never very far from the highways. For the most part they stand upon either side of the Fosse Way. What the Manor was to the men of the Middle Ages the villa was to the Romans; an estate, that is, the property of a great landowner who dwelt in the "great" or, as we should say, the Manor House, and cultivated his land partly perhaps with slave labour and partly by letting it to *coloni*, possibly semi-servile in condition. The landowners generally would seem to have been Romanised Britons, nobles or men of the upper classes of the native population, not Roman officials, or Italians. Their peasantry lived about them in huts or small hamlets, and though they seem to have had few comforts and no luxuries, their civilisation was Roman. Roman too were the art and furniture of their life; and if the houses both in town and country do not conform to those we know so well in Pompeii for instance, but rather to those of Northern Gaul, and are, in fact, what we know as Corridor houses, consisting of a straight row of rooms opening upon a corridor, they would seem to have been none the less Roman on that account. For the Roman has always been known rather for what he has adapted to his use than for what he has invented, and he would have been the first to see that what was useful in the heat of the south would be useless in the northern cold and wet.

The last feature that we are aware of in the Roman civilisation in Somerset is industrial; the Mendip lead mines. They too, like the hot mineral springs of Bath, were known to the pre-Roman Celts and they at once became among the most important industries of Roman Britain.

It remains to account for the government and the administration of "Roman Somerset." We know very little about it, but dimly we may distinguish in Britain three units of administration under the Romans; that of the five *municipia*, each with its own territory, which of course had no place in Somerset; that of the Imperial domains under Imperial officials; and that of those parts of Britain which were neither municipal nor Imperial areas, which were ruled, as in Northern Gaul, by Cantonal authorities. In Somerset only the Mendip Lead Mines and their region were Imperial property; the rest of what is now Somerset was probably ruled by the Cantonal authorities: the nobles and chiefs of pre-Roman days, who ruled under Roman powers and administered Roman Law, and were called *duoviri* and their assembly the *Ordo*. Of such a government in Somerset we have no trace as yet, and it seems unlikely that we shall now find any evidence of what we may think nevertheless certainly existed.

What then may we say of the Romans in Britain and in Somerset? This certainly, that to south Britain at any rate they brought an old and an ordered civilisation, the Christian religion, an universal language, a great literature, and an immutable peace. All this grew up and endured during some three hundred and fifty years. Suddenly, during the lifetime of one man, all was swept away.

By the year 407 the Legions had been called away; three years later, in the August of 410, Alaric sacked the City. In that tremendous disaster not for Rome only but for the whole world it is something to know that we did what we could even though Britain fell by that act. For those Legions which departed one after another down the long roads through Britain, through Gaul, for the defence of Italy were filled with the strength, the hope, and the endurance of our forefathers. These were no Italian troops but the same as many a time since have held a breach as desperate in a new cause, yet the same, and—*Deo gratias*—with a better success.

The Legions departed and with them our youth, our hope, and our confidence. Already before Alaric thundered at the iron gates of Italy or the watchmen on the towers of Aquileia descried far off upon the mountains the barbarian hosts, or red Verona heard the Gothic shouting, sometimes in the summer mists, or hardly through the foam of the winter seas, we had seen the beaked ships of the barbarian hovering about our coasts, in the night we had been afraid, fancying their voices, and in the day time had threatened our children with their mystery and terror. But when our youth and strength were gone with the Legions, when the Wall was deserted, the little Picts already at their work, and strange ships from the east, without fear any more, raided our coasts and sacked our villages, we must at last have understood that the end was at hand. Many of us left Britain for Armorica; how many we can never know. Of those of us who remained, if we may believe the legend, the only literature of the Fall, it can be said that we did not altogether disgrace ourselves though we failed to hold our island.

It may well be that the heroic defence which was made by the Romano-British chiefs and peoples centred at last in Somerset and perhaps in Glastonbury, as it was to do again four hundred years later against a more cruel but less successful foe. What we know is this, and it is so little that it goes for nothing. It seems that of true invasions as distinct from raids, that of the Jutes was first, and befell in 408, we may think; they landed as our auxiliaries against the Picts; they betrayed us and seized a kingdom in Kent. In the following year, 409, according to Prosper Tiro, the friend of St. Austin, "the provinces of Britain were laid waste by the incursions of the Saxons." Later, the same chronicler tells us that "the provinces of Britain, which up to this time had been torn by various slaughters and disasters, are brought under the dominion of the Saxons." That is all we know about it, and that is hearsay. We said to ourselves, The Empire is fallen.

The Empire was fallen. From the year 407 when the Legions had departed till the year 596 when they returned as the Benedictines of St. Augustine, there is a space of near two centuries in Britain when all is night. We know nothing of what then befell, only we see shapes in the darkness, some terrible and confused, bearing uncouth names, eager only for slaughter; some beautiful and heroic, which seem to sum up all Romance and will live for ever in the legends of our island. Such is Arthur and his knights, who here and now if at all appear upon the scene of history.

For the barbarians were not to have it altogether their own way. Even then there was one who in the midst of despair stood for the Faith and our past and to whom—surely he knew it—the whole future belonged. *Hic jacet Arthurus, rex quondam, rexque futurus.*

It may well have been now that we built the Wansdyke to keep out the invaders who came at first from the north-east. But according to the Saxon Chronicle, in the year 495 a new invasion of Britain was achieved by Cerdic and Cynric, who seem to have landed in Southampton Water. Slowly they subdued Hampshire and part of Wiltshire and about the year 516 were signally defeated in the battle of Mount Badonicus, probably at Badbury in Dorset, by Arthur and his knights. Here and elsewhere that heroic figure flung back the invasion from Somerset and Glastonbury, so that we read when Old Sarum fell at last to the invader in 552 the church of Amesbury had to be deserted and we took up the precious dust of Guinevere and bore it with us, Lancelot did, to the island of Glaston to lie for ever beside Arthur. Such is the legend which would seem to speak truth, at least in this, that Glastonbury was safe when all Wessex proper was in the hands of the Saxons.

Even when in 577 the Battle of Deorham in Gloucestershire had given Ceawlin of Wessex, Gloucester, Cirencester, Bath, and Somerset as far as the crest of the Mendips, the marshes of Glastonbury were still inviolate.[1] And so slow was the

[1] What has been considered as the earliest piece of real history with regard to Glastonbury is the grant of Gwrgan, King of Damnonia, in 601 of the land of Ynyswitrin to the "old church." Freeman believed this document, which W. of Malmesbury copied, to be genuine. In 601 then the "old church" was still safe.

progress of the Barbarian invaders that it was not till Cenwalh's time a century later, after the battles of Bradford-on-Avon and Penselwood in 658, that the Saxon border was advanced from the Mendips to the Parret and the larger and wealthier part of Somerset came into Saxon hands. Before then, however, the Legions had returned, St. Augustine was in Canterbury, St. Birinus had converted the West Saxons and had been laid to rest in the church at Winchester which Cenwalh had built. Glastonbury was safe[1] and with Glaston the future. For she was not only the oldest centre of Christianity in Britain, which possibly from apostolic times stood inviolate till the Reformation; she was something more than that; a kind of symbol assuring us of our past and of all that out of which we are come.

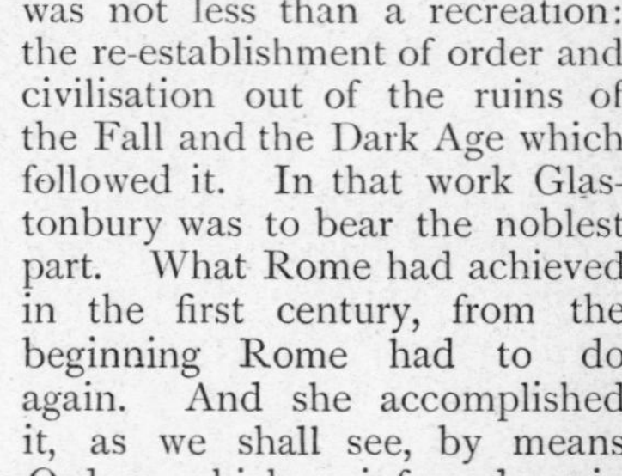

Wells Cathedral.
The Apple Stealer.

What had now to be achieved was not less than a recreation: the re-establishment of order and civilisation out of the ruins of the Fall and the Dark Age which followed it. In that work Glastonbury was to bear the noblest part. What Rome had achieved in the first century, from the beginning Rome had to do again. And she accomplished it, as we shall see, by means of the monks, the Religious Orders, which, reinforced again and again century after century, here as elsewhere rebuilt Europe.

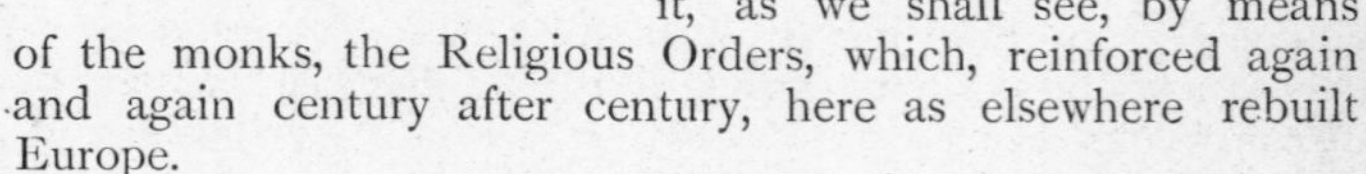

II.

THE fate of Bath in the Fall of the Empire, the failure of the Roman administrative power in Britain and the terror which followed it, remains, as does indeed the fate of every British city at that crisis, obscure and uncertain. We know that Somerset, that part of Western England we now call Somerset, was free from Saxon invasion till Ceawlin had won the battle

[1] W. of Malmesbury tells us that Cenwalh was even a benefactor to Glastonbury, but the charter which claims to be his is spurious.

of Deorham in 577, which certainly brought Bath into his power, and probably gave him all Somerset to the crest of the Mendips or the edge of the difficult if not impassable marshes to the south of those great hills. But whether the Saxons took Bath by storm as tradition has it, or whether, as the moderns suggest, the city was abandoned at their approach we do not know. This much seems certain, however, that in either case Aquae Sulis was not left for any length of time without inhabitants, that there is no real hiatus here any more than there is elsewhere in our history.

The evidence we have, it must be admitted, is meagre enough and indeed in so far as it is archaeological—and it is almost entirely archaeological—proves almost nothing, for similar evidence might be advanced to prove the desertion and abandonment of Rome. It is asserted that the inhabitation of the site of Bath must have ceased, because in 1755 a Saxon cemetery, not in date earlier than 978, was discovered under the Abbey House and above the eastern parts of the Baths. Obviously, it is said, the Roman ruins were covered with earth when these burials were made, and, therefore, a great gap must exist between Romano-British Aquae Sulis and English Bath. Similar evidence, as I have said, might be brought forward to prove that a great gap must exist between the Rome of the Kings and the Rome of the Republic, between the Republican and the Imperial city, between the Rome of the Emperors and the Rome of the Popes, between the Mediaeval and the Renaissance city. We know that no such gap does in fact exist, that civilisation in the City is continuous and unbroken, and we may well believe that the same is true here in Bath.

But indeed if it were necessary to support a view so merely reasonable one might refer the sceptic to the lines of that unknown poet of the eighth century who describes the ruin of Aquae Sulis, that beautiful place, and the wonder with which even then the relics of Roman greatness struck the mind:—

"Wondrous to behold is the wall stone, that fate hath broken, the stronghold burst asunder, the work of giants decaying, the roofs fallen, the grey gates despoiled, the mouldering palaces roofless, the weather-marked masonry, the shattered shelters time scarred, tempest marred, undermined of old. Earth's grasp holdeth its mighty builders, tumbled, crumbled, in the earth's hard grip till a hundred generations of men pass away. Often this wall, now fern-tufted and lichen spotted, withstood chieftain after chieftain rising in storm. Bright was the borough place, and many the princely halls and high the roof of gold. And the court is dreary and the crowned roof lies in the shadow of the purple arch. . . . Princes of old time, joyous and goldbright and splendidly decked, proud and with wine elated in war-gear they share. They looked on their treasures, on silver and gems, and on stones of price and on this bright borough of their broad realm. The stone court stands, the hot stream hath whelmed it, there where the bath was hot on the breast." [1]

If this beautiful description refer to Bath, as seems indeed most likely, and if, as is generally allowed, it were written in the eighth century, at least it proves the existence, above ground, of vast ruins at that time. But certainly, by then, and probably much earlier, a convent had been founded at Bath. Are we to believe that this was established, in those uncertain days, in an utterly desolate and deserted place? It is impossible. If, as we have good authority for believing, Osric, the under-King of the Huiccas in the kingdom of Mercia, founded a convent in Bath on the 6th November, 676, we must consider the city as at least sparsely inhabited; and with the nuns Rome herself had returned.

Between the victory of Ceawlin at Deorham in 577 and the establishment of that nunnery by Osric there is a space of just ninety-nine years. How are we to fill them? Where all is theory he is wisest who holds most closely to commonsense. It is probable, as we have seen, that in the height of her splendour Aquae Sulis was an unwalled city, that the walls were built only when the long decline of Roman power began. That decline antedated the final departure of the Legions by certainly three generations. It was never arrested, and it is possible and even probable that the latter half of the fourth century saw Bath already in a sort of decay. The public buildings were not kept in due repair, the roads even may have been neglected, and a long drawn out financial crisis probably caused men to hoard what money they possessed. When the first pirates landed they found in Britain an administration already ruined, and their long series of attacks, ending at last probably in regular but always barbarian invasions, would seem to bear witness to an already decentralised social system and government. But weak and isolated as that civilisation was, and more and more became, it lived and continued to live

[1] Compare Earle in *Bath Field Club*, ii, 266 *et seq.*, and C. Elton in *Proc. Som. Arch. Soc.*, xxviii (1883), p. 16.

until, with the advent of St. Augustine, Rome once more took up her interrupted task.

Into Bath, as it seems, the heathen did not penetrate at all till the year 577; and all that, without any particular and definite evidence, we can presume to have happened then is that a condition of barbarism, of neglect that is, rather than of active destruction, took the place of the Romano-British civilisation, which, little by little, leavened the barbarian lump. The tradition was not lost, it endured till, reinforced from Rome, it was able to rise again in all its strength and to involve us all, victor and vanquished alike, in its own past and in its own future.

Till it was reinforced from Rome! Just that is what the founding of that convent perhaps as early as 676 really meant. Henceforth Aquae Sulis becomes a village grouped about a church and a convent, and this it remained till its transformation in the eighteenth century. The place does not even lose its name. What has been Aquae Sulis and in the later and Christian Roman times simply Aquae, becomes Akemanceaster[1] while Sul or Sulis would seem to survive in the name of that hill above Batheaston, Little Solsbury.

The nunnery of Bath lived for less than a century; but in 758 we find Cynewulf, King of the West Saxons, with the consent of Offa of Mercia granting land at North Stoke to the monks and their monastic church of St. Peter, at Bath. We know nothing of the foundation of this monastery, though according to tradition it was established by King Offa; we are equally ignorant of how it came to take the place of the convent founded by Osric, but perhaps the religious decline and abuse of monasticism that marked the opening years of the eighth century may account for the supersession of the nuns by the monks. It is at least significant that the monastery was at first made dependent upon Haethered, Bishop of Worcester, though only a few years later, in 781, we find the "celebrated monastery" at Bath a part of the royal demesne of Offa. But of this monastery and these monks, if monks they were, and not, as Leland has it, a college of secular priests, we know

[1] The derivation of the name is still a subject of controversy. Ake, according to some and perhaps the best authorities, is Aquae, Akeman meaning the place of the Bath. Others prefer to derive it from some chieftain Akeman.

nothing. It might seem probable that it was in some sort a monastery that Offa founded, that it suffered in the Danish wars, its discipline relaxed, and what happened elsewhere happened here in Bath, a hybrid order of *canonici*, seculars, that is, leading a collegiate life, bound to chastity and obedience but not to the renunciation of private property, gradually filched the house and lands of the monks. At any rate we find some sort of effort at reparation made in the earlier part of the tenth century by Athelstan, by Edmund and Edwy, and this, with the accession of Edgar, is immediately followed by the restoration and reform of the monasteries by St. Dunstan and certainly not less radically at Bath than elsewhere,[1] for there Edgar was crowned King on Whit Sunday, 973, "surrounded by a numerous crowd of priests, monks and nobles, with the utmost pomp, magnificence and festivity." What seems then to have been achieved was the introduction or the re-establishment of the Benedictines and their rule in Bath, and it is now for the first time we hear of an abbot, Aescwig by name.

It is, however, a more famous name than Aescwig's we connect with the abbey at this time. About the year 980 St. Elphege came to Bath as a hermit from the monastery of Deerhurst, with the laxity and worldliness of which he was dissatisfied. According to the *Golden Legend*, "St. Elphege the holy bishop and martyr was born in the shire of Gloucester,[2] and he came of a noble kin and was his father's heir, but he forsook all for God's love, and became a monk at Deerhurst, five miles from Gloucester; but afterwards good King Edward gave that home of Deerhurst to the house of St. Denys in France. And when St. Elphege had been monk there a long time living a full holy life, then he went from thence to the Abbey of Bath to be there in more contemplation and rest of

[1] Britton, *History and Antiquities of Bath Abbey Church*, says: "About this period (970) an important change was effected in the state of this foundation through the influence of the Papal See and the active bigotry of Archbishop Dunstan. . . . The Church of Rome finding the monks more completely devoted to its ambitious purposes than the Secular clergy, exerted the most strenuous efforts to expel the latter. . . . These measures were most zealously supported by King Edgar at the instigation of the bold and unprincipled Dunstan: . . . The canons of Bath were ejected about 970 and a convent of Benedictine monks were introduced."

[2] Others say at Weston, near Bath.

soul. And he builded there that fair abbey and established therein black monks and endowed it, and was himself therein the first abbot and founder. But he led there a full holy life, and much well he guided the monks in holy and virtuous living."

St. Elphege became successively Bishop of Winchester in 983 and Archbishop of Canterbury and was martyred by the Danes at Greenwich in 1012; and whether or no he was ever Abbot of Bath, the monastery probably owed a large increase in its fame and numbers to his presence there. At any rate it seems to have increased in influence and in wealth, and though we know little of it till the Norman Conquest, Domesday Survey credits it besides numerous and wide possessions in Somerset and Gloucester with the Manor of Bath and "in the same borough twenty-four burgesses who paid twenty shillings," a mill which produced the same sum and twelve acres of meadow. The church was also rich in relics.

A certain confusion here as elsewhere seems to have fallen upon the Abbey with the Conquest; we hear of two abbots ruling at the same time, but in 1087 both were dead and the Abbey seems to have been involved in the conspiracy of Odo, Bishop of Bayeaux, Geoffrey, Bishop of Coutances, and other Norman Barons against William Rufus, in which business the town had suffered and, as some have it, had been burned. However that may be, the Abbey, wanting an abbot, was seized by the king, who had just conferred the Bishopric of Wells upon his friend John de Villula, a native of Tours. This man was a skilful physician and is said by some to have practised his art at Tours. In 1075 the Council of London, no doubt moved by Rome, had urged the removal of Episcopal Sees from villages to towns, for such was the Roman plan of Christendom. Probably in furtherance of this design the Bishop John obtained from the King and Archbishop Lanfranc the Abbey of Bath and moved his See thither from Wells. At the same time the Bishop bought from the King the city of Bath "in free alms with all its appurtances, to hold and possess in as free and honourable a manner as the King himself held any city in England; together with its mint and all accustomed rights both within and without the same, with the toll money arising as well in the parks as the woods as well in the market as the meadows and other lands, that with the greater honour he may fix his pontifical seat there." John paid the King 500 silver marks for Bath in 1091. Thus the Abbey of Bath became a Cathedral church. Under the rule of Bishop John the small family of religious grew into a large and well organised community, the office of Abbot was lost in that of Bishop, the Prior and monks became the Bishop's chapter and the Bishop became lord of the City. John de Villula, himself a learned and successful man, loved the society of scholars, and no doubt the members of his community at Bath were swelled by the admission of many a Norman; but it is an English scholar who conferred the greatest lustre upon the Priory in the twelfth century, Adelard, who was born at Bath and who, having acquired his education at the Priory, studied at Tours and lectured upon philosophy in the school of Caen, and travelled as widely as any man of his time: in Spain, in North Africa, in Greece and Asia Minor, and lived in Sicily. He certainly knew Greek and probably Arabic, and wrote that notable philosophic treatise *De Eodem et Diverso*, in which he offers a solution of the difficulty of reconciling the real existence of the individual with the equally real existence of the species or genus.

John de Villula, with all his love of learning, was a great builder. He probably found the church of Bath, if not in ruins after the affair of 1087, at any rate too mean for his ambitions. Everywhere in England great buildings were rising with an extraordinary rapidity and an immense splendour, and here in Bath the little Saxon church seemed like a barn. The bishop devoted all his revenues both from the city and the See to the building of a new church and this with such enthusiasm that he had completed it as far as the lower vaultings before his death. In this great work—the nave alone of his vast Norman minster would have contained all the present church—he was assisted by two great Norman barons in Somerset. William de Moion gave him the church of Dunster and its possessions, which thus became a cell of Bath, and Walter de Douai gave the church of Bampton in Devon and half a hide of land. John de Villula also built himself a house, known as the Bishop's Bower, one great tower of which was still standing when after the suppression in the sixteenth century Leland visited Bath. For the public good he is said to have enclosed and conserved the mineral springs of the city and to have built there two baths, the Bishop's bath and the Prior's bath, though possibly these were restorations of Roman remains. Jovial and courteous in all his ways, he died of old age on December 29th, 1122, and was buried in the sanctuary of his new church.[1]

He left behind him the following document *ad perficieneum novum opus quod incepi*:—

"In the name of the Father and of the Son and of the Holy Ghost, Amen. I, John, by the grace of God, Bishop of Bath, to all Bishops my successors and to all the sons of Holy Church, greeting. Be it known unto you all that for the honour of God and S. Peter I have laboured, and at length effected with all decent authority that the Head and Mother Church of the Bishopric of Somerset shall be in the City of Bath, in the Church of S. Peter; to which holy Apostle, and to the monks his servants I have restored their lands which I formerly held unjustly in my own hands, in as free and ample a manner as Aldsius the late Abbot held them before me; and if I have improved them, and whatever of mine shall be found thereon, I give to them to their own use and property. I also give them for farther supply of their food and clothing and to increase the convent of the holy brethren serving God there, and to reimburse the Treasury which I took from the Church, those lands which I have acquired by my own travail, or bought with my own money;—to wit, those five hides in Weston, which I purchased of Patricius de Caurica and the land of Hugh *cum Barba*, to wit, Claverton, Docne, Mersfield, and Eston, together with Herley and Arnemunde on the sea coast, and whatsoever belongs to them; and one house in Bath and one other in Winchester. But as to the city of Bath, which first of all King William and after him his brother King Henry gave to S. Peter for their alms, I have pursuant to my vows determined that all issues and profits arising from it be laid out in perfecting the new work I have begun. Besides which I have acquired of church ornaments, in copes, in palls, in curtains, in dorsals, in tapestries, in crucifixes, in robes, in chalices, in phylacteries; and whatsoever of my own I have added in the episcopal chapel, my whole armoury, my clothes, my bowls, my plate, and all my household furniture I give to S. Peter and his monks for ever to their own use and property for the remission of my sins. Whosoever therefore shall infringe on this my gift, may the curse of God and of His Holy Apostles and Saints light on him and by the authority of me, though a sinner, let him be accursed and for ever cut off from the community of the Church.

"Done A.D. 1106 in the reign of Henry son of William Duke of Normandy and King of England, Anselm being Archbishop; of my ordination the nineteenth and of the induction the twelfth, and that this

[1] Leland says: "This John pulled down the old church of St. Peter at Bath and erected a new much fairer and was buried in the middle of the Presbyteri thereof, whose Image I saw lyng ther . . . at which Tyme all the Church that he made lay to wast, and was unrofed, and wedes grew about this John of Tours sepulchre." It was probably Bishop John who first properly walled the city.

my Deed may remain more firm and unshaken, I have with my own hand signed it with the sign of the Holy Cross ✠."

John de Villula, the greatest Bishop Bath was to know, was succeeded by Godfrey, the Queen's chaplain, in 1123. He ruled in Bath uneventfully for thirteen years and dying in 1136, Robert, a Cluniac[1] monk of Lewes, was appointed by King Stephen. At this time the whole country was devastated by civil war. Faction fights between neighbouring cities and the private war and depredations of the great nobles threatened the whole country with utter ruin. Bath, under her new Bishop, supported the cause of Stephen; Bristol on the contrary opposed him, and in the course of the struggle between them on July 29th, 1137, the Church of Bath was burned. In the following year Stephen came to Bath and laid siege to Bristol, and in the course of the struggle Bishop Robert was taken prisoner, but presently, much to Stephen's disgust, he was exchanged for Geoffrey Talbot, an important adherent of the Empress Matilda.

Robert was almost as notable a builder in Bath as John de Villula had been; he repaired what the wars had spoilt, and he built a chapter house, a cloister, dormitory, refectory and infirmary, and other buildings for his monks. He did what he could to reconcile the claims of the canons in Wells and the monks in Bath with regard to the Bishopric, but at any rate so late as 1157 he did not contemplate any return to Wells from Bath for his episcopal seat. A charter of Pope Hadrian IV, the Englishman, in 1157, formally recognised Bath as the Bishop's seat, and sanctioned the title of Bishop of Bath; a charter of the succeeding Pope, Alexander III (1157–81), however, while it conferred the title recognised the following compromise between the secular canons of Wells and the monks of Bath. There we find that the two churches of Bath and Wells were equally to be the seat of the bishop; that the Bishop was for the future to be elected by representatives of both chapters; that the Bishop was to be enthroned in both churches, but first in the church of Bath; and that the Prior of Bath was to give notice of the election to the Archbishop of Canterbury.[2]

[1] The Cluniac abbey of Lewes had been founded in 1077.

[2] *Cf.* C. M. Church, *Four Somerset Bishops*, 1136–1242 (Taunton: Barnicott & Pearce, 1909).

Bath Abbey.

In 1166 Bishop Robert died and for seven years the See was vacant. In 1173 the new proposals for the election of a Bishop[1] seem to have been acted upon, and we find the monks of Bath and the canons of Wells at the instigation of Henry II electing Reginald Fitzjocelin, the opponent of Becket, as Bishop.[2] Bishop Reginald was the son of that Jocelin de Bohun who became Bishop of Salisbury and was excommunicated by Becket. He had been brought up in Italy, and was known in England as "the Lombard." Immediately on his election to the See of Bath, he went in company with the Archbishop elect of Canterbury to procure the Pope's confirmation. He found Alexander at Anagni, but though the Archbishop was there consecrated, Reginald was not, his consecration being deferred under various pretexts until his return to England. On their way home they crossed the Mont Cenis and stopped for some time at S. Jean de Maurienne in Savoy. Here Reginald was consecrated Bishop of Bath, why we do not know.

From St. Jean de Maurienne Reginald went to the Grande Chartreuse, and there, on the King's behalf, persuaded St. Hugh of Avalon[3] to come to England and govern the first Carthusian monastery in this country, which Henry II had founded at Witham, in Somerset, as part of his penance for Becket's murder.

Bishop Reginald did not build much in Bath; his chief work there was the foundation of the Hospital of St. John for the succour of the sick poor who came to use the Baths. He greatly enriched the Church of Wells, refounded and to a large extent built the Cathedral we know, and certainly seems to have contemplated the transference of his throne thither probably as a better and more convenient centre from which to watch and oppose the growth of the powers of the Abbey of Glastonbury. To the same end we find him making the Abbot of Glaston a member of the Wells chapter and the Liberty of the Abbey he turned into an archdeaconry. In all this we see the growing importance of the great Religious Orders and especially, here in Somerset, of that ancient Bene-

[1] The charter only received the formal sanction of the Roman Court in 1176.

[2] Becket was canonised in the very year of Reginald's election, 1173.

[3] See *infra.*

Interior of Bath Abbey, looking East.

dictine House entrenched in the marshes. How the Bishopric finally dealt with the Abbey we shall see later.

Reginald, however, was, if not a great Bishop, a fine sportsman. When he had been his father's archdeacon at Salisbury in his youth, he had loved hawking, and as Bishop of Bath he obtained from the King the right of keeping sporting dogs throughout Somerset. And some idea of his power may be gathered from the fact that at the coronation of Richard I in 1189, he walked on the left hand of the King's Majesty, the Bishop of Durham being upon his right; he even aspired to the Chancellorship. Finally, in 1191, he was elected by the monks of Christ Church Archbishop of Canterbury; but he did not live to be Primate, dying on December 24th at his Manor of Dogmersfield in Hampshire. He was buried before the high altar of the church of Bath, on the festival of his old enemy St. Thomas à Becket.

In all his later work at any rate he had been signally assisted by his kinsman Savaric, Archdeacon of Northampton, and cousin, as he said, of the Emperor. It was this man who was chosen to succeed him. It seems he had taken the Cross with Richard I, and at Messina in 1191 upon the elevation of his kinsman Reginald to the See of Canterbury he obtained a letter from the King to the end that he should be chosen Bishop. The monks of Bath elected him, and without waiting for the consent of the chapter of Wells, which in fact protested, the King's justiciar, Walter, Archbishop of Rouen, confirmed the election. At this time Savaric was not in priest's orders; but these he received and was consecrated in Rome on August 8, 1192, by the Cardinal Bishop of Albano.

The truth was that the King was in need of a friend. Early in 1193 we find Savaric negotiating with his cousin the Emperor for Richard's release from his captivity in Germany, and as his part of the bargain demanding the annexation of the oldest Abbey in England, the Abbey of Glastonbury, to the Bishopric, in exchange for which he was ready to surrender to the Crown the city of Bath. He even dreamed of Canterbury; but this was denied him. He gained however the consent of the Pope Celestine III to his annexation of Glaston, and on his return to England, as it is said, summoned the Abbot to Bath and proclaimed himself Abbot in his place. The monks appealed to the Pope in vain. In 1195 Celestine declared the union of the churches of Bath and Glastonbury under Savaric, making Glastonbury equally with Bath a Cathedral church, and directing that Savaric and his successors should be entitled Bishops of Bath and Glastonbury. Again the monks appealed and again in vain. In 1196 the Pope ordered them to give up their Abbey into the hands of the Bishop and inhibited them from electing an Abbot. And all this was done in spite of the efforts of the Archbishop of Canterbury and later of the King, who had repented him of the evil bargain he had made.

In 1198, however, Pope Celestine III died, and a man of very different calibre was set upon the Papal throne. Innocent III, for all his strength, was nevertheless largely committed by the so recent acts of his predecessor and was doubtless confirmed in the course they seemed to insist upon when the King, seizing the opportunity of Celestine's death, took Glastonbury into his own hands and bade the monks elect an Abbot. The monks chose William Pica, and in November, without reference to the Holy See, the King's justiciar confirmed the election. Savaric, then at his manor of Wells, in Somerset, immediately excommunicated his rival and laid an interdict upon the Abbey. Abbot Pica at once set out for Rome to appeal to the Pope in person; in his absence the monks submitted to Savaric's authority. It was at this moment that King Richard died on April 6, 1199, and John reigned in his stead. In this, Savaric, who had followed Abbot Pica to Rome, saw his opportunity. Returning in haste to England he obtained by bribes from John what Richard had always denied him, namely, material possession of the Abbey and lands of Glastonbury and his public installation as Abbot. On June 8th the Archbishop of Ragusa and the Archdeacon of Canterbury were sent by the King with Royal letters to enthrone Savaric in the Abbey Church. This was, in spite of the monks' previous submission, not to be done without a struggle. Savaric appeared surrounded by armed men, the closed gates of Glastonbury were forced, and amid a scene of violence such as even then must have been rare, Savaric of Bath was enthroned Bishop of Glastonbury. In the year 1200, the Pope annulled Abbot Pica's election, confirmed the union of the churches of Bath and Glastonbury, and ordered

Savaric, who had been guilty of the greatest violence, to desist from persecution.

Savaric had thus gained his end. The greatest Abbey in Somerset was in his hands; the second monastery, Bath, he had always held; there only remained Athelney and Muchelney, and these in the persons of their respective Abbots he attached as prebends to the See. Even Cleeve, a Cistercian house, he was not content to leave in freedom. He persuaded the Abbot of Bec in Normandy to hold the church of Cleeve as a prebend of Wells.[1]

Of the last years of Savaric we know little or nothing. He died in Italy in 1205, and was buried before the high altar at Bath, and over his tomb it is said the following epitaph was set up:

> Notus erat mundo per mundum semper eundo
> Et necis ista dies est tibi prima quies.

Indeed one who had been such a traveller "going to and fro through the earth" can have had but little time to administer the diocese he was so busy to enlarge. Nevertheless, we know, that to the monks of Bath he was not ungenerous; the money they should have found for the ransom of King Richard he found himself and saved the treasure of their Church, and he strengthened the position of Wells, which eagerly assisted him against Glastonbury, and founded a daily Mass in honour of the Blessed Virgin in the Cathedral. He died in enormous debt, but apparently in England, though not in Rome, his credit was still good, for we hear of a man as praying that he might be included in the legion of Savaric's creditors.

Immediately upon his death, however, all his work fell to pieces. From all over the country, and indeed from all over Christendom petitions poured in on behalf of the Abbey of Glastonbury. Nothing was changed, however, during the life of Innocent III. But when Honorius succeeded him in 1216, the Abbey regained its freedom, the union was dissolved, and this was but the prelude to further changes which were to leave Bath after nearly a hundred years of domination little more than an appendage of Wells.

[1] Montacute (Cluniac), Witham, and Hinton (Carthusian) were probably too unimportant for him to trouble about.

Savaric was succeeded in the See of Bath and Glastonbury by Jocelin of Wells in 1206, the canons of Wells concurring in the election of one of their own members who had been born and bred in their city. Two years later he made one of the five bishops who left England in consequence of the Papal Interdict. He returned in 1213, and thereafter sided with John, and was one of the councillors named in the preamble of the great Charter. In 1218, Honorius having succeeded Innocent, he surrendered his claims to Glastonbury and resumed the title of Bishop of Bath and Wells. In him we see the movement, begun by Bishop John de Villula, come full circle. The movement which had exalted Bath during the whole of the twelfth century left her in full decline. John de Villula had made the change from Wells to Bath largely for Roman reasons and in accordance with the design upon which Christendom had been built. That change too brought under his close authority the second of the great monasteries within the diocese; yet the growing splendour and fame and wealth of Glastonbury slowly but surely undermined all this. The absorption of the great Abbey by the See of Bath was an attempt to save the situation, but it could not endure, the true solution lay in a return of the Cathedral to Wells, whose position was such that thence the Bishop was able to mark, and in some sort to dominate, the great Abbey. Thus here as elsewhere, and for local reasons, the Roman plan in England broke down; the Primate did not sit in London but in Canterbury; the Bishopric of Somerset had not its seat in Bath but in Wells, an isolated village far from any highway, on the verge of the impassable marsh, in the shadow of the great forest upon the hills.

From this time forward until the suppression Bath remains little more than a small town grouped about its Priory. It had become the property of the Crown again when in 1189 Savaric surrendered it to Richard I in exchange for Glastonbury, and shortly afterwards had been invested by the King with the privileges of a free borough; that is to say, the citizens were given the right to trade free of all toll, and customs, etc.,[1] and of course a certain measure of trouble was

[1] *Cf. Som. Arch. Proc.*, XXII (ii), 6–7. The date 1189 is the first of legal memory and the year in which a Mayor of London was first elected. The charter of Richard to Bath, dated in that year, reads as follows :—

certain between the monks and the burgesses, the Church and the King. In the civil war of Henry III's time (1264–6) the Priory sided with the Barons, and was excommunicated therefor. But with the accession of Edward I, who was in Bath on two occasions, in 1276 and in 1285, the privileges of the town were increased, the right to hold an annual fair at Twerton was granted by the King, at which a great trade in woollen goods appears to have been done, but Bath was at a disadvantage in matters of trade with the town of Bristol, so much more fortunately situated on the Severn Sea.[1]

The town was certainly visited and probably half depopulated by the Black Death of 1348, which so greatly injured the monastery that it never recovered; even the fabric began to fall into decay and was never repaired, and whereas it had supported between thirty and forty monks all through the twelfth and thirteenth centuries, from the Black Death to the suppression it seldom if ever numbered more than sixteen.

So in Bath the years passed, not indeed we may be sure uneventfully, but without leaving any great mark or record in history. As the seat of the Bishop it was overshadowed by Wells, as a place of trade by Bristol. It had no shrine to attract pilgrims as Glaston had[2]; and indeed when we come

"Richard, by the grace of God King of England, Duke of Normandy and Aquitaine, Count of Anjou, to the justiciars, sheriffs, barons, provosts, ministers, and all other his faithful subjects of the whole of England and of the ports of the sea, Greeting. We do commend that the citizens of Bath who are of their merchant guild shall have in all things the same acquitance and freedom as to all their markets, wherever they shall come by land or by water of toll, of herbage and of all other customs and demand and matters, as fully and freely as our citizens of Winton of their merchant guild have, and we do forbid that anyone disturb or molest them herein or their property on pain of forfeiting 10£."

[1] Under the auspices of the monks, however, the art of weaving woollen cloth was established here about 1333, and carried to great perfection during the fourteenth century, when Bath became famous for this manufacture. *Cf.* Chaucer, *Wife of Bathe*.

[2] The monks endeavoured to obtain such a shrine and to attract pilgrims by setting up an altar of the Holy Trinity, and there miracles were said to be worked. In 1459 we hear of a certain Agnes Cole of Bath who was prosecuted in the ecclesiastical court at Wells, and sentenced to recant before all the congregation in the great church at Bath for having said "that it was but waste to give to the Holy Trinity at Bath." The Holy Trinity, however, worked at least one miracle there, as we shall see, when Bishop King was inspired to begin the new church.

upon it at the end of the fifteenth century its great Norman Church is in utter ruin even to the foundations.

It was in this miserable state that Dr. Oliver King found it when in 1496 he became Bishop of Bath and Wells. Bishop King was a statesman, and served Edward IV, Edward V, Henry VI, and Henry VII as Secretary of State. He came to Bath three years after his election to the See to institute William Bird as Prior of Bath, and it was, according to Sir John Harrington, upon this occasion that, warned in a dream, he determined to rebuild the abbey church. "Lying at Bathe and musing or meditating one night late after his devotions and prayers for the prosperity of Henry VII and his children, to which King he was principal Secretary and by him preferred to his bishoprick; he saw or supposed he saw a vision of the Holy Trynitie with angels ascending and descending by a ladder neer to the foote of which there was a fayre olive tree supporting a crowne, and a voyce that said:—'Let an Olive establish the Crowne and let a King restore the Church.' Of this dream or vision he took exceeding great comfort and told it divers of his friends. . . . He was so transported with his dream for the tyme, that he presently set in hand with this church (the ruins whereof I rue to behold even in theis times) and at the west end thereof he caused a representation to be carved of this his vision of the Trynitie, the angels and the ladder; and on the north side the olive and crown with certain French wordes which I could not reade; but in English is this verse taken out of the book of Judges, cap. 9:—

> Trees going to chose their King,
> Said, 'Be to us the Olive King.'

All which is so curiously cut and carved as in the west part of England is no better work than in the west end of this poor church; and to make the credit of all this more authentique he added this worde to it, '*de sursum est*,' ('it is from on high'). This much the stones and walls (though dumb witnesses, yet credible) doe playnly testifie."

Such was the genesis of the church we now see. It was begun in the year 1500 in the western part of the old abbey, and altogether as we see it would not have filled its nave. If Bishop King began it, he was eagerly supported by Prior Bird who, when he died in 1525, had expended his whole fortune upon it, and by the last Prior, Prior Holleway alias Gybbs; but when Henry VIII decided upon the suppression

Tomb of Bishop Montague, Bath Abbey.

of the religious houses it was not nearly finished, but remained a mere shell standing in the mighty remains of the older church.

In the summer of 1535, Layton, Dean of York, and one of Thomas Cromwell's chief agents in the ghastly business of the suppression, came to Bath to discover material for his "Black Book." On the 7th August he wrote to the Vicar General a letter full of lying statements—for he was a masterly liar, though a poor parson—in which we find the following indictment:—

"If it may please yor goodness to understand that we have visited Bathe, whereas we found the prior [William Holleway] a right vertuose man and I suppose no better of his cote, a man simple and not of the greteste wit, his monkes worse than I founde yet both in . . . and adulterie, sum one of them haveyng X women, some VIII, and the rest no fewer. The house well repared but foure hundred poundes in debt. . . . Ye shall receive a bowke of o^r lades miracles well able to mache the canterberie tailles. Such a bowke of dremes as ye never saw which I founde in the librarie. . . ."

It is curious to find such a man as Layton speaking well of the Prior, but Holleway seems to have been rather interested in alchemy than in theology, and like too many others of his kind at that time, he stooped to send Cromwell presents, probably in the hope of saving his monastery. He received a pension of £80 a year and a house in Stall Street.[1]

After the suppression, in 1539, the commissioners, says Harrington, "in reverence and compassion of the place did so far strayne their commission that they offered to sell the whole Church to the towne under 500 marks; but the townsmen fearing they might be thought to cosen the king if they bought it so cheape, or that it might after (as many things were) be found conceal'd, utterly refused. Whereupon certain merchants bought all the glass, iron, bells, and lead; of which lead alone was accompted for (as I have crediblie heard) 480 tonne, worth at this day £4,800."

Not much later the monastic estates were granted to Humphrey Colles, who sold the site and buildings of the Priory to Matthew Colthurst, whose son Edmund, in the beginning of 1560, "made the city a present of the carcase of

[1] It is possible that it was from Prior Holleway that Shorthouse drew his Prior of Westacre in "John Inglesant," for in an old poem we read:

"He had our stone, our medicine, our Elixir and all,
Which when the abbie was supprest he hid in a wall."

St. Peter's church with the ground upon the east, west, and north sides of it."

Thus the house founded by Osric in 676 came to an end, materially as well as spiritually.

In 1572 something was done to put the church into some sort of repair; and again in 1597 through the importunity of Sir John Harrington, who really seems to have loved the old building, and in 1608, with difficulty, persuaded Bishop Montague to roof it by leading him there to the roofless fabric for shelter in a shower of rain. More was done later in the seventeenth and throughout the eighteenth centuries; but it was not till 1859 that the entire fabric was overhauled and then it was delivered to Sir Gilbert Scott. It is well to remember that what we have in Bath "Abbey" to-day has never been a monastic church, that in all probability Mass has never been said within it, and that it can have no appeal but such as may be made by its own cold and lifeless beauty. It is a work of the sixteenth and following centuries, built without inspiration or hope and littered with the tombs and epitaphs of the fashionable world whose existence was organised by Beau Nash, who himself lies there, in the eighteenth century.

Wells Cathedral.
Capital Bird.

III.

The suppression of its monastery, upon which it had largely depended ever since the fall of the Empire, marks the end of a great period in Bath as elsewhere. Even in Roman times, as we have seen, the city had been very small, never exceeding the twenty-three acres enclosed within the walls. These limits were maintained throughout the Middle Ages, and indeed were not broken until the wonderful renaissance of the eighteenth century. The history of Bath between the suppression of the Abbey and the famous visit of Queen Anne in 1702 can be given in a few lines.

Leland, writing just after the suppression, but with a memory of Bath before that disaster, thus describes it: "Bath," he says, "is sette booth yn a fruteful and pleasant botom which is invironed on every side with great walls out of which cum many springes of pure water that be conveyid by dyverse ways to serve the Cyte. There be four gates yn the town by the names of Est, etc. The waulle within the town is of no great height to the eyes, but without it is a fundamentis of a reasonable heighth; and it standith allmoste alle, lakking but a peace about 'Gascoyne tower.' This took its name from one Gascoyne, who 'in hominum memoria' built a peace of walle as amends for a fault committed in the city."

Chapman writing later, in the seventeenth century, tells us: "The streets are of the narrowest size, especially that nearest the centre, called Cheap Street."

Evelyn, who visited Bath from Cadenham, June 27, 1654, says: "We all went to see Bathe where I bathed in the Crosse Bathe. Amongst the rest of the idle diversions of the toune one musitian was famous for acting a changeling, which indeede he personated strangely. The *faciate* of this cathedrall is remarkable for its historical carving. The King's Bathe is esteem'd ye fairest in Europe. The toune is entirely built of stone, but the streetes narrow uneven and unpleasant."

While Pepys, who was in Bath in 1688, found the baths "not so large as I expected but yet pleasant; and the town most of stone, and clean, though the streets generally narrow."

All these descriptions, though written at such various dates and by such various pens, wonderfully agree, and this is not surprising when we know that from the suppression to Queen Anne's visit the city was absolutely stagnant and did not increase by so much as twenty houses. During that period, however, Bath was visited in state by many of the kings and queens of England, and other distinguished personages. Queen Elizabeth came in 1574. She spent Sunday, August 22nd, in the town, occupying, it is said, the royal apartments at the Westgate, which had been built two years previously. In her honour, we hear—such was the abject condition of the "cathederall"—"Quaresters were brought over from Wells at a cost of 10s."

In 1616 Anne of Denmark, the wife of James I, came to

Bath to take the waters, as did Queen Henrietta Maria in 1644. In the same year Charles I on his way westward stayed two nights in Bath, leaving the city for Wells on July 17th. In the Civil War, Bath was overshadowed by Bristol, though in the heights above (on Lansdown) one of the famous battles of that miserable rebellion took place and cost the life of one of the noblest of West countrymen, Sir Bevile Grenville, in 1643; and Sir William Waller, the Parliamentary general, used Bath as his headquarters in 1645, and lies in the "Abbey" church.

In 1663 Charles II, with his queen and his brother (afterwards James II) and Prince Rupert, visited the city for the sake of the waters, as did Mary of Modena, James's second wife, in 1687.

Two years before that Bath had closed its gates against Monmouth and become thus the cause of that retreat which ended so fatally at Sedgemoor. During all this period, indeed, Bath appears as a mere watering place, existing upon the reputation of her baths which later, in more favourable circumstances, were to bring her honour, wealth, and a great population. Of all the writers who speak of her during this time it is, I think, Fuller who gives the best and truest description of her. He speaks of the town as a mere invalid's resort, infested with beggars; whilst Wood, writing in the eighteenth century, when, largely through his efforts, the city had become the noble and beautiful town we know, tells us of the meanness of the houses and the dirt everywhere, hidden within doors with a mixture "of soot and small beer."

From this abject condition Bath was raised, and suddenly, to splendour by the efforts, in a fortunate moment, of two men, Ralph Allen and Richard Nash; that moment was, as we know and the city itself everywhere bears witness, the eighteenth century.

Really, I suppose the Bath of the eighteenth century was the unconscious creation of the *malade imaginaire.* The place had already been famous for more than seventeen hundred years for its healing springs, and had flourished exceedingly for this reason in the first four Roman centuries, when a high and complex civilisation had obtained in Britain. During the Middle Ages, in the shadow of its church, it had shared the fortunes of the monastery, and when that was suppressed it fell into wretchedness. But the gradual amelioration of the world at the beginning of the eighteenth century, the recovery of Britain from the economic disaster of the Reformation, and the revolution in manners then just beginning, consequent upon that recovery, gave Bath a new opportunity, which was, in fact, in some sort a reproduction of Roman conditions. It was due to two men, Allen and Nash, that Bath was able to seize that opportunity and to make the utmost of those conditions.

At the beginning of the eighteenth century, as at the end of the first, the great need of England was a new reconciliation of classes, of society. The people of the countryside, of the provinces generally, the fox-hunting squirearchy, the country gentleman, his wife and daughters, found in Bath the means of social intercourse with the new aristocracy, the *habitué* of St. James's Street, the bureaucracy and the governing class, just as previously the British landowner and provincial had found there the means for the same intercourse with the Roman officialdom; in fact the existence of the governing class in both periods depended upon the establishment of such an intercourse. It is curious, and surely a proof of the continuity of our civilisation, that, though separated by much more than a millennium, in both periods the same means were found and in the same place. Looking at the matter in this way, and it is thus it must be regarded, Beau Nash appears as a saviour of society; one may well believe that all such have been adventurers of his kidney.

The rise of Bath as the great social centre, the only one where the upper and middle classes could meet upon equal terms, was due to the following causes.

More and more as the new society, created by the Reformation and ensured by the Great Rebellion, matured and entered upon its final form, Bath had become a resort for those in search of health; but it was not primarily to these it owed its immediate success—this was the work of the wealthy and aristocratic *malades imaginaires.* They found there a pleasant climate and situation within a reasonable distance from London, at the meeting place of the great roads that served all southern and midland England—all England, that is, that was in any sense wealthy. Around these *dilettanti* gathered men of letters and wits, and to them again were added little by little as the place became fashionable—for Bath was nearer and less expensive than London, and a true pleasure resort with a sober excuse for its existence—the squires of southern England and their womenfolk, who, if they regarded the wits and men about town as wanting in all manly qualities, were themselves, and justly it would seem, looked upon as barbarous, without manners or education. Gradually in Bath, in the continual social intercourse of the "seasons," these people, so strange and antagonistic, whose reconciliation was so necessary for the existence of the State, became known to one another; the fox-hunting squire was taught manners, and from the mere barbarian of those days became the courteous and delightful gentleman that Goldsmith shows us so perfectly in *She Stoops to Conquer*. Of course all this was largely the work of women; it was, however, primarily the work of Nash, without whose enterprise woman could not have found her opportunity.

"At this time," says Goldsmith, by far the best authority, "London was the only theatre in England for pleasure and intrigue. A spirit of gaming had been introduced in the licentious age of Charles II, and had by this time thriven surprisingly. Yet all its devastations were confined to London alone. To this great mart of every folly, sharpers from every country daily arrived for the winter; but were obliged to leave the kingdom at the approach of summer in order to open a new campaign at Aix, Spa or The Hague. Bath, and other places of the same kind here, were then frequented only by such as really went for relief; the pleasures they afforded were merely rural; the company splenetic, rustic, and vulgar. In this situation of things people of fashion had no agreeable summer retreat from the town, and usually spent that season amidst a solitude of country squires, parsons' wives, and visiting tenants or farmers; they wanted some place where they might have each other's company and win each other's money, as they had done during the winter in town. . . Probably upon this principle and by the arrival of Queen Anne there for her health, about the year 1703, the city of Bath became in some measure frequented by people of distinction. The company was numerous enough to form a country dance upon the bowling green; they were amused with a fiddle and hautboy, and diverted with the romantic walks round the city. . . Still, however, the amusements of this place were neither elegant nor conducted with delicacy. General society among people of rank or fortune was by no means established. The nobility still preserved a tincture of Gothic haughtiness and refused to keep company with the gentry at any of the public entertainments of the place. Smoking in the rooms was permitted; gentlemen and ladies appeared in a disrespectful manner at public entertainments in aprons and boots. With an eagerness common to those whose pleasures come but seldom, they generally continued them too long; and thus they were rendered disgusting by too free an enjoyment . . ."

Thus Goldsmith shows us the extraordinary difference in culture and civilisation that separated the upper and the middle classes at that time in England; it was the social reconciliation of these classes, in culture and manners, that was achieved at Bath and by "Beau" Nash.

He arrived in the midst of the hurly-burly of barbarism and horseplay described by Goldsmith, he organised the entertainment of this crowd of ill-assorted people, was apparently at once recognised as the necessary leader and "the sovereignty of the city was decreed to him by every rank of people." As "Master of the Ceremonies," or "King of Bath," he presently drew up a set of "Rules to be observed at Bath," and posted them in the Pump Room. These rules, written by himself, seem to us both insolent and stupid, but they were then regarded as witty, and as such they were accepted and obeyed, and Goldsmith tells us that even the Royal Family themselves had not influence enough to make him change them. "The Princess Amelia, once applying to him for one dance more after he had given the signal to withdraw, he answered her royal highness that the established rules of Bath resembled the law of Lycurgus, which would admit of no alteration without an utter subversion of all his authority." And one day when, breaking his rules, the Duchess of Queensberry appeared on a ball night in a white apron, he "stript it off and threw it at one of the hinder benches among the ladies' women," observing that none but Abigails appeared in white aprons. "This," says Goldsmith, "from another would be an insult; in him it was considered a just reprimand, and the good-natured duchess acquiesced in his censure."

The man who thus ruled so despotically, and, incidentally and quite unconsciously, rendered so great a service to England, was the merest adventurer. Born in 1674 at Swansea, he had been "sent down" from the University of Oxford, and as a student at the Temple had been notorious for his dissipation. He went to Bath as a gambler for the purpose of getting a living by gambling, and, apparently seeing his opportunity and seizing it, got himself appointed "Master of the Ceremonies" about 1704, on the death of Captain Webster. He is described as "an agreeable and ingenious person of organising capacity," and he seems to have been endowed with that combination of impudence and discretion which is so often in all ages socially successful. Dropping the character of a spendthrift, he became a real social power, and the great days of the city are practically conterminous with his life. In his old age he fell into some contempt and poverty, for his work was done, but when he died, in 1762, he received a public funeral, and lies under a resounding epitaph in the "Abbey" Church, amid the innumerable dust of that fashionable society he had known so well how to organise and to intimidate.

But if Bath owes much to Beau Nash, she owes more to Ralph Allen, without whose noble and attractive character the eighteenth century city over which Nash ruled with so frivolous a despotism would have lacked both its charm and its permanence. It was, perhaps, inevitable that English society should deliver itself to the first adventurer of talent or genius who attempted to govern it, but it was by no means inevitable that that age should have expressed all that was best in it in enduring stone, and raised, at so late a day, upon Leland's "great and rocky hills," when all is said, perhaps the noblest modern city in England. This was the work of a greater man than Nash.

Ralph Allen, the constant friend of Pope, the intimate friend of Fielding and of Warburton, was the son of a small innkeeper at St. Blazey in Cornwall, where he was born in 1694. His grandmother had kept the post office at St. Columb Major, and at the age of eighteen Ralph Allen had entered the post office of Bath. There he attracted the notice of General Wade by detecting a Jacobite plot and soon after married the general's natural daughter. He became deputy postmaster at Bath, and, seeing the inconveniences of the postal system of that day—a letter from Bath to Worcester being sent by London—"he devised a system of cross posts for England and Wales and forwarded them himself." His scheme came into practice upon 16th April, 1720, and from that time till 1764 his average profits were some £12,000 a year, amounting in all to about half a million of money. Nor was he content with this; he had become proprietor of the Combe Down quarries, and, having invented a means of conveying the great blocks of hewn stone from the quarries to the canal, he did a huge business in stone also. He became thus the great capitalist in Bath, and though only once mayor, in 1742, as a fact he always ruled the city. His first house, which still stands between York Street and Lilliput Alley, to enhance the view from which he built the Sham Castle upon Hampton Down, he left in 1743 for his new palace under Combe Down, above Widcombe within three or four miles of Bath, which he had begun to build in 1736. His architect was John Wood, of Bath, and Prior Park remains one of the finest eighteenth century palaces in the country. Here he entertained like a prince a succession of distinguished guests, including members of the Royal Family and some of the greatest men of letters and painters of his day. His friendship with Pope, it is true, was interrupted by the poet's attempt to foist Martha Blount upon him, but Pope immortalised him in the lines—

> Let humble Allen, with an awkward shame
> Do good by stealth and blush to find it fame. . . .

and his letters prove that Allen overwhelmed him with kindness, while Warburton, the poet's friend, here met and married Allen's favourite niece and got his appointment, by Allen's influence with Pitt, to the bishopric of Gloucester. Pitt, for long Member of Parliament for Bath, was the intimate friend of Allen, who left him a thousand pounds in his will. While Fielding, who drew Allen's portrait in "Tom Jones" as Squire Allworthy, received a gift of two hundred guineas "in admiration of his genius" before he knew Allen personally; and in acknowledgment of friendship dedicated his *Amelia* to his frequent host. On the novelist's death, in 1754, Allen provided for his family.

But the true monument of Allen is not to be found in the praise and affection of his contemporaries; nor even in the marble lines of Pope; his true memorial is the city of Bath, as we see it, with its noble buildings, its squares and terraces and parades, that give it so classic an air beside the loveliness of our, perhaps, truer English cities, Winchester, Canterbury, or Oxford. Bath was fortunate in that, being a Roman city, the moment ordained for her resurrection was that of the eighteenth century, and that in Allen she had a Maecenas and in the Woods architects singularly capable of the recreation proper to her.

John Wood, a Yorkshireman, born in 1704, was probably introduced to Bath by Allen, first displaying his powers of design in the North and South Parades, which have suffered

Royal Crescent, Bath.

much from modern alterations. At any rate, by the end of the year 1725 he had at the suggestion of Allen formed a noble plan, really for the rebuilding of the city, its tremendous enlargement upon the hillsides, with that old walled town so close about the "Abbey" Church for citadel. In this plan there was to be, we are told, "a grand place of assembly," to be called "the Royal Forum of Bath;" another, for the exhibition of games and sports, to be called "The Grand Circus," and in 1727 these noble and grand ideas for the transformation of a city, the greatest that had appeared in England since the Reformation, began to be carried out.

Queen's Square, Gay Street, The Circus, finished by the younger Wood in 1785, the Parades, the old Assembly Rooms (destroyed by fire in 1820) were built. And when Wood died, in 1754, his work was continued by his son, John Wood junior, who had been associated with many of his father's works. To him we owe the Royal Crescent, the Upper Assembly Rooms (begun in 1769), the Hot Bath and the Royal Private Bath in Hot Bath Street, the York House Hotel, and, indeed, all York Buildings, Brook Street, St. Margaret's Chapel (now a skating rink), Edgar Buildings, Princess Buildings, Alfred Street, Russell Street, Belmont, and Nelson Park. To his successor, Baldwin, we owe Pulteney Street and Laura Place. Monsieur Barbeau, the excellent historian of Bath in the eighteenth century, thus sums up the work of the Woods in Bath under the patronage of Allen: "The peculiar merit of the Woods in proposing and accomplishing their tasks was that they were architects and not mere builders, that they had the beauty of the city they were transforming always before their eyes, that they conceived and carried out a vast and harmonious whole. Their ideal is no longer ours altogether; their academic style is far from having retained the universal favour, the exclusive respect it enjoyed about a century and a half ago. Rigorous criticism will find their regularity a little cold sometimes, their solemnity a little heavy, their decoration somewhat poor, their invention somewhat circumscribed. But, granting all this, their conceptions remained original, dignified and happy enough in Macaulay's opinion "to charm even eyes familiar with the masterpieces of Bramante and Palladio."

As famous as any of these buildings, though not from their hands, was the Octagon Chapel, now a warehouse, which Selina, Countess of Huntingdon, built in 1765 for the "Methodists." Wesley had visited Bath and encountered Nash as early as 1739, and it must be confessed that probably no city in England was more in need of his services; Charles Wesley indeed considered Bath at this time as "the headquarters of Satan," and however we may regard so rash a statement we must admit that the fashionable, frivolous, and sceptical society, unfamiliar with the manifestation of religion, and wholly at the mercy of a mean materialism stood certainly in need of admonition.

In 1739 therefore John Wesley appeared in Bath and preached twice, drawing enormous congregations,[1] but almost at once Nash, who had not been present at his sermons, seeing in him a rival, determined to turn him out of Bath. In this he was unsuccessful, through no fault of his own; but even in the encounter of wits he came off (according to Wesley) second best.

That naïve journal of Wesley's gives us a lively description of the evangelist's meeting with the "King of Bath":—

"There was," says he, "great expectation at Bath of what a noted man was to do with me there: and I was much intreated 'not to preach, because no one knew what might happen.' By this report I also gained a much larger audience, among whom were many of the rich and great. I told them plainly '*the Scripture had concluded them all under sin*,' high and low, rich and poor, one with another. Many of them seemed to be not a little surprised and were sinking apace into seriousness when the champion appeared, and coming close to me, asked, 'By what authority I did these things?' I replied, 'By the authority of Jesus Christ, conveyed to me by the (now) Archbishop of Canterbury, when he laid his hands upon me, and said, "Take thou authority to preach the Gospel."' He said, 'This is contrary to Act of Parliament. This is a Conventicle.' I answered, 'Sir, the Conventicles mentioned in the Act (as the Preamble shows) are seditious meetings. But this is not such. Here is no shadow of sedition. Therefore it is not contrary to the Act.' He replied, 'I say it is. But besides, your preaching frightens people out of their wits.' 'Sir, did you ever hear me preach?' 'No.' 'How then can you judge of what you never heard?' 'Sir, by common report.' 'Common report is not enough. Give me leave, sir, to ask, is not your name Nash?' 'My name is Nash.' 'Sir, I dare not judge of you by common report. I believe it is not enough to judge by.'"

But in spite of his wit Wesley would probably have failed to make any real impression upon that vigorous but corrupt society, had he not been openly championed in Bath by a great lady, the Countess of Huntingdon. She came to Bath in the same year he did, with her husband, a friend of Ralph Allen's. Warburton was there at the same time and did not hesitate to attack the doctrines of the Methodists, though Allen, his host, sided with them. In 1747 Lady Huntingdon as a widow returned to Bath, and became as it were the head of the new church. Whitefield trembled before her; she made one (in spite of St. Paul) of the directing Council, which consisted of herself, the three Wesleys, and Whitefield, and

[1] On the first occasion four hundred heard him, on the second a thousand.

ruled the whole movement with a rod of iron. It was largely this domination which caused Wesley's rupture with her in 1770. According to Southey, he "neither wanted nor would have admitted patron or patroness to be temporal head of the societies he had formed and he gradually grew into disfavour." The whole movement had indeed its comic if not its ridiculous side, and it does not need the caustic notice of Horace Walpole to point it out. "Mr. Wesley's Opera," he calls the new service. "I have been at one opera," he writes, "Mr. Wesley's. They have boys and girls with charming voices that sing hymns, in parts, to Scotch ballad tunes; but indeed so long that one would think they were already in eternity, and knew how much time they had before them. The chapel is very neat with true Gothic windows (yet I am not converted); but I was glad to see that luxury is creeping in upon them before persecution; they have very neat mahogany for benches and brackets of the same in taste. At the upper end is a broad *hautpas* of four steps, advancing in the middle; at each end of the broadest part are two of my eagles [possibly a gift of Walpole's to Lady Huntingdon] with red cushions for the parson and clerk. Behind them rise three more steps in the midst of which is a third eagle for pulpit, scarlet arm-chairs to all three. On either hand a balcony for elect ladies. The rest of the congregation sit on forms. Behind the pulpit, in a dark niche, is a plain table within rails; so you see the throne is for the apostle. Wesley is a lean, elderly man, fresh coloured, his hair smoothly combed, but with a *soupçon* of curls at the end. Wondrous clean, but as evidently an actor as Garrick . . . towards the end he exalted his voice and acted very ugly enthusiasm; decried learning, and told stories like Latimer of the fool of his college who said: 'I *thanks* God for everything.' Except a few from curiosity and some *honourable women* the congregation was mean. . . ."

All this barbarism within sight of John de Villula's monastery and the memories which stood for Europe!

The Octagon Chapel however was, in spite of itself as it were, to bear witness to something beside a provincial Christianity rank with heresy. Walpole's remaining letter, from which, though the scarlet armchairs are there, the Scarlet Woman is unaccountably absent, was written in 1766. In that same year a certain William Herschel, a Hanoverian, a musician, accepted "the agreeable and lucrative situation" of organist to the Octagon Chapel in Bath; and for many years directed concerts and oratorios there, composed anthems, chants, and gave music lessons. Notwithstanding his busy professional life Herschel retained an insatiable thirst for knowledge. The study of music led him to a study of mathematics, and from mathematics to optics was for him but a step. He began the practical study of this science in a very modest way, using a small and imperfect telescope. But he soon determined to have a better instrument, and since the price demanded by the dealers was too great, he determined to make one, for to genius and enthusiasm nothing is impossible. "From conducting a brilliant concert in Bath he would rush home and without even delaying to take off his lace ruffles he would plunge into his manual labours of grinding specula and polishing lenses." He transformed his house into a laboratory; of his drawing room he made a carpenter's shop. Turning-lathes were the furniture of his best bedroom. As he progressed he determined not only to have a good telescope, but a very good one, and he ultimately succeeded in constructing the greatest that the world had up to that time ever seen. He finished it in 1774. In 1780 he removed to King Street, and it was there with his new instrument on March 13th, 1781, that he discovered the planet Uranus, perhaps the greatest of his marvellous discoveries. In the following year upon his appointment as Court astronomer with a salary of £200 a year, he left Bath after a residence of fifteen years.

But Bath was not only the birthplace of the new civilisation, of the new architecture, and of the new science, it was the mother or at any rate the patron of the new school of painting which was to place England in this, too, beside the very greatest the world had known.

As early as 1736 we find Mrs. Barber writing to Swift, of the success of painters in Bath. "I never saw a painter that came hither, fail of getting more business than he could do, be he never so indifferent," and reminding herself of this she has hope even for her son. A little later we hear of William Hoare as painting there portraits of Pitt, Pope, Ralph Allen, and Lord Camden, and a picture of Christ Bearing His Cross for St. Michael's Church, and another of the Pool of Bethesda, so appropriate to Bath we may think, for the Octagon Chapel.[1] "Barker of Bath," too, a painter of landscape and rural life, born in 1769, though not in Somerset, is known to everyone by his two pictures in the National Gallery; "A Woodman and his Dog in a Storm," and a "Landscape upon the Somerset Downs."[2]

It is not however of them we think when we speak of that new school of painting, the greatest school England has ever known, but of the work of Sir Thomas Lawrence who was born in Bristol in 1769, and, more especially, of Gainsborough who, like Hoare, was born in Suffolk in 1727.

Gainsborough, at the suggestion of Philip Thicknesse, came to Bath in 1760, and thereby took his first step to fame and fortune. He occupied an apartment in the new built Circus, for which he paid £50 a year. He began to paint portraits there for five guineas, but his success was so great that he quickly raised his price to eight, and before long was able to obtain forty guineas for a half length, and as much as a hundred for a full length. He remained in Bath for fourteen years, and painted there some of his best works, among them, according to Sir Walter Armstrong, the Blue Boy; but certainly very many of the beautiful women and notable persons who visited Bath at that time sat to him, and though it is impossible to give a full list of the pictures he painted while at Bath, the following may be mentioned: the Miss Hurley and her brother, now at Knole; the General Honeywood, which is in the hands of Sir William Agnew; three portraits of Garrick, the Lady Sussex and Lady Barbara Yelverton, belonging to Lord Burton; the two landscapes of the Tweedmouth collection, the landscape belonging to Mr. Lionel Phillips, the "Going to Market," belonging to Lord Bateman; the marvellous canvas of the two Miss Linleys, at Dulwich; the two great landscapes. "The Cottage Door," in the Duke of Westminster's collection, and "The Watering Place," now in the National Gallery, and the beautiful portrait of Orpin, the Parish Clerk of Bradford-on-Avon, in the same collection.

[1] Portraits of Chatham, Lord Camden, and Allen remain in Bath in the Banqueting Hall, another of Derrick is in the Assembly Rooms. The Hospital, St. Michael's Church, and the Octagon Chapel still retain canvases painted by him.

[2] Many works by Barker are to be found in the Holburne Museum.

Famous and busy as he was, Gainsborough, in Bath, had very frequent need of the services of the public carrier between Bath and London. This man was one Wiltshire, who came to have so great an admiration for the painter that he never would accept any payment for his services. "No, no," he protested, "I love painting too much." At last, however, Gainsborough insisted, and Wiltshire replied, "When you think that I have carried to the value of a little painting, I beg you will let me have one, sir, and I shall be more than paid." It was for him that Gainsborough painted the beautiful landscape, "The Return from Harvest," in which Wiltshire's own waggon and the favourite horse he had proposed to Gainsborough as a model, as well as the artist's two daughters as peasant girls were introduced. The portrait of Orpin was another of these payments.[1]

Gainsborough was an eager if unstable musician, and many of the *virtuosi* resident in Bath he immortalised by his portraits; among them were Abel, the *viol di gamba* player; Giardini, the violinist; Fischer, the haut-boy player; later, his son-in-law, Samuel Foote, and Edwin and John Henderson. Of Abel he painted many portraits. "Doubtless," says a contemporary, "it was in exchange for the notes of his *viol di gamba* that he obtained so many drafts upon the genius of the painter."

Nor must we forget that the two Miss Linleys, whom Gainsborough painted so often, were singers, were the "Miss Linnets" before they became Mrs. Sheridan and Mrs. Tickell.

Thomas Linley, the father of these two ladies, was a great singing master, according to Parke[2] "almost unrivalled in England. He was born at Wells in 1732, the son of a carpenter. He studied first at Bath and afterwards at Naples, and on his return to England set up as a singing master at Bath, and for many years, assisted by his children, but especially by his two daughters, who were both very beautiful, he carried on the concerts in the Bath Assembly Rooms. Sheridan, whose father had come to Bath in 1770 to teach elocution fell in love with the elder of Linley's two daughters,

[1] See Sir W. Armstrong's *Thomas Gainsborough* (1905), p. 32. A list of Gainsborough's works done in Bath would be very difficult if not impossible to make.

[2] *Musical Memories*, I, 203.

who though she was but a child, just sixteen years old, already had several suitors, among them Sheridan's elder brother Charles and his friend Halhed, and in the year 1771 actually became engaged by her parent's wish to a rich sexagenarian named Long. The romantic story with all its dramatic details of Eliza Linley and Richard Brinsley Sheridan is too long and too well known to be told here save in outline. It is plain that even in so corrupt a society as that of Bath in 1771, the marriage of so young and so beautiful a girl as Eliza Linley with an old roué such as Long, appeared impossible and disgusting. Public protests were made and in June of that year Foote voiced the universal feeling in his play, "The Maid of Bath," which was produced at the Haymarket Theatre on June 26, 1771. There Eliza Linley appears under the name of Miss Linnett and her aged lover as a fool and a miser, called Flint. The engagement of these two is in the *dénouement* broken off, Miss Linnett exclaiming, "I beg to remain in the station I am in; my little talents have hitherto received the public protection, nor whilst I continue to deserve, am I the least afraid of losing my patrons." As in the play so it was in reality. Miss Linley found herself in love with Richard Sheridan and wrote to Long to ask for her release. He, very unlike the Flint of the play—and indeed his worst fault was his age—set her free and settled £3,000 upon her. This, however, did not altogether smooth the way for the young lovers. Another villain in Foote's play, a certain Major Hackett, in real life Major Matthews, continued to molest her and to escape him she resolved to flee to a convent at St. Quentin. While her father and sister were busy at a concert, she, having feigned indisposition, left the city with Sheridan and a maid. Sheridan seems to have realised that he had hopelessly compromised the girl and so—for he asked nothing better—he secretly married her at a village near Calais. He was then twenty-one years of age, Eliza Linley was nineteen. In spite of the marriage, which was an entire secret, Mrs. Sheridan went into a convent at Lille and was later brought home to Bath by her father, who knew nothing of her marriage. Meantime Matthews, cheated of his mistress, like the ill-bred fool he was, inserted a notice in the *Bath Chronicle* to say that Sheridan was no gentleman and to challenge him to a duel. When Sheridan heard of this he hurried back, fought Matthews in a tavern, and forced an apology from him. Matthews emigrated to Wales, but presently returned to Bath, and unable to hold his tongue was forced to fight a second duel upon Kingsdown. In this it would appear that Sheridan had the worst of it. Even this did not bring husband and wife together; for though Mrs. Sheridan, when she heard of the plight Sheridan was in, insisted on going to him, saying she was his wife; no one believed her and, indeed, it was not till April 13, 1773, that the pair were re-married in London.[1]

Sheridan brings us to the last and not the least important set of people who have helped to make the eighteenth century famous in Bath—the authors whose genius has, as Macaulay declared "made it classic ground." There Rochester wrote his fine historic dialogue "Alexis and Strephon." There Wycherley and Congreve and Defoe went to recruit, Addison took the waters, and Steele found material for his satire. Fielding and Pope were often there as the guests of Ralph Allen, and from Anstey to Dickens, through Smollett, Frances Burney, and Miss Austen, the three literary pillars of Bath society, there is scarcely a great name in literature that has not its connection with Bath: Bolingbroke, Arbuthnot, Gay, who there witnessed a performance of his *Beggar's Opera*, Cowper in 1748, Lady Mary Wortley Montagu, who wept when she left the place, if we may believe her verses:

> To all you ladies now in Bath
> And eke, ye beaus, to you
> With aching heart and wat'ry eyes,
> I bid my last adieu. . . .

Butler and Berkeley, Smollett who wrote a treatise on the Bath waters and filled "Roderick Random" and "Peregrine Pickle" with his reminiscences of the town; Young, the author of "Night Thoughts," who was there in 1757; Hume, and Goldsmith, who was there in 1762, and whose *Life of Beau*

[1] *The Rivals* has been thought to be founded upon his own romantic love story. Lydia is the romantic "Maid of Bath"; her elopement is planned, but not carried out. Sir Anthony stands for Sheridan's own dictatorial father, Acres for Matthews, Sir Lucius for Captain Paumier, and Mrs. Malaprop is surely a character common enough in the Bath of her day. Faulkland is Sheridan himself, and so is Absolute. There is, however, no real analogy between the plot of the play and the story of the lovers.

Nash was the result of his visit, Sterne who was there painted by Gainsborough in 1765, Scott and Southey, Johnson and the Thrale family and the faithful Boswell, Gibbon and Hannah More, Porson and Coleridge and Hazlitt and Beckford and Napier and Carlyle and Forster and Landor they are all in the picture and helped to make Bath what in their day she was, the epitome of England, the polite metropolis of our civilisation.

And now that Bath is become, in any superficial view of her, almost as any other town in England, though at least to the seeing eye still that stately and beautiful city which the Woods made her, it is with these great ghosts of the eighteenth century we people her, as idling about her terraces and squares we pass the languid days in so great a quietness. If you will but have patience any day it may chance you will see Burke steal out of his door on the North Parade, or pass the "Saviour of Europe," carefully making his way through the Abbey Churchyard. Just round the corner in Pierpont Street you shall meet little Lord Nelson with his empty sleeve and it is lovely Miss Linley herself who will drop you a curtsey and make you happy for a whole day on her way to the Assembly Rooms.

And yet the Romans are not more dead than they. Nay in Bath it is, amid all the ghosts, only Rome that continually endures, that does not pass away, that cannot be denied. Akemanceaster, the great Norman Abbey, the mediaeval city, where shall we find a stone of them or anything to remind us they ever were? Yet that which was the root of them all; out of which they were created, and because of which they had a being, remains, astonishing and even tremendous, something that even time has not been able to destroy or to erase from the memory of men.

CHAPTER II

SOME BATH VILLAGES

To realise the beauty and the delight of Bath it is not enough to have seen the Roman Thermae, to have wandered in and out of the Abbey Church, to have felt the nobility of the eighteenth century city, to have lingered in the gardens and by the river communing with the great ghosts of yesterday; you may have done all these things and yet not have understood half of the delight of Bath which is to be found as much in the beauty of her environs, in the villages and country places, the hills and valleys about her, as in the city herself.

I have said that Bath is full of Latin memories, but these are something more than the mere ruins, formidable though they be, of the Roman Thermae. These are dead and discarded, but the Latin memories I mean, which more and more press upon the traveller as he lingers here, are living things, sprung, as I like to think, from those beautiful broken buildings, which like the gods themselves, as men found of old, do not rest in their graves. I suppose no man well acquainted with Italy, with Florence for instance and its environs, can come from Charlcombe over the shoulder of Lansdown without remembering Settignano and its white villa-walls crowned with roses and hung with stone crop; and certainly no one can visit Prior Park with its vast empty rooms, its stony corridors, and shadowy church, in which the scent of incense lingers vaguely even yet, without recalling to mind those Tuscan villas, often enough empty or half empty too, which in their curious summer stillness and their beauty of park or garden are among the delights of the Italian country-side.

As no one will visit Prior Park without thinking of Ralph Allen, for it was his country house, that is a good way if you have time for a ramble and will go afoot which leads you first up on to Bathwick Hill to that Sham Castle, an artificial ruin, which he built to stand in the view from his town house, still to be found, with its eighteenth century façade, buried now in the houses at the end of the North Parade.[1]

An artificial ruin! It is perhaps difficult for us to understand the point of view of men who could desire such a thing with sincerity. It is true that England is littered with ruins beyond any other country in Christendom, but we in our day at least cannot look upon these with satisfaction, nor indeed without regret, I think, for what they once were. No man in our time has come to Glastonbury or Tintern, surely, without wishing they were whole again, without feeling angered at the memory of their murder and saddened by the spectacle of so much beauty that can never be replaced, wantonly spoilt and destroyed by folly and greed. But to build a ruin. . . . It is what you might expect maybe of a South African millionaire, but not of a European. Well, in the eighteenth century they thought differently. Sham castles were not rare and I suppose served their purpose, whatever that may have been.

A ruin, by no means sham, stands not far beyond Sham Castle upon Hampton Down, the ruin of the Wansdyke and of a large British encampment. Thence it is easy to follow westward across Claverton Down to Prior Park under Combe Down where Allen built that great palace he called his country house.

Prior Park, once as its name suggests a possession of the Priory of Bath, which there had a grange and fish ponds and a well-stocked deer-park, though the deer were gone in Leland's day, came, at the Suppression in 1539, with the rest of the monastic property, into the hands of Humphrey Colles. This person shortly after sold the place to Matthew Colthurst whose son Edmund, as we have seen, gave the Abbey Church, dilapidated and dismantled as it was, to the Mayor and citizens of Bath. The Prior's Park, however, he sold to Fulk Morley, from whose descendants it devolved through the Duke of

[1] Wood's first work on settling in Bath in 1727 had been to rebuild this town house of Allen's.

Kingston to Lord Newark, from whom Ralph Allen bought it. Allen hoped to work the quarries, but meeting with very considerable opposition he commissioned the elder Wood in 1736 to build him the great "classical" country house we see to show the virtue and beauty of his stone. A story, probably untrue, is told concerning this commission. For it seems that Wood was doubtful even of Allen's ability to pay for the building of so great a palace till he led him into his house and shewed him strong box after strong box full of gold. Prior Park was finished in 1743, and is indeed, apart from the eastern wing, the flight of steps on the north, and the delightful Palladian Bridge, which are later works, perhaps Wood's masterpiece. The great hexastyle portico, the Corinthian columns of which are some three feet in diameter, is certainly one of the finest compositions of a great time.

It was here, at Prior Park, that Allen entertained his friends, William Pitt, Pope, Fielding, Richardson, Garrick, and Warburton, to name no others. To Allen, Pitt largely owed the fact that he sat in the House of Commons as one of the representatives of Bath. He repaid his obligation in many ways; among others by making Warburton first Dean of Bristol and later Bishop of Gloucester. Pope, though he was under many obligations to Allen, finally quarrelled with him; but it was at Prior Park he finished the "Dunciad," and a lane between Perrymead and Combe Down is still known as Pope's Walk. As for Fielding, if it cannot be said that Prior Park is described in "Tom Jones," it certainly served as the model for Allworthy's estate, as its owner did for the genial squire.

When Allen died in 1764, Prior Park came to Warburton, Bishop of Gloucester since 1759, who had married Allen's favourite niece. In 1769, however, he gave it up and went to live in his Cathedral city. After his death in 1779 Prior Park came into the hands of another parson, a Mr. Smith, who had married Warburton's widow; so it passed to Lord Hawarden from whom in 1829 Bishop Baines, who had received the Benedictine habit at Ampleforth in 1804 and had been created by the Pope Vicar Apostolic of the Western District in 1829, bought the estate for £22,000. Thus Prior Park came again, after nearly three hundred years, into Catholic, and what is more curious, into Benedictine hands.

Bishop Baines had bought Prior Park for his episcopal

Palace, and he founded in connection with it a College for the Catholic youth of England. It was he who built the superb

Bath. Prior Park from the Palladian Bridge.

flight of steps leading to the portico, which he designed, it is said, for religious processions; the eastern wing known as St. Paul's College is also his work. His college, however, was scarcely started when in 1836 Prior Park was gutted by fire.

The Bishop, however, bravely set to work and rebuilt the interior of the mansion which thus no longer dates from Allen's day. In this rebuilding much material, for instance the ceiling of the entrance hall, the fireplaces, and pilasters, came from Houndstreet House in Shepton Mallet which Beckford had built.

In 1842 Bishop Baines died and was succeeded by Bishop Baggs, who a year later began the "Corinthian" church to the west of the house. The college, however, was not a success, and in 1856 Bishop Burgen, who had succeeded Bishop Baggs, closed it. Ten years later, however, Prior Park was bought by Bishop Clifford, who resuscitated the college. He died in 1893, and the place is once more empty and deserted.

There is nothing more lovely than Prior Park, with its gardens and meadows sloping down to Widcombe and overlooking the city, anywhere within reach of Bath. And indeed that is the best as well as the pleasantest way home.

Widcombe, which stands at the foot of the high hills, but well above the city, is the parish in which Prior Park stands. It too, of course, was a part of the Priory Estates, and the ivy-mantled tower of its old church, built by Prior Bird, is perhaps worth a visit: and no one who cares for Fielding and *Tom Jones* will pass quite unnoticed Widcombe Lodge, close to the church, where that famous novel was finished. But here certainly the chief interest lies in the beauty of the way, its gaiety and delight, the gardens and villas which seem too fair and happy for England, and the noble view of the city at one's feet.

A visit to Sham Castle, to the Wansdyke, to the Camp upon Hampton Down with its curious great rocks, and best of all to Prior Park under Combe Down, may well fill the morning of the most energetic wayfarer. But let no one imagine that he has exhausted the interest of these great hills, thrust like a wedge into the valley of the Avon, when he has seen but these.

From the top of Combe Down, from the Cross Keys Inn, for instance, looking south you may see one of the noblest views that even upon these hills will open before you. Beneath you three valleys meet under a great wooded hillside and the villages of Claverton, Freshford, and Midford, with its curious castle, lie clustered there. By the firs to the east stands the tower that Warburton built in memory of Allen, and only half a mile away southward is the little village of South Stoke, the most southern of the immediate possessions of the Priory of Bath in Norman times. The church dedicated to St. James has a very fine Norman doorway of beautiful design and a picturesque perpendicular tower, and in the village is a great gabled tithe barn about which the pigeons still gather, for it is their home.

About three times as far to the west of the Cross Keys Inn as South Stoke is to the south of it, stands English Combe above two valleys and to the north of the Wansdyke, which here again appears as a visible thing, as it does upon Odd Down and Claverton Down. English Combe was English, I suppose, as against the Welsh on the other side of the Wansdyke. The little place is full of interest. In 1086 it formed part of the vast estates of the Bishop of Coutances, but later the rectory and advowson came into the hands of the Priory of Bath. To the Priory the very large and imposing tithe barn at the top of the hill above the churchyard with its fine but simple roof and pretty window belonged. There were stowed the tithes of many manors and the surrounding parishes, among them the tithes of the "vineyards of Lyncombe," which, alas! have altogether disappeared. The church, its dedication is unknown, dates from Norman times and was probably modelled upon John de Villula's great church in Bath. It has a central tower and retains a fine Norman doorway and a good piece of Norman arcading on the northern side of the choir space beneath the tower. On the south side is a large chapel said to have belonged to the Gournay family, whose chief seat was at East Harptree, though they had a castle here, of which nothing remains. On the inside of the west wall of the chancel is a curious figure of the infant Saviour, wrapped in swaddling clothes. Perhaps the sentimental traveller will care to note that two of the bells here date from before the change in religion and that one, probably the "Ave" bell, bears the inscription, *Sancta Maria: Ora pro nobis.*

But if the hills of Bath are thus full of interest and beauty, so are the valleys.

The London road upon the left bank of the Avon brings one in some two and a half miles to Batheaston, at the foot of Solsbury Hill, in whose name perhaps we may find all that is left of Sulis, the Romano-British Minerva.

Batheaston is not very interesting; indeed, the only memorable thing about it is the fact that Batheaston Villa was the scene of those famous and ridiculous contests of poetasters, of which Walpole rightly made so much fun. A certain John Miller, a retired officer, and his wife, the owners of this villa, established these contests, and continued them during some twelve years from 1769. The competitors were probably the merest fribblers, though some among them seem to have taken themselves sufficiently seriously to hope "to convince Pope and Swift that there are more Poets in England than themselves."

Walpole describes the place as a "new built house with a bow window directly opposite to which the Avon falls in a wide cascade, a church behind it in a vale, into which two mountains descend, leaving an opening into the distant country. . . . Here they hold a Parnassus fair every Thursday, give out rhymes and themes, and all the flux of quality at Bath contend for the prizes. A Roman vase, dressed with pink ribands and myrtles, receives the poetry, which is drawn out every festival; six judges of these Olympic Games retire and select the brightest compositions, which the respective successful acknowledge, kneel to Mrs. Calliope, kiss her fair hand and are crowned by it with myrtle—with I don't know what. You may think this a fiction, or exaggeration. Be dumb, unbelievers! The collection is printed, published—yes, on my faith! . . . In short, since folly which never ripens to madness but in this climate, ran distracted, there never was anything so entertaining or so dull." A very foolish affair.

A quarter of a mile southward from Batheaston, across the Avon, stands Bathampton, which, at least after 1086, was a manor belonging to the Priory of Bath. The church dedicated to St. Nicholas is of considerable interest even yet. For the most part, a Perpendicular building, with remnants of Early English work in the chancel, it has in the porch two figures of the time of Edward III. But the most remarkable object is a figure let into the outside of the east wall. This represents a figure of a Bishop of the eleventh or twelfth century, possibly John de Villula himself, who, it may be said, presented an estate he had bought for £60, which included Bathampton, to the new body of monks he had got together in 1106. This figure, which many, without any foundation, I think, take to be the representation of a woman, was, with the two in the porch,

removed from the interior of the church when it was restored by Ralph Allen, who owned and occasionally lived at the Manor House close by.

It is said to have been in connection with this house that Pope quarrelled with Allen. The story is that Pope wished his host to give up the Manor House here to Martha Blount. Allen refused, and the quarrel which followed endured till Pope's death. In his will the poet directed his executors to

St. Catherine's Court, near Bath.

pay Allen £150 as the amount due for his entertainment at Prior Park. Allen paid the sum thus received into the funds of the Bath General Hospital, quietly observing that at the best of times Mr. Pope was not a good accountant, and when he mentioned £150 as measuring the amount of his obligation he had omitted a cipher in the amount.

From Bathampton one returns to Batheaston and so, still following the London road for a quarter of a mile, comes to a by-way on the left which follows St. Catherine's Brook (which here flows into the Avon), up to St. Catherine, another manor of the Priory of Bath. Here is a Grange built by Prior Cantlow at the end of the fifteenth century, surrounded by terraced gardens. Its fine porch is of the time of Charles I, and within there is said to remain a beautiful "hall-screen" of the time of Henry VII. The church, which Cantlow restored and in part rebuilt, was originally a Norman building, as the font bears witness. The most interesting thing remaining there to-day, however, is the glass and especially that in the east window which would seem to date from Prior Cantlow's time; whilst the roof, the choir, the carved pulpit, and the tomb of William Blanchard and his wife are of the first half of the seventeenth century.

Another characteristic and pleasant walk from Batheaston brings one, on the other side of Solsbury Hill, into another valley where the chief village is Swainswick.

Swainswick is said, I wonder with how much truth, to get its name from the Danish leader, but is much more likely to owe it to the descendants of Bladud the swineherd and his pigs. Who held it at the time of the Domesday Inquest we do not know, but that it was then in being would appear certain from the evidence its church affords of Norman builders. The south doorway certainly dates from that time and the tower is early English. But the chief claim of Swainswick to notoriety—I will not say to fame—is the fact that it was the birthplace of that notorious Puritan William Prynne, to whose parents monuments remain in the church. The famous author of *The Unlovelinesse of Love-Lockes* and *Healthes Sicknesse*, a windy tract against the jolly custom of drinking healths, was, I regret to have to admit it, a Somersetshire man. In 1633 he had the cruel audacity to publish a libel upon the virtue of Henrietta Maria for which he paid a fine of £5,000, and lost both his ears. Two years later he attacked little Laud and the Bishops, for which he paid another £5,000 and was branded on both cheeks with the letters S.L., that is, seditious libeller. This restless agitator presently quarrelled with his own side; for when Cromwell and the Independents decided to murder the King he opposed them and then became one of those of whom the House was "purged." The years 1650 to 1652 he spent in prison in Dunster Castle, a grimmer keep doubtless then than now, at the hands of the Commonwealth, just as he had spent the years 1637-1640 in prison at the hands of the

Royalists. The truth seems to have been that Prynne, like those of his kidney to-day, was bent on serving himself. Charles II knew how to deal with this kind of rascal. He made him keeper of the Tower records to "keep him quiet" till he died in 1669.

Swainswick like Batheaston lies under Solsbury Hill, which, crowned by its camp, is so fine a feature in all this landscape. The steep valley which divides it from Lansdown is the road to two of the finest little villages which are set about that vast bastion which so completely dominates Bath. Of Woolley, the village opposite Swainswick, there is nothing I think to say, but of Langridge at the head of the valley there would seem to be much, for it is as completely Norman a place as anything in the country. Norman it is, even in its rather bleak situation, its air of an outpost or a stronghold; and its little lonely church, as lonely as a castle on this high hillside, is almost wholly Norman though it has not altogether escaped the hand of the restorer. The only exception indeed to the Norman air of the place will be found in the beautiful fourteenth century manor house, with its additions of the sixteenth century, the home of the Walsh family, to whose memory there remain some fifteenth century brasses in the church.

From Langridge one follows the road on to the long crest of Lansdown, and turning north there along the high road in about a mile comes to the monument to Sir Bevil Grenville upon the site of the most bloody encounter of the Civil War.

The Great Rebellion which confirmed the new aristocracy in their church lands, in their newly acquired oligarchical power, and broke the Crown, the last bastion of English freedom, was begun in August 1642. In October of that year, Sir Ralph Hopton, a Somersetshire man and one of the best Generals the Royalists had—indeed, as Clarendon calls him, the "soul of the army"—was in Cornwall with Sir Bevil, where in May 1643 they won the battle of Stratton not far from Sir Bevil's home at Stow. This was all very well, but in Cornwall they were useless and isolated, and their need was to join the main body of the King's army with their Western contingent, with as little delay as might be. Therefore, early in June they marched into Somerset, and at Chard joined their forces with those of Prince Maurice and the Marquis of Hertford. Thus was formed an army of some six thousand men, with which was compelled the surrender of Taunton, Bridgewater, and the stronghold of Dunster. Sir William Waller was then at Bath, his chief business being to prevent the Western army joining the King. The Royalists, sure of defeating him, advanced to Wells, and thence by way of Frome to Bradford-on-Avon where Waller faced them upon Claverton Down, which he held very strongly. Finding him too strong for them, the Royalists decided to march to Oxford leaving Waller to follow if he would. That he would was certain, for his chief object was to prevent the Western army reinforcing the King. Therefore they went to Marshfield and thence, apparently unable to control themselves or their army which was thirsting for battle, they made a direct attack upon the great northern ridge of Lansdown held by Waller's forces.

The following letter from one of the combatants upon the rebel side puts the whole matter in a nutshell, at any rate from the rebel point of view:—

"*Captain Edward Harley to Sir Robert Harley at Westminster.*

"1643, *July* 15, BRISTOL.—Monday, the third of July, we heard the enemy began to advance from Froome . . . towards Bath; upon which we drew up all our horse and foot upon Clirkton (*i.e.* Claverton) Downe, fronting towards the enemy, and Colonel Burghill with his regiment of horse and some comanded foote advanced something neerer the enemy to make good a passe which led to Bathe, and this proved one of our greatest disadvantages, for we were not able to send seconds in time, so that party was forced to quitt the place to the enemy and our army to retreate to Bathe. The next day we marched to a hill called Lansdown towards Glostershire, where we continued all day in battaglia, the enemy being in the same posture upon a hill over against us. In the afternoon we saluted them with three pieces of canon, which they liked so ill they presently began to remove, and wheeling somewhat to the left marched to a town called Marshfield almost behind us. Wee fell upon their reare guard and beate them. Wednesday morning the enemy drew out towards us and presently began to retreate; which Sir William Waller perceiving, he sent out a party of horse with musketiers to fall upon them, which they did with very good success; but other parties of our horse being engaged in places of disadvantage were forced to retire to the hill which wee possessed. The enemy pursued hotly and got that ground where our ordinance was planted, but then our whole body of horse charged them with as much resolution as could be, and in particular Sir Arthur Heselrig and his regiment; he received there a push in the thigh with a pike. Our regiment charged twice, and in the second charge my bay horse was killed under mee, but I thank God brought me off well in this hot service. The enemy lost many of their bravest men, and the next morning it pleased God that most of their powder was blowne up, by which Sir Ralph Hopton and some others of quality were very sorely wounded."

All that can properly be said against this letter is that it omits three facts; that the battle of Lansdown was a Royalist victory; that the powder which blew up was that captured from the rebels, and that Sir Bevil Grenville was among the dead.

The victory of Lansdown was dearly purchased with the death of such a man as Sir Bevil Grenville; and the miserable misfortune of the powder which next day robbed the army of the services of Sir Ralph Hopton certainly completed the discomfiture of the troops. As for Sir Bevil, he had taken his young son, John Grenville, a lad of sixteen, with him. When he fell it is said that Anthony Payne, his Cornish servant, caught his master's horse and set the lad thereon and placed him at the head of the Cornishmen. The charge which followed completed the rout of the rebels. Nothing could have been more in keeping with the Grenville traditions. "I cannot contain myself within doors when the King of England's standard waves in the field upon so just an occasion," Sir Bevil had written before Launceston, and it is of him that the Cornish poet sings:—

> Ride! ride! with red spur, there is death in delay,
> 'Tis a race for dear life with the devil;
> If dark Cromwell prevail, and the King must give way,
> This earth is no place for Sir Bevil.
>
> So at Stamford he fought and at Lansdown he fell,
> But vain were the visions he cherished;
> For the great Cornish heart that the King loved so well,
> In the grave of the Grenvilles it perished.

Returning from the battlefield along the high road to Bath, nearly two miles from the monument, we pass the village of Lansdown, where are the few remains of a chapel dedicated to St. Laurence, probably attached to a hostelry for pilgrims. A mile nearer Bath we come upon Beckford's Tower whence its eccentric builder could see his home, Fonthill Abbey in Wiltshire, twenty-six miles away. From the platform at the top a wide and splendid prospect lies before the adventurer. Beckford's body lies beneath his Tower, which with the grounds about it, on his death, came to his daughter the Duchess of Hamilton, who gave the place to the city of Bath to form a public cemetery. Beckford's life was a wasted one. Extravagance brought him to sell the magnificent house he had built upon the ruins of the old manor which had belonged to his ancestors and where he was born, together with the wonderful collections he had made. As a writer he was a brilliant amateur, and indeed *Vathek*, written, it is said, at a sitting, impresses the imagination as does no other piece of Oriental fiction written by a European. But he was as extravagant in the use of his talents as he was with his money, and neither his genius nor his fortune yielded what they would have produced to a wiser and a better man.

From Beckford's Tower you may go straight on into Bath; but there is a way eastward across the fields which leads down into Charlcombe, a pleasant way to a romantic and delightful village. Charlcombe, where upon 28 November, 1734, Fielding married his first wife, Charlotte Cradock, is beautifully situated, looking into the Avon valley, and its tiny and ancient church is well worth seeing with its Norman font and south doorway. Thence by the fairest way about Bath, perhaps, one climbs by the road over the shoulder of Lansdown and comes steeply into Bath by the Lansdown road.

There remain under Lansdown three villages upon the western side of it, which generally form the business of a separate excursion from Bath; I mean Weston, Kelston, and North Stoke.

Weston, less than two miles west of the city, upon what was in Roman days the Via Julia and in the eighteenth century the most fashionable promenade in the neighbourhood of Bath, is chiefly notable as the birthplace of St. Elphege, of whom I spoke in the last chapter; and Kelston, under Kelston Round Hill, was the home of that Sir John Harrington to whom the Bath "Abbey" owes so much. His home was destroyed in 1760, when Sir Caesar Hawkins employed Wood to build the present house near the church. The church is a modern rebuilding of an older fabric of which only the tower and the north porch remain. The last village, North Stoke, is the prettiest of the three, and perhaps the finest view of the whole neighbourhood of Bath is to be had from Prospect Stile, easily reached in less than a mile from the village. It is well that the last of the Bath villages should afford us so wonderful a panorama, for thence we may see Bath itself in the cup of its hills, Bristol to the west on the verge of the Severn sea, to the east the height of Savernake Forest and

Salisbury Plain, to the north the Forest of Dean and the Cotswold Hills, and to the south the great line of the Mendips which seem to shut out from this part of the county, as indeed they do, the true Somerset, and to act, as it were, as an inner gate to that mysterious country of mere and torr, where so much of the secret and the story of England seems to lie hid.

Wells. Detail Bracket.
Figure of a Knight.

CHAPTER III

THE AVON VALLEY

Is there, I wonder, in all Somerset a road more delightful or more nobly English than that which leads through the upper Avon valley from Bath to Freshford, where that gentle stream, not yet sobered with the experience of any city, first comes into the county?

I remember very well the day I first traversed this road, for it was spring and the young leaves were fresh and tender, the soft and uncertain notes of young birds filled the air, and the whole valley was bright with blossom.

The road I followed, and all by chance, that spring morning led me out of the city by way of the Pulteney Bridge and Sydney Gardens, and, climbing as it went, round Hampton Down, past Hampton Rocks, suddenly turned southward as the valley turned and narrowed, and in a moment the world was filled with a new gaiety and a new light, which was the sun shining upon the steep escarpment of Wiltshire as it stood up in a great ridge across the river hung with fresh woods all joyful in the wind and the sun.

So it was with a light heart I went on to Claverton, which is all in a garden about its church, and there in a great tomb upon three steps lies the man of Bath, Ralph Allen, buried there in 1766, his friend, Richard Graves, reading the service.

Allen we all know, but who now remembers any more the author of *The Spiritual Quixote*? Yet I think he should be remembered, at any rate, in his own Claverton, for he was a remarkable man. He was presented to the living of Claverton in 1748 by the lord of the manor, William Skrine, and from the time he came into residence there, in 1750, he was never absent from his parish for a month together till his death in his ninetieth year, in 1804. In the old rectory house at Claverton, which Allen had built for him in 1760 and which he enlarged, he received pupils whom he educated with his own children, among them being Warburton's only son, Henry Skrine, the son of his patron, Malthus, the famous economist, who was taught "little but Latin and good behaviour," and Hoare, the painter. Indeed, as a schoolmaster, Graves was so successful that he was presently able to buy the Manor of Combe Monkton, two miles farther up the valley. He is said to have been short and slender, and an eccentric both in dress and gait, his conversation marked by "a sportive gaiety." Here at Claverton, Shenstone, who was his oldest friend, paid him many visits. Their letters are very numerous, and touch lightly as such men would upon literature. It was to Graves that Shenstone confided that he thought Richardson deserved a bishopric. In his last illness Malthus, his old pupil, attended him and administered the sacrament to him. On the verge of ninety it was no uncommon sight to see him walking into Bath "with all the briskness of youth." The old man lies in the church he served so long.

In Claverton churchyard lie four soldiers of an older England than Allen and Graves knew; men of the Civil War, a Royalist and three rebels killed near the ferry in an affair of outposts in the summer dusk just before the battle of Lansdown.

Claverton, Limpley Stoke, Freshford, are three flowers on the stalk of Avon, each fairer than the other and all together a morning's delight. Yet, save at Claverton, there is nothing but their own country beauty to bring you to see them. Nevertheless if Freshford has nothing old and rare to offer you itself, it is the best key to three splendours—Farleigh Hungerford, Norton St. Philip, and Hinton Charterhouse—that are, in fact, worth almost any trouble to see.

Farleigh, Farleigh Montfort, Farleigh Hungerford, the place has been known at different periods of its history by all these names, lies very beautifully on the last Somerset hillsides looking towards Wiltshire over the valley of the Frome. There in a delightful world of old parklands, of aged oaks and elms, above fair meadows, from which, according to Collinson, Farleigh gets its name, stands the little village with its ruined castle, now no more than a broken great gateway and the desecrated chapel of St. Leonard, within which is the silent chantry of St. Anne, with its beautiful fifteenth century tomb unmatched, I think, in all Somerset, and its monuments of the Hungerfords who held Farleigh for so long and lost it at last through the reckless extravagance of the last of the race, that Sir Edward Hungerford who died in 1711 as a poor knight of Windsor.

What was the fortune of Farleigh before Norman William landed we do not know, but its story since, till in 1369 it came into the hands of the Hungerfords, can be told in a few words. William the Norman granted the little village to his follower, Sir Roger de Courcelle; but when Roger died Farleigh reverted to the Crown and William Rufus granted it, together with the manors of Wellow and Claverton, to Hugh de Montfort, the son of that Thurstan de Bastenburgh who had come with Duke William into England. This Hugh—*cum barba*, as he was called, for he wore a great beard—was presently slain in a duel. His son Hugh sold Claverton to John de Villula. He was an unfortunate man, for his two sons died upon pilgrimage and he left only a daughter to succeed him. She married Gilbert de Gant and had a son whom she named Hugh, who assumed the name of De Montfort and succeeded to Farleigh, which his descendants held till 1336, when Sir Reginald de Montfort sold the place with Wellow to Bartholomew Lord Burghersh.

This great Baron and his son had held Farleigh for thirty-three years when in 1369—the second Bartholomew having but a daughter to follow him, and she married to Edward Lord Despenser and a childless widow—he sold Farleigh to Sir Thomas Hungerford, the friend of John of Gaunt and later the Speaker of the House of Commons. Thus Farleigh Montfort became Farleigh Hungerford.

The great family who now came to make their home at Farleigh for more than three hundred years were of Wiltshire stock; they were seated in that county in the twelfth century and Sir Thomas's father had sat in the House of Commons for Wiltshire in the Parliaments of 1331–2, 1333–4, and 1336, and Sir Thomas himself had been returned for the county in 1357, and was re-elected many times after. Those were troublesome days, and it is not surprising to find that in 1383 Sir Thomas

Hungerford obtained permission to convert his manor house at Farleigh into a castle.

This castle consisted of two courts lying north and south, surrounded by a lofty wall with a moat on the south and west. The outer court on the south had two entrances, that on the east guarded by a drawbridge before an embattled gateway. It is the shell of this gateway which remains; over the arch is a single sickle, one of the devices of the Hungerfords, beneath their crest, a wheatsheaf between two sickles. Within this south court stood the stables, guard rooms, and so forth, and the chapel and gardens. Within the northern court which had a tower at each of its four corners was the dwelling-house, the great dining hall and other buildings.

The chapel which is dedicated to St. Leonard had been in ancient times the parish church, but when Sir Thomas Hungerford converted his manor house into a castle it was soon necessary to build a new church for the people, and thus was founded, in 1443, the present church of Farleigh on the hill to the south of the castle.

The chapel of St. Leonard has attached to it a chantry church dedicated to St. Anne. This was probably built by Sir Thomas while the chapel of St. Leonard served as the parish church, and it came to serve as the mortuary chapel of himself, his wife, and his family. When he died in 1398 it is there he was buried, and in 1412, in accordance with her will, his wife Joan was laid beside him in a magnificent tomb, a master work of the fifteenth century upon which we may still see lying the life-size figures of Sir Thomas Hungerford and Joan his wife, perhaps, apart from the thirteenth century work at Wells, the two most beautiful statues in the county.

The Hungerfords, as I have said, were retainers of John of Gaunt, and Walter Hungerford, the only surviving son of Sir Thomas, was very strongly attached to the Lancastrian cause. When Henry IV seized the throne in 1399 he was knighted. His life was full of adventure. In 1401 he was fighting in France, and is said outside Calais to have met and worsted the King of France in a duel. In 1451 he was with Henry V in France, and it seems that it was he, and not the Earl of Westmoreland, as Shakespeare has it, who on the eve of Agincourt drew from the King his famous rebuke. Before that, in 1413, like his father he had been Speaker of the

House of Commons, while in 1417 he was Admiral of the Fleet, and in 1425 was summoned to the House of Lords as Baron Hungerford. He died in 1447, and was buried beside his first wife in Salisbury Cathedral within the iron chapel, which still exists, built by himself. His very successful life added largely to the estates and wealth of the family; and he was a man of piety too. "He founded a chantry at the altar of the Blessed Virgin Mary in the Chapel of S. Leonard and endowed the same with lands to the amount of ten pounds per annum for the maintenance of one priest to pray for the good estate of him the said Walter and Catherine his wife during their lives and for their souls after their decease; and also for the souls of Sir Thomas Hungerford his father and Joan his mother and all his progenitors. He also established a chaplain there, to celebrate mass every day in the chapel, and upon every third day of December, being the anniversary of the said Sir Thomas, to keep his obit, as also the obit of the said Joan his wife, and then to assemble seven other priests to sing with note the exequies of the dead, and the next day perform solemn mass; each of them to receive from the hands of the chaplain four pence, and thirteen pence to be distributed to as many poor persons . . ."

The chaplain of this, as well as of the other chantry he had founded there, was given his residence in a messuage to the east side of the chapel, where it still remains. The first chaplain appointed was one John Gody, and it is very possibly his tomb we see in the larger chapel between the entrance steps and the font, but the inscription is now illegible.

Sir Walter Hungerford was succeeded by his son Robert, the second Lord Hungerford. He, too, was a great soldier, but as unsuccessful as his father had been successful; for the Lancastrian cause, which he like all his family espoused, was failing. He fought at Towtonfield, and was presently taken prisoner and beheaded at Newcastle. On account of the great dignity of his family they were permitted to bury him beside his father in Salisbury Cathedral. Farleigh became forfeit to the crown.

His eldest son, Sir Thomas, perhaps hoping to get back his estates, sided with the House of York, but half-heartedly, we may think; for presently he was found employing all his power and interest towards the restoration of Henry VI. He too was tried for his life, condemned, and beheaded. Farleigh was granted to John Howard Duke of Norfolk by Richard III. In the first year of Henry VII, however, the attainder of both father and son was taken off and Farleigh came to Walter, second son of Robert, third Lord Hungerford,

This man had fought at Bosworth, and had been knighted upon the field. Later he helped to dispose of Perkin Warbeck.

His son Edward succeeded him, and married as his first wife Jane, daughter of Lord Zouche of Haryngworth, by whom he had a son, Walter, who succeeded him. As his second wife he married Agnes, the widow of John Cotell. It appears that this woman strangled her first husband at Farleigh on July 26th, 1518, with the aid of two yeomen, and after burying the body married Sir Edward Hungerford. Proceedings were not taken against her till Sir Edward's death. She was then convicted and hanged with one of her accomplices at Tyburn, in February 1523.

Sir Walter was then twenty years old and a squire of the body to Henry VIII. In 1532 his father-in-law by his third wife, Lord Hussey of Sleaford, introduced him to Cromwell, to whom he proved very useful in Wiltshire in the matter of the suppression of the Religious Houses, and Cromwell in June 1535 made a memorandum that he should be rewarded.

Not far from Farleigh, through his park, there stood the little Carthusian monastery of Hinton, the second of the Order to be founded in England, dating from 1227. This, no doubt, for such was the wretched condition of the time, Sir Walter Hungerford coveted, as Ahab did Naboth's vineyard. At any rate, when Henry, persuaded by Cromwell, had decided upon the suppression of the religious houses, Hinton was sold at once by Tregonwell, who took the surrender on behalf of the King, to Sir Walter Hungerford. But, as it happens, the spoiler was spoiled. For "through a misunderstanding," Sir Thomas Arundel coming to survey the Charterhouse while Sir Walter Hungerford was absent, "sold and despoiled and quite carried away a great part of the church and other superfluous buildings," so that Sir Walter, on his return, writes to his friend Cromwell to get him recompense, to wit, the manors of Hinton and Norton St. Philip; but happily he perished, and upon Tower Hill, too soon to receive them.

His tragic fate befell him in this wise. In spite of his covetousness, so characteristic of the time, for the property of the Church, he seems to have been a loyal Catholic to the day of his death. In 1540 his chaplain, William Bird, was under suspicion of sympathising with the Pilgrimage of Grace, and Walter Hungerford with him. He was attainted and charged with employing Bird as chaplain, knowing him to be a traitor, and other of his offences were now remembered. On July 28th, 1540, he was beheaded upon Tower Hill, together with his patron Cromwell. There is some suspicion that he was not altogether sane, and his treatment of his third wife would certainly seem to strengthen such a suggestion. In 1536 she addressed the following letter to Cromwell, in which she asserts that her husband had kept her locked up in one of the towers of Farleigh for three or four years. "Here," she writes, "I have byn these three or fower yeares past without comfort of any creature, and under the custodie of my Lord's Chaplain, Sir John a Lee, which hath once or twice poyson'd me, as he will not deny upon examination. He hath promised my Lord that he would 'soon rid him of me;' and I am sure he intended to keep his promise, for I have none other meat and drink but such as cometh from the said Priest, and brought me by my Lord's fool, which meat and drink I have oft feared, and yet do every day more than another, to taste; so that I have been well-nigh starved, and sometimes of a truth I should die for lacke of sustenance, and had, long ere this time, had not poor women of the country, of their charity, knowing my Lord's demayne always to his wives, brought me to my great window in the night such meat or drink as they had, and gave me for the love of God; for money have I none wherewith to pay them, nor yet have had of my Lord, these fower yeares, fower groats."

The great days of the Hungerfords came to an end with the execution of Walter Hungerford, first Baron Hungerford of Heytesbury, for such was his title. He was succeeded by his son, Walter Hungerford, born in 1532, and called "the Knight of Farleigh," to whom the confiscated estate was restored by Queen Mary in 1554. He, too, had trouble with his wife, the second, for he had two, whom he accused of trying to poison him in 1564, and of having committed adultery with William Darrell of Littlecote in 1560 and 1568. She was acquitted of both these charges, however, and her husband refusing to pay the heavy costs was committed to the Fleet. His wife went to live with the English Catholics at Louvain. He died in 1596, leaving all his property to his brother Edward. He lies in the south-east corner of the large chapel in a great altar tomb bearing curiously arranged the following inscription :—

"TIME. TRYETH. TRUTH. QUOD WALTER. HUNGERFORD. KNYGHT. WHO. LYETH. HERE. AND EDWARD. HYS. SONNE. TO. GD'S. MERCY IN. WHOM. HE. STRUST. FOR. EVER. ANo. DO. 1585. THE VI. OF. DESBR."

The Knight of Farleigh left, as I have said, all his property to his brother Edward, who died in 1607, and is also buried at Farleigh in the north-east corner of the smaller chapel. His tomb bears the following inscription :—

EDWARD. HUNGERFORD. KNIGHT. SONNE.
TO. WALTER. LORD. HUNGERFORD. AND.
LATE. HEIRE. TO. SIR. WALTER. HUNGERFORD.
DECEASED. THE. 5TH. DAIE. OF.
DECEMBER. 1607. AND. LIETH.
HERE. WITH. DAME. JANE. HIS. WIFE.
DAUGHTER. TO. SIR. ANTHONY.
HUNGERFORD. OF. DOWNE. AMNY."

The fate of Farleigh Castle in the Civil War has never been satisfactorily explained. That it was held for the King and by a Colonel John Hungerford we know, but we cannot connect this man with the Farleigh family, though he is said to have been the owner's half-brother. This owner was Sir Edward Hungerford, commanding the Wiltshire forces for the Parliament. In 1643 Sir Edward had a violent quarrel with Sir Edward Boynton, the Parliamentary governor of Malmesbury, each accusing the other of treachery. Subsequently he attacked Farleigh, and took it in September 1645. He died in 1648, and was buried in the middle of the smaller chapel in a magnificent altar tomb of black and white marble. He was the son of Sir Anthony Hungerford of Black Bourton in Oxfordshire, who married as his second wife Lucy, daughter of the Knight of Farleigh. He was succeeded by the son of his half-brother, Anthony Hungerford, the Royalist. This was that Sir Edward, the last of his race, who was born in 1632. He was a keen Royalist, and at Charles II's coronation was made a Knight of the Bath, just as the Sir Edward whom he succeeded had been in 1632. He was known everywhere for his reckless extravagance, and when he had, as it is said, made away with some thirty manors, he obtained permission to hold a market on the site of his London house which had been destroyed by fire. So was established Hungerford market; the market house was removed in 1860, when Charing Cross Station was built in its place. A ruined man in 1686, he sold the manor and castle of Farleigh to Henry Boynton of Spye Park, a descendant of the parliamentary general who had quarrelled with Sir Edward Hungerford in Malmesbury in 1643. He got £56,000 for Farleigh, which in 1700 Boynton sold to Joseph Houlbridge of Trowbridge, with whose descendants it remained till Lord Donington bought it in 1891. The last Hungerford thus stripped himself of his possessions, of which Farleigh had been in his family for more than three hundred years. He died a poor Knight of Windsor in 1711, and was buried in London.

Little remains to be said of Farleigh. All we have to-day there is a ruin save the chapel, and that is desecrated, and rather a museum than a church. Nevertheless it is one of the most precious things in Somerset, lying as it does there unannounced by the side of the white road among its old trees still looking over the wide meadows of England.

It is hard to leave Farleigh, but it would be harder if it were not that it is for Norton St. Philip and Hinton we are bent:—Norton St. Philip, "a pratie Market Town about a mile from Farley Castelle," as Leland describes it.

Norman William gave the manor of Norton with that of Hinton to Edward of Salisbury, and from this Edward the manor descended to Ella Countess of Salisbury, who in 1292 bestowed it upon the Carthusian house she had founded at Hinton. The monks held in Norton a charter of free warren and other privileges, among them the market of which Leland speaks, "a meane market . . . most maynteyned by clothing." The fine old Inn, the great sight at Norton, a half-timbered house of the fifteenth century excellently preserved, was probably always used as a hostelry even by the monks, but they may also have turned it to account for the purposes of the wool trade of the Priory. Here it was that the Duke of Monmouth slept upon the night of June 26, 1685, in his march from Glastonbury to Keynsham before the Battle of Sedgemoor. "While he was at the Inne a man hoping for the reward that had been offered for the life of the Duke fired at him as he stood at a window; but according to the ballad the Duke

> " . . gently turned him round
> And said, 'my man, you've missed your mark
> And lost your thousand pound.'"

The church dedicated to St. Philip and St. James is a curious building with a curious tower; indeed, Freeman said

Norton St. Philip. The George Inn.

of it that it was built by a man who had devised it out of his own head without reference to any other building. That it does not accord with Somerset traditions is not curious after all, if the monks, who administered and owned it, built it, and then it was much restored in 1847. It is possible that the church originally consisted of a chancel and nave, that later chapels were added to the nave, and that these were at some time, possibly after the Reformation, turned into aisles. In the floor of the nave Collinson records there were in his day "the mutilated portraitures in stone of two females close to each other, called by the inhabitants 'The Fair Maidens of Foscot,' a neighbouring hamlet now depopulated. There is a tradition

Norton St. Philip. Courtyard of the George Inn.

that the persons they represent were twins whose bodies were at their birth enjoined together; that they arrived at a state of maturity, and that one of them dying the survivor was constrained to drag about her lifeless companion till death released her of her burden."

One comes upon Hinton Priory, about a mile from Freshford, in a country that is still all a parkland and shadowy with ancient trees almost without knowing. For the Manor House, which occupies the site of the Prior's dwelling, stands well back from the road, half hidden even by the foliage of spring, before great lawns, white with daisies as with snow, with scarce a hint of its presence. The Manor House empty, and to be let when I was last there, is for the most part a building of the sixteenth century, and probably the work of the Colthursts, who it will be remembered acquired Bath Abbey. They seem to have built the house, without any sort of scruple, out of the materials of the monastic buildings, and it must be confessed they achieved something we could not do to-day. For I can imagine few more delicious places than Hinton Abbey, as it is called, with its curious stone staircase, and its sunny rooms, its gables and tall chimneys and mullioned windows looking out across vast lawns to the belt of old trees, where what is left of the monastery stands in all its Early English beauty.

Hinton Priory was a Carthusian House, the second of that Order to be founded in England. In 1181, Henry II, as part of his penance for Becket's murder, which touched Somerset so nearly, for more than one of the assassins was a Somerset man, founded at Witham the first English Carthusian House and presently obtained St. Hugh as Prior there. And though Henry had nothing to do with the foundation of this second house at Hinton, still indirectly he is connected with it, for it was founded by his son and Fair Rosamund's, William Longespée, who had married Ella, Countess of Salisbury. After all, however, it must be admitted that Hinton owes more to the Countess than to her husband. The Carthusian house that he actually founded, in thanksgiving, it is said, for deliverance from shipwreck on his way home from the Crusades, was at Hatherop, near Fairford, in Gloucester. This for some reason or other did not take root, and so, after her husband's death, the Countess of Salisbury refounded it at Hinton, on the same day, it is said, upon which she founded the nunnery at Lacock, not far away in Wiltshire; Primo mane apud Lacock, et Hinton post nonam. Lacock in the morning and Hinton after Nones.

This refoundation took place as it seems in 1227, Henry III being King of England; presently the Countess, as a widow, herself took the veil, and for more than fifteen years ruled her Nunnery of Lacock as Abbess, and was buried in the choir there. Her husband lies in Salisbury Cathedral.

Hinton Charterhouse was dedicated in honour of the Blessed Virgin, St. John Baptist, and All Saints, as was Witham, and it was from the first called Locus Dei. This would seem to

Hinton Charterhouse.

mark it as a place of great sanctity. Unfortunately we know very little of its life; we have documents in which we find certain lands and certain privileges granted to the monks of Hinton Priory, but we know almost nothing of the life of the monks there. And now all is silence. Yet it was for some human touch, some incident of sanctity, or of heroism, or of sacrifice that I longed, for already I loved the place as I passed across those beautiful deserted lawns under the great old trees to the few exquisite fragments which remain of Hinton Priory. There to my disappointment—for in these sentimental journeys one prefers to be alone—I found a man upon the same errand as myself. Avoiding him as far as I could, I examined the ruins. These consist of a chapel lighted only at the eastern end by three lancets, above which is a chamber that is called the library, and above again a columbarium. This group of buildings is very beautiful and in the Early English style. To the north is a more recent building consisting of a vaulted corridor below and above a small chamber. To the south-west lies what is generally said to be the Refectory, a great chamber borne upon pillars thirty feet by twenty, half full of earth, above which is a dormitory. Beyond the refectory is the kitchen, measuring some twenty-two feet by twelve, with a large fire-place and serving hatch.

I had got so far in my examination and was about to return to the chapel when the fellow I had seen looking about the buildings and whom I had tried to avoid, for he seemed of a truculent sort and yet timid withal, a man of sudden resolutions, came striding on and up to me and suddenly asked whether I thought of "taking the place."

"I did not know it was to be had," I answered.

"Yes," said he, "it is, and I hope you have no designs upon it, for I want it myself."

"You may be quite easy in your mind," said I, "I could not afford it."

"Neither can I; neither can I," said he hastily. "But have you ever thought what could be done with such a place as this? Of course you haven't. Have you ever tried to reconstruct it? It's perhaps impossible, as you can see, for the destruction has been very complete with regard to the main buildings, and even those which remain have been the subject of dispute. The chapel, for instance, has been called the chapter-house, an impossible suggestion, for its shape and dimness unfit it for any such business. However, it was certainly not the church of the monks; it was probably the chapel of the *conversi*, the lay brothers, for you know this was a Carthusian house."

"You evidently know the place well," I said, hoping, I confess, to have done with him.

"Yes," he answered after a pause. "I have known it ever since I was a boy, and I have always wanted to buy it—not for myself . . . Do you know the whole story of the place?"

"Why," said I, "I was only telling myself just now that it has no story, no human story that is, nothing but facts, and precious few of them."

He turned away and I thought I had got rid of him, when he wheeled round and digging in the turf with his stick demanded:—

"Of course you know that the Nicholas Henton in *Henry VIII* was a monk here. The man I mean who was Confessor to the Duke of Buckingham? How does it go? Someone says to the king when he asks what brought Buckingham to think of the throne:

> "'He was brought to this
> By a vain prophecy of Nicholas Henton.'

"And the king asks:

> "'What was that Henton?'

"And is answered

> "'Sir, a Chartreux friar.
> His confessor; who fed him every minute
> With words of sovereignty.'

"But you recollect the whole story, I see. However, you probably never heard of Dom Stephen of Hinton, yet Petrus Dorlandus speaks much of him in his chronicle of the Carthusian Order."

Something at once pedantic, charming and a little pathetic in this lonely and sentimental traveller mooning so seriously about the ruins of Hinton and evidently with too much understanding and love for his peace of mind, touched me. "Tell me," said I, "of this Stephen." "Sir," said he, "I would tell you very gladly if you would believe me (but you will not) all there is to tell. As it is, let this suffice. One day under these apple trees here at Hinton this Stephen saw and spoke with the Blessed Mary Magdalen, yes, as though Hinton were Italy and Somerset as blessed as Umbria—and she blest him."

"And that," said I, "is why you love the place and want it?"

"Yes," said he, "that is it. And yet not altogether; but of what other place in England is such a thing credibly reported? That is why I love it, and then, besides its beauty—those Early English buildings, the chapel, the dove-cote, the library among those great trees—there is its hard fate. Even this little

Hinton Cromwell could not spare. When the Priory was dissolved in 1539, the last Prior Edmund Hurd could do nothing but surrender it. There is a letter of his I have read written to his brother Alan in London about this very thing. He had then sixteen monks: all signed the surrender, for there was nothing else to do. Hungry Hungerford of Farleigh was appointed chief steward and surveyor, and the buildings were sold to him by Tregonwell, the King's Commissioner. Within three months the place was a ruin. Hungerford, however, did not long enjoy his ill-gotten gains, for, in 1540, both he and Cromwell were beheaded together upon Tower Hill.

"Hinton presently came into the hands of the Colthursts, those land jobbers of the period of whom we hear more than enough. They probably built the Manor House there out of the ruins, and then sold all again to the Hungerfords in or about 1578. . . . But I weary you."

"Not at all," said I. "But I am curious to know what you would do with Hinton if you had it."

"Why," said he, "what should I do with it but restore it as far as I could to them that built it. Are there not Carthusians to-day at Parkminster?"

"You would return it then to the Carthusians? You are a Catholic?"

He bowed. "And failing them," said he, "I would get me a loud-voiced priest from Downside, and, since I am a Christian, I would establish here in this chapel at Hinton a daily mass of Requiem for the repose of the soul of Henry VIII."

There was a pause. Then, said I: "I think you would do well, for I, too, hold it fundamentally a Christian act to have pity upon mere wretchedness."

And when I had said this I bade him farewell and went on my way.

And I came by way of the village of Hinton Charterhouse, where, in the church, an Anthony Hungerford, who had held command in Ireland, and died in 1594, lies buried, to Wellow, with its beautiful church, built by Sir Walter Hungerford in 1372. The manor house of the family, now a farm, still stands near the school. The church, however, is the chief beauty of Wellow. It is dedicated to St. Julian, a rare dedication, pointing, probably, to a Christian sanctuary here as old as the Roman occupation, of which there are many signs in Wellow, pavements and a sudatory, discovered as early as the seventeenth century. The church, in spite of restoration—the chancel is all new—is very fine both within and without, the tower being among the noblest in these parts. The roof is beautifully panelled, and the nave still boasts a fine oak screen and some old benches. The font is Early English, and there is on the south side the effigy of a priest, possibly of the fifteenth century. The Hungerford chapel, now spoilt by an organ, has a rather charming roof and two seventeenth century Hungerford tombs. To the east of the church is the well of St. Julian.

From Wellow that same day I went on over the hills northward through Combe Hay, where in the church Sir Lewis Dyver, who held Sherborne Castle for the king, lies buried, to Midford, and so back to Bath.

Then on the following morning I set out again by Avon side to explore the valley below Bath. It was very early when I came out of Southgate Street by way of the Old Bridge which joins Bath and Holloway—originally they say erected in the reign of Edward III; before which happy time, if one may believe the historians, one crossed by a little ford just above it. The bridge was granted in 1304 to the monks, who doubtless kept it in repair and so well that it endured till 1754, when it was pulled down and the present structure, still called the Old Bridge, was erected by the Corporation.

Just across the Old Bridge, instead of climbing up Holloway, I turned to the right beside the Avon, into the now rather dingy suburb of Twerton. Twerton, however, is not to be altogether despised, for it is very old. It was here that the old industry of Bath, the weaving of cloth, was set up and established by the monks in the fourteenth century, and presently came to surpass in excellence them "of Ypres and of Gaunt," as Chaucer tells us. It must have been from Twerton that his Wyf of Bathe came:

> A good wyf was there of bisyde Bathe. . . .
> Of clooth-making she hadde swiche an haunt,
> She passed hem of Ypres and of Gaunt.

Of later years Twerton, though cloth is still manufactured there, has lost all its charm and character and exists merely as a suburb of Bath. Yet even so late as the days of Fielding it was a village separate from the city and full of delight. There Fielding lived, and there part of *Tom Jones* was written; while of the great antiquity of the place we are assured by that Norman doorway which still remains in its rebuilt and restored church, reminding one of the days of John de Villula.

Here it must be confessed that the valley of the Avon below Bath has none of the charms it has in such plenty above the city, nor any of the gay delight we find in its course through Bath itself. As the hills draw away from it and the valley widens, the river loses its liveliness and becomes at once the sluggish and somnolent stream hidden in green fields, which it remains till lost in the murk and noise of Bristol. Nor is the valley itself below Bath other than monotonous. The railway runs on either side the stream as far as Keynsham, and the broad highway is too well used to afford the wayfarer much pleasure. For this cause, many travellers bent on exploring the Chew Valley take the train between Bath and Keynsham, and in this they are perhaps wise. Nevertheless, once in a way, the road should be followed, for there is more than one quiet village upon it which should not be missed. Of these the first is Newton St. Loe, a little place just off the highway, some four miles from Bath before you come to Corston.

Newton St. Loe, a very pretty and well-cared-for village which you may easily miss, stands well above the highway to the south upon a little isolated hill. The church, which stands high, looking down upon the churchyard over the trees of Newton Park, is, or was, a Perpendicular building of which various restorations have left very little but the arcade on the south side and the curious squint between the chancel and the south aisle. The heavy roof is modern and out of place in a Somerset church. Newton St. Loe has, however, memories older than the church, of Roman times, and a villa was discovered in the neighbourhood together with many Roman fragments at the time when the railway was being built. At the Domesday Inquest the Manor belonged to the Bishop of Coutances, but by the time Henry III sat upon the throne of England it had come into the hands of the family of St. Loe from which it gets its name. This family is said to take its name from St. Laud in Normandy, over the gates of which town its arms were to be seen as late as the seventeenth century. It is uncertain when the St. Loes came into England; their name is not in the Battle Abbey Roll and the first mention of them in Somerset shews them as holding "half a fee in Niweton and Puppelow, 47 Henry III." Here, in Newton, they built a castle in which they are reported to have imprisoned King John, and it is possible that it is the remains of this building we see in the vaulted gateway in the park of the present eighteenth century house. John de Sancto Laudo was, however, sheriff of Dorset and Somerset from 1284 to 1290 in Edward I's reign, and the lists of their manors shew the St. Loes to have been a great family. We shall come upon them again at Chew Magna.

Just as Newton St. Loe lies off the high road a little to the south of it, so does Corston, a pretty old world village, where in the ancient manor house, now a farm, Southey went to school. Robert Southey was the son of a linendraper, and grandson of a farmer of Lydeard St. Laurence in the Quantocks, who was descended from a great clothier of Wellington. The poet was brought up at Bath by his aunt, Elizabeth Tyler, and before the age of eight he had read all the plays in her library. From her rather too tender care he was sent to school at Corston, where his master, whose wife had been his housekeeper and was given to drink, taught him nothing, and he must have been very wretched. "Here," says he, in his reminiscences,[1] "one year of my life was spent with little profit and with a good deal of suffering. There could not be a worse school in all respects." Yet he sentimentalises the place charmingly enough in *The Retrospect*:—

> Corston, twelve years in various fortunes fled
> Have pass'd with restless progress o'er my hea
> Since in thy vale beneath the master's rule
> I dwelt an inmate of the village school.
> Yet still will Memory's busy eye retrace
> Each little vestige of the well-known place;
> Each wonted haunt and scene of youthful joy
> Where merriment has cheer'd the careless boy;
> Well pleased will fancy still the spot survey
> Where once he triumphed in the boyish play
> Without one care, where every morn he rose,
> Where every evening sunk to calm repose.

[1] *Life and Corespondence*, i, 46–58. Southey was at Corston, 1781–2.

Large was the house, though fallen in course of fate
From its old grandeur and manorial state.
Lord of the manor, here the jovial squire
Once called his tenants round the crackling fire;
Here, while the glow of joy suffused his face,
He told his ancient exploits in the chase,
And proud his rival sportsmen to surpass
He lit again the pipe and fill'd again the glass.

. . . . .

There now in petty empire o'er the school
The mighty master held despotic rule.
Trembling in silence, all his deeds we saw,
His look a mandate and his word a law.

. . . . .

Such was my state in those remembered years
When two small acres bounded all my fears,
And therefore still with pleasure I recall
The tapestried school, the bright, brown-boarded hall,
The murmuring brook that every morning saw
The due observance of the cleanly law;
The walnuts, where, when favour would allow,
Full oft I went to search each well-stript bough;
The crab-tree, which supplied a secret hoard
With roasted crabs to deck the wintry board.

It was a Sunday evening when I set out from Corston, and darkness had fallen solemnly upon all the valley and the now distant hills, when I came into the village of Keynsham where the river Chew flows into the Avon.

CHAPTER IV

THE CHEW VALLEY

THERE is a valley—happy is he who knows it—which winds quite through that great hill country one sees when looking southward from Prospect Stile, above Kelston and North Stoke, upon Lansdown, opening a way from the Avon valley to the great barrier of the Mendips. This valley is the valley of the Chew, and at the very foot and end of it, where the Chew flows into the Avon, stands Keynsham, a famous place.

"It has always been the popular opinion," says Collinson, "that Keynsham derived its name from one *Keyna*, a British Virgin who lived about the year of Christ 490, and according to Capgrave, a writer of the fourteenth century, was daughter of Braganus, prince of that province in Wales which from him was afterwards called *Brecknockshire*. When this lady arrived at years of maturity she attracted many admirers, and many noble personages sought her in marriage; but she was deaf to all their overtures, having consecrated her virginity by a perpetual vow, for which cause she was denominated by the Britons *Keyna the Virgin*. At length she determined to forsake her native country and seek some desert place where to indulge in private her religious contemplations. Directing her journey beyond the Severn, she met with a certain woody place in these parts, and made her request to the prince of the country that she might be permitted to serve God in that spot in solitude and retirement. The prince informed her he was ready to grant her petition, but that the place so swarmed with serpents that neither man nor beast could live therein; to which the virgin replied that she firmly trusted she should be able to drive the venomous brood out of all that country; thereupon the place was granted her, and by her prayers all the snakes and vipers were converted into stones. And to this day the stones in that country resemble the windings of serpents through all the fields and villages as if they had been so framed by the hand of the engraver."

Keynsham to-day, too big for a village and too small for a town, is not a very charming place, consisting for the most part of one very long street. From Domesday Book it appears that the King held it; but later it came into the hands of the Earls of Gloucester, where it remained till in 1170 William, Earl of Gloucester, at the request of Robert, his son, when on his death bed, founded in Keynsham a house of Black Canons, which he dedicated to the honour of God, the Blessed Virgin Mary, and St. Peter and St. Paul, and endowed the same with the whole manor, and hundred of Keynsham, which donation was confirmed by his successor, Gilbert de Clare, and ratified by King Edward II, in 1318. The canons of Keynsham were of the Order of St. Austin and followed the Rule of St. Victor. There were two other similar houses of this Order and Rule in Somerset, but both of later date than Keynsham Abbey, Worspring Priory, founded in 1210, and Stavordale Priory, founded in 1263; in all England there were apparently but three beside.[1] The order was conventual, that is, its members were professed for a special house and not for a province, or a congregation, like the Friars; but they were not so closely bound to their house as were the monks. They were allowed to serve parishes that were impropriated to their houses; for instance, the canons of Keynsham may well have served Keynsham Church and parish, whereas the monks of Hinton were obliged to employ a secular vicar to serve Hinton and Norton.

Keynsham at the time of the dissolution was ruled by Abbot John Sturton and was served by eleven canons. It was received as was Hinton by Tregonwell. The whole place was thrown down and a certain Richard Walter was paid twelve pounds for melting the lead upon the church, the cloisters, and the steeple. The bells were sold as old metal at so much a hundredweight. Immediately after the spoliation the king let the site of the Abbey to John Panter for twenty-one years together with a close called Covent Orchard. The manor he settled upon the Queen Consort Catherine Parr, who as we know survived him and lived to marry Sir Thomas Seymour, Lord High Admiral of England. She died, however, in 1548,

[1] St. Austin's Abbey, Bristol, Warmsley Priory, Hereford, and Wigmore Abbey, Hereford. The Austin Canons, however, following the so-called Rule of St. Austin, were very numerous. At the dissolution they had some 164 houses, the oldest of which was St. Botolph, Colchester, founded in 1100; two were mitred abbeys, Waltham Cross and Cirencester.

and King Edward VI, upon May 12, 1550, granted the Manor and Hundred of Keynsham, together with the parsonage and church and other manors belonging to the Abbey, to Sir John St. Loe of Newton St. Loe for sixty years. But in 1552 this lease was in part surrendered and for a sum a little above nine hundred pounds the King granted to Thomas Bridges, Esq., Keynsham and Eastover and Westover and other properties. This Thomas Bridges was the second son of Sir Giles Bridges of Coberley in Gloucester, and brother of the Sir John Bridges who in 1554 was created Baron Chandos. Henceforth this family held Keynsham, destroyed everything that was of old, mended the road with the abbey church, and in fact obliterated in Keynsham everything that might have served to remind folk of their so lately lost freedom. Even the chancel of the parish church they succeeded in appropriating to themselves and turning it into their mortuary chapel.

Practically nothing remains of the abbey buildings, which seem even in Leland's day to have wholly disappeared; but the site has been excavated in our own time.

The parish church, however, remains a very spacious building with a beautiful though late western tower. This tower is Laudian, and was begun in 1634 when the old tower which then stood at the east end of the north aisle was destroyed by lightning (1632). The chancel, in which the Early English lancets still remain, is, as I have said, full of the memorials of the Bridges family, some of which are of much interest. The south aisle is of the plainest Decorated style and there is a fine Perpendicular screen, a small fragment of that which once stretched right across the church. Later the north aisle was added in the Perpendicular style, and then the south aisle was raised to correspond with it. When this was done and before the western tower was built the west front of the church must have been very noble. The fall of the northern tower in 1632 destroyed the chancel wall where the organ stands and no doubt much of the furniture of the church including the screen. This was re-erected in the Jacobean style and a part of it is now placed in front of the organ. The pulpit, too, dates from this time. There are two sundials: on that set over the main door of the church one reads "Festina lente." Can this be a motto of the Bridges family;

or was it they who wrote so frankly upon the southern dial "Venio ut fur"—I come as a thief?

In the old days a noted place of pilgrimage stood not far from Keynsham in the parish of Brislington, and though it has entirely disappeared the site is still pointed out by the cottagers. This was the Chapel of St. Anne in the wood. It stood upon the other side of Avon, and a ferry still in use conveyed pilgrims thither. Founded by Roger, first Lord de la Warre, in the end of the thirteenth century, it was a notable place even at the end of the fifteenth when King Henry VII rode from Bristol on pilgrimage to its shrine, and again upon August 22, 1502, both he and his Queen paid their devotions there.

I left Keynsham early one morning on my way up the valley of the Chew, but I had not gone further than Chewton Keynsham when I turned more than a mile out of my way to visit Queen Charlton, a little village some two miles from Keynsham upon the old road to Bath, according to Collinson.

Queen Charlton got its name from Queen Edith, the Confessor's wife, whose property it was, and as it happened it earned its title twice over, for when Henry VIII suppressed the monastery of Keynsham and stole its goods, and this manor too among them, he bestowed it as he did Keynsham itself upon Queen Catherine Parr. When the Abbey held it the abbots had here a court house of which nothing now remains but an old gateway, the arch of which is Norman and which is generally considered, I think wrongly, to be the gateway of the abbey itself. The church is deserving of particular notice, for it is not only an exceedingly pretty village church, but one very characteristic, though not perhaps as much so as that of Whitchurch a mile away to the west, of the early Somerset manner. It remains in part a Norman building with a central tower which Norman arches still support. The original Norman tower was low and presumably unbuttressed. In the Perpendicular period a new storey was added to the tower, which was strengthened as we see with diagonal buttresses. The manor house beside the church is of great interest and antiquity, and it was here in the present gardens the abbot of Keynsham had his Court House.

So I went on my way through the beautiful vale past

Compton Dando of which I find nothing to say save that it came at one time into the possession of the Hungerfords of Farleigh by marriage, and that into the south buttress of the eastern end of its church a Roman altar has anciently been built just as the figure at Bathampton has, probably to preserve it, been built into the wall of the church there. I came to Publow beside the water with its magnificent church tower of four great storeys.

Publow anciently belonged to the St. Loes of Newton, and later came with Compton Dando into the hands of the Hungerfords. The beautiful tower of Publow church is as well seen from Pensford, the next place in this valley, and the only one save Keynsham that can boast of a railway station. But though Pensford is now more important than Publow, it was not always so, for its old name was Publow St. Thomas, and it was a chapelry of Publow. The St. Thomas of Pensford is St. Thomas à Becket, to whom the church, a Late Perpendicular building with a Jacobean pulpit, is dedicated. The old chapel was demolished in the seventeenth century, and the chantry, anciently founded here by the St. Loes, disappeared at the Suppression. It was a place of some importance in the cloth trade of Somerset, and Leland describes it in his day as "a praty market townlet occupied with clothinge. Browne of London yn Limesstrete was owner of it. The toune stands much by clothinge."

Following the road and the stream up the valley I came about a mile above Pensford to the great spectacle of this vale, and one of the most remarkable antiquities in England, I mean the stones at Stanton Drew, " secret as the thoughts of God." And, indeed. the whole place is full of an indefinable sense of mystery and stillness, perhaps by reason of the immemorial elms which stand everywhere about it like a curtain.

The "megalithic remains" lie in the fields beyond the church to the south-east of the road. They cannot of course compare with the great work at Stonehenge, but they are a sufficiently remarkable memorial, apparently of the Neolithic age.

They consist so far as is known of one great circle with an avenue, and of two smaller circles, one to the north-east of the great circle, also with an avenue, and one to the south-west. Besides these there are three mighty fragments which are certainly connected with them. One is the triangle of stones known as the Cove near the Church, the second a vast boulder now much smaller than of old, for it has been hewn to mend the roads, known as Hauteville's Coit upon the northern side of the river and close to the road as one comes into Stanton; the last is as far the other way and upon the southern side of the river, it consists of two stones.

The local tradition with regard to the circles, which are known as the "Fiddlers and the Maids," or "The Wedding," is that a pair of lovers "were married on a Sunday and the friends and guests were so profane as to dance upon the green together, and by a divine judgment were turned into stones." I do not think this tradition can be older than the Reformation, for in Catholic England I hope no one would have thought it evil to dance upon Sunday. With regard to Hauteville's Quoit the local tradition is quite different, and does not in any way connect it with the circle. It is said the Sir John Hauteville, of Norton Hauteville or Hawkfield, threw this vast stone from the top of Maes Knoll hard by.[1] As for the Cove I can find no local tradition concerning it nor the derivation of its name. But the feeling is strong that (as Wood of Bath records) the people say: "No one was ever able to reckon the number of these metamorphosed stones, or to take a draught of them, though several have attempted to do both and proceeded until they were either struck dead upon the spot, or with such illness as soon carried them off."

The question remains unsolved as to what purpose these stones served, who erected them, and when and how it was done. In fact, we know absolutely nothing about these great ruined circles, nor can we be sure to what age they belong. It seems certain that the stones of the north-east circle one and all come from the Harptree neighbourhood, at best some five miles away, and since the stones of the great and south-west circles are smaller and differ from them geologically, we may perhaps conclude that they belong to a different age, but whether earlier or later it is impossible to say.

[1] "Sir John Hauteville lived in the time of Henry III, and was engaged in all the wars of that Prince, and 54th of that reign was signed with the Cross in order to his going to the Holy Land with Prince Edward. In his old age he is said to have resided at Norton, where he seems to have been somewhat of a terror to the inhabitants inasmuch as they termed him a *giant*."

But if we assume, as most of us do, that the stones are the ruins of a Temple, then it is evident that the church of Stanton Drew, the church of St. Mary, stands within precincts which, whether Druidic or no, have for ages been considered holy. This church is an uninteresting building, but its font belongs to Norman if not to earlier times. But if the church is disappointing, "the parsonage house," as Collinson says, "is a curious piece of antiquity. On a dead window which has horrid figures at the corner are two armorial shields cut in the stone." One of these bears the arms of Bishop Beckington.

Chew Magna, a mile above Stanton Drew, and anciently the most important place in the valley, stands upon the north side of the river which, with the Winford water, makes an island of the little town so that it must of necessity be approached by one of its three bridges, the Tun Bridge, over the Chew, the Port Bridge, over the Winford stream, and Sprat's Bridge.

Chew, as I have said, has seen better and perhaps happier days. At the Domesday Inquest it was held by the Bishops of Wells, and hence comes one of its names, Bishops' Chew. It remained a part of the Bishops' property all through Catholic times, and it was not till Edward VI sat on the throne of England, and Bishop Barlow the vandal and the married man in the See of Wells, that the manor was alienated from the Bishopric. Bishop Barlow surrendered it to the Protector Somerset, upon whose attainder it came to the Crown. Elizabeth granted it in part to Edward Baber and in part to Sir Francis Popham, in whose family it remained till 1766, when it passed by sale to the Summers.

Though to-day it is one of the quietest places in a county that seems the very home of eternal summer, Chew keeps about it much of the aspect of its more prosperous days. Its street has a raised causeway upon the northern side of it, and more than one notable old house; but its chief splendour is its church with its noble Perpendicular tower. This is generally said to have been built by Bishop Beckington, and possibly with some truth as regards the building we see which, nevertheless, has still some signs of late Norman and Early English work. It is probable that the Early English church that certainly stood here was of very simple plan, consisting of a nave and chancel and dated from 1215. But this has almost entirely disappeared, and what we see now is a building of the

Chew Magna Church.

fifteenth century with a wide nave and aisles, chancel, and chapel. The arcade upon the south side, however, would seem to be Early English. The screen which runs right across the church is poor, and probably a reconstruction from fragments of the old original. In the end of the south aisle is a chapel with two windows, one above the other, which suggests that it originally consisted of two chapels, one above the other. This is confirmed by the doorway which, though filled up, is still visible from the inside, high up in the wall. It seems that the old Manor House of Chew which belonged to the Bishops of Bath and Wells stood upon this side of the church, and that at one time a gallery ran from the house to the church where in the upper storey of this chapel the Bishop had his private pew. In this south chapel are the rather heavy tombs of Edward Baber and his wife, dating from 1578, not good specimens of what the Elizabethans considered fitting as monuments for a church.

In the north chapel is a fine though restored monument of the fifteenth century to Sir John St. Loe and his wife of Sutton Court. This dates from about 1475. Sir John is in complete armour and his wife in a horned head-dress with a robe over a long dress fastened with a cord and tassels. Both wear the Lancastrian collar. The effigy of Sir John is more than seven feet long, and is supposed to represent him as in fact he was.

In the south aisle, in a recess beneath a window, is an enormous and painted figure, carved in oak, which was brought hither from the Church of Norton Hauteville. It is popularly supposed to represent Sir John Hauteville, the giant, but he lived in the time of Henry III, whereas this figure is of 1450, temp. Henry VII.

Above the south porch there are indications of a gallery, which may have been used upon Palm Sunday, in the procession, when the *Gloria Laus et Honor* was sung here, as it still is in Catholic churches, in antiphon, within and without the church.

At the gate of the church yard there still stands an old mediæval house, "the Church House," which in earlier times served as a club or public house of the parish. There the churchwardens brewed their ale and baked their bread, and held their "Church Ales." Those happy days are gone;

alas! when will they return? It uplifts the heart and increases our respect for our fathers to dwell in mind upon them, and to know that there was no charge made for admittance to those entertainments. The old ancient Church was a very human as well as a divine institution.

From Chew Magna it is good to visit Dundry, which, though little or nothing remains within the church for admiration, yet offers us, from its church-yard, and better still, from its very noble tower, one of the greatest views in Somerset. The manor has always gone with that of Chew, but nothing could be more different than their situations. The village of Dundry, upon its abrupt and noble hill, stands some 800 feet above the sea, and it is difficult to say how much country it is there able to command. On a clear day you may very easily see to the east Bath and the hills about Calne and Devizes beyond it. To the north, Bristol and the hills near Berkeley and Stroud, in Gloucester, perhaps the lights of Gloucester itself, and as far as the heights of Malvern, while all the west is bounded by the solemnity of the Welsh mountains, across the Severn Sea, and close beneath you is the noble view over the lakes of Barrow Gurney to Long Ashton. To the south-west appear the Quantocks, and on a very clear day Exmoor and Dunkery Beacon, the noble range of the Mendips in the foreground, and, away to the south-east, the high lands about Shaftesbury. Altogether, Dundry offers us a prospect which should not be missed, and the glorious air to be had there, after the heaviness of the valley, will entice the wayfarer to remain and to explore the Wansdyke hereabout, and the great Camp, upon Maes Knoll, an outlier of Dundry, towards Keynsham.

There is another visit to be paid from Chew Magna. This will bring us to Sutton Court. Several places, all demesnes of the manor of Chew Magna, stand up against the high land to the east of the Chew; there is Bishop's Sutton, so called because it belonged to the Bishops of the diocese, there are Sutton Wick and Sutton North.

Sutton Court was anciently in the possession of the great family of St. Loe. In Leyland's time the fine old manor house of the St. Loes here was evidently one of his stations in surveying the county. He made several excursions thence. The St. Loes continued to hold the place till Sir William St.

Loe, captain of the Guards to Queen Elizabeth and styled chief butler of England, settled it, with other possessions hereabout and in Gloucester, upon his wife the celebrated Bess of Hardwicke. This lady had four husbands; her second being Sir William Cavendish, by whom she had six children. By Sir William St. Loe she had no issue, and therefore she gave the greater part of the estates she had from him to her second son, Charles Cavendish. Charles Cavendish had a son William, who afterwards became Earl of Newcastle. He held Newcastle for Charles I, and eventually became Duke of Newcastle. But he was on the losing side. His lands were confiscated by the Commonwealth, and Sutton Court was purchased in trust by Elizabeth the wife of Edward Baber of Chew for the use of her son. He died without issue and she settled the place upon John Strachey, her stepson by her second husband, and in that family it remains to this day. The beautiful old house, as we see it, is in part the work of the St. Loes, in part of Bess of Hardwicke, and of course it has been well cared for by its present owners. John Locke often stayed here with his friend Mr. Strachey. There is nothing in England lovelier than the views and vistas of the hills here, where the enchanted valleys lead up into the blue Mendips.

A mile south of Chew Magna, in the valley, stands Chew Stoke. This manor, in the Conqueror's time, belonged to Gilbert Thorold, one of the most prominent of the conspirators against William Rufus. For his great share in that business his lands were all confiscated and in process of time Chew Stoke came to the St. Loes. The church is, save as to one feature, an uninteresting modern building, but its tower is one of the loveliest in this part of Somerset. It is small, but its niches perfect with figures, its battlements, and spire make a charming work of art. The figure in the niche toward the church is that of St. Andrew, to whom the church is dedicated. One of the altars within, in the old days, was dedicated, we are told, to "Maid Uncumber," otherwise "St. Wilgefort," not a very orthodox Saint we might suppose, for she was invoked by wives who wanted to get rid of their husbands; her favourite offering was of course wild oats. As a matter of fact, however, St. Wilgefort herself was of the most strict integrity. When someone offered her marriage she was so bewildered that she fled away, and, as it is said, to prevent a repetition of the offence grew a beard and as a "bearded lady" she is always represented. She had an altar in St. Paul's in London and in Bristol at St. Mary-le-Port. There were but few dioceses in England that had not four or five altars in her honour. Clôse to the church is a fine old parsonage of the fifteenth century, with the arms of the St. Loes.

Not far from Chew Stoke, within its parish, at a place called St. Cross, was, of old, a cell for four nuns, and near by was a well called St. Mary's. This cell was founded by Elizabeth de Sancta Cruce, of a family which held the manor of Moreton among others. Nothing remains of this little nunnery.

From Chew Stoke I followed the road southward, over the hill through Stoke Villice and Moreton, the manor of the St. Cross's, and climbed a little way thence into the roots of Mendip, to the beautiful village of Compton Martin. Before me all the way now the Mendips stood up, shutting out all Somerset, a noble great wall of limestone, a real mountain range.

The great sight of Compton Martin, apart from its own beauty, is its unique church, a really glorious building of the latest Norman time, the twelfth century, consisting of nave, chancel, north and south aisles, and clerestory. The roof is vaulted, and the vaulting of the chancel is especially noteworthy, and has been compared with that in Durham Cathedral, which dates from 1130. The chancel, in its proportions, has been spoilt by later building, and the chancel arch is an alteration of the late Perpendicular period, the old arch was narrower, and the east window is a substitute for a substitute, being of nineteenth century "Norman," replacing a Perpendicular window. The side windows are of the plain Decorated style the Chew valley knows so well.

The nave of the church is very noble, and contains a curious and beautiful pillar upon the south, with a fluted shaft recalling again work at Durham. The north and south aisles are Perpendicular. The tomb seen in the former is of their date, though the figure it holds is earlier. Until the middle of the nineteenth century there was a fine screen here, a light Perpendicular work, very like those still standing at Wellow and West Pennard. What has become of it no one seems to know. The small screens which remain enclosed the chapel in the south aisle, and are very fine indeed of their kind, especially that which might seem to be part of the old Rood Screen. It would appear that we owe this beautiful Norman church to the family which gave Compton its additional name. Martin de Treves, the first of this stock, was a great founder of monasteries and churches, and his son Robert Fitz-Martin was like him. Indeed, the whole family, which was not without lustre, was always founding, or building, or endowing churches and monasteries.

In the time when this church was building a saint was born in Compton Martin, whom we shall certainly not forget to invoke ere we pass on our way, though, alas! he has no shrine to-day in unhappy Compton. This was St. Wulfric, of whom Roger of Wendover has so much to say, and who prophesied the accession of King Stephen. He lived in a cell at Haselbury Plucknett, near Crewkerne.

Not far from Compton Martin is a fine old moated house of the fifteenth century called Bykefold Manor. It is rather hard to find, however, and there is not much to see.

From Compton Martin I turned eastward back into the Chew valley, and on my way in about a mile of good going came down hill into the pretty village of West Harptree. The churchyard here has seven splendid yews within it, and the church, alas! as we see it is not so old as they. Only the tower remains unspoiled Norman work with a wooden spire upon it.

Opposite the church is a fine house of the time of James I called Gournay Court. On the caps of the two pillars of the outer door jamb are the words "altogether vanity." Who it was that wrote these words so strangely over his house as though every day at his in-coming and out-going to be reminded of them, we do not know. But Tilly Manor, another old house beside the church, was the house of "a most pious and seraphical person," as Wood calls him, a celebrated Catholic divine who was born there in 1564. He was born a Protestant and went to Merchant Taylors' school in 1571, and in 1579 proceeded to Magdalen College in Oxford, but before he took his degree he became "inflamed with a love to the Roman Catholic religion, left his parents, country, and the prospects of a fair inheritance, and went to the English College at Rheims. In 1588 he was ordained priest and returned to England to labour in that vineyard just then first tangled and lost. He was banished in 1606 and died in 1611, leaving behind him the character of a person 'who went beyond all of his time in pious devotion.'"

East Harptree, a mile away, with its glen behind it, its curious cavern in the hills, and its remains of the famous Richemont Castle, is an interesting and a pretty place; but its church is not more important than is that at West Harptree, save that it can boast of an Elizabethan monument in the south porch rather remarkable than beautiful. It is that of Sir John Newton, ob. 1568.

Richemont Castle, the old fortress of the Gournays, lies about half a mile further up in the hills than the village. It was probably useful in the Norman conquest of Somersetshire, and in 1138 it was held for Maud the Empress against King Stephen who, after the siege of Bristol, took the place. He did not burn or in any way demolish it. This, however, was done in Henry VIII's time, when Sir John Newton built his new house Eastwood out of its ruins—a fine house which is still standing.

As for the cavern it is still further in the hills, and is reached by "a perpendicular shaft about 70 fathoms in depth; at the bottom is a large vault extending in length about 40 fathoms. . . . This cavern crosses many veins of lead ore." It is locally known as the *Lamb's Lair*, though how it got that name I have not properly been able to discover.

From East Harptree I continued up the valley past the reservoirs, whence Bristol gets a part of its water, and where the Chew now rises. Presently I came to Litton and found nothing, and then just at sunset I entered the long street of Chewton Mendip, having seen already above me the glorious double-windowed tower of its church.

The great sight in Chewton is its church. It is a building of many periods, of the twelfth, of the thirteenth, of the fourteenth and fifteenth centuries, and a very beautiful and interesting affair.

Domesday book tells us that there was a church at Chewton so early as the Conquest, and that this church was held with the appendant lands by the Abbot of the great Abbey of St. Peter at Jumièges in the diocese of Rouen in Normandy. The Abbot and convent of Jumièges continued during a long series of years patrons of the rectory.

That old Norman church of which Domesday Book speaks might seem to have disappeared altogether but for the northern doorway, but there remains of a Norman church of the twelfth century the chancel arch with some thirteenth century fresco work upon it. The font and the arcade on the south side of the chancel are both Early English work of that century, as is the nave arcade in the eastern portion. The western half seems to be of the fourteenth century, it is neither Decorated nor Perpendicular. The bench ends are fine fifteenth century work, about 1480, according to Mr. Bligh Bond. The lectern is Jacobean, as is the Bible upon it. To the south of the chancel is a chantry containing an altar tomb of the fifteenth century, with the figures of Sir H. Fitzroger and his wife lying upon it.

The tower, as I have said, is among the finest in Somersetshire, and of its kind is actually the masterpiece. Nor anywhere do I know a tower that in its own way is more lovely. Over the western door still stands the figure of our Lord between adoring angels.

In the churchyard there is a fine fifteenth century canopied cross with Crucifixion groups sculptured upon it. And there is this, too, to be said of Chewton: it possesses the chalice and paten which were used here before the change in religion: beautiful sixteenth century silver, holy, too, as we know. Only two other parishes in the county can make such a boast as this; Nettlecombe, which actually possesses fifteenth century vessels, and Newton St. Loe, which, like Chewton, retains its chalice and paten of the first half of the sixteenth century.

Toothache in the Middle Ages.
Capital. Wells Cathedral.

CHAPTER V

THE MENDIPS

THAT mysterious and beautiful valley which runs up from the Avon southward and which we have followed past so many strange and old world places, brings us at Chewton into the roots of the hills, the great range of the Mendips which from far or near, from the north or the south, seems to rise like a vast wall sheer into the sky and to cut off so decisively all that broken country to the north from what lies to the southward. There is nothing that remains more steadfast in the mind of the traveller on foot in Somerset than this range of hills which runs quite across the county from a little south of east to a little north of west cleanly as a wall might do from the Wiltshire border to the sea.

Mendip, as one soon finds as one trudges along its highways —for it has highways very definite, lonely, and walled with hedges of unmortared stone—or wanders along its vague tracks and byways, is a vast mountain table-land, worn to a bare stump of limestone by countless centuries of time, meagrely clothed with a shallow, poor soil; a lonely, windy place, as grey as a winter sky and as mysterious as the last few days of the year, a place of rolling and empty fields, of sudden and immense views, of a strange and grim enchantment.

For Mendip holds the secrets of men and civilisations older far than Rome, and, here alone, more enduring. Maesbury Camp, the lonely and forbidding Barrows upon Blackdown, weigh upon one as nothing that Rome has abandoned here is able to do;. they seem to speak to one of a life that is so old it is an agony to think of it, and they threaten us with their enormous wisdom: the vast labour which has ended only in a few gigantic heaps of barren earth. For upon the Mendips as upon no other mountains in the world, perhaps because few are so old as they, man and his efforts fade into nothing; their futility is exposed by the emptiness of space and the passing of time. And if, as he will, the traveller turns to the sky for assurance and for comfort that sky is too often a grey immensity of cloud, of great clouds hurrying no whither before the south-west wind, laden with the memory of the emptiness of the sea.

The loneliness of Mendip is a real loneliness. A man turns to the sky because he must; he is shut away there from the great and fruitful world he knows, the towns, the villages, the ploughlands, and the steadings beneath him, not only by the height, but also by the breadth and flatness of the great plateau which the roads, purposeless for the most part, shepherded by their loose walls of grey stone, traverse so swiftly, anxious only to pass on their endless ways. One is caught as it were in an empty space, a featureless desolation, a solitude that is like no other solitude. A man there is utterly alone, he cannot stay, he passes on with deliberate step down the roads that only lead away. And there is no one who has persisted in the exploration of these hills but has been astonished by their silence, the absence of trees, of cattle, of sheep, of all voices, and of the sound of bells, a sound, one thinks, that might break the spell that lies over all this great desolate upland. Yet such a man will know too that Mendip has voices and sounds of its own that are a part of the silence.

For the hills of Mendip are hollow and are full of secrets; secret springs, secret underground rivers whose courses you may not know, but whose voices you may sometimes hear suddenly on a still day as you lie on the shady side of one of the many swallets or pits, a curious murmuring hollow sound, rising and falling; and sometimes as you pass by where no visible spring is to be found you will be drenched with spray suddenly in the face; but whence it comes you will not know. It is not everyone who in such a loneliness can bear such music or encounter such natural malice and still remain in firm possession of his soul.

Yes, the hills are full of secrets; they are dreadful for they are very old; they are full of caves where are mingled the bones of men and of beasts that are dateless and have no history;

they are full of deserted camps and barrows that were once used and defended and meant something to someone of whom we may know nothing; every height or headland is bastioned or crowned with the work of man, work that was already crumbling, nay, already a forgotten ruin, before the beginning of history. These remain. But the work of the Romans, those deserted mines beyond Charterhouse, what is there left of them? What is there to be found of those two religious houses of the Carthusians, Charterhouse a cell of Witham, and Green Ore a cell of Hinton? Not a stone, not a single foundation. For them no man can say here they stood or there. It is as though Mendip were outside History and Christendom.

And yet on a day of wind, a clear day after rain, this great plateau which a man fears almost as much as he loves is capable of offering you endless reward. On such a day Mendip awakes; the thin grass laughs like an old man in the sun, the grey rock shines golden with lichen, the spare woods are filled with the strength and the joy of the wind, and suddenly you find as you come up southward out of the plateau on to the height, on to Beacon Hill or Pen Hill or Maesbury for instance, all the world spread out at your feet.

It is a glory that passes and yet cannot pass away. For when, as a man, suddenly and without warning, after years of absence, I looked one evening from that great height, I saw not this; I saw my home. Spread out beneath me lay a vast and mysterious plain, blue and grey and gold in the setting sun, and beyond far and far away the great hills of the West Country. To one returning after long absence that view must always be the most beautiful and the most consoling in the world, for it gives him at a glance all his childhood and his home.

Setting out from Chewton Mendip to explore the hills, one will take the straight road to Wells, passing Chewton Priory, the seat of Earl Waldegrave, whose family has held Chewton so long. The Priory stands upon the site of a Benedictine house belonging to the monks of Jumièges; when the alien priories were suppressed the King, Henry V, granted this appropriation to the Carthusian priory of Sheen, which he had founded in 1413.

Climbing steadily past the Priory, one comes to Green Ore, in about half an hour, and here the road to Wells is crossed at right angles by the old Roman Road to the lead mines, and, perhaps, to Uphill on the coast. Turning along this road, to the left, on the hollow top of Mendip, in three miles the traveller will come to Maesbury Camp, through which the Roman Way passes as a mere track, onward to Beacon Hill, where at the Inn, which sells as good cider as is to be had in the known world, the Roman Road is continued for half a mile as a modern highway, to be lost again at Long Cross, where the modern road swerves to the north for Leigh-upon-Mendip and Frome.

Maesbury Camp is chiefly celebrated for the great view it offers south and west of the county of Somerset. It is an ancient fortress, how ancient who shall say,[1] upon a hill top, with artificial defences following the natural line of the hill. Its very name means hill-fort, and it must have been a very strong one.

Returning from Maesbury to Green Ore, one again follows the Wells Road for half a mile, and then turns westward, to the right, at Hill Grove, and, continuing past Hunter's Lodge Inn, near which is one of the many Mendip caverns, one comes to Priddy.

There is not, in all the Mendip country, a more desolate village than Priddy, yet it is the chief place upon these heights.

The church, as indeed we might expect, is very plain, but it contains a font of the eleventh century, though it is mainly, as we see it, a building of the Perpendicular period. It

[1] Prof. Boyd Dawkins assigns it to the Prehistoric Iron Age; Mr. St. George Gray to the Bronze Age "and it may subsequently have been occupied in the Prehistoric Iron Age." Only excavation can decide the question.

"We are at present only on the threshold of our knowledge as regards the hundreds of camps, fortifications, and ancient enclosures with which the whole of England is studded, and which as a rule occupy the most elevated and commanding positions. . . . Wherever we find isolated encampments of *prehistoric* date on the top of hills we may be pretty sure that they were simply places of refuge for local tribes . . . to which they resorted when attacked. Endeavours to differentiate the Stone Age and Bronze Age camps from Roman, post-Roman, and Norman camps in Britain are for the future. . . . As a rule the art of castramentation was very much the same in all periods . . . the only real method of throwing light upon the subject is by means of the pick and shovel, provided these potent instruments are wielded in the right manner."—H. St. George Gray in *Som. Arch. Soc. Proc.*, 1903, pp. 27, 28.

possesses several fine ornaments, among them two ancient screens, one the rood screen still in position, and the other across the north aisle. That across the south aisle is modern. Here, too, is a curious stone pulpit and a very beautiful altar cloth of mediæval needlework.

Priddy, as its little church would lead us to believe, is a very old place. A chapel of Westbury, it was anciently a part of the estates of the Bishop of Wells, but in 1164 the rectory of Westbury, near Priddy, was added to the endowments of the Augustinian Priory of Bruton, by Bishop Robert. The Canons, in return, were obliged, among other payments, to supply a wax taper to burn continually before the High Altar of the Cathedral Church of Wells.

In 1225 a curious murder was committed at Priddy. The account of the outrage runs: "John Swete-bi-the-bone killed Richard, the Shepherd, and fled. He was of the mainpast of the Abbot of Bruere, in his sheepcote of Bridie (Priddy). Therefore, he (the abbot) is in mercy, and he (John) is suspected, and no one else. Therefore, let him be exacted and outlawed. He had no chattels." This verdict was given at Ilchester Assizes, in 1225. To be of the mainpast of the abbot, was to have the abbot for surety; the abbot, therefore, was held at the mercy of the court.[1]

The mention of Richard the shepherd brings us to the subject of sheep. A very peculiar and valuable breed once inhabited the Mendip Hills. They bore a considerable resemblance to the Exmoor sheep and to the Dorsets. Perhaps they were an intermediate breed between the two. The horns were smaller and the countenance wilder, the sheep altogether more diminutive and the wool finer, and the flesh more finely flavoured than the Dorsets. "They were," says Youatt, "a hardy breed, and would thrive upon the poorest soil. They covered the Mendips in immense numbers, and were alternately changed from the moors to the hills as the season demanded. They bred, too, twice a year. When a considerable tract of the hills became enclosed the number of sheep diminished, and the character little by little was changed. The old wild Mendips were crossed with the heavier Devons and others, and the genuine Mendip sheep became extinct."

[1] See Rev. Preb. J. Coleman, "Historical Notes on Priddy" (*Som. Arch. Soc. Proc.*, LV, (ii), 138 *et seq.*

A fair, famous all through this part of Somerset, has been held in Priddy on August 21 for over 500 years. It is said that it was held in Wells till 1348, but that then it was removed to Priddy on account of the Black Death, and never returned to the Cathedral city. Everyone knows the proverb, "the first rain after Priddy Fair is the first rain of winter." It is equivalent to the Tuscan saying that the first rain after the Assumption (August 15) breaks the summer.

From Priddy it is a journey of some three miles across bleak Mendip to Charterhouse and the Roman lead mines. The plateau of Mendip was, like the similar limestone uplands of Derbyshire, rich in lead, which was worked by the Britons before the Romans came to the land, just as it was worked later by the mediaeval miners. The Romans with less excuse than their predecessors seem to have mined with astonishing extravagance, leaving more than twenty-five per cent. of the metal in the slag they cast away. Their operations, Mr. Haverfield tells us, extended over a very considerable area of Mendip between Black Down and Priddy, but the centre of their works lay here by Charterhouse in the valley of Blackmoor. Here many movable objects, including several inscribed pigs of lead, dating from within four or five years of the occupation to about A.D. 170, have been found, but practically no traces of building. Close by is a small Roman camp or amphitheatre, where apparently the mining population played their games, fought their cocks, and enjoyed other pastimes. The place is rather small to be dignified with the name of amphitheatre, which raises false ideas of space and grandeur, Professor Haverfield, however, says that the "notion of a tiny amphitheatre is not wholly absurd," and the excavations undertaken by Mr. St. George Gray have proved the earthwork to be Roman, though they have not thrown any light upon its uses.

It was in the Middle Ages that Charterhouse-on-Mendip got the name we know it by. About the middle of the thirteenth century the Carthusians of Witham, in Selwood, built a cell here on Mendip, which stood where we now see the manor-house, but no trace of the monkish dwelling remains. It was a desolate and lonely place for a religious house, and one may well believe that only the Carthusians would have chosen it.

From Charterhouse the more adventurous traveller will pursue his way across Black Down, the highest and perhaps the loneliest part of the hills, to Burrington, which boasts of a curious ravine, similar to, but not so fine as, the gorge at Cheddar. It also boasts of a cavern something like Wookey Hole, but by no means so interesting. From Burrington a delightful road takes one eastward to Blagdon, notable chiefly for its noble church tower, all that is left to it of its old church. It was while curate at Blagdon that Toplady wrote the well-known hymn, "Rock of Ages." It seems he had taken refuge one day in Burrington Combe from a passing

Market Cross, Cheddar.

thunderstorm, and the impression of the great cleft rocks remained in his mind.

The less strenuous traveller, however, will return from Charterhouse on the road to Priddy, and take the way for the greatest sight upon Mendip, the Cheddar Gorge.

It is impossible to describe the really tremendous effect of this great and enormous cleft in the bare hills. It is something so big that we are surprised to find it in England where our effects are generally without bigness or grandeur. The mere height of these great rugged cliffs that rise so sheer on either side of the narrow road that winds down the gorge is in its effect astonishing and certainly unique in southern England. In some cases these cliffs rise sheer from the road to a height of 450 feet, but they might be a thousand so majestic is their formation, so narrow the cleft by which you creep between them, and so tortuous is the road. The wise traveller will always approach Cheddar from the hills, thus descending the gorge, and this for two reasons. In the first place the mere effect is infinitely more astonishing, for the spectacle increases in splendour and height as he descends. In the second place the rabble of touts, the confusion of bristling advertisements, and the air of Bank Holiday that have overwhelmed the town of Cheddar at the foot of the gorge are enough to spoil most people's enjoyment in any work of nature. If one descends from the silence of the great plateau one comes into all this noise when the great spectacle has passed, and disgusting as it is one can pass through it without delay. It is for this reason I have never seen any of the caves of Cheddar, nor shall I do so till the mountebanks who exploit them have been cleared out, the obnoxious advertisements swept away, and the gorge is hushed and at peace from their raucous voices.

I think the church of Cheddar, though it has a noble triple-windowed tower of the second class, must have suffered from the continual air of Bank Holiday that affects the town, for it is as highly coloured and gaudy as a genuine mediaeval building. It is not very impressive, however, though it has many good, and even fine, details, including a splendid roof, a stone pulpit of the fifteenth century, and a south chapel devoted to the Fitz Walter family. All, however, is so full of colour as to be dazzling to modern eyes.

Cheddar was the true centre of the Forest of Mendip. This term, Forest of Mendip, was used in many variable senses. It meant, for the ordinary man, the great unenclosed area on the heights some twenty miles east and west. In the records it was, of course, closely defined, but it never meant what, for us, the word forest has come to mean, that is, a great wood. "Forest" was really a legal term, and meant a privileged hunting area, administered not by the Common Law but by Forest Law. It was an unenclosed wild place, containing generally both woodland and moorland, but it was necessarily vested in the Crown and it could not be created by a subject. The forest laws of England were older than Canute, who renewed them in a code which Henry II revived.

There were, mainly within the county of Somerset, five forests, Selwood, Mendip, North Petherton, Neroche, and Exmoor. They were, though, so widely distributed under the general control of one chief warder, or keeper. This was a member of the Du Plessis family. William du Plessis was hereditary Master Forester in the middle of the thirteenth century, and Sabine Peeche, his descendant, held the office in the year 1300.

The Forest of Mendip would seem to have consisted of two parts, namely, the hunting forest and the mining forest. This last was at some unknown period broken into four lordships, and granted to subjects called Lords Royal, for they held Royalties. These four Lords Royal were the Bishop of Bath and Wells, the Abbot of Glaston, the Lord of the Honour of Richmont in East Harptree, and the Lord of Chewton.

As for the hunting forest it was a favourite summer hunting resort of the Saxon Kings; *Interdum aestivabunt circa forestam de Mendep* we read (V.C.H.) and we have a spirited account of the celebrated hunt at Cheddar by King Edmund when the stag fell over Cheddar Cliffs and was dashed to pieces. Leland tells us that "at such hunt as Gournay loved, the forest of Mendepe was well furnished with dere but anon after, for riots and trespassys done in huntyngs it was deforestyd and so yet remaineth."

The forest has gone, a great part of the free hills has been enclosed since 1770, when an Act was passed, the first of its kind, enclosing that part of Mendip which lies between the parishes of East and West Cranmore; but at least one thing remains to Cheddar, if it is no longer the heart of the forest, it still makes its world-famed cheeses.

Somersetshire cheese was already well known in the eleventh century, and in the seventeenth we find Cheddar cheese still in high estimation, and, indeed, we read that these cheeses had "lately grown to be in such high esteem at Court" that they were all "bespoke before they were made." And if it is not so bad as that to-day, yet he is wise who sees Mr. Small, of Cheddar, in good time, and trusts to his discretion.

Some few miles to the west of the town of Cheddar, at the

foot of Shute-Shelve Hill where Mendip begins to break into isolated steep islands of limestone, very high and notable lies the ancient town of Axbridge, which holds a charter it is said from Edmund, who as we know was saved from death while hunting in Mendip Forest, and certainly others granted by Henry VI, by Philip and Mary, by Elizabeth, which, till 1886, was the governing charter of the town, and by James I. The town was originally a part of the huge demesne of Cheddar, and so it remained till the end of the twelfth century when King John granted it to the archdeacon of Wells. Henry III granted it to the Bishop, and save for an interval in the reign of Edward I, when it passed to the Bishop of Lincoln, the Bishop of Wells held it till the change of religion. The most interesting thing in Axbridge to-day is, of course its church, which stands in the middle of the town on a hill to the east of the old market place. It is a cruciform building with central triple windowed tower, transepts, nave, and aisles of four and chancel of two bays, with two chapels, a small south and a large west porch with stone benches. The church was restored in 1636 and in 1879; the plaster ceiling of lace work with a pendant to each alternate rib which covers the nave dates from the former restoration, but the chancel roof is quite modern. The really interesting feature of the interior is the arrangement for what would appear to have been a double rood screen. For in addition to the rood screen in its usual position west of the tower with its stair, here on the south side, there is a second stair east of the tower on its north side, opening from the chapel there. It may have been that the two screens formed and supported a platform upon which miracle plays were acted (we know one was played in the church in 1581) or it may have been that these two screens bore a great rood to which the people ascended on Good Friday when they "crept to the Cross" to kiss the feet of the Crucified. On the other hand it may well be that the eastern end of the church is older than the nave, and that when the church was enlarged the rood screen was moved westward.

The tower is also interesting; it is ceiled with a fan tracery roof having a bell aperture, and is a triple windowed tower of good design. It still possesses two statues in its niches; that on the east being a figure of the patron of the Church of

Axbridge Church.

St. John the Baptist; that on the west of the best patron of the town, Henry VI.

West of the church is a two storeyed building called the Treasury, where in the upper room is a chest with three locks; the window has double gratings. Near the north side of the chancel there once stood a sacristy with a squint into the church, that remains.

Axbridge itself is full of antiquity, and lying as it does to-day in the midst of gardens, makes a very pleasant place for a halt. It is, too, an excellent centre from which to visit the surrounding places: Cheddar, for instance, and Compton Bishop, with its interesting little church, its Norman font, carved stone pulpit and ancient glass, under Wavering Down and Crook's Peak, that well-known horn of the first island hill of Mendip towards the sea. And seeing that it lies at the very foot of what I may call continental Mendip, it is, perhaps, the best place from which to start to visit those little places which, between Axbridge and the Cathedral city, crouch under the shadow of Mendip at the base of the great hills. Cheddar again, Rodney Stoke, and Westbury with the great spectacle of Ebbor Rocks, not so fine as Cheddar Gorge and Wookey Hole, the finest cavern in all this country.

Rodney Stoke, one of the prettiest places in all this delightful and strange country, is chiefly noteworthy for the family which gave it its name. The village was originally Stoke, simply; then in the time of King John it came into the hands of the Giffards and was known as Stoke Giffard; the last Giffard, a daughter named Maud, married in the time of Edward I Sir Richard de Rodney, and brought him the manor which thereafter was known as Stoke Rodney.

The church is dedicated to St. Edward, and was doubtless, before the addition of the Rodney Chapel, a very plain fifteenth century building of tower, nave and chancel. It was, however, greatly adorned by Sir Edward Rodney under the influence of the Laudian revival in 1625. It was he who built the rood loft upon which a music gallery stood in comparatively recent times. To him, too, the pulpit and the octagonal font-cover are due. But the chief sight here is the Rodney tombs. The oldest of these is under the canopied arch in the south wall of the chancel. It bears the recumbent effigy of a young man, that Sir Thomas Rodney, the son of Sir Walter, who married

Margaret, daughter of Lord Hungerford of Farleigh, and died in 1478. In the panels below are five female figures kneeling, two of them with rosaries, one with an open book. On the other side we see a bishop seated, his pastoral staff upon his left arm and, perhaps, a windlass in his right hand; this may represent St. Elmo. Next to him is a woman nursing two babies, which some think represents St. Anne, and next again a man is seated with what looks like a pair of manacles and a book; this may be St. Leonard. Close by to the east is the tomb of Sir John Rodney, Sir Thomas's son. To the north

Rodney Stoke. Monument of George Rodney.

opens the Rodney chapel built at the end of the fifteenth century; its altar is gone, but under the east window we see the effigy of a woman under a canopy; this is Anna Lake, the wife of George Rodney, who died in 1630. To the south lies George, her husband; and to the west his father, Sir Edward, who died in the same year as his son, 1651.

The Rodneys appear again at Westbury, another village, a mile further east, on the road to Wells, and still in the shadow of the hills. The church, which has a tower, Norman in its lowest storey, and a south aisle of the time of Edward IV, with a Norman doorway upon the north, has a now disused chapel, which contains the tomb of George Rodney, who died in 1586.

Above the village is the chasm, known as Ebbor Rocks, and beneath it lies Wookey Hole, the most remarkable of all those many caves which are the mystery of Mendip, and here the River Axe is marvellously born.

If a man stands within Maesbury Camp, on Mendip top, he may see, at least with the eye of the mind, running east and west, a track across which the Romans drove their Way, older far than Rome. Whither does it lead us? Into the darkness.

That track has little or no place in history, for it was hoary, and perhaps forgotten when history began; but, if we follow it, it will lead us to the beginning of things, in so far as anything may be said to have had a beginning.

The landscape it will show us there, from the long crest of Mendip, we should not recognise as our home. In those days the British Islands stood some 1,000 feet higher than now they do, and formed a part of the continent of Europe. To the west there was land so far as the hundred fathom line, the English Channel was a great valley, down which a mighty river, fordable at the Straits of Dover, flowed into the Atlantic. The Bristol Channel was another broad valley through which the Severn ran; and Exmoor and the Devon and Cornish highlands were the great watershed dividing them.

Britain then endured a continental climate, that is to say, a blazing summer and a freezing winter, and not only possessed the mammalia she still has, as well as the wolf, the bear, the wild boar, and the bison, animals of the temperate zone, but those of the cold and heat also, such as the reindeer and the arctic fox, the lion, the leopard, the spotted hyaena, the hippopotamus, the elephant, the mammoth, the woolly rhinoceros, and the Irish elk, whose bones have all been found here, in Somerset, in the caves of Wookey Hole, or Bleadon, or Durdham Down.

As for man, the first we have any trace of, the earliest inhabitant of these islands who has left any mark of his presence is known to us as the River Drift Man. He came from the South, as a hunter, but he knew not the use of the dog; he was armed with a feeble weapon of flint, and was largely at the mercy of the beast. He entered Somerset by the valley of the southern Axe, and we find his implements at Broom, near Axminster, on our borders.

In the course of ages River Drift man was followed and apparently conquered by a better armed race, whom we know as the Cave Man; he came from the North. He, too, fought with the flint, but he made of it a better weapon, and he was in possession of a higher culture than his predecessor. Yet he, too, was terribly at the mercy of the beast. His presence in Somerset is well attested by the discovery of his implements in Wookey Hole.

This large cavern in the Mendip limestone the Cave Man may be said to have shared with the beast. Vast quantities of the bones of the hyæna, the woolly rhinoceros, the lion, the bear, the mammoth, and other animals have been discovered there, and all of the same period. Wookey Hole, however, really belonged to the hyæna, and it might seem that the other animals whose remains have been found there were its prey. It hunted in packs and drove its quarry over the precipice above the Hole, and having thus killed or injured it, dragged the carcase into the cavern and devoured it. Presently the Cave Man, without a true weapon, followed its example. From time to time he seems to have driven out the hyæna from Wookey, to have lighted fires, and on his hunting expeditions to have used the cavern as a shelter. His weapons, flakes, scrapers, cutters, and hatches of flint and cheet have been found for the most part on the floor of the chamber near the entrance to the Hole.

Such was Paleolithic Man in the Pleistocene period in that part of England we now call Somerset. The earlier comer, the River Drift man, entered Somerset from the south in the wake of the southern mammalia; then later the Cave-man came in the wake of the reindeer and the Arctic fox, and as the former probably departed with the animals he followed, so did the latter. What their relation was to the enormous change that in the course of ages overwhelmed all England so far South as a line drawn through the estuary of the Thames to the Severn, we do not know.

It is possible, however, that some of these hunters stood where we stand on Mendip and watched the sun on the peaks of the glaciers that had slowly overwhelmed Wales and the North, for here on Mendip, where the ice never descended, Paleolithic man was probably pre-Glacial, Glacial, and post-

Glacial.[1] However that may be, he disappeared, and has left no trace of himself in the existing population of Europe, nor any vestige of his culture in what we know of those Neolithic peoples that came after him. It is of these, our forefathers, we think as, leaving Wookey Hole and the loud voice of the new-born Axe, we set out upon the way to Wells.

[1] *V. C. H.* (*Somerset*), vol. i, p. 178.

Wells Cathedral. Detail Bracket.
Figure of a Countryman.

Wells Cathedral. Distant View.

CHAPTER VI

WELLS

THERE are places in the world so beautiful, so happy, or so sacred, that to speak of them now without a certain reverent hesitation might seem impossible; of these Wells is one.

As you come over Milton Hill, perhaps very early in the morning, and lingering there, as I did, gaze upon the city in the meadows at your feet, you might think it still a city of that divine and joyful kind, uplifting the heart, which was once common in England, and, indeed, typical of this country; and, for all its silence and its isolation, it remains in its beauty and completeness perhaps the best example of all that we have been compelled to sacrifice to that Moloch of Industrialism which has risen to enslave us upon the ruins of the Protestant heresy. For, from any modern point of view, Wells remains, in its essence, an inexplicable mystery, a denial of everything that is fundamental in modern philosophy, a negation of that strange theory of "progress" which is one of the more amusing obsessions of the modern spirit, an unanswerable confutation of all the ridiculous assertions of the modern world. In Wells, we not only believe, we know and we feel, that men have been happy; in Sheffield who could even dream of it?

Therefore rejoice and be glad on Milton Hill, for there, at your feet, lie your origins to which you shall return. If you have any happiness in your heart, here it shall blossom; if you have dreams here they shall come true; for, though men have forgotten and been silent so long, those towers still sing *Te Deum*, and cry aloud in antiphon with the hills out of which they were hewn: *Sanctus, Sanctus, Sanctus, Dominus Deus Sabaoth; Pleni sunt coeli et terra majestatis gloriae tuae.*

. . . . . .

No man who comes to Wells believing, as I do, that all which it once stood for and expressed shall rise again, can be indifferent to its origin and its history. At first, and, indeed, at last, too, the sheer beauty of the city, its miraculous

Wells Cathedral. From the Deanery Garden.

completeness, the enthusiasm and the force of its marvellous church, the dignity and repose of its great palace, of its noble deanery, of all its ecclesiastical buildings, the loveliness of its situation by those living waters, amid meadows and orchards at the foot of the great hills, overwhelms one with a sense of beatitude, of pleasure and of joy; but the more deeply one is thus moved, the more irresistibly one desires to know the story of such a place, to learn of its origins and to follow it through all the vicissitudes of its long and noble life.

Let the traveller filled with such an enthusiastic curiosity not be content with the view of Wells, fine as it is, which

Milton Hill gives him. Let him seek out Tor Hill, upon the road to Shepton Mallet, and thence obtain a view of the general aspect of Wells such as no other point will give him. Thence he may see grouped about the Cathedral, the Palace, the Cloister, the Chapter House, the Vicar's Close, the Deanery, the detached houses of the Canons, the three cemeteries, and, more distant, the beautiful tower of the Parish Church, which, altogether, make up this unique and lovely city, still almost perfect, still almost as it was in the Middle Ages. That view is, as I say, unique; it cannot, in its completeness, be matched in Europe, and, as it were at a glance, it gives you the whole history of Wells from its beginning in the eighth century till our own day.

For, let it be said at once, Wells is wholly ecclesiastical both in its origin and in its development. No doubt some sort of municipal history can be found for it, but the more that is examined the more it will appear merely a part of its ecclesiastical history. The city never had any military or political importance, it had no castle, nor town walls, it has never been the seat of any Earldom or of any secular provincial government, it is wholly without commercial importance. It is simply a small town that has grown up about a great ecclesiastical foundation which is the reason of its being, and without which it would cease to exist.

The city, then, such as it was and such as it is, grew up gradually about a little church founded, if we may believe tradition—and the tradition is strong—by King Ine at the suggestion of St. Aldhelm in honour of St. Andrew the Apostle in the beginning of the eighth century. The site was probably chosen—it is possible that it had long been sacred—on account of those living springs of water, which here well forth from the secret places of Mendip and enrich the vale; but it was not till the year 909, two centuries after its foundation, in the time of Edward the Elder, that the church of St. Andrew became the seat of a bishop, and Athelm, a monk of Glastonbury, first sat upon its throne, when for the second time the great diocese of Wessex was divided, and a Bishopric of Somerset was cut out of the greater See of Sherborne.

Of the church which Ine built, save that it was served by a college of priests, we know nothing. We are ignorant alike of its history and of its buildings, and this ignorance remains complete until the time of Bishop Giso of Lorraine, who was consecrated in Rome in 1061. He asserts that on taking possession of his See of Wells he found the church to be but mediocre, that it boasted of but four or five clerks who had no cloister or frater, and that he began at once to prepare not only a cloister and a frater but a dorter also, and "everything that was necessary and fitting for them according to the manner of my own country." Giso also placed his clerks who were thus known as Canons, under the Rule of St. Chrode-gang, and having reigned for twenty-eight years, died in 1088, and

Wells. The Deanery from the Garden.

was buried "in the church which he had ruled, in a recess made in the wall on the north side near the altar, as Dudoc his predecessor was buried on the south side beside the altar."

Giso was succeeded by John de Villula, who, as we have seen, in 1090, removed his seat from Wells to Bath. He destroyed the buildings of Giso: "the canons he turned out of doors, and they were driven to live a common life with the people,"[1] and it is said that he built a house for himself upon

[1] These quotations are from the *Historiola de primordiis Episcopatus Somersetensis*, etc. (Camden Society, 8), 16–22. See also "The First Cathedral Church of Wells," by W. H. St. John Hope, in *Proc. Som. Arch. Soc.*, vol. lv (ii), 85, *et seq.*

the site, where they had dwelt. He was succeeded in 1123 by Bishop Godfrey, who, in his turn, was succeeded in 1136 by Bishop Robert, who did something to restore Wells from the ruin that John de Villula had thrust upon it. He rebuilt the church which seems to have been utterly spoilt and reconsecrated it in the presence of the Bishops of Sarum, Worcester, and Hereford. But, what exactly Bishop Robert did, still remains a mystery. The probabilities are that he repaired the old Saxon church, and extended it eastward. When he died the See was vacant for some years, till, in fact, Bishop Reginald was appointed in 1174.

It is to Bishop Reginald we owe the foundation, the ground plan, and a considerable portion of the existing church, which must in no way be confounded with the Saxon building. That church, founded by Ine, cherished by Giso, and repaired and added to by Bishop Robert, has utterly disappeared, so that no stone of it remains above ground. Nor must we look for it as forming the foundations of the present building. It would seem to have been utterly destroyed, and its disappearance is a mystery, that until to-day our scholarship has been unable to solve. In the year 1909, however, Mr. St. John Hope offered us a solution, that as one studies it more and more recommends itself. It will be noticed by anyone who takes up a map of the city of Wells, that the buildings and the streets and the squares are all set north-east and south-west,[1] but that the present Cathedral is an exception. So long ago as 1850, excavations were made in the Vicar's old cemetery to the south of the present church and the foundations of two buildings, one rectangular and the other octagonal, were discovered. In 1894 the site was again opened, and those fragmentary foundations were shown by Mr. Buckle to have belonged to two distinct buildings, the later of which was now proved to have been cruciform and to have formed the Lady chapel, known to have been built in the time of Edward IV. The other buildings were shown to be of totally different character, and to belong to more than one period. These buildings stood obliquely to the present cathedral, but were exactly in line with the city,

[1] The general axis of the city is some twelve degrees north of east; only the Cathedral, the contemporary cloister, and Palace stand due east and west. See article, already referred to, by W. H. St. John Hope.

that is to say, their axis was some twelves degrees north of east. Here then, as is thought, to the south of the present church and not beneath it, stood the old Saxon Cathedral which Bishop Robert repaired and added to, and which stood apparently from 709, at any rate till 1174, when Bishop Reginald began the present church, that is to say, for more than four hundred and fifty years.

Now let a man stand in the noble close, perhaps the noblest in England, before the most splendid of our façades, and consider this matter for it will, if rightly understood, explain much to him that is difficult to understand.

The Cathedral one sees before one is in its main parts, and altogether in its ground plan, the work of Bishop Reginald (1174–1191). The west front, all that glorious façade with its great outstanding towers, is later work, is work of the first years of the thirteenth century, the splendid achievement of Bishop Jocelin (1206–1242). Let us ignore it for the moment.

When Bishop Reginald began to build the great church we see, the old Saxon church to the south, which Bishop Robert had repaired and extended, was still standing and was still, of course, the centre of worship. It is probable then, that the first part of the present church to be built was the south transept near the old church and the house of the Bishop.[1] Thus the first door of the church was that in the south transept. If this is doubted it is necessary to find another explanation for the remarkable and unusual position of the Font here at the door of the south transept.

There would follow, and somewhat in this order, the north transept, the eastern limb, that is the choir with the high altar, and then the nave with the beautiful north porch, one of the loveliest things in the church

We have seen that the first entrance to the present church was probabıy in the south transept from the older building, but as the present church grew—the *major ecclesia* as it is called in the earlier documents—and the older church was dismantled, that entrance would cease to be of the old importance. A new and grand approach would have to be built and this we find in the north porch which is, in fact, as it is at Westminster and perhaps at Salisbury, the true entrance to the

[1] Canon Church in *Proc. Som. Arch. Soc.*, lv (i), 55, *et seq.*

Wells Cathedral. The West Front.

Church. It is called in the documents the *magna porta canonicorum* "the great door of the canons," the *alta porta*,

Wells. The South-West Tower from the Cloisters.

and it opened upon the area which Reginald had given to the canons, that northern quarter where were to be built the houses for the dean and chapter and the vicars, for the schools and for that district called the Liberty. Now just as Westminster is a Coronation Church, and the great entrance is designed there in the north transept near to the King's Palace,

Wells. Detail of North Porch.

and for his official use, so here at Wells, the main entrance, now as then, to the Cathedral stands here on the north, near the Canon's dwellings, and for their use who were the chief users of the Cathedral. For the Cathedral of Wells was not built for the people either of Wells or of England, but for the glory of God which the Canons served.

Thus far then had the Cathedral proceeded towards completion when in 1191 Bishop Reginald died. He was succeeded by Bishop Savaric (1192–1205) of "Bath and Glastonbury" who, as we might suppose, did little, if anything, to the Church at Wells. The work was at a standstill when Bishop Jocelyn "of Wells" was elected Bishop in 1206. It is to this man, a native of the city, we owe the completion of the main church and above all the conception and the building of the magnificent western façade.

There can be no one who has ever stood in that green Close which is now spread out before the Cathedral but has noticed, after all his wonder at one of the greater glories of England and the world, the smallness of those doors in the west front, and sought, for the most part in vain, for an answer. But, let us admit it at once, those doors in the western façade were never meant to be the main entrances to the church. The glory of that mighty frontal was not intended, as we should undoubtedly now intend it, as a sort of boast; it was never meant for the vague enlarging and the pride of man, but for a definite purpose quite other. Indeed, it is only in comparatively modern times when an indolent luxury, the vested interest of married men of the upper classes, have turned our cathedrals into a sort of dead and national monuments, that that great, green close has stood before the church. Of old upon the southern and the western sides, the cathedral was quite surrounded, not by gardens or closes, but by three cemeteries; to the south the Vicars' and the Canons' graveyards, to the west the cemetery for the laymen of the city. It was not through a graveyard we may be sure that of old one came to the church—one entered by the south transept or the north porch. The doors on the western front gave access not to the great open air atrium we have there to-day, but to a cemetery, and it was over the dead that that mighty façade rose as it were with its hymn to Madonna: *Regina Coeli laetare, Alleluia.*

Bishop Jocelyn, to whom we owe that glorious façade with its multitude of statues, as a first act upon entering his bishopric, founded, in 1207, a daily Mass in honour of the

Blessed Virgin.[1] This Mass was generally sung at the earliest dawn with all ritual solemnity, accompanied by organ and choristers chanting the sweetest and most learned music of those times. So it was sung at Sarum by order of Bishop Richard Poore; so at St. Albans as Matthew Paris relates.[2] And this Mass which Bishop Jocelyn founded was sung in the

Wells Cathedral. The Lady Chapel and Chapter House from the Palace Garden.

Lady Chapel; not in that which stood near the cloister upon the foundations of Bishop Robert's church, for that was now

[1] Not "to the Blessed Virgin," as Canon Church has it. His little monograph upon *Five Somerset Bishops* is a delightful work, and should be in every traveller's hand.

[2] The custom became general in the thirteenth century all over England. It remained to the end. Cardinal Wolsey orders all the houses of Canons Regular in England to sing their choir services in Plain-Song, but the Masses of our Blessed Lady sung in her chapel were to be sung in figured music or, as it was then called, Prick-Song. What marvellous and exquisite music this could be Dr. Terry is recalling for us day by day at Westminster Cathedral.

in the thirteenth century set apart for mortuary devotions, but in the new Lady Chapel at the extreme eastern end of the cathedral, though not, of course, in that we now see; for Madonna is the Morning Star of our redemption, and Mass was sung in her honour where the earliest dawn crept first into the dark church.

Of Bishop Jocelyn we read again that both in 1215 and in 1239, when the western façade was finished and he consecrated the church, he "further endowed" this Mass; that is to say, he made it more splendid. Now if he thus glorified our Lady, as we have seen, in the earliest dawn, he would not be likely to forget her when all, though they forgot her all day, remember her at evening. Nor did he. It was in her honour, and particularly in honour of her Coronation, that he built the great façade,[1] with its pillars and shafts of Purbeck marble, towards the sunset; the greatest thing of its kind, the most noble and the most beautiful in England.

Whatever fantastic and nationalist theories may once have been held as to the meaning of the façade, really a vast piece of tabernacle work, containing more than four hundred statues, it may now, I think, with confidence be asserted that it spreads, and for the first time in the history of Gothic sculpture, one great sculptural drama over the entire front, and that its subject matter is the Coronation of the Blessed Virgin.

It would seem to be hopeless now to expect the identification of more than a very few of that multitude of figures which surrounds the central act of the drama over the central porch. Here and there we may be sure of the identity of a figure, however, as of King Solomon and the Queen of Sheba between the tall Early English windows above the great scene of the Coronation; of St Eustace on the eastern face of the north tower, and of course of certain groups of figures, as the Majesty which crowns the whole work, the twelve Apostles immediately beneath it, the Archangels and angels beneath the Apostles, the Resurrection groups that are spread right across the west front and towers, forming the topmost tier of sculpture upon the latter. And then roughly we may say as seems always to have been known, though too often forgotten,

[1] The façade proper, not the towers above it; these are perpendicular work.

that the general scheme was to bring together the Old and the New Dispensations, the nine orders of Angels and a great assembly of Saints, Prophets, and Kings about the central act, the Coronation of the Blessed Virgin. But we may, I think, more fully understand the idea of the whole if we turn to the account of the Death, Assumption, and Coronation of the Virgin, as given in *The Golden Legend* of Voragine.

Wells Cathedral. The Chain Gate.

There we read that at her death all the Apostles were gathered about her, and "at the third hour of the night Christ came with sweet melody, with the Orders of Angels, the Companies of the Patriarchs, the Assemblies of Martyrs, the Covenants of Confessors, the Carols of Virgins, in order and with sweet song and melody." It is the continual celebration of this great Feast that is here set forth with so much splendour amid the "Chivalry of Heaven." More than that I fear we shall never know.

What the ancient glory of that mighty frontal must have

been, when it was covered with silver and gold, with scarlet and purple and blue, and the beauty of all colours, we cannot, perhaps, realise. It must have been like a page from some glorious book of hours; yet when on a fortunate evening the sun falls upon it still at sunset, it shines even now with so great and dazzling a splendour that I have thought to see there that work of praise and worship as it was when new from Bishop Jocelyn's hands. There can have been nothing like it in England nor perhaps in the world; though it was done with a knowledge of the still earlier work at Amiens and Chartres, in size and in splendour and unity it surpassed them both, and it is perhaps needless to say that there is nothing comparable to it left upon earth.[1]

In the year 1242, when Bishop Jocelyn died, the main parts of the church, as we see them to-day, were finished. Indeed, from outside we may say that all we see was then in being except the three towers, the chapter house, and the Lady Chapel. Let us now examine the church more particularly within.

I have said that the nave, the transepts, and the choir, as we see them, were the work of Bishop Reginald (1174–1191).[2] This being so, quite apart from their beauty, they are worthy of the closest attention, for they are the earliest piece of complete Gothic building in England. Not in 1192 with the building of St. Hugh's choir at Lincoln, but in 1174, with the building of the choir of Wells, English Gothic began. "It was," says Mr. Francis Bond, "in the west of England that the art of Gothic vaulting was first mastered, and it was in the west, first apparently at Wells, that every arch was pointed, and the semi-circular arch was exterminated." The work at Wells is in fact a little earlier than the French choir of Canterbury and the delightful presbytery of Chichester, and yet it is more Gothic than either. That some Romanesque feeling should remain, as it does for instance in the zigzag ornament in the doorways of the south porch, in several of the beautiful foliage capitals, and above all in the square abacus everywhere to be seen, is not surprising; it is only surprising that the

[1] Some dim idea of its effect may perhaps be had from the façade of Orvieto Cathedral.

[2] Of course this does not include the "St. Andrew Crosses" built to support the central tower.

The Steps to the Chapter House, Wells.

Romanesque is not overwhelming, as it was later than this, at Glastonbury. Indeed, Wells Cathedral would seem to allow us to assert that Gothic architecture in England does not trace its descent from the French choir of Canterbury, but is "native and indigenous to the soil."

But the nave of Wells has the supreme importance of its own beauty and distinction. It is but sixty-seven feet high, and is thus one of the lowest naves in England, yet so perfect are its proportions, so noble the tall clerestory, that it does not appear low at all. Nor does it seem, thanks to the fine unbroken triforium, as short as it is.

We thus have in Wells an unique example of the very earliest English Gothic, while in the west front and in the two chapels within the towers, the chapels of the Holy Cross and of St. Edmund, we have some of the finest Early English work anywhere to be found. Nor did the splendour of the work at Wells stop there. In the undercroft of the Chapter House, in the romantic and lovely staircase beside it, and in the Chapter House itself we have some of the very finest work in England of the Geometrical period, and perhaps the best work in Wells. The undercroft which as at Westminster was possibly used as a Treasury, was built about 1280. It was apparently finished in 1286, and the staircase was then begun, to be followed by the very beautiful Chapter House, an octagonal chamber of light, upheld as it seems by a single palm-tree, which was not finished before 1320. It is impossible to praise adequately these most beautiful works; they endure for ever to remind us what a very different England from our own was able to achieve.

When the Chapter House was finished with its beautiful staircase, which led not only to that great chamber, but also to the Close of the Vicars, the very important work of extending the choir eastward was undertaken. This had already been accomplished in many of the English cathedrals. The Angel choir at Lincoln, for instance, was built about 1280. But at Wells, the extension of the choir was not begun till 1320: this involved the rebuilding of the Lady Chapel, and thus, as it happened, gave to Wells as priceless an example of the Decorated style, as it already possessed of the Transitional, the Early English, and the Geometrical.

The Lady Chapel at Wells would seem to have been built

really as a separate building, and, itself the work of genius, to have been joined again by nothing less than genius to the Transitional bays of Bishop Reginald's choir. It thus formed

Wells Cathedral.

the most beautiful east end to be found in England, a thing beyond criticism or praise, an immortal and perfect loveliness. Here, at Wells, the usual English east end, square and blunt, lacking in fancy and imagination as many have thought, is magically avoided, and all that the subtle French builder achieved with his apsidal chapels is suddenly won by a stroke of genius for this English Church, but in a simpler fashion. The Wells builder avoids the usual English squareness by making his Lady Chapel not rectangular but octagonal. "To get this octagon," says Mr. Bond, "of which only five sides were supported by walls, he had to plant in the retro-choir two piers to support the remaining three sides; and these piers are necessarily out of line with the piers of the choir. He had got his continental vista. He saw it; but he saw also that it could be improved upon. And he did improve it, by putting up an outer ring of four more piers round the western part of the octagon of the Lady Chapel. It was an intuition of genius; it makes the vistas into the retro-choir and Lady Chapel a veritable glimpse into fairy land; and provides here alone in England, a rival to the glorious eastern terminations of Amiens and Le Mans." It would seem that the builder of this marvellous chapel had studied the magical effect of light and space which had already been attained in the Chapter House and had learned his lesson there. However that may be, we have here an effect unique in England and perhaps in the world. From the choir we look through three marvellous arches into a wonderland of light and air, a heaven upheld by four palm trees of marble and of stone, or are they the stalks of lilies that tower there and burst into blossom upholding the house of Our Lady? In the early dawn the effects of the faint light streaming through the coloured glass of the windows and reflecting their glory upon the slender grey shafts of Purbeck marble must have been incomparably lovely; but no one ever sees them now, for the Protestants do not open the Cathedral, now in their possession, till nine o'clock.

The Lady Chapel would seem to have been completed in 1324. It is thus an early work of that period of English Gothic known as the Curvilinear, and it is the masterpiece of that moment.

The choir, as we have it to-day, completely modified by the Lady Chapel, consists in its work of three parts, the three new eastern bays that were built at this time to join the new Lady Chapel to the western bays of Bishop Reginald, and the great Jesse window over the high altar, one of the glories of the church; the transformation of the western bays to chime with the new work; and the unfortunate but characteristic vaulting.

Wells Cathedral. The Choir.

The piers and arches of the western bays remain as they originally were, and are repeated in the three eastern bays but the triforium has been replaced by exquisite tabernacle work of great richness and beauty, and the windows, four of which still retain their fourteenth century glass, both here and in the aisles have been renewed in the Curvilinear style. It is only the vault which is really a failure, and that for many is redeemed by the fact that it is peculiarly Somerset in character, indeed it is copied or adapted from many a wooden vault in the parish churches of the county.

The work done at this time involved the rebuilding of the central lantern in 1318-21, which in 1248 had been thrown down by an earthquake. This noble tower, however, proved too heavy for the piers upon which it stood, and the ugly expedient was adopted of supporting these with arches carrying inverted arches, known from the shape they assume as St. Andrew's Crosses; this was found to be successful in preventing any further damage. The central lantern which is no lantern closed as it is, was thus built and saved, and it now became the business of the authorities to complete the western towers. Work was begun upon the southern tower in the last ten or twelve years of the fourteenth century, and it is thus in the Perpendicular style of the day, as is the northern tower a work of the fifteenth century. They both, of course, lack their spires. At the same time the windows in the clerestory of the nave and in the aisles were tampered with and Perpendicular tracery inserted.

All this Perpendicular work upon the northern tower, and in the windows, was the achievement of Bishop Beckington (1443-1464). To this Bishop, who was a great benefactor of Wells, and whose executors had already built the northern tower, a chantry was erected under the last bay but one, towards the east, on the south side of the choir. This exquisite tomb has been utterly spoilt, and is now in pieces in the chapel of St. Calixtus, where is also the beautiful alabaster tomb of Dean Husee, d. 1305. Close by is the thirteenth century stone which marks the grave of Bishop William Bytton, 1266-1274, and in the south transept is the spoilt tomb of Bishop William de Marchia (1293-1302). Here, too, the curious and beautiful fourteenth century clock should be noticed. It does not seem to have come, as is generally asserted, from Glaston, but was probably made for the cathedral by one of the scholars of Peter Lightfoot, a Glastonbury monk. The figures without are very fine, and splendid work of the period.

In the north choir aisle is the tomb of the great rebuilder

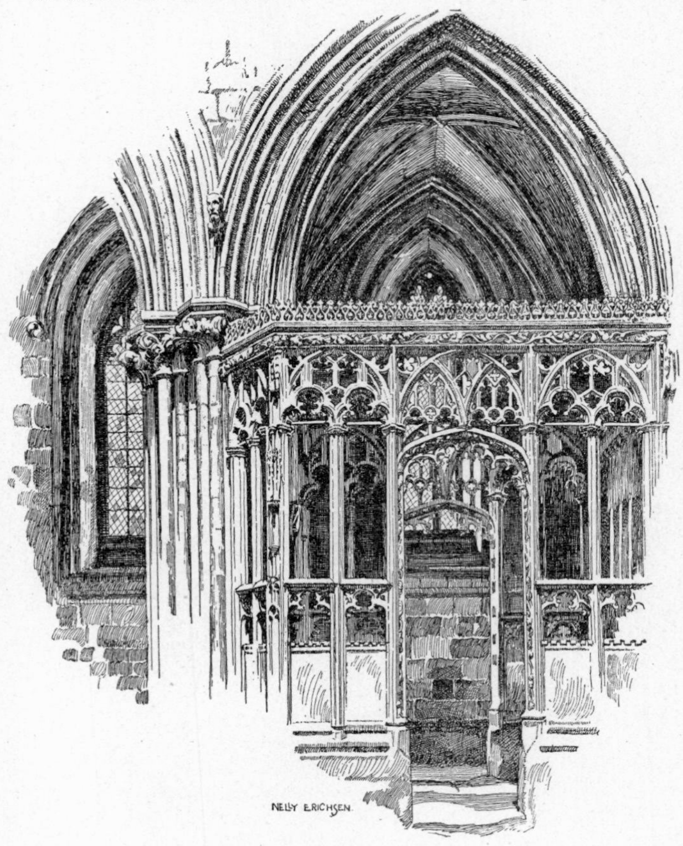

The Bubwith Chantry, Wells.

of the choir, Bishop Ralph de Salopia (1329–1363). But what, of course, will attract every visitor most are the two beautiful, and now useless, chantry chapels, of Bishop

Bubwith (1407–1424) and of Hugh Sugar, Treasurer of Wells (1460–1489), in the nave. They are both beautiful Perpendicular chapels, in which Mass was designed to be said for the repose of the souls of those whose names they bear. For nearly four hundred years now they have been empty of meaning and useless.

The great church of Wells, so full of sweetness and all delight, in spite of the stale odour of Anglicanism, which, alas! everywhere prevades it, and which its beauty, gaiety, and enthusiasm continually deny, is complete in all its parts. It can boast of one of the noblest Chapter Houses in England, its Lady Chapel is perhaps the loveliest anywhere to be found, and it has always possessed a Cloister.

This, as we see it, is a fifteenth century rebuilding of an Early English Cloister, to which the outer walls and the two lovely doorways still belong. The Palm Churchyard, as it is called, within the Cloister, which has but three walks, was the cemetery of the Canons. To the east of this was the Vicar's cemetery, and to the west, what is now the Close, was the great cemetery, as we have seen, of the people of Wells.

Over the eastern walk of the Cloister is the Library of the Chapter, built by the executors of Bishop Bubwith about 1428. It contains many fragments of some interest, and a number of books, among them many that belonged to Bishop Ken. Over the southern and western walks Bishop Beckington built a school of music, and to the west a house for the master of the choristers, which effectually blocked the western processional door.

Leaving the Cathedral by the eastern walk of the cloister we may reach, by its southern door, the drawbridge and the fourteenth century gate-house of the Bishop's Palace. This noble and beautiful place, with its gardens and battlemented walls and ruins of the Great Hall of the thirteenth century where the last Abbot of Glastonbury was shamefully tried and condemned, is entirely surrounded by a great moat which is fed from St. Andrew's Well in the Vicar's Churchyard. All this was the work of Bishop Ralph de Salopia, but the Palace itself was built by Bishop Jocelyn and substantially, apart from the upper storey, what remains may be said to be of Bishop Jocelyn's time. The beautiful and lofty chapel, however, is the work of Bishop Burnell. But it is not of Jocelyn or of any great mediæval churchman, I suppose, we think here, but of a lesser spirit and yet one who was not lacking in courage, in holiness, and in poetry. For it was, as it is said, while pacing up and down that terrace walk southward above the gardens that Ken, who was Bishop here from 1685–1691, composed that well-known and simple Evening Hymn, "Glory to Thee my God this night," an adaptation both fortunate and lovely of the lovelier Latin Hymn of Compline, *Te lucis ante terminum*, and sung, curiously enough, all over the English world to-day to the tune that Tallis wrote for the Latin.

Wells. Gateway of Bishop's Palace.

The Well House of Bishop Beckington, whence the city was freely supplied with water, and Bishop Bubwith's Barn remain, the former in the Palace Garden, the latter not far away to the south-west.

The Palace of Wells, so incomparably lovely and peaceful now and full of a beauty we can well understand, has suffered a good deal more than the Cathedral in the course of time. The Cathedral, of course, has been stripped of its altars, its pictures, a great deal of its sculpture, and last, of its soul; but it has kept—if there is any consolation in reminding ourselves of it, and I think there is—its body almost intact. This, the Palace, which had no soul to lose, has been unable to do.

As Bishop Jocelyn built it, it consisted of buildings about

Wells. Part of the Bishop's Palace.

a quadrangle, the western side of which, consisting of a curtain-wall and a gate house, has been destroyed. As for the Great Hall which Bishop Burnell built, it was dismantled by Sir John Gates in 1552 when he bought it after the

Gateway known as the Bishop's Eye.

execution of the Duke of Somerset, to whom Barlow, the Bishop who first disgraced the See by heresy, to say nothing

of his other crimes, had alienated it in 1550. Gates was happily executed for high treason in the following year, but, what was left of the Great Hall was utterly despoiled by Dr. Cornelius Burgess, an egregious person of Puritan opinions, to whom palace, deanery and chapter-house, and other church property were sold by the Parliament, who had appointed him to "preach God's word in the late Cathedral Church of St. Andrews, Wells." That sentence astonishes one on a first reading; but, later maybe, one comes to think it not unjust. The Catholic Church and the Catholic Faith were gone in every sense of the word; the Cathedral Church was dead as it has ever since remained. Nor can we regard with more than a very fleeting regret the destruction of the Great Hall at the hands of Sir John Gates and his extraordinary successor. The place had seen the mock trial and foul torture of Abbot Whiting in 1539. It deserved only to be swept away.

After leaving the Palace, one turns westward through the great Palace Gate, known as the Bishop's Eye, the work of Bishop Beckington, and comes into the Market Place originally designed by that Bishop in 1443, the houses upon the north, though spoilt, still being substantially his work. At their north-eastern end stands a narrow approach to the Close, the only one from the Market Place, called the Penniless Porch, with Bishop Beckington's *Rebus* upon it on either side of his arms and Henry VI's. Due north across the Close, from this gate, stands the Deanery, a noble building somewhat modernised, but still in the main the house Dean Gunthorpe built at the end of the fifteenth century, and in which Henry VII was entertained upon September 30th, 1497, when on his march against Perkin Warbeck. Its north façade is especially fine.

Following the road eastward past the Deanery we see the beautiful bridge that connects the Vicar's Close with the Chapter House, and before we reach it we have on the left the Archdeaconry, a house originally of the thirteenth century, which, since the time of Polydore Vergil, who here wrote his history, has ceased to be church property.

The northern side of the Cathedral is of very great beauty, and should be lingered over with love. I know of nothing better in England than the composition made by the north porch, the north transept, the lofty Chapter House and the Chain Gate. This Chain-Gate and Bridge were built by Bishop Beckington in 1459, as I have said, to give access to the Vicars' Close, a Close of houses built in the middle of the fourteenth century by Bishop Ralph de Salopia for the Canon's vicars, the assistants and substitutes of the Canons of the Cathedral. There were at that time fifty Canons, and therefore fifty vicars, and though the predecessors of these priests

Wells. The Chapel in the Vicars' Close.

had been organised by Bishop Jocelin, they would seem till Bishop Ralph's time to have lodged anywhere in the town. The little houses which all together are very picturesque and charming, have been much altered, but so far as their roofs and chimneys and general appearance go they would seem to be much as they have always been. At the north end of the Close is a beautiful fifteenth century chantry which Bishop Bubwith built for the vicars, and over which the executors of Bishop Beckington built a library. To-day, the Close of the old vicars is used by the students of Wells Theological College. A perhaps stranger fate has befallen the Vicars' Hall, in part a building of the sixteenth century, over the south entrance to the Close. This has come into the hands of the Freemasons!

I began this account of Wells by saying that the city was of little or no interest apart from its ecclesiastical history and buildings. Indeed, apart from the Cathedral and its subject buildings, there is nothing whatever to see in Wells except it be the very noble parish church of St. Cuthbert and the almshouse of Bishop Bubwith close to it. The double-windowed tower of St. Cuthbert is one of the finest in Somerset, and it groups so well with the Cathedral tower in every distant view of the city that no one can approach Wells without wondering about it. But it is not only the tower which is splendid. The church itself is very spacious, and comes of long lineage, for there stood here, probably to the east of the present south porch, a Saxon chapel, under the same dedication, already in Alfred's time, and certainly a Norman chapel was endowed here in the time of Bishop Robert, of which a fragment of the piscina remains, the only Norman thing in Wells. The present church dates from about the middle of the thirteenth century, from Bishop Jocelyn's time that is, but the only parts which remain of what was probably a cruciform church with a central tower are the upper parts of the pillars and the capitals, and a few bases, an Early English window in the south transept, and another on the north side of the church in what is usually known as "the Exchequer."

During the fifteenth century the church was evidently rebuilt and remains for the most part of Perpendicular style. The central tower, which outlasted this rebuilding, fell in 1561, and was not rebuilt, the beautiful western tower we see, begun in 1410, and finished about 1430, alone remaining. The church, as we now see it, is then a building of the fifteenth century restored in the latter half of the sixteenth. It consists of nave with clerestory, and singularly fine roof, aisles, and chantry chapels upon both sides, transeptal chapels, north and south porches, each with a chamber above, chancel with aisles, and the original sacristy now called "the Exchequer" upon the north.

The chantry in the south transept was founded in 1402 by

Gateway known as Penniless Porch, Wells.

Thomas Tanner, of Wells, in the Lady Chapel. There was another altar dedicated in honour of Our Lady in the north transept ; both these altars were magnificently decorated, and both were, of course, mutilated at the Reformation. The

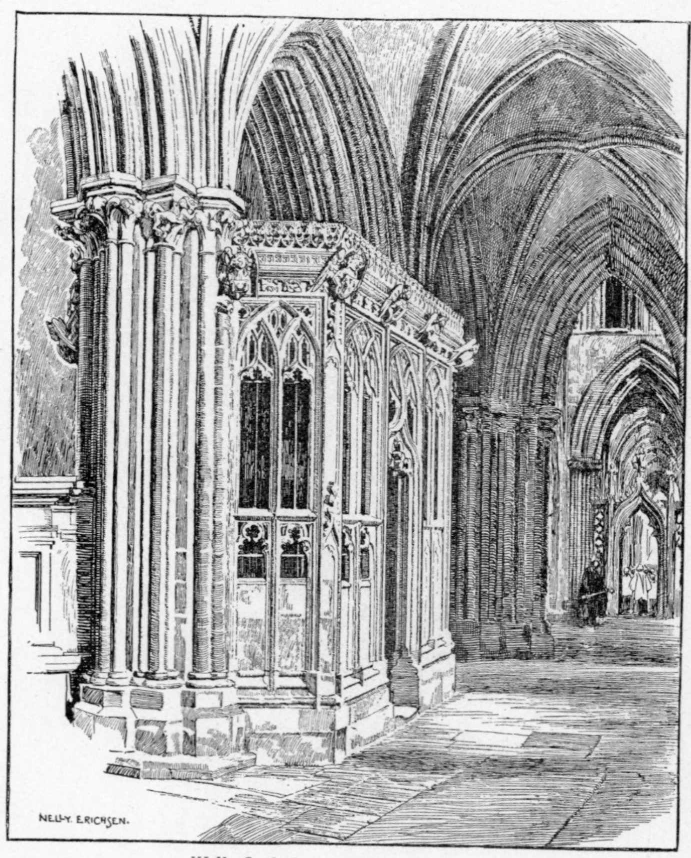

Wells Cathedral. The Sugar Chantry.

reredos of the altar in the south transept represented the Tree of Jesse ; it was made in 1471, and, though spoiled, re-erected in 1848. The altar in the north transept was found at the same time to have possessed a reredos even finer. It would seem to have been of somewhat earlier date; but it was completely ruined, and only a few figures were placed at the south-west of the Church. The finely carved seventeenth century pulpit should be noticed.

But when all this is seen and perhaps done with, then is the time come, not to leave, but to enjoy Wells. For the charm and the delight of the city are not to be had in the most careful sight-seeing, but, if at all, then in those long quiet days in which one does nothing, but by chance wanders about the city, watching the daws that for so many centuries have made their home, really as gulls might do, upon the great cliff of the Cathedral front, or lingering in the palace gardens, or lying in the shadow of the old and beautiful trees or wandering upon the hills, while all unconsciously the unique beauty of Wells sinks into the mind and remains ever after to influence it with a certain quietness, beauty, and peace. For dead though she be Wells yet speaketh of all that is best worth having in the world.

Wells Cathedral. The Cloisters.

CHAPTER VII

GLASTONBURY

No one I suppose can tread the hard way from Wells due south across the marsh to Glastonbury, at least for the first time, with a light heart; for whether it be that the country over which that causeway has been driven is in itself gloomy and sombre, or whether too much that is wretched and unfortunate in our history has passed this way, so that it still haunts our thoughts, and colours our mood as we go; this is certain, that those six miles are always full of a sense of discomfort and tragedy.

Nor will the arrival in Glastonbury lighten the heart. Here where our fathers, through how many changes and revolutions, found a shrine, the first and the holiest Christian altar in Britain, we find a rather aimless town and a ruin so beautiful and so appalling in its dead eloquence that after a few hours we are eager to hasten away and to forget that for more than a millennium Glastonbury was the day star of England, the cradle of Christ in Britain, the foundation and the root of our happiness and our civilisation.

That ruin lies upon the hillside as it were a little behind the present town, and till recently was reached by a devious way through an old yard opposite the Tribunal in the High Street, built by Abbot Beere before 1517. And coming upon it thus perhaps without much understanding of what it is that lies there forsaken in the meadows, it is with nothing less than astonishment one sees the splendour of the ruin which remains.

Perhaps I am not far wrong when I assert that but few of those who through the long summers come to Glastonbury to see her ruined Abbey know or realise at all what it is upon which they look.

We talk of "old" England, and think perhaps of Alfred,

Glastonbury Abbey. Looking West.

perhaps of the Conqueror, forgetful that the church at Glastonbury was already older when William landed than it would have been now if he had founded it. For if it be true, as the legend asserts and not our latest poet only has told us,

> "That Joseph came of old to Glastonbury,
> And there the heathen prince Arviragus
> Gave him an isle of marsh whereon to build,
> And there he built with wattles from the marsh
> A little lonely church in days of yore. . . ."

then, as we may believe, it certainly remained when the Legions were withdrawn for the last time, and it stood there in the marshes, hidden from all evil men till St. Augustine and St. Birinus had converted barbarian Wessex, so that when Rome returned in the person of the Benedictines she found here, alone perhaps in England, a native Christian church in being, dating, too, from the Apostolic Age. Upon it doubtless Alfred based his defence in that second and worse barbarian invasion from which he saved at last all that could be saved. It certainly, and perhaps alone, was never violated. It held the whole of our traditions as a reasonable people, a part of Christendom—safe and intact; and it shone there like a sign over all our history till the sixteenth century. When Henry murdered it he killed in us something that should have been immortal, that we shall never have again.

But the sacredness of Glastonbury, dating, for us, from the first years of our religion, would seem in fact to be older far than Christianity. Before Glastonbury was, the isle of Avalon was a holy place, known perhaps far and wide through Europe. It was the Island of the Blest, Avalon the place of departed spirits, and this mysterious fame it owed perhaps to its strangeness and the suddenness of its height, towering there as it does five hundred feet out of the marsh.

A man making his way in prehistoric times westward from the Straits of Dover along the great Chalk Downs would have seen from the high ridge of Wiltshire the great white curtain of mist like a sea lying over the vast marsh of Somerset, and out of the mist the high Tor thrust up, a green island, lonely, beautiful, and radiant with the sun. To him as perhaps to us such a place can only have seemed holy and unapproachable. It is, then, little wonderful that such a spot should have gathered to itself or even created such a legend as that of the coming of St. Joseph, the Cup of the Grail in his hands, to be hidden there under the Wirrall Hill; his staff, like that other Joseph's, the husband of the Blessed Virgin, which blossoms suddenly when thrust into the ground in midwinter, and the little church

The Tribunal, Glastonbury.

built there out of mud and reeds, the first church, as we like to think, that was ever built in all the world, and by one who had seen and loved our Lord and laid Him in his own sepulchre.

We shall never know now whether that legend is indeed true or whether, as some men take a curious pleasure in asserting, it is utterly false. Every sane and human heart must surely wish it true; for who would not rejoice to know that one who had actually stood beside the Cross, and served our Lord and seen Madonna's tears, first brought the news of it all to Britain? I cannot imagine a man so brutish. But little or rather nothing is to be gained from the "arguments" of any man in a matter like this, for arguments suppose evidence, and we have no evidence upon which an argument can be founded; only we have the legend, and for that, since it is so fair and so fine, let us be thankful and especially if we can believe it.

I suppose the earliest piece of history as distinct from legend which we have in regard to Glastonbury is the grant of Gwrgan, King of Damnonia, in 601 A.D. He gave land to the "old church" in the time of Abbot Worgret. The document which bears witness to Gwrgan's grant was copied by William of Malmesbury, the historian of the Abbey, and was, I believe, accepted by Freeman as genuine. It is not, however, till a hundred years later—in 704—that we have positive evidence of the existence of that little church of wattle; this is contained in a charter of the inevitable King Ine, which is dated "Lignea Basilica"—the wooden church. That this church, already called "the old church" in 601, was still in existence in 1032 we know from a charter of King Cnut, which in that year was signed within its walls. According to Malmesbury the bodies of St. Gildas, St. Patrick, and many others were buried in this "old church," which was presently encased in stone for its preservation, and endured till 1184, when on May 25th a great fire swept it away, "then venerable with the weight of perhaps a thousand years," and indeed everything else at Glastonbury, including other churches and the monastic buildings, which in the course of ages had grown up about it, the holiest and the oldest thing in England, were then destroyed. But such a miserable misfortune could not be endured by the men of that day, and Henry II, in whose hands the Abbey was at the time, immediately set about rebuilding it in the loveliest manner of that age. It is the ruin of this church we have in the so-called "chapel of St. Joseph," really the church of St. Mary in whose honour

St. Joseph of Arimathea had first founded it. It endured perfect, beautiful, and in use from 1186, in which year Reginald of Bath consecrated it, till its destruction by Henry VIII.

A man lying upon the green sward there on a summer afternoon in the shadow of what is left, shamefully roofless, of that little church of St. Mary may be sure at least of this amid all his astonishment at the beauty of the Norman work so delicate there, and his scepticism of anything so living as a legend: that he is certainly lying on the very place where that wattle church stood of old and that he is gazing upon its successor. Lying there one tries to grasp something of all that must have happened in that place between the foundation of that little wooden church and its rebuilding in 1184. And I think what strikes one most is the way in which that earlier Glastonbury gathers up all that is most fundamental in our history. If St. Joseph was indeed the apostle of Britain, if it is to him we owe the news of the Son of God, here he lies. Here it is said St. Patrick, the apostle of Ireland, ended his days and was buried on the right of the high altar. And it is here, too, St. David, the apostle of Wales, came with seven bishops to consecrate the old church, but our Lord appearing to him prevented him, wounding him in the hand as a sign of his displeasure with a wound that was healed the next day at morn. It is St. David who builds the first church beside St. Mary's, and it is he who gives to Glastonbury the famous sapphire altar which we shall never see, for it was stolen by Henry. Relics of St. David were brought to Glaston by King Edgar, that great benefactor of the Abbey. Why, in Glastonbury we were one ages before any King or statesman conceived of a United Kingdom.

But it is not only as the burial place of our saints that Glastonbury seems to be the sanctuary of England; there, too, lie how many of those Kings whom we delight most to honour; Arthur, beside whom Lancelot presently lays Guinevere, bearing her all a summer's day from Amesbury; and Ine marks their graves; Edmund the Elder, Edgar, and Edmund Ironside, too, lie down beside them. And all the Kings bring gifts, not only of lands and wealth (so that at the Norman inquest those twelve hides of Arviragus have grown to eight hundred and thirty), but gifts more precious, as Alfred a piece of the True Cross, and Edmund the bones of St. Beda, the bones of St. David.

Yet of all the great men, saints and kings, who at one time or another stood for England and still lie at Glastonbury, he is not the least who was her own son, whom she loved and taught to rule himself and her and England: I mean St. Dunstan.

There is a tale told by Voragine in the *Golden Legend* how on the Feast of the Purification the people went with great devotion to the church of Our Lady at Glaston, amongst others, Herstan, the father of St. Dunstan, and Kinedrida, his mother, who was then with child of him :—

"It was so that on a Candlemas day, as all the people were in the church with tapers in their hands, suddenly all the lights in the church were quenched at once, save only the taper which St. Dunstan's mother bare, for that burned still fair. Whereof all the people marvelled greatly; howbeit her taper was out, but by the power of our Lord it lighted again by itself, and burned full bright, so that all the others came and lighted their tapers at the taper of St. Dunstan's mother. Wherefore all the people gave laud and thankings unto our Lord God for his great miracle. And then there was a holy man that said that 'the child that she then bare should give light to all England by his holy living.'

That was true for Glaston as well as for England. Born and educated at Glaston, learned in music, painting, and metal work, St. Dunstan in the year 945 became Abbot, and "for thirty years was the mainstay of the safety and glory of the English." Here at Glaston he fought with the devil, certainly, of lax discipline and disorganisation, taking him as we know by the nose with his tongs as he hammered out a chalice. Voragine tells the tale :—

"And on a time as he sat at his work his heart was on Jesu Christ, his mouth occupied with holy prayers, and his hands busy on his work. But the devil, which ever had great envy at him, came to him in an eventide in the likeness of a woman, as he was busy to make a chalice, and with smiling said that she had great things to tell him, and then he bade her say what she would, and then she began to tell him many nice trifles, and no manner of virtue therein, and then he supposed that she was a wicked spirit, and anon caught her by the nose with a pair of tongs of iron, burning hot, and then the devil began to roar and cry, and fast drew away, but St. Dunstan held fast till it was far within the night, and then let her go, and the fiend departed with a horrible noise and cry, and said, that all might hear: 'Alas! what shame hath this carle done to me, how may I best quit him again?' But never after the devil had lust to tempt him in that craft."

The devil that Dunstan chased from Glaston was in fact that of a decayed discipline. He would seem to have found the whole organisation there in disorder, and to have established for the first time the full Benedictine Rule before King Edgar made him Bishop of Worcester. From Worcester he went to London as Bishop, and from London to Canterbury, where he died and was buried. Yet in a moment of disaster his bones were returned, as it is said, and brought for safer keeping to Glastonbury, where they were long one of the chief relics and treasures.

Dunstan was the third primate Glastonbury had given to England; but so greatly had he established the abbey that his six immediate successors in the primacy may be said to have been Glastonbury men. This being so, it is not wonderful that one of Norman William's first acts should have been the curtailment of the powers of the great abbey of the west. Aegelnoth, its abbot, he took to himself as a hostage, and seized several of Glastonbury's best manors. In 1077 he thrust upon the abbey Thurstin, a Norman whose business it was to break the long English traditions of the place. He began by certain ritual reforms which the monks refused. He then called in his men at arms, and two English monks were killed at the altar. This was too much even for William. He sent Thurstin back to Normandy, and made grants of land to Our Lady of Glaston. Thurstin, however, was restored by William Rufus, and it must be confessed not without success. Great days began again for Glastonbury. It was an age of great buildings, and between Thurstin's restoration and the year 1171 undoubtedly the abbey was transformed, rebuilt, and vastly added to. This was largely the work of Abbot Henry of Blois, nephew of Henry I., who was so successful in obtaining the crown for his brother Stephen. He is said to have built a palace at Glaston, or rather a castle, a chapter house, cloister, lavatory, refectory, dormitory, infirmary, a great gateway of stone and a bell tower, and to have filled the library with books. When he became Bishop of Winchester he still ruled by sub-abbots, and when he died in 1171 he had undoubtedly refounded Glaston in the new nation the Normans had made. The possessions and estates of the Abbey at this time were perhaps the greatest in England. At the Domesday Inquest they stretched unbroken from Mells in the east to Middlezoy in the west, and from the Mendips to High Ham in the south.[1] Many isolated manors also were the property of the Abbey, as Camerton, Marksbury, Wrington, Winscombe, Lympsham, East Brent, Brent Knoll, West Monkton, Podimore, Blackford, Maperton and Holton; and indeed, when in 1178 Robert of Winchester died, and

St. Mary's Chapel, Glastonbury.

the Abbey and its domain came into the hands of Henry II, its revenues were great enough to tempt him successfully to keep it in his own hands. This he did for near six years when, as was generally believed, as a punishment for this act the great fire arose and swept all away on May 25, 1184.

It is from this terrible fire which swept everything away save Abbot Henry's bell tower and a chapel built by Abbot Robert, and which utterly destroyed the "old church," the *vetusta ecclesia* of St. Mary, that the buildings we now see in

[1] See the excellent coloured map in *Som. Arch. Soc. Proc.*, vol. xxxv (1889).

ruin begin to date. The first work the King, who undertook the great scheme of rebuilding, began upon, was naturally the church of St. Mary on the site of the old wattle church, and as we may think very much in its original dimensions. The exquisitely beautiful church we now see in ruin, known falsely as St. Joseph's chapel, and the first of the buildings we now approach, was the result. It would seem to have been practically finished within three years if we may believe Adam de Domerham, who tells us that it was consecrated by Bishop Reginald of Bath on St. Barnabas Day about the year 1186; and the great church to the east of it was already begun, when in 1189 the King died and nothing further would seem to have been done for more than forty years; in the midst of which Savaric made his piratical incursion; till, indeed, in 1235, Michael of Amesbury was elected Abbot.

Abbot Michael is known to have been a great builder at Glastonbury, and it is probable that he completed, during his twenty years of rule, the choir and transepts of the great church, in the north transept of which he was buried in 1255. Then in Holy Week, 1278, upon the 13th of April, Edward I and his Queen came on a visit to the Abbey, and were present at the great ceremony in which the bones of King Arthur and Queen Guinevere were exhumed and placed in a *sepulchrum*, before the High Altar. Adam de Domerham, who was present, has left us a very full account of the proceedings. It seems the King and Queen, with a great retinue, came in state, upon Wednesday in Holy Week; and upon the following day, Maundy Thursday, the Archbishop of Canterbury arrived in state at Glaston. Upon the vigil of Easter, he held an ordination, and for the three great days, doubles of the first class, he officiated Pontifically. Upon the Tuesday in Easter Week, in the presence of the Royal party, the Abbot proceeded to open the tomb of King Arthur. On the Wednesday, the King bore the bones of Arthur, and the Queen those of Guinevere, wrapped in the most precious palls, to the *sepulchrum* which had been made for them before the High Altar, and affixed their seals to a document which stated that "these were the bones of King Arthur."

In all his long and extremely valuable account of this ceremony, of which he was an eye-witness, Adam de Domerham does not say a word as to the condition of the church. This would be understandable, if, as we may suppose, it had been completed between 1235 and 1255, in the time of Abbot Michael; but if the fabric was then complete, the church itself must, one would think, still have been in the hands of the workmen, and it may be that the great ceremony at which Edward I and his Queen assisted with the Archbishop was in fact the consecration of the High Altar, quite lost sight of in the wonder and enthusiasm of the discovery of the bones of Arthur and Guinevere. At any rate, with the completion of the nave in the time of Abbot Sodbury, who was elected in 1323, the interior of the great church of SS. Peter and Paul was finished and it was then decided to throw open the church of St. Mary to the new, through the Galilee which joined them, and which would seem to have been a part of the original scheme of building. To effect this the eastern wall of St. Mary's church was thrown down and an arch built in its place, thus making the entire range of buildings one.

Abbot Sodbury, who not only completed the nave but vaulted it and covered it with paintings, gave the Abbey its famous clock, its seven great bells of the central tower, and the five in "the steeple" as well as the organ and many altars and ornaments, died in 1334. His successor completed the great Hall of the monastery at the cost of £1,000, but did little for the Church. Abbot Walter de Monyngton, who became Abbot in 1342, also added very largely to the monastery, and Leland tells us that he also lengthened the choir by two bays, and revaulted the whole of it, as well as building eastward the retro-choir and chapels, and the western part of the great Chapter House. His successor rebuilt the Cloisters with Dormitory and Fratry, finished the Chapter House, and built the Abbot's Kitchen, which remains to the south-west of the Abbey ruins.

The last great builder was Abbot Richard Beere, 1493-1524, the last abbot but one, to whom was due the Edgar Chapel to the east of the church; he restored the eastern end of the church and built the St. Andrew's crosses to support the tower, as had been done at Wells. To the north of the body of the church he made a chapel in honour of our Lady of Loreto, this when he came "from his Embassadrie out of Italie"; and to the south "he made the chapelle of the Sepulchre" for the solemnity of Holy Week.

Abbot Beere died in 1524 and was succeeded by Abbot Richard Whiting, brutally martyred by Henry VIII in 1539. This good man was a son of Glaston, for he had been educated there before he went to Cambridge, where he graduated in 1483. He returned to Glaston to make his profession as monk, and for some time under Abbot Beere he held the office of *camerarius*. In February, 1525, he was appointed abbot by Wolsey, to whom forty-seven of the monks had given their rights of election. At this time the Abbey was educating nearly three hundred boys of the nobility and gentry beside other meaner folk, and the Abbot often entertained some five hundred persons at a time, and on Wednesday and Friday fed all the poor of the neighbourhood. Leland, who knew him and had stayed with him, describes him as "homo sane candidissimus et amicus meus singularis." In 1534 he, with his prior and some fifty monks, took the oath of supremacy, the refusal of which cost Blessed Thomas More his life; and in fact when the first investigators came to Glaston they were able to find no fault at all with the Abbey or its administration. Even the brigand Layton writes to Cromwell in August, 1534, to say that the monks "are so strait kept that they cannot offend, but fain they would."

In 1536, however, a friar, preaching in the Abbey, denounced "the new fangylles and new men," very rightly, but unwisely, considering the unscrupulous revolutionaries "the new men" were; and this seems to have been seized upon as an excuse for attack, and "the property of the abbey" we read "was constantly being granted on leases to courtiers." However, at the beginning of 1539 Glastonbury was still untouched, but it was the only religious house left in Somerset; such was the greed of the Crown and the devilish rapacity of Cromwell. In the face of these even Glastonbury, the oldest and holiest house in England, might not stand, for the appetite grows by what it feeds upon. In September, to compass its fall, a new visitation was decided upon. The infamous Layton was once more despatched, and on September 16th Abbot Whiting, whom formerly this creature had praised, "now appears to have no part of a Christian man."

On the nineteenth of the month Layton and the other commissioners, Pollard and Moyle, arrested Whiting at his manor of Sharpham, brought him to Glaston and later to

London, where he lay in the Tower. The charge against him has never been clear; some suppose that it had to do, not with the Royal Supremacy, but with the Succession, since a book of "arguments" in favour of Queen Katherine is said to have been found by the Commissioners in the Abbey. The truth was that Cromwell and the King were determined upon his murder, though he was but "a very weak man and sickly." This is clear from Cromwell's own hand. In October we find him noting: "The Abbot of Glaston to be tried at Glaston and *also executed there with his complycys. . . . See the evidence be well sorted and the indictments well drawn.*" In November Abbot Whiting was sent down to Wells, and on November 14, in the Great Hall of the Palace at Wells, he was arraigned and condemned and his murder decided upon. He was then dragged upon a hurdle all the way from Wells to Glaston, where upon Tor Hill he was hanged with his companions John Thorne and Roger James. His head was set upon the Abbey gate and his quarters sent to Wells, Bath, Ilchester, and Bridgwater. In the year 1896 Richard Whiting, last Abbot of Glaston, was beatified.

The fate of the Abbey, the most ancient in England, whose abbot had precedence of all the abbots of England till the year 1154, when Pope Adrian IV, the Englishman, gave that honour to the Abbot of St. Alban's because there he had received his education and because our proto-martyr St. Alban suffered there, was not left long in doubt. Its riches were stolen away by the King and his minions, its buildings which for so long had borne witness to an universal religion, sunk into decay, and presently, in the miserable times which followed, were used to mend the roads, and particularly that causeway across the moor which leads from Wells to Glastonbury. In 1547 the Abbey and Manor of Glastonbury were granted to the Duke of Somerset, and he, not knowing what to do with the already ruined buildings, in the summer of 1550 introduced a colony of Flemings. In 1552, however, he was executed, and in 1553 Queen Mary sent them home. In 1539 Queen Elizabeth granted the Abbey and Manor to Sir Peter Carew, but on his death without heirs it came back to the Crown. Eventually the place came into the hands of the Dukes of Devonshire, who in 1773 sold it to a Thomas Bladen for £12,700.

Scarce a fragment remains in the world of all those treasures which helped to make Glastonbury famous. The sapphire altar, that wonder of the earliest Middle Age, is gone for ever. Only—and by a miracle—a Thorn from the Crown of Thorns, mentioned by John of Glaston as one of the most precious relics of Glaston, is still preserved in the Nunnery of Stanbrook in Worcestershire. Nothing else remains from Glaston but the vast ruins in the beautiful meadow among the trees at the foot of the Tor.

Those ruins consist of the church of St. Mary, built by Henry II to replace the *vetusta ecclesia* of wattles destroyed by fire in 1171, and of certain walls and arches very fragmentary and despoiled of the great church of SS. Peter and Paul. All the domestic buildings are utterly gone save the Abbot's Kitchen built by Abbot Beere and the Abbey Barn which was probably built by Abbot Nicholas Frome in 1420. Both these buildings are very well worth inspection; but what will attract the visitor most, and rightly, is the wonderfully preserved ruin of the little church of St. Mary.

This building, which is commonly called the chapel of St. Joseph, perhaps because it stands upon the ground on which he built his wattle church in honour of the Mother of God, was begun in the year 1184, and originally appeared as a detached rectangular building with a tower at each angle. It is built, as John of Glaston says, "of squared stones of the most beautiful workmanship, omitting no possible ornament," and is probably the most exquisite piece of late twelfth century architecture ever achieved in these islands. According to Mr. Bligh Bond, an almost infallible authority, who, since the ironical and amusing purchase of the ruins by the Anglican Bishop of Bath and Wells, has been in charge of them, "the chapel does not appear to be altogether of native design but is more nearly related to a late type of Romanesque found in France. It is very possibly of Burgundian French conception though to some extent English in its interpretation."[1]

However that may be, the church of St. Mary was without doubt one of the loveliest buildings of its day, and it remains,

[1] See *An Architectural Handbook to Glastonbury Abbey*, by F. Bligh Bond (Bristol, 1909). This is by far the best guide to the ruins, both historical and architectural.

even in ruin, one of the most astonishingly beautiful things in Somerset.

The church was, as I have said, a rectangular building with a tower or turret at each corner. The walls were richly panelled with arcades of semi-circular arches supported upon a colonnade of shafts of Purbeck marble with carved capitals and moulded bases all of this precious material; and this both within and without. The Purbeck shafts have all been stolen away or have been destroyed by time and weather, but the work in Doulting stone still remains almost perfect in its beauty.

In the upper part of the walls are the round arched windows, exquisite and various in their details, originally of one clear light, but, later, in the Perpendicular time, altered into two lights. The buttresses of Romanesque type, really pilasters, set against the wall, and the turrets at the angles of exquisite design should especially be noticed, but what will most interest the traveller is the doorways of the chapel, especially that upon the north.

This contains some very remarkable reliefs in four bands or rings, alternately of foliage or decorative ornament and of figures. In the innermost band or ring, beginning upon the left, we see the Annunciation, the Salutation, the Nativity, and the Journey of the Magi and their Adoration. This subject of the Magi is continued or repeated in the outer band or ring, which beginning again upon the left shows us the Adoration of the Magi and their return to their own country after their warning in a dream that they should not return to Herod. Then we see the Flight into Egypt, the Massacre of the Innocents, the Annunciation of the Death of Herod to Joseph, and the Return from Egypt. It is to be hoped that the present owners will, unlike their predecessors, do something for the preservation of this chapel, at least by supplying it with some sort of roof and perhaps a flooring over the crypt. This crypt was not a part of the original church, but was excavated and vaulted in the fifteenth century. It contains a well, known as St. Dunstan's, of which, however, nothing is recorded.

As for the great church of SS. Peter and Paul, nothing comparable with the ruin of St. Mary's remains of it. Its few exquisite arches, the mighty piers of the chancel arch, here a wall and there a pile of stones, are all that is left to remind us of this great and beautiful abbey church—the longest in England, with the exception of old St. Paul's, for it was, with St. Mary's, 580 feet long.

Nothing, I suppose, can take away from the bitterness of a visit to these appalling ruins amid the beautiful trees in that meadow at the head of the vale of Avalon at the foot of the Tor Hill. In summer they seem, in the silence and the sunshine, like something spell-bound, to await the advent of some deliverer, who shall restore all things in Christ our Lord. Under the winter's snow they seem to be caught in a beauty so marvellous that it appals and terrifies us, when we remember the crime which robbed God of this the perfect gift of countless generations of men. No one can look upon these ruins and be at peace. For if he be of the faith which is founded upon this shameful and cruel ruin, these poor stones are a continual and unanswerable reproach before which he can but hang his head; and if he be of the old Faith, how can he restrain his tears, or remembering modern England and our misery, how shall he not be angry and afraid? But it is impossible and useless to comment upon a murder and a sacrilege so foul and bloody; it is better to be silent, for there is no reason or excuse which may explain them.

When not great Arthur's tomb nor holy Joseph's grave
From sacrilege had power their sacred bones to save;
He who that God in man to his sepulchre brought,
Or he which for the Faith twelve famous battles fought.
What! did so many kings do honour to that place
For avarice at last so vilely to deface!

. . . .

As we return into the High Street from that disastrous meadow, we pass on the left, between the Abbey ruins and the old entrance to them in the High Street, the Almshouse or Hospital for women founded by Abbot Beere. Its chief interest lies in its chapel, where the altar still remains from Catholic times, apparently undisturbed and still marked with its consecration crosses.

Coming into the High Street we turn up to the right, and, at the cross roads, turn again to the right, about Chalice Hill on the left, to make our way to the Tor Hill, which towers 500 feet over the moors. It was at the foot of Chalice Hill (a little way to the left, before one takes the footpath for the

Tor, leaving the Abbey Barn on the right), according to the legend, that St. Joseph hid the cup of the Grail.

> "The cup, the cup itself from which our Lord
> Drank at the last sad supper with his own.
> This, from the blessed land of Aromat—
> After the day of darkness, when the dead
> Went wandering o'er Moriah—the good saint
> Arimathæan Joseph, journeying brought
> To Glastonbury, where the winter thorn
> Blossoms at Christmas, mindful of our Lord."

Glastonbury Tor.

Here at the foot of Chalice Hill, it is said St. Joseph hid this cup; but others assert that not the cup, but two phials of our Lord's Blood, were buried here, and the cup placed in a great tower upon a hill. However that may be, and the legends with regard to all that Joseph did are very various and will not allow of a clear story, it has been believed at Glastonbury for many ages that the spring which rises at the foot of Chalice Hill, and from which flow two streams of water, an upper and a lower, is peculiarly holy and, indeed,

impregnated with the Precious Blood of our Redeemer. It is impossible to say when this belief arose, though some assert that it was in the ignorance and superstition which followed the Suppression, and that it is not older than the change of religion. However that may be, in the year 1750, the people of Glastonbury suddenly declared that this water was possessed of miraculous virtues, that it healed the sick, and especially those afflicted with asthma. For a time pilgrimage was made to it; and on May 5th, 1751, some ten thousand persons from all Somerset gathered there to taste of these waters.

I have said that the legend of St. Joseph, as we have received it by many channels, is full of variations and contradictions, as in this matter of the Chalice. It is so, too, with regard to the famous Holy Thorn, which is said by some to have sprung from his staff thrust into the ground as he rested at the foot of Wirrall or Weary-all Hill. Others say that it was a walnut tree which sprung from St. Joseph's staff, and that this was cut down and destroyed by the Flemings, introduced by the Duke of Somerset. This walnut tree stood in the abbey cemetery, as the life of St. Joseph printed by Richard Pynson in 1530 has it:—

> "Great mervaylles men may se at Glastenbury,
> One of a walnut tree that there dooth stande
> In the holy grounde called the semetery
> Harde by the place where Kynge Arthur was founde
> South fro Joseph's chapell it is walled in rounde. . . .
> Three hawthornes also that groweth in Werall
> Do burge and bere grene leaves at Christmas
> As fresh as other in May, when the nightyngals
> Wrestes out her notes musycall as pure as glas."

These hawthorns originally sprang, according to one version of the legend, not from St. Joseph's staff, but from a Thorn from the Crown of our Saviour which St. Joseph brought with him. Whatever we may think of the story, it is a fact that there is a thorn at Glaston still which does "burge and bere" at Christmas, and often I believe the altars of the churches there are decorated with it for the Feast. The original Thorn doubtless grew upon Weary-all Hill, but in the seventeenth century some blackguard Puritan cut down a great limb of it, but happily cut his own foot off at the same time. A little later his vandalism was completed by one of

Cromwell's soldiery, but not before many a whitethorn had been budded from the original tree. One of these children of the Holy Thorn is growing to-day in the Abbey precincts and several are to be found up and down Somerset, notably at Bath.

To return to the Tor. It is a long and rather tiring climb from the Chalice Well to the top, but the view will well repay the effort. For how many ages beyond history men must have

View from Glastonbury Tor.

stood here to question the sea and the mystery of the moors. St. Joseph is said to have likened it to Mount Tabor, the Mount of the Transfiguration, and indeed it is said to resemble it closely, and according to one of the legends it was in a tower upon a high hill that St. Joseph hid the Cup of the Grail, and the name of that hill was Corbenicy. Perhaps this hill was the Tor we see, upon which St. Patrick and his companions are said to have built a chapel in place of the oratory built there by those pilgrims of the second century, Phaganus and

Diruvianus, in honour of St. Michael the Archangel. Here certainly there was a church in the time of Henry I, and the tower we see with its image of St. Michael is all that is left of a building of the fourteenth century. Here Blessed Abbot Whiting and his companions were martyred upon November 15th, 1539.

. . . .

The town of Glastonbury is in itself of little interest. Its principal church, that of St. John the Baptist in the High

St. John's Church, Glastonbury.

Street, has a very noble and beautiful double windowed tower of three storeys in the well-known Perpendicular style of the county. It is perhaps more rich than most, and in Freeman's opinion it should rank third in order of beauty and merit after those of Wrington and St. Cuthbert's in Wells. The church, which is cruciform, is, as we see it, the work of Abbot Selwood at the end of the fifteenth century, but originally a Norman building with a central tower stood here, which was pulled down by Selwood in 1457. Nothing remains of this early building, the present noble church being wholly in the Perpendicular style. It is certain that Abbot Selwood was not the only builder of the church. Richard Atwell and his wife Joan, who are buried on the north and south of the chancel, were also considerable benefactors to the church and had a part in the great rebuilding as well as the Abbot. The curious tomb of John Camel, once in the south transept, but now at the west end of the south aisle in the nave, should be noted for its fine and curious sculpture. Camel appears to have been the chapman or bursar of the Abbey, and it is possible that as a Glastonbury man he too assisted largely in the rebuilding of this church. Outside the church upon the north side are the spoiled remains of two mortuary crucifixes with St. Mary and St. John, one on the bottom of the stairway leading to the rood-loft and the other on the north side of the tower.

The other church of Glastonbury dedicated to St. Benignus, the young companion of St. Patrick, was in mediaeval times merely a chapel dependent on St. John's. It was, however, restored by Abbot Beere, and part of the work on the north side of the church, the north porch and the double-windowed tower, are due to him.

In Magdalen Street there is an almshouse under the protection of St. Mary Magdalen, of which the interesting chapel with a charming bell-cot with a figure upon it yet remains, though called St. Margaret's Chapel. In the present decayed state of religion, people are not sure of their saints; thus in Wells they call St. Eustace "the pancake man" because they have never been taught his true name, and here in Glaston they call St. Benignus St. Benedict, and St. Mary Magdalen St. Margaret.

Three or four pieces of domestic architecture of the happy time before the Spoliation are to be found in the town, all of them connected with the Abbey: the old entrance to the Monastery, now restored, the George Inn, and the Tribunal in the High Street. The George Inn—the *novum hospitium* as John of Glaston calls it—was built by Abbot Selwood for the use of pilgrims and travellers who wished to remain in the place. The Abbey itself offered free hospitality, for two nights, to all who came, but beyond this all remained at their own charges, and it was for such that the *novum hospitium* was built. The Tribunal a little higher up the street was built by Abbot Beere. Here the Lord Abbot tried such as had offended against the laws of the land.

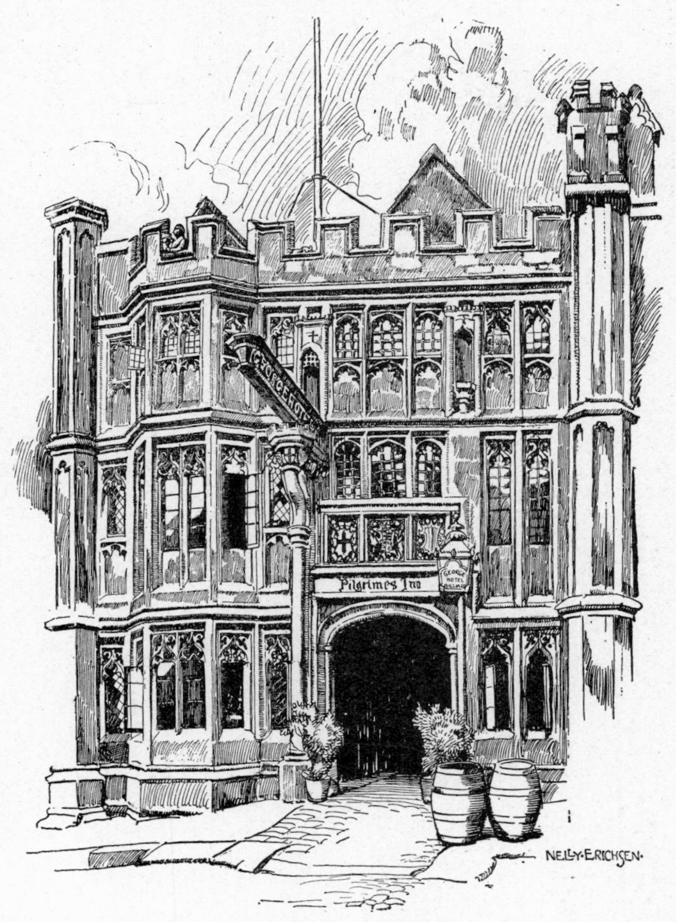

The George Inn, Glastonbury.

I do not know whether Glastonbury appears so melancholy and yet so beautiful a place to all those who visit it as it did and does to me. I would always be gone, yet can scarce drag

myself away. Surely it holds in some mysterious way something safe for us that all unconsciously we would willingly have again. As one paces up and down among the trees about the old Abbey remembering a thousand things—St. Joseph, the Cup of the Grail, the gold of Guinevere's hair, the holiness and the long endeavour that seem to have come utterly to nothing—one recalls, and perhaps with a new meaning, that legend upon the hidden tomb of Arthur which men believed in once upon a time:

Hic jacet Arthurus
Quondam rex, rexque futurus. . . .

CHAPTER VIII

THE VALE OF AVALON

THE vast flats or moors of central Somerset, out of which Glastonbury rises so suddenly and almost precipitously, a towering island five hundred feet at its summit, are from many points of view the most characteristic feature of the county, and, indeed, rather than any other part of it, may be called the true Somerset. These moors, the landscape of Glastonbury, lie between the two great hill ranges of our county, the Mendips and the Quantocks, and from east to west they stretch from the broken hill country of the Wiltshire border to the sea. Known still in the greater part of their extent as Sedgemoor they are roughly divided into two not unequal parts by the low range of the Polden Hills, but everywhere they are scattered with islands often of considerable extent; and drained though they are, for the most part, by three sluggish rivers, the Axe and the Brue to the north, the Parret to the south, of the Polden Hills, in every corner, nowadays, they are crossed and recrossed by ditches and drains known as Rhines bordered by pollarded willows, which little by little through many hundred years have turned what was once a shallow sea, or at best a marsh, into some of the richest grazing land in England. Nevertheless this country, still so strange, remains often among the loneliest, as it is certainly the flattest and lowest, in Britain; as full of surprises for the modern traveller as ever it was of old, when the monks of Glastonbury, Athelney, and Muchelney first set about draining it and bringing it, as far as might be, within the service of man.

I say that these moors were once covered by a shallow sea,

from which such high land as Glastonbury and its Tor, Brent Knoll, the Polden Hills, Somerton Hill, High Ham, the long ridge of Curry Rivel, and a hundred lower and smaller bits of good land, stood up as islands, from which the moors were conquered; and, indeed, even to-day they seem to fling themselves, just as the sea might do, against the high hills which are their shore, beating against a thousand headlands and thrusting themselves into innumerable creeks and bays.

It is easy to see from Glastonbury Tor that Avalon is an island, but, though, looking westward, we are scarcely aware of anything but the great sea-moor stretching out for mile after grey mile till it is lost in the midst of the sea; looking eastward we see at once how narrow is the channel which here makes Glaston an island, and how near is the high land here thrust out far into the moors, in a great headland, very steep upon its seaward side. This headland is called West Pennard, and it may be said always to have threatened the island safety of Glastonbury; for thus far there is good land and good going all the way from the eastern uplands, and though the marsh lies between the Isle of Avalon and West Pennard there is yet a narrow pass of fair land almost all the way between. Thus Glastonbury, safe upon all sides but this, was here not naturally impregnable and it is upon this side, as we might expect, that we shall find the fort, which guarded it.

If a man set out, then, upon the road to Shepton to the south of the Tor he will find the fort some two miles out of Glaston at Ponter's Ball. Ponter's Ball, really *Pontis Vallum*, the fort of the bridge, for the fairly good land here offers a road, though a narrow one, almost as far as the island, is an earthwork about fifteen feet high with a ditch upon the eastern side. Who were the original builders of this defence it is impossible to say, but doubtless it was used by us through countless generations as each wave of invasion swept about Glaston.

The road at Ponter's Ball stands some fifty feet above the sea and it rises gradually all the way till we stand in the woods of West Pennard. The beautiful church here, as though rejoicing to stand on good and firm land, seems itself to climb the hill, for it slopes gradually from the west right up to the east end, a curious thing. Originally the church we see—a Perpendicular building which is dedicated to St. Nicholas—doubtless consisted of a nave and chancel only, but when the tower was built, an aisle was added and the nave arcaded upon the north side. Later, the south aisle and the south arcade were built. The north arcade consists as we see of four equal arches, but the arcade on the south not only has unequal arches, but it does not in any way at all chime with that on the north. The wide arch with which it begins at the eastern end may possibly bear witness to the existence of a chantry chapel here, before the building of the south aisle was decided upon.[1] The fine screen is of early sixteenth century date. The tower built in Edward IV's time is exceedingly good and has a timber spire covered with lead; it is this which has given it its "corkscrew twist," for the lead covering subjected the green oak of the structure to enormous changes of temperature under which it warped and shrank and twisted. The carved angels in the string course over the doorway are beautiful, and should be noted. In 1813, a fives court was built at the foot of the tower on the south. The churchyard cross, of which the shaft only remains, is a fine one, having on three sides emblems of the Passion, and on the north the initials of its builder, Abbot Beere of Glaston (1493–1524).

To the south of West Pennard, at the foot of the hills, lies the little village of West Bradley. On the way we pass a fine fifteenth century Tithe Barn built by Abbot Beere. The church, a rather earlier building than that of West Pennard, is small and consists of nave, chancel, and tower. The font is Norman, and the east window is square with an interesting mediaeval cross on the gable over it. The windows in the nave however are fine Perpendicular work. The tower dates from about the year 1400.

To the south of West Bradley and in the marsh lies Baltonsborough on the river Brue, whose manor was given in A.D. 745 to the monks of Glaston by a certain Lulla, a devout lady and great benefactress of the Abbey according to William of Malmesbury. There was in the Conqueror's time a mill

[1] It is possible that the great width of the arcade here was caused by the removal of a Rood-loft which originally existed here. See *Som. Arch. Soc. Proc.*, vol. xxxvi (i), 71.

here, which was broken down by Bishop Jocelyn of Bath. This broken mill was one of the complaints the monks brought against the Bishop in their suits about the government of Glaston. At the Suppression the manor of Baltonsborough was granted to the Duke of Somerset. The church, which is dedicated to St. Dunstan, is wholly of the fifteenth century, and consists of a curiously wide nave, chancel, and tower, a

The Abbot's Barn, Glastonbury.

single design apparently. The gable crosses should be noted, especially those upon the east gable and the south porch. The south door, too, boasts a fine fifteenth century handle and escutcheon. Within, the bench ends are of the fifteenth century and are interesting. In the nave there is, or was, a curious Jacobean stool, called "the stool of repentance," where sinners of old did penance during service. In the south wall of the nave by the pulpit a piscina marks the site of an old altar. In the chancel the sedilia with panelled shields remain as well as an aumbry upon the north. The fine oak cornice should be noted, but the screen as we see it is modern, as is the cross in the churchyard save for the crucifix which was found buried hard by. In the chancel we find the following verse to the memory of Thomas Walton, son and heir of the Richard Walton, armiger, who died here in 1581:—

A shroude, a coffin, and a marble stone
Are dead men's due; and may the living teach
That when to ripeness they are fully growen
Death will the best and fairest flowers reach.
For coulde a piouse life have stay'd death's force
Hee yet hadd lived that's here a lifeless corse.

From Baltonsborough we pass south-west across the old marsh, but through a picturesque country, to the charming village of Butleigh, on the north side of the Polden Hills. Butleigh was given to the monks of Glaston in the time of King Egbert, and the church there is still under the protection of St. Benedict. It has, however, been practically rebuilt in modern times. Of old it consisted of nave and porch, central tower and chancel. The original plan was doubtless Norman and had no transepts. The nave and chancel as we see them, however, date at least from the fourteenth century. The western window, which contains some fragments of old glass, is Perpendicular, and there on the left we see still the Glastonbury shield. The transepts date at earliest from 1608, when Christopher Simcox, the son of that Thomas Simcox to whom there remains a monument, now in the chancel, built one as a family burial-place. The church was renovated out of all recognition in 1850.

Butleigh Court is a fine great house with some ancient features and a fine collection of family portraits. More interesting, perhaps, is Ivythorne Manor close by, a building of the fifteenth century.

But the proper interest of Butleigh lies in the fact that it was the birthplace of Admiral Viscount Hood, the eldest son of Samuel Hood, vicar of Butleigh, whose monument in the woods upon the ridge above Butleigh is a landmark hereabout. When Hood, who was a magnificent seaman, was superseded in 1795, Nelson was full of indignation and wrote, "The fleet must regret the loss of Lord Hood, the best officer, take him altogether, that England has to boast of; great in all situations which an Admiral can be placed in." His brother Alexander, Viscount Bridport, was also a fine sailor and shared in the "glorious first of June" off Ushant.

Their kinsmen, Arthur, Alexander, and Samuel Hood, of the Dorset branch of the family, are commemorated by Southey in the following long epitaph upon their monument in Butleigh Church:—

"Divided far by death were they, whose names
In honour here united, as in birth
This monumental verse records. They drew
In Dorset's healthy vales their natal breath,
And from these shores beheld the ocean first
Whereon in early youth with one accord
They chose their way to fortune; to that course,
By Hood and Bridport's bright example drawn,
Their kinsmen, children of this place and sons
Of one who in his faithful ministry
Inculcated within these hallow'd walls
The truths in mercy to mankind reveal'd.
Worthy were these three brethren each to add
New honours to the already honour'd name;
But Arthur, in the morning of his day,
Perished amid the Caribbean sea,
When the *Pomona*, by a hurricane
Whirl'd, riven and overwhelm'd, with all her crew
Into the deep went down. A longer date
To Alexander was assign'd, for hope,
For fair ambition, and for fond regret,
Alas, how short! for duty, for desert,
Sufficing; and while Time preserves the roll
Of Britain's naval feats, for good report.
A boy, with Cook he rounded the great globe;
A youth, in many a celebrated fight
With Rodney had his part; and having reach'd
Life's middle stage, engaging ship to ship
When the French *Hercules*, a gallant foe,
Struck to the British *Mars* his three-striped flag,
He fell, in the moment of his victory.
Here his remains, in sure and certain hope
Are laid, until the hour when Earth and Sea
Shall render up their dead. One brother yet
Survived, with Keppel and with Rodney train'd
In battles, with the Lord of Nile approved,
Ere in command he worthily upheld
Old England's high prerogative. In the East,

The West, the Baltic and the Midland seas,
Yea, wheresoever hostile fleets have plough'd
The ensanguined deep, his thunders have been heard,
His flag in brave defiance hath been seen;
And bravest enemies at Sir Samuel's name
Felt fatal presage in their inmost heart
Of unavertible defeat foredoomed.
Thus in the path of glory he rode on,
Victorious alway, adding praise to praise;
Till full of honours, not of years, beneath
The venom of the infected clime he sunk,
On Coromandel's coast, completing there
His service, only when his life was spent.

To the three Brethren, Alexander's son
(Sole scion he in whom their line survived),
With English feeling, and the deeper sense
Of filial duty, consecrates this tomb."

A little to the north-east of Butleigh, and also at the foot of the Poldens, lies Barton St. David, another dependency of the Abbey of Glaston, which gets its name of St. David from its church, a cruciform building of the Perpendicular period with north and south transepts; but the south transept has been destroyed. A Norman church originally stood here, of which apparently the sole remaining witness is the fine old north doorway. The tower is unusual for Somerset, being octagonal from the base, and placed in the angle formed by the north transept and the chancel. In the churchyard there are remains of an old cross, on the west side of the shaft of which is the figure of a bishop with a mitre and maniple. It is believed to represent St. David, who, it will be remembered, was a pilgrim to Glastonbury, where he is said to have restored the *vetusta ecclesia*.

The country about Butleigh is delightful and full of the variety of the wooded hills. It is pleasant going hereabout and the way over the little foothills of the low Polden range—its steeper escarpment here looks south—is good enough whether you are making your way to Barton St. David or westward through Butleigh Wooton into Street, a place that in its appearance, built, as it is, almost entirely along the road, suggests a Roman origin, as I suppose does its name. Its only modern interest would seem to be that it is the scene of one of the most successful of those experiments in co-operative chicken farming which have been made so commonly up and down England. It is also—and this is its proper industry—engaged in the manufacture of boots and shoes. Close to Street is the small village of Walton, which boasts of a small parsonage house and a farm of the fifteenth century, and in the church which is a comparatively modern building, much restored, there is a recumbent figure of a priest in alb and chasuble.

From Street it is but a couple of miles into Glastonbury. Setting out thence for Sharpham across the moor the best way lies again through Street and Walton. At Sharpham there is a fine old Manor House pertaining to the Abbey of Glaston, but of somewhat uncertain date, though it is thought to have been built by Abbot Beere. Here was a park of four hundred deer and some forty large cattle, and here the unfortunate Abbot Whiting, last abbot of Glaston, was arrested by the minions of Cromwell, who had already decided upon his murder. The main interest of the place for the traveller, however, would seem to be the fact that it was the birthplace of Sir Edward Dyer, the Elizabethan poet, and of Henry Fielding, the novelist, who was born here in what is known as "The Harlequin's chamber," a small room over the chapel, on April 23rd, 1707.

Sir Edward Dyer was born at Sharpham Park in the sixteenth century. He died in 1607. He is a forgotten poet, I fear, yet in his day Sir Philip Sidney himself was not ashamed to bandy verses with him.

His most famous poem—here in Somerset we should not forget it for it is in praise of contentment—was set to music by so great a master, second indeed to none, as William Byrd, Here it is:—

CONTENTMENT

My mind to me a kingdom is;
  Such perfect joy therein I find,
As far exceeds all earthly bliss
  That world affords, or grows by kind:
Though much I want what most men have,
Yet doth my mind forbid me crave.

Content I live—this is my stay;
  I seek no more than may suffice,
I press to bear no haughty sway;
  Look—what I lack my mind supplies!
Lo! thus I triumph like a king,
Content with that my mind doth bring.

I see how plenty surfeits oft,
And hasty climbers soonest fall;
I see how those that sit aloft
Mishap doth threaten most of all:
These get with toil and keep with fear
Such cares my mind could never bear.

I laugh not at another's loss,
I grudge not at another's gain;
No worldly wave my mind can toss,
I brook that is another's pain.
I fear no foe; I scorn no friend;
I dread no death; I fear no end.

Some have too much, yet still they crave;
I little have, yet seek no more;
They are but poor, though much they have,
And I am rich, with little store.
They poor, I rich; they beg, I give;
They lack, I lend; they pine, I live.

I wish but what I have at will;
I wander not to seek for more:
I like the plain; I climb no hill;
In greatest storms I sit on shore
And laugh at those that toil in vain
To get what must be lost again.
—This is my choice; for why?—I find
No wealth is like a quiet mind.

We follow the road about the hills to Buscott and then turn straight across the moor to Meare. Here, and at Godney too, and better still, about a mile and a half to the north of Glaston, in the moors, have been found examples of those prehistoric Lake Villages dating, it is thought, about 200 B.C., which doubtless once abounded in the marsh. These curious excavations will, however, scarcely succeed in interesting the ordinary traveller. The great sight at Meare, itself little more than an encampment in the marsh beside the Brue, surrounded by rhines and famous for its peat which the women dig among the reeds and osiers, is the Fish House. This is a really fine example of a fourteenth century cottage in excellent preservation. Why it is called the Fish House no one seems to know, but it is not an inexplicable title seeing that it stands on the edge of the old pool rich in "a great abundance of pikes, tenches, roaches and eels" drained a hundred years ago; and that, as we know, the chief fisherman of the Abbey of Glaston lived here. Within, the house is curious; there is no communication between the two floors, the upper doubtless being approached by a flight of outside steps. This upper floor was the dwelling house, which consisted of two rooms, one large and one small. Some years ago the Fish House was fired, it is said by an incendiary, and the fine fourteenth century timber roof was destroyed.

Close to the Fish House stands the church and manor house. The latter was erected by Abbot Godbury it seems to replace a smaller house built in 1300, itself the successor of an earlier house that was certainly standing in 1252, when Abbot Michael of Amesbury lived in it. Here, too, we find the chief room upstairs, no doubt, as in the case of the Fish House, on account of the danger of floods. The great Hall of the manor house on the first floor is a noble apartment with a very fine fireplace, with a five-sided chimney-hood and a pair of carved corbel brackets to bear lights. Nor should the windows be missed; they are very good indeed, with an inner cusped and pierced canopy, and still with the pegs and hangers for shutters.

The church, too, is very well worth seeing. In the main it belongs to two periods, the chancel being of the fourteenth century and the nave and aisles of the fifteenth, the work of Abbot Selwood. The pulpit, of stone, is a very fine one, also of this date, and the wooden roof is good and was made by one John Jackman, whose name appears in a stone corbel in the south aisle. The tracery of the east window should be noted, for it is fine and uncommon, and the parapet without is extremely charming.

Close to Meare, and indeed within the parish, on Honeygore Farm, Westhay Heath, in the year 1873, was uncovered a part of the "Abbots' Way," a causeway of wooden beams across the moor; when this road was built, whither it led, and what was its proper purpose, remain uncertain.

We proceed across the moor, with marshy grazing fields on either side the road, cut by many a willowed rhine where the wrens sing loud from dawn to dark. Knee deep in the fields are groups of red cattle, while the plover cries continually as you go, till, out of the marsh and the moor—the vale of Avalon indeed—rises the long low island upon which the village of Wedmore stands out of the flood.

Wedmore, famous long ago as the place of Guthrum's Chrisom-loosing and of the great treaty Alfred there made with the Danes which saved England for Christendom, and the better and nobler half of England at once for Christian men, is a charming place enough. Materially, I suppose its chief claim upon our notice is its fine church, one of those "quarter cathedrals" as they are called in Somerset, of which St. Cuthbert's, Wells, is another example. It is a cruciform building with a central triple-windowed tower, and dates originally, perhaps, from the twelfth century, the doorway in the south porch being perhaps of that time. But this church was certainly altered in the thirteenth and largely rebuilt in the fifteenth century, when it got the spacious appearance it now has. Its chief fault is the lowness of its nave in comparison with its lofty aisles. The chancel is aisled too, and upon the south, curiously isolated, there is a chantry or chapel, formerly the chapel of the Confraternity of the Blessed Virgin, which once existed here, though the church itself is dedicated in honour of the Blessed Virgin. This chapel was not originally to be entered from the church, but it had a large squint so that people within it might follow Mass said at the high altar.

On the north of the west tower arch is a remarkable wall painting of St. Christopher, beneath which are remains of another picture of the same Saint; one very appropriate to these marshes so liable to flood.

At the end of the south aisle there remains a stone altar from the time before the change of religion, similar to that in the Women's Almshouse chapel at Glaston. The north chapel by the chancel is covered with a magnificent roof of panelled oak, each panel being painted with the figure of an angel. There was here, as at Axbridge, originally a double Rood loft, and the suggested explanation is that here too it was the custom to act miracle plays upon this great platform. The south porch over the, perhaps, twelfth century doorway is interesting. It once contained a gallery, and over this of old was placed the canopied niche, not empty then, which is now over the doorway within the church.

The Jacobean pulpit and reading desk are among the finest in Somerset. And the brass, to a member of the Hodges family, in the north chapel of the chancel, should not be missed: it is said to be one of the latest military brasses in England. In the village is a very lovely fourteenth century cross with a canopied head on which are sculptures of the Crucifixion, the Madonna and Child, a bishop and a knight. It is said that Jeffreys hanged a doctor there because he had dressed the wounds of one of Monmouth's soldiers.

Wedmore is a good centre from which to visit this part of the Moor, or, at any rate, one place in it, I mean the village of Mark.

Mark, which lies some five miles to the west of Wedmore, is said to get its name from the Apostle, but perhaps a better derivation derives it from the Saxon *Mearc*, meaning a boundary.

In Fielding's *Tom Jones* it appears as the birthplace of the "Man of Mark." The church is a fine building in the Perpendicular style, but the south porch and perhaps the south wall are of the thirteenth century. Mr. C. E. Giles, one of the founders of the Somersetshire Archaelogical Society and the rebuilder of Allerton church, asserts that "Mark church was reconstructed in the XV century in the same manner as were more than half of the smaller Somersetshire churches, viz., by first of all rebuilding the western part of the nave and adding a tower; then rebuilding the eastern part which until then was retained, because the tower generally stood in that part, and was required for the bells until the new tower was complete. Then the old aisles (if there were any) were altered or rebuilt; and if only one existed a second was added; and finally the chancel was altered, not rebuilt." It might seem doubtful whether this method could quite fit in with what we see at Mark, but no doubt in the main the explanation tallies with the facts. At Mark perhaps the best thing within the church—for it is much handsomer without than within—is the noble roof in the porch, though there it is hidden by a foolish ceiling. The fine triple-windowed tower is a good one of the third class.

From Wedmore we turn east and take the road across the moors for Wells through Wookey which has little to show us now besides its church, which has been restored of late years out of recognition. It was originally a building of the twelfth century, perhaps the work of Bishop Robert of Wells (1136-1166).

CHAPTER IX

THE MENDIPS AGAIN

CURIOUS and even beautiful as the moors are with their strange lights, their absolute subjection to the great clouds of their limitless sky, Wells seems more marvellous than ever when one comes into it out of their loneliness; and if the traveller sets out, as I did, immediately for the hills, he will find them more precious, after the monotony of the marsh, than ever they were when we found them first, coming up out of the beautiful valley of the Chew.

It was very early one still autumn morning that I set out from Wells on my way to Frome intending to go slow and to linger on my way; for the weather, golden and firm, invited me to spend all my day in the open air in a country so fair and noble as that which I knew lay before me. Therefore I did not deny myself the pleasure of leaving the road as I came out of Wells in order to traverse Dulcote Hill from end to end, for there, as I knew well, I should get as fine a view of the delectable city as was anywhere to be had, and there, as I knew too, I must bid it farewell. All this I did in due form and with reverence; and then, the sun being well up, the day very clear, and the mist departed, I lifted up my heart and prepared to go on my way. But even as I turned a new wonder met my gaze; for by chance I looked out westward and south and there in that fortunate morning I saw what I had never seen before from this place, the blue goodness of the moors, the splendour of the western hills, and beyond—this was the miracle—the mighty headland of Countisbury in Devon rising out of the sea and hiding behind it the height of Lynton. Nor as I think can this splendour have been less than fifty miles away across the world.

Now as I came down from Dulcote Hill, the first church I came to was Dinder, the valley of the stream, and the stream is the Sheppey; and there, had I been in Italy, or had I had the good fortune to have been living in England before the miserable change of religion I should have heard Mass; as it was, I was forced to go without. Nevertheless though the church was fast shut, I lingered there, for in the churchyard I found as fine and ancient a yew, certainly Catholic,[1] as ever I saw in my life; and by my rough and ready methods I reckoned that about three feet from the ground it measured at least thirty feet round.

Dinder church, is dedicated to St. Michael and All Angels and is even more various than the usual Somersetshire parish church. Small parts of it, the south wall of the nave for instance, date from the twelfth century perhaps, but it seems to have been rebuilt in the thirteenth century, and it is possible that the five consecration crosses which remain in the south wall date from this time or even earlier, as certainly do the two dragon heads now placed over the small and modern chancel window near the chancel steps. The other windows in the chancel, which was built in 1871 when the old building was removed, are of the fourteenth century, as are the piscina there within, and the head and base of the cross in the churchyard. Towards the end of this century the north wall of the nave was broken down and an arcade built in its place, and an aisle and porch added. To this time belong the east window and the side windows in the nave. In the following century and probably towards the end of it, the tower was built. Nothing but evil was apparently done anywhere in the sixteenth century, but in the seventeenth the change of religion is marked for us here at Dinder by the magnification of the pulpit as opposed to the altar; and in 1621 a stone pulpit was built here. The screen with its Rood had then long since been swept away. The restorations of 1839 and 1871 have left us too little of this beautiful church. Some fragments of the old glass collected in

[1] I see that some authorities put the age of this yew at 1200 years, which would bring us back to Ine and Aldhelm, and make the tree as old as the See and vastly older than the Cathedral Church. A very Catholic yew indeed.

1871 have been placed in the "rood loft" window, where we may still see a representation of the Blessed Trinity and St. Michael in his armour weighing us in the balances.

Leaving Dinder I went on by the beautiful road between the hills to Croscombe. Here the church is a very noble building. From the outside it seems altogether of the fifteenth century, when undoubtedly it underwent a very considerable restoration and rebuilding; but on closer examination it is seen that the south doorway is earlier. The restoration took place in the earlier half of the fifteenth century, and to it are due the tower, the nave with its roof and clerestory, the greater part of the chancel, and the windows. In the beginning of the sixteenth century and still in Catholic times the present vestry, then a chapel, was added, and the east end of the chancel was rebuilt. Probably at the same time the curious storeyed building at the south-west corner of the south aisle was built. Part of this with its strongly barred windows was used as a treasury, but part of it was used also as a meeting place of the seven Guilds which Croscombe then boasted. These were The Young Men, The Maidens, The Webbers, The Fullers, The Hogglers, The Archers, and The Wives.

Especially should be noted here at Croscombe the fine carpentry work, the carved roof and benches of the fifteenth century, the Laudian pulpit and the very lovely screen, also of the seventeenth century. Two brasses of 1606 and 1625 respectively commemorate members of the Bisse family; but the great benefactors here would seem to have been Sir William Palton and Hugh Fortescue, lord of the manor in 1616, whose arms with those of the Bishop of the Diocese appear on the screen and pulpit. The chancel roof is a fine work of 1664.

Croscombe is full of old houses, and is one of the most charming villages in all this country.

Some two miles beyond Croscombe I came into the town of Shepton Mallet, which is now dreadful to live in on account of the exertions of an "Anglo-Bavarian" Brewery and its steam sirens. Poor Shepton seems like a town gone mad, and the traveller will do wisely if he takes a look at the church, which in spite of some dreadful Reformation and Victorian vandalism is an interesting building, at the Market Place, and Shambles, and then hurries away into the silent and peaceful hills.

Shepton Mallet, standing practically upon the Fosse Way, which here begins to take the hills, was given by Ine, as Croscombe was, to the Abbey of Glaston. At the Conquest it came to be held of the Abbot by Roger de Courcelle, but later it was held by the Mallets, from whom it takes its second name. For many years it was famous for the manufacture of woollen-cloth, in which, even in Collinson's day, some four thousand persons were employed. But all this has come to nothing, and to-day, the "Anglo-Bavarian" Brewery, I suppose, accounts for much of the "industry" here. The church, with its very glorious triple windowed tower, the noblest of all towers of this type, is almost all that remains of old Shepton, and that, as I have said, has suffered much from villains and fools, both in the time of the change in religion and in our own day. What remains, however, in spite of this vandalism. is of very considerable interest and beauty. This consists of the ancient font, of the late Transition arcade of the nave, the thirteenth century chancel arch, with its fine responds, the beautiful double piscina, the glorious tower of the early Perpendicular period, perhaps the earliest Perpendicular tower in Somerset, the magnificent late fifteenth century oak roof, perhaps the finest in the county, consisting of three hundred and fifty carved panels, all of different design, with bosses and rosettes, and thirty-six angels, and the very lovely stone-pulpit. The chancel is low, and no doubt over the chancel arch, where now the ugly and forbidding tables of the old law hang, there was originally a Rood, or perhaps a picture of the Last Judgment. Originally, of course, the church had no clerestory, hence the great height over the low chancel arch. The horrible galleries that now spoil the church should be done away with.

From the church we proceed to the Market Place, where I suppose the rare old shambles now so ruinous, the last mediaeval shambles left in England, it is said, should certainly be examined. They date from the fifteenth century. Only about half of them is left; another row, a generation ago, ran along the other side of the market place. Here, of course, meat was sold. The Market Cross, the lower part of which, including the shelter, is ancient, was built in the year 1500. The upper part, which fell in the eighteenth century, was rebuilt in 1841. The original brass remains, with the following inscription: "Of your charyte pray for the soules of Walter Buklond and Agnes hys wyff with whoys goods thys Crosse was made in the yere of our Lord God 1500 whoys obbyt

Shepton Mallet. Market Cross.

shall be kepte for Ever in thys parisshe Churche of Shepton Mallett ye 28 day of November whoys soules Jesu pardon."

With the Market Place it would seem one has done with Shepton, a singularly unfortunate town, very irregularly built, and with less visible antiquity about it than one would expect from its undoubted ancientness. What remains to it of old appearance will be found at Longbridge, where some of the houses seem to have belonged to the clothiers and to be old.

From Shepton it is well to visit Pilton, some two miles or so away to the south upon the road to Glaston, a pleasant road. Pilton was the original great parish of all the little places in this country, as Croscombe and Shepton, Pylle and North Wooton. It belonged to the Abbey of Glaston as part of the original grant of King Ine, but in 1174 Bishop Reginald got possession of the Rectory of Pilton and with the Bishopric it remained. The church has been destroyed almost out of all recognition, but the chancel arch is fine and should be noted: the old screen which once stood here is now with modern additions at North Cheriton, and perhaps the loveliest thing left to us is the fragment of glass in the south-east window of the chancel, where we see Overay (not as in the inscription, Overall), precentor of Wells, 1471–1493, at a fald-stool. Over his head is a scroll where is written *Sancta Trinitas, bonus Deus, miserere nobis.* Here, too, is a Paten of silver-gilt dating from the fifteenth century, and presented to the church by a vicar, one Sir John Dier. The screen in the north aisle is very noble and lovely, its gates, for it has gates, giving access to what was once a chantry chapel, are of the seventeenth century. The screen itself is earlier. Not far away is a great barn where the monks of old stored their crops grown on their estate of Pilton.

From Shepton the beautiful road under Beacon Hill climbs eastward to Doulting, also appertaining to Glastonbury. Here too the church was spoiled when it was rebuilt in 1869. Mr. Bligh Bond, for instance—and there can be no better authority—tells us that the nave as we see it is practically all modern; the south porch is all new work copied from the old, the old stones being built into the vicarage garden wall, and the inner door head on the north, he says, is a Norman one reversed and altered in shape.

The Tithe Barn, some little distance away upon the road to Bramble Ditch and Stony Stratton, should be visited; it is a fine and large structure, larger than the barns at Pilton and Glastonbury, of the end of the fourteenth century.

Doulting was the place where the great apostle of all this

country, St. Aldhelm, Bishop of Sherborne, died in 709. He, as Bishop, was continually making preaching expeditions through his diocese, and these he performed on foot. It was as he was thus journeying in May, 709, that he came through the pleasant country to Doulting and died in the wooden church here. A well, still to be seen in the Vicarage garden, is known, even yet, by his name.

Another of the Glastonbury churches is to be found in the

Porch of Mells Church.

village of West Cranmore, not much more than a mile west of Doulting, just south of the road to Frome. This has a triple windowed tower, smaller, it is true, but very like that of Shepton—a beautiful piece of work. It boasts, too, of a figure of St. Bartholomew, to whom the church is dedicated, to say nothing of a spoiled sundial.

It was St. Elphege who gave Cranmore to Glaston in 959, and the Abbey held it till 1259, when the Bishop got it as part of the price the Abbey had to pay for its independence.

Like so very much of the Abbey property, Cranmore came to the Duke of Somerset at the Spoliation; but it is the Strode family whom we chiefly connect with the place, though they did not come in till 1627. James Strode, the first of them, died in 1698, when he desired to be buried beneath the Communion table here, "I being the first Strode that lived and inhabited there and that will be buried there." It was only in 1896 that the Manor passed from the Strodes to Mr. Spencer. The Strodes lived not at Cranmore Hall in East Cranmore, but at Southill House, half a mile to the south of the church of West Cranmore.

From Doulting I took to the Mendips again on my way to Leigh-upon-Mendip, going past the famous quarries whence came most of the stone for Glastonbury Abbey and, I suppose, some for the Cathedral. From Cranmore, however, the road is less steep, and you go through Downhead, a manor of the great Abbey, a lonely village with a fine view, a chapelry of Doulting. This part of the Mendips is less impressive than that I have already described, for it is less lonely. Yet nothing can, I think, be finer than the view to the east, to the high land of Wiltshire beyond Frome across the long valley of the Frome river, in which under the Wiltshire woods so much beauty lies hid.

The glory of Leigh lies in its glorious church tower—a triple windowed tower of double tiers, the noblest of its kind, a thing really that lifts up the heart, but the church, dedicated to St. Giles, late Perpendicular in style, like the tower, looks mean beside it, though in fact it is a fine building with a Norman font, a very splendid chancel roof, and some fine old benches. Leigh was originally a chapelry in the large parish of Mells, which appertained to Glaston, and hence, I suppose, the beauty of its church. The glass in the west window is lovely and is said to be untouched from the fifteenth century. From Leigh to Mells that is a good way which takes you into Chantry and so through Whatley, where for Mells you must turn north again. At Chantry there is a modern church built by Sir Gilbert Scott; and everyone should pause a moment in Whatley if only to visit the little church where in the south of the chancel Dean Church, who was for about twenty years vicar here before he went to St. Paul's, lies buried.

Mells stands beautifully in Wadbury Vale, a lovely winding

rocky valley looking to the woods of Orchardleigh. In 942 King Edmund bestowed the *Parochia Mellis*, the "village of honey," upon Earl Athelstan and he gave it presently to the Abbey of Glaston. Soon after the Conquest the Abbey was robbed of Mells and Leigh, but after litigation got them back and retained them till Cobbett's "old wife killer" sat upon the

Mells. Manor House and Church.

English throne, when the manors came to the Crown and were purchased by John Horner, as the old rhyme has it

> Horner, Paget, Portman, Thynne
> When the monks stepped out you stepped in.[1]

Here in Mells a Horner has remained ever since.

[1] The nursery rhyme,

> Little Jack Horner,
> Sat in a corner,
> Eating a Christmas pie,
> He put in his thumb,
> And pulled out a plum,
> And cried, "What a good boy am I,

though ironically appropriate, seems to be of earlier date than the sixteenth century.

Mells church—a decorated and late Perpendicular building —Leland speaks of it as built "in time of mind"—is dedicated to St. Andrew, and is a fine though not a very fine specimen of a Somersetshire parish church. The tower is an example of the type that we have seen at its best at Leigh-upon-Mendip, and is a very noble thing. The porch is elaborate with a great niche, now empty, over it and another on either side; within it is elaborately groined. But the most

Mells. Manor House and Garden.

charming part of the church from outside is the octagonal vestry to the south, a two-storeyed building also with fine but empty canopied niches. The font is Norman, or, rather, was Norman, for it seems to have suffered some sort of restoration. On the north wall of the tower is a mural tablet by Burne-Jones with the emblem of a peacock. The glass in the windows was made in Mells, and that is its excuse.

Close by the church is the noble Manor House of the Horners, built originally in the form of the letter H, as so many Elizabethan manor houses were built in the form of the

Mells. Manor House from the Garden.

letter E. Here Charles I slept, in 1644, on his way from Bath to Exeter. "The King lay at Sir John Horner's howse at Mells, a faire large howse of stone, very strong, in the form of an H; two courts. The church is very large and faire adjoyning. Horner is in rebellion, his estates sequestered £1000 per annum."[1]

Of course Horner was in rebellion; was he not in enjoyment of Church property, was he not one of those new men made by the Suppression and the change of religion, whose object it was to bring the Crown into subjection and to put all things under their feet? Thus was the Whig aristocracy founded, and thus it riveted its power upon the nation. With the fall of the Crown there was nothing in England to outface such men as these, for the Church had already been ruined. Yes, Sir John Horner was in rebellion and so were most of those like him. Thinking of the time before the disaster and comparing it with ours, it is interesting to read Leland's account of Mells: "*Melles* stondith sumwhat clyving, and hath bene a praty Townelet of Clothing. It longgid onto *Glessenbyri*. *Selwood Abbate* of *Glessenbyri*, seing the Welthiness there of the People, had thought to have reedified the Townelet with mene Houses of square Stones to the Figure of an *Antonie* Crosse, whereof yn deade he made but one Streatelet. The Chirch is faire and buildid yn tyme of mynde *ex lapide quadrato* by the hole Paroche. One *Garlande* a Draper of *London*, gave frely to the Building of the Vestiarie, a fine and curiose Pece of Worke. One . . . a Gentilman dwelling ther yn the Paroche made a fair Chapelle in the North Side of the Chirch. There is a praty Maner Place of Stone harde at the West Ende of the Chirche. This be likelihod was partely buildid by Abbate *Selwodde* of *Glasteinbyri*. Syns it servid the Fermer of the Lordeship. Now Mr *Horner* hath boute the Lordeship of the King."

Mells village is a very charming and delightful one, with its pretty thatched cottages, covered with roses, its glorious trees and its fine church tower; but somehow one thinks the Abbot intended better than this, and certainly one is not to-day struck by the "welthines there of the People." Other times, other manners, I suppose; but it is more than time to take the straight road for Frome.

[1] See R. Symonds' *Diary of the Marches by the Royal Army during the Civil War*. Ed. C. E. Long. (Camden Soc.)

CHAPTER X

FROME AND ITS VILLAGES AND WITHAM FRIARY

As we come into Frome we come also into the ancient Forest of Selwood stretching some fifteen miles from north to south and some six from east to west through which our way will be in this chapter.

The town of Frome gets its name from the river over which it stands, upon the north-east side of the last Somerset hills, outliers of the Mendip range, looking towards Wiltshire and the White Horse above Edington, which is plainly seen from here.

Of old, Frome was devoted largely to the manufacture of woollen-cloth, a trade which was already declining in Collinson's day, but it still persists and employs a large number of people. The streets of Frome are for the most part steep and somewhat narrow and irregular, and seem to promise at first sight much of antiquity to the traveller. This impression, however, soon wears off and, as a fact, I suppose there is not another town of its age in Somerset which has less that is old to shew us. Cheap Street indeed, a narrow and paved lane down which a stream flows, might seem to be old, but in fact its houses, gabled though they be, are modern enough; nor shall we be more fortunate in regard to churches. The Parish Church is curious but absolutely modern, a work of the Oxford Movement with a new *Via Crucis*, statues, and a Rood, which are not very successful or charming. In fact nothing of the old church, which was originally Norman, remains but the plan and I suppose the foundations. No doubt some such wholesale rebuilding as we see here was necessary; that the old church was in a bad state we may well believe; but if this was the best that was to be had at the time, and everything is so handsome that we may well believe no expense was spared, it only serves to reassure us in the belief that in modern England we have no longer the art of building in which our Catholic forefathers excelled. In the churchyard, under the east window of the church, is the grave and monument, rather an expensive than a beautiful one, of modern manufacture, enclosing the old iron tomb of Bishop Ken, who died in retirement at Longleat, across the valley in Wiltshire, in 1711. He was a holy and brave man and refused the oath of allegiance to that Dutchman, William III. His desire was to be buried "in the churchyard of the nearest parish within his diocese under the east window of the chancel just at sunrising—was it not he who wrote that morning hymn:—

> Awake, my soul, and with the sun,
> Thy daily stage of duty run. . . .

—he had his wish.

One must not leave the parish church of Frome without saying something of two of its vicars. The earlier of these two was that Joseph Glanvill (1636–1680), a Devonshire man, "the first English writer who had thrown scepticism into a definite form." He was the author of *The Vanity of Dogmatising*, and in 1662—for he conformed at the Restoration—he was presented to the vicarage of Frome Selwood by Sir James Thynne (remember the Somersetshire rhyme) in place of John Humphrey, expelled for non-conformity. This thorough-going sceptic was a superstitious person of course, and firmly believed in witchcraft like most of his fellows. Later he became rector of the "Abbey" church of Bath, chaplain to Charles II, and was jobbed into a prebend at Worcester.

It might seem impossible to find a greater contrast to this man than we have in his successor, the builder of the present church, the late Rev. W. G. E. Bennett (1804–1886). Bennett had been brought up like Newman in a "low church" atmosphere, but in 1840 he was nominated minister of the new district of St. Paul's, Knightsbridge, and there he built the church we have. He was also very active in promoting the building of St. Barnabas, Pimlico, another ritualistic sanctuary. At St. Paul's, Knightsbridge, he had to face riots owing to his ritualism, and both his church and his house were guarded by the police, and in 1850, partly owing to a stupid letter from Lord John Russell, then one of his parishioners, he was compelled to resign his living. He was befriended by the Marchioness of Bath, who appointed him in 1852 to the vicarage of Frome-Selwood, where he met with much opposition, for the parish was notoriously Protestant. Here too, however, he won his way and began to build or rebuild the church, which was in a bad state of repair. Maybe he did this in too thorough a manner, but then he was the builder of St. Paul's, Knightsbridge, and part builder of St. Barnabas, Pimlico—what was an old country church to such a master? He died in 1886 in harness to the end, and he lies near Bishop Ken, in the churchyard here, on the south side of the chancel.

But the loveliest thing left to Frome is Vallis, a delightful valley or glen across the meadows north-west of the town, where the woods close in and two valleys and two streams meet in their shadow, under the last rocks of Mendip.

In the old days before the Conquest the king held Frome, but in the time of Henry II we find it in the possession of the family of Fitz Bernard, and in Henry IV's time the Manor of Frome-Valleyse was granted to John Payne of London. His daughter and heiress married Edmund Leversege, and as late as James I's time the manor was in the possession of this family. In the eighth year of James I it came by sale into the hands of Sir Thomas Thynne, with whose family it still remained in Collinson's day; it is now the property of the Earl of Cork.

Adjoining the old Vallis Farm, the Manor House of the Leversege's remains, though in a terribly spoiled condition, as a carpenter's and wheelwright's shop. The house is of the time of Henry VII., and though the interior is in little better condition than the outside, the fine old roof remains almost perfect.

Close to Vallis, between it and Mells, is Great Elm, over the valley, and from here a road runs north through a pleasant lowland to Buckland Denham on a steep hillside. This place was once of some importance and consideration, which it owed to its lords, the Denhames or Dinhams, really it seems the Dinants who came in with Norman William. The church is interesting rather than fine, with a Norman font and twelfth-century south doorway, a thirteenth century chamber also on the south and on the north a fourteenth century mortuary chapel of the Denhams, where on the floor are the figures of a knight and his lady. A large piscina in the chancel should be noted, and there are others in the chapels.

But, perhaps the most delightful and surprising thing to be seen within a walk from Frome is Orchardleigh Park and the old broken manor of the Champneys and the island church therein. All this may be reached over Murtry Hill from Buckland. Murtry Hill, besides the noble view it gives you, can boast of a cromlech surrounded by an earthen bank, and is supposed to be haunted by a lady in white.

The Champneys got Orchardleigh by marriage from the Ramseys in the time of Henry VI, and held it till modern times. Their old manor house stood in a hollow beneath the modern mansion. Nothing is left of it; but the church is delightful. This stands upon a small island in the midst of a lake, and is, even after the restoration of Sir Gilbert Scott in 1879, largely a building of the fourteenth century. The font, however, is Norman, but the rarest and loveliest thing here is the Priest's Door on the north side. Within is a finely carved piscina and two small figures in the chancel which once held up the Lenten veil. In 1879 all the old benches were taken away, but the west window was freed and there is still left a little of the fine old glass. In the window over the north door we see the Blessed Trinity; in the north and south windows are eight figures of apostles, and in the west window the fragmentary figure of a king, and another of St. Michael battling with the Devil.

Going north-west, through Orchardleigh Park, in something more than a mile, we come to Lullington. Lullington, like Orchardleigh, was part of the great domain granted at the Conquest to the Bishop of Coutances. Earl Harold held it in the time of King Edward, and later it was conferred upon the Priory of Longleat, in Wiltshire. At the Spoliation Lullington fell, first to the Earl of Hertford, but presently, in 1542, with the rest of the Longleat estate, to Sir John Thynne. It is now a pretty and quiet village, with a curious church, consisting of chancel and nave without aisles, a large south transept, and a central tower in the Perpendicular style.

The earliest, and one of the most remarkable things in the

church, is the font, which is a fine piece of Norman work with the following inscription: HOC FONTIS SACRO PEREUNT DELICTA LAVACRO, and another which is undecipherable.

Norman, too, is the beautiful north doorway with a figure of Our Lord in benediction above it in a niche under five coats-of-arms [?]. Beneath this the tympanum of the arch is filled

Norman Font. Lullington Church.

with a relief of two animals, apparently gryphons, supporting what looks like a tree.[1]

Within, the piers which support the tower are also Norman, and the arch from the tower into the nave is probably Norman altered in the tenth century, as is, I think, that from the tower into the chancel. The south transept, which is divided from the nave by a decorated arch, was built in 1280, and is charm-

[1] Perhaps these are the Faithful feeding upon the Tree of Life.

ing. The chancel dates from some forty years later. The east window of three lights is curious, having the centre light pointed and the other two with rounded heads. The other windows here are poor work of the Decorated period. On the whole, the main fabric of the church would seem to be transitional Norman, but the chantry dates wholly from 1280.

From Lullington I returned towards Frome, crossing the

Norman Doorway. Lullington Church, near Frome.

river at Old Ford, and then through a beautiful country, but on the main road to Bath, I made my way north again to Beckington.

This is a beautiful old village once famous for its woollen-cloth, with some interesting houses and a fine church, the birthplace about 1390 of Bishop Beckington of Wells. The manor was held for many years by the Erleigh family, from whom it passed in the time of the Black Prince to the

Seymours, whose manor house, Seymour's Court, still stands, a farm house now to the north-east of Beckington.

The church, dedicated to St. Gregory, stands well and has a fine but mutilated Norman tower. The church itself is Perpendicular, but its original character is more or less obvious. It consists of nave and clerestory and aisles, and chancel. The font, which is, or appears to be, of the thirteenth century, is in the south aisle, where there is a piscina, as there is in the chancel. In the north aisle is the grave with stone and bust of the poet Samuel Daniel, a Taunton man, born in 1652. He tells us:

> I know I shall be read among the rest
> So long as men speak Englishe and so long
> As verse and vertue shall be in request
> Or grace to honest industry belong.

But it would seem that, as he found in his life,

> . . . yeeres hath done this wrong
> To make me write too much and live too long.

Here, however, by his grave we may well recall his beautiful sonnet:—

> Care-charmer Sleep, son of the sable Night,
> Brother to Death, in silent darkness born,
> Relieve my languish and restore my light;
> With dark forgetting of my care return.
> And let the day be fine enough to mourn
> The shipwreck of my ill-adventured youth;
> Let waking eyes suffice to wail their scorn,
> Without the torment of the night's untruth.
> Cease, dreams, the images of day-desires,
> To model forth the passions of the morrow;
> Never let rising Sun approve you liars
> To add more grief to aggravate my sorrow;
> Still let me sleep, embracing clouds in vain,
> And never wake to feel the day's disdain.

He died in 1619. It seems that since 1603 he had been "living in the country," forsaking London. "In his old age," says Fuller, "he turned husbandman and rented a farm in Wiltshire, near Devizes." This was called "Ridge" and was not far from Beckington. There he died. Wood tells us he was "in animo Catholicus"; it is to be hoped and believed. His old pupil "in gratitude to him a long time after (his death) when she was Countess Dowager of Pembroke" erected the monument above his grave here in Beckington church.

In the chancel of the church is the effigy of a knight in armour—one of the Erleigh family it is thought—with his wife, dating from the middle of the fourteenth century; the effigy of a lady above this is that of Mary Erleigh, dating from the first part of the fifteenth century. On the floor is a fifteenth century brass to Sir John Seymour.

In the quiet village of Beckington there is more than one old house which deserves to be noted. Perhaps the most interesting is that known as the Castle, a many-gabled stone house with many mullioned windows, and a porch and turret stair. Scarcely inferior to it in interest though not in preservation is the house right in the village known as the Abbey. This was probably a grange, either of some religious house or of the Bishops of Bath and Wells. Its history is obscure; but there does not appear to be any warrant for numbering it among the Somerset Religious Houses. Without, it is very fair and picturesque, but within it has been much tampered with, and is at present in a miserable state of confusion.

It is worth while, on the way back to Frome, to visit the small village of Berkley, upon the Wiltshire border under Black Dog Hill. Here is an amazing little church, true to its period of classical eighteenth century design. It doubtless owes its existence to the glory of Bath at that time. There is another wonder, too, upon this road to Frome, I mean the Laudian church of Rodden, which stands without village or road near it in a farmyard.

The country about Frome is so delightful that one could wish to spend many weeks wandering in its neighbourhood; nor, indeed, are the villages to the south less lovely than those to the north of it.

Just off the road to Bruton, to the west of it, in a delicious valley, stands the village of Nunney, famous for its noble and beautiful castle, now, alas, a none too well cared for ruin. The Inn—the George at Nunney—must attract everyone's attention, for it is not only a fine old house, but its sign, a splendid one, swings quite across the road.

The de Montforts held Nunney while the Delameres were still in Wiltshire, but certainly, by 1315, this family, with which Nunney will always be connected, came in, and in 1373

Sir John Delamere received the following licence from the king for "kernellating his house," a manor house, in other words for fortifying it:

"The King, to all whom, etc., greeting. Know ye that of Our special grace We have granted and given license for Us and Our Heirs (as much as is in us) to Our loving and faithful John de la Mere, chevalier, that he may fortify and crenellate his house at Nunney in the county of Somerset with a wall of stone and lime, and the aforesaid house so fortified and embattled may hold to himself and his heirs for ever without occasion or impediment of Us or Our Heirs, Justices, Escheators, Sheriffs, or others Our Bailiffs, or Ministers whatsoever. . . ."

Thus was created the "castle" we see. It is a four-square building with a round tower butting out at each angle,

Nunney Castle.

surrounded by a moat. Within, it was probably divided into four storeys by wooden floors. In one of the towers, in the upper part of it, there remains the window, perhaps with the altar, and certainly with the piscina of a chapel or oratory. In another we may still find some signs of a staircase, and other signs are to be found of the drawbridge by which the castle was approached from the village. In the fifteenth century Nunney passed by marriage to the Paulets, who in the time of Elizabeth sold it to the Praters. It was a Colonel

Prater who defended the castle in the Great Rebellion for the King, when it fell to Fairfax, who sent artillery against it in 1645. At the time Colonel Prater was flying a crimson standard, "and in the midst thereof a fair Crucifix cross." He was evidently a sympathiser with the old religion, if not himself a Papist, and he had many Catholics in the castle with him. His standard was sent to London and exhibited to the Parliament. Colonel Prater presently saw fit to make friends with the stronger party, but he did not save his lands.

It was a Delamere, so it is said, who built the church, the greater part of which is in the Early English style, but the tower, the south porch, the east windows of the transepts, and the screen are Perpendicular. A good deal of modern work appears to have been done especially in the west of the church. The screen has been replaced in recent times and a curious wall-painting over the arches in the south aisle should be noted. But by far the most interesting things in the church are the Delamere tombs. The founder of the "castle," Sir John Delamere, lies in effigy upon the window sill in the north aisle, but behind the organ here is a fifteenth century altar tomb with recumbent figures, the man in a tabard and Lancastrian collar and the lady in a long veil. The tomb is surrounded with coats-of-arms, among them, one of the Paulet and Delamere coats quarterly, which assures us that it was later than 1427 when marriage connected the two families. In the north-west corner is another altar tomb also bearing two figures which were once surrounded by children. These figures are in Elizabethan costumes and no doubt represent Richard Prater and his wife, the successors to the Paulets. Note, too, the Mawdley Samborne tombstones; she died Nov. 13, 1690; he Dec. 7 of the same year. How often do we find this; as though indeed man and wife grown together through many years were in truth one flesh and could not be parted.

Close to the church some vestiges of the old manor court house remain, now used as a shed. Within is a fine roof or gallery.

From Nunney I went on through Cloford to Wanstrow, where I took the train for Witham Friary, for it is a difficult place to approach by road and I greatly desired to see it, for it was here the first Carthusian monastery erected in England was founded, and the little church there is all that remains of it. Witham lies right in the valley in the midst of Selwood Forest in which it was a liberty, under the noble great ridge of Wiltshire and not more than half a mile south of the old and, as is thought, Roman road between the Mendips and Maiden Bradley. It will be remembered that after the murder of Becket, and King Henry II's public repentance for his part in all that evil, the Pope gave him for penance a Crusade of three years in the Holy Land, but when that was found inconvenient he commuted it for the building of three monasteries of which one was to be Carthusian, for the Carthusians at that time had no house in all England.

The place chosen for this convent was Witham, then in the King's hands, for the Rule of the Order demanded a solitude, and if Witham was not so bleak and lonely as the Grande Chartreuse, at any rate it was in the heart of the Forest. Indeed, whether the place, even to-day difficult of access by road, was too hard for the monks, or whether there was some other hindrance, of which we know nothing, certain it is that Witham did not flourish, and the first two Priors, though both from the Grande Chartreuse, failed to establish the house. Then it was that Henry was advised to beg of the mother house, Hugh of Avalon, her shining light. So the King seized the opportunity of the presence in the Alps, at St. Jean de Maurienne, on his way back from Rome, of Bishop Reginald of Wells, and sent him to beg Hugh of the Prior of the Grande Chartreuse. In this embassy Bishop Reginald was successful, and though the Prior declared that it would widow his house of that "most sweet and necessary presence," Hugh came, though reluctantly, with the Bishop, who conducted him with great honour to Witham, where he was received "as the angel of the Lord." It was this great and holy man, later Bishop of Lincoln, and known to us all as St. Hugh of Avalon, who firmly established the Carthusian Order in these islands, and in whose honour the only house of the Order in modern England is dedicated.

The presence of this saint in our Somerset, his holy, brave, and laborious life in Selwood, should make of Witham a place of pilgrimage among the most glorious in our country, so despoiled of shrines and all its noble past. St. Hugh was the third Prior, but the true founder of this monastery, which, like its successor, was dedicated in honour of the Blessed Virgin, St. John Baptist and All Saints. That was in 1175. He ruled there for ten years, and for just three hundred and sixty-three years Witham was a light and glory in Selwood and in Somerset. In 1539, when Dom John Mychell was Prior, that light was extinguished and that glory put out. Dom Mychell succeeded, in 1526, Dom Henry Man, who was in fact a traitor, "the assuryd beydesman and servant" of Cromwell, as he signs himself, though perhaps only in customary wise. However that may be, he became Bishop of Sodor and Man. It remained for Dom Mychell to surrender the house, having acknowledged the King's supremacy, in 1539.

Ah, there lay the great and fundamental error that brought down not only English monasticism but the very Church herself in England. Once it had been decided, if only by way of escape, that the Pope's supremacy was not one of the vital points of the Catholic Faith, once it had been agreed to acknowledge the supremacy of the King, we were helpless and could deny Henry nothing. Thus fell Witham and more than six hundred other houses; thus fell the Church in England, because we could not understand that Sir Thomas More was right, and that the verities of the Catholic Church were bound up with the supremacy of Peter.

After the Suppression, Witham was given by Henry VIII to Ralph Hopton, and later it came to the Wyndham family, who sold it to William Beckford, the author of *Vathek*.

And so, instead of a beautiful refuge here in Somerset, to-day we have only a little church in the hands of an alien religion. It is a small and simple vaulted building, the work of St. Hugh and in the Norman style, with an apse. The windows are curious, the splay inside being nearly three feet wide and half as much outside instead of a few inches. This is explained by the fact that the walls of the church not being strong enough to bear the stone vault were surrounded by others, so that they are now together some twenty inches thick. A small window in the apse is said to be that through which lepers were given Holy Communion. The Restoration of 1876 added to the length of the church; but, so far as such things can be, seems to have been otherwise conservative. But much damage seems to have been done in 1832, when the fine screen was destroyed. The bell-cote we see is modern. The church, which as a monastery had for centuries no font at all, now boasts two. Apparently in or about 1458 the older of the two was placed here, and later was lost. The other was presented in 1843 by a gentleman who wished to be baptised here.

It is a matter of controversy what purpose this church served in the time of the monks. But, as at Hinton, it would seem that we have here the church of the lay brothers, and that this explains the second name which Witham bears to-day —Witham Friary or Frery.

And when I had thought all this out and offered a prayer to St. Hugh for such wandering men as he was reluctantly, and I with all my heart, I went on by the train to Bruton.

Longleat.

CHAPTER XI

BRUTON AND ITS NEIGHBOURHOOD.

It was already dark when I came into Bruton, but in some way I knew at once that I had come to one of those places, growing rarer every day, but perhaps more common in Somerset than elsewhere, which still keep about them a spirit and an atmosphere of that old English world which is so surely passing away. The station is some little distance from the town, which lies in a valley beneath it, but I preferred to walk to the "Blue Bell Inn" where I had determined to sleep. As it happened, this proved a foolish decision, for the night was very dark, and so far as I could find Bruton had dispensed herself from any public lighting of the way, or for that matter of the town, so that it was only after many vague questions and vaguer answers given in the dark that I found myself standing in the doorway of that extraordinary Inn.

Next morning, after as weird a night as I can ever remember to have spent, I went out to explore the little town, and soon found that my first impression had been right and that Bruton was nearly everything that I could desire, or at any rate expect.

In truth Bruton is of a very high antiquity; it was already in possession of a mint in the time of Cnut, and there was certainly a church here dedicated to St. Peter in those days. It is said to have been founded by St. Aldhelm, and to have been in possession of a piece of white marble which he had brought from Rome, possibly from St. Peter's Church or tomb there. This Saxon church, after the Norman Conquest, seems to have given place to another building with a new dedication—St. Aldhelm and St. Mary—and of this, too, nothing remains but the merest fragments. At the time of the Domesday Inquest Bruton was in the possession of Roger de Courcelles, and the much larger and neighbouring manor of Brewham in that of the Mohuns. It would seem to remain a matter of controversy as to which of them founded the Priory of Bruton; but the latest opinion would seem to assure us that in 1142 Earl William de Mohun was lord of the manor of Bruton and North Brewham, and that it was he who in that year founded here a house of Augustinian Canons "who were the impropriate rectors of the parish church." From this time the Prior of Bruton held the manors of Bruton and North Brewham with those of Charlton Adam and Stow Easton. Earl William de Mohun is said to have rebuilt the chancel of the church for the use of his religious with a crypt under it as a burial place for himself and his successors. And so it was, for there lay Mohuns and Luttrells and Montagues till the year 1743 when De Mohun's chancel was pulled down and a new one built in a foreign and fantastic style, the crypt cleared and the bones reburied in the churchyard to make way for the Berkeley tombs. The foundation of this Priory and the building of the chancel explain the double dedication of the church though not the disappearance of the dedication to St. Peter. Perhaps the crypt was in his keeping. However that may be, the church was now a double one; the new chancel, the church of the Canons, was dedicated to St. Mary; and the nave, the parish church, remained St. Aldhelm's. Practically nothing but perhaps the small north tower remains of these buildings.

What we now see in the noble church of Bruton is a fine Perpendicular building, of which the oldest part is the most beautiful triple-windowed west tower, dating from the middle of the fifteenth century and the Priorate of John Henton. This rebuilding was completed by his successor, Gilbert, who about 1510, we are told, "obtained a Bull elevating the Priory into an Abbey, and he it was who thus became the first Abbot of Bruton." To him are due the glorious nave with its carved roof and the aisles of the present church. He lies at the west gate. We know practically nothing of the Priory from the end of the twelfth century to the Priorate of John Henton. At the Spoliation in 1541, it and its estate with the patronage of the church were leased and then sold to Sir Maurice Berkeley, Constable of the Tower and Standard-Bearer to Henry VIII, whose tomb we still see with that of his wives in the chancel. It would seem that the Abbot's house, or what Sir Maurice Berkeley had made out of it, remained till 1763, when it was gutted by fire and finally destroyed in 1786. Nothing now remains of the Abbey save the ruined *columbarium*,

Bruton.

a four-gabled tower of two storeys on a rising ground close to the church.

Near by, opposite the vicarage, is the old school, founded in 1520 by Richard Fitz James, Bishop of London, his nephew, the Lord Chief Justice, and John Edmondes, clerk. It was suppressed at the Spoliation but revived by Edward VI, by whose name it now goes. It still possesses many delightful corners and windows of architectural interest.

But Bruton has more to show than its church and school, and other things to interest us besides the vague story of its ruined Priory. Leland tells us that when he was here the town was "much occupied with making of clothe." It is divided into two parts by the river Brue. Leland mentions that "the Paroche Church and Thabbay by it stande beyond the Ryver, hard over the Est Bridge in Bruton. This Bridge is of 3. Archys of Stone." There is another bridge over the river by the Abbey, and it formed the nearest way from the Abbey to the town. This is an extremely narrow foot or pack-horse bridge of a single arch of very picturesque design just below the other; it is known as Bruton Bow.

Everything in Bruton is charming and worthy of attention, and the traveller may, if he will, spend more than one happy day there pottering about the old streets. For instance, in the High Street may still be seen the old Abbey *Hospitium*, or, perhaps, the steward's house, with the rebus and initials of Prior John Henton over a shield bearing the Mohun arms. Another shield here also bears another Mohun coat. The Abbey used the former as its own.

Then there is the Sexey Hospital close by. This was founded in the time of Elizabeth by Hugh Sexey, a poor boy of Bruton, who rose to be auditor to the Queen and to her successor, James I. The estates he devised for the upkeep and administration of the hospital are still held by the feoffees. The hospital is a fine specimen of the work of that time. Over the door we see the bust of the founder with an inscription and coat-of-arms. The building is surprising by reason of its delightful triple windows and of its chapel, where there is some fine carving.

In the Civil War Bruton and the Berkeleys stood for the King, who, in 1644, stayed here, quartering at "the Abbey" for two nights. Two years before this loyal town had been threatened with outrage by the rabble of Batcombe, hence the glorious verses of relief and *Deo Gratias*,

> All praise and thanks to God still give
> For our deliverance Matthias' eve.
> By His great power we put to flight
> Our raging foes the Batcombites
> Who came to plunder, burn, and slay,
> And quite consume our town this day.

Batcombe, which is some three miles to the north of Bruton, was it seems, in spite of the Bisse family, who had got it by fair means or foul at the Spoliation, for it was a part of the Glaston estates, suffering under a certain Richard Bernard, a "puritan divine," author of "The Isle of Man, or Legal Proceedings in Man's Hart against Sin," who died here in 1691.[1] Batcombe, however, in spite of its evil behaviour, must be visited, for it is a pleasant village with a very fine triple windowed tower of the second class, but unique of its kind, and if the church is disappointing it is at any rate curious. The tower is very noble indeed, and has upon its western face a niche which, in spite of Mr. Richard Bernard, still contains a figure of our Lord with six angels, two swinging censers, two bearing instruments of the Passion, and two with scrolls; and —what can the Batcombites have been thinking of?—a Crucifix upon the eastern gable of the nave. Within, the clerestory is fine, and there is a beautiful staircase, which of old led to the rood-loft, but the church is desolate, and that is all that can be said about it.

But if the Batcombe tower is fine, what are we to say of Evercreech, a jolly village some three miles to the west of it? It might seem to be one of the loveliest in all Somerset of those double-windowed towers of which St. Cuthbert's in Wells is the prototype, and it was built probably by the same masons who erected the tower of Batcombe church, and may have studied at Wells. The church for the most part is of the same date as the tower, which is of the latter half of the fifteenth century. It is a noble building with a lofty nave, clerestory, open timber roof and large windows. The chancel is older, possibly of the fourteenth century; its windows are certainly of that time. The south aisle is of our time. It replaced a chapel possibly of the Hoptons, who for a time lived at Park House, Evercreech. The only monument in the church of any interest is one to a former vicar, one James Dugdale, who held the living from 1619 to 1641. He, unlike his brother of Batcombe, was a King's man and endured much for his loyalty. It is stated that he was much beloved, and that when a troop of rebel horse came to arrest him, the women of Evercreech "beat them off with stones."

Some two miles or a little more to the south of Evercreech lies Ditcheat, on no account to be missed, for it has a fine cruciform church and a manor house, the descendant of that

[1] Bunyan is said to have taken his plan of *The Pilgrim's Progress* from this work. Master Richard Bernard was succeeded by Richard Alleine, who was ejected for nonconformity.

belonging to the abbots of Glaston to whom the manor of Ditcheat appertained. The church differs very much from that usually found in this part of Somerset, and owes, I suppose, much of its beauty to Glaston. It is, as I have already said, cruciform with a central tower, the lower part of which is Norman. This lower part is extraordinarily massive, with small arches which might seem almost to have been hewn out of the solid masonry, and it most effectually divides nave and chancel. No doubt the whole of the Norman tower of the original church remains, and is now surmounted

Ditcheat Church and Manor House.

by a Perpendicular belfry with niches, in which remain statues of St. Mary Magdalen, to whom the church is dedicated, and St. John Baptist. Even so it is dwarfed by the noble church that in the thirteenth, fourteenth, and fifteenth centuries supplanted the old Norman structure. From the thirteenth century there remain to us the south transept and the lower part of the chancel. The lower windows in the chancel are exquisite work of the fourteenth century, and the rest of the church is a fine fifteenth century building. It was then the chancel was heightened and its clerestory built, the nave entirely rebuilt with aisles and clerestory, and oak roof the beams of which spring from finely carved angel-corbels, which still retain traces of their ancient colouring. To this time, too, the font is due, but the pulpit and reading desk are Jacobean, "adapted to the purpose when the Leir family pew was lately (1889) removed from the north aisle."

The manor house standing near the church is of the seventeenth century.

From Ditcheat it is three miles of good going, in which we cross both the Alham and the Brue to Castle Cary. Nothing in all Somerset is finer or lovelier than the country here, lovely with woodland and beautiful with hill and valley. Nor is there, I suppose, anywhere in the county a finer view to be had than that from Lodgehill, overhanging the little town of Cary. Looking thence to the south we see the hills of Corton Denham and the dark height of Camelot: further to the west we see the sharp crater-like Tor of Montacute and the great bulwark of Hamdon Hill. In the true west rises the long line of Blackdown with the Wellington monument and the darkness of Castle Neroche. There, too, at Burton Pynsent we may see the Chatham monument, and on the low Poldens over the marsh the pillar set up to Hood. Beyond this, far away, rise the blue Quantocks, and behind them faintly the Brendon range. To the north appear Glastonbury Tor, Brent Knoll, and the Severn Sea, the long line of the Mendips and the noble escarpment of Wiltshire bearing, what I have not mentioned till now, though it has been visible for days, the foolish "Alfred's Tower" among the woods. Beneath us at our feet, amidst its rich pastures and woods, lies Castle Cary beside the little river Cary, which rises in five springs upon this very hill. One of these springs is called of Our Lady, and another after turning the wheels of three mills pursues its course across Somerset through Babcary, Cary Fitzpaine, Lyte's Cary, and Cook's Cary, marking its course in the names of all these places till upon bleak Sedgemoor it is lost in the Parrett.

Castle Cary, lovely as it is, is poor in visible antiquities. Yet it is, I suppose, literally as old as the hills. At any rate, there has been a castle here since Norman times, when it was built or occupied by the Lovells. What part—though we may be sure it was an important one—this castle played in the

Norman occupation of Somerset we do not know; but in the days of private war, which were King Stephen's, it certainly ruled all this country and ravaged it so that King Stephen attacked and took it in 1138. But the castle disappeared, and it is only in recent times that its site has been discovered and excavated, when the foundations of a great square Norman keep—marked now by pillars—were brought to light.

The church, which is nobly placed, is not very interesting, for it has been restored and rebuilt out of all recognition. It still possesses, however, a finely-carved pulpit and a font of the time of Henry VII.

Castle Cary, which had no great part in the Civil War, yet gave unwilling sanctuary to Charles II in his flight after the battle of Worcester in 1651. It seems that though there is no mention of the Castle of Cary after the twelfth century, by the middle of the fourteenth a large manor house of the Seymour's had been erected not far from its site. This, too, has disappeared, but it was here that Charles II slept, coming from Leigh Court disguised as Mrs. Jane Lane's postillion, on September 16th, 1651. The house was then in the occupation of Mr. Edward Kirton, steward of William Seymour, Marquis of Hertford, and later Duke of Somerset.

If the road through Ansford be taken back to Bruton from Castle Cary, a mile from the little town we shall pass through Wyke Champflower, where there is a chapel built in 1624 in the same style as the Sexey Hospital of Bruton. Close by is the manor house under some noble old elms, those mysterious trees which seem to be full of magic and ancientry.

For beauty the road from Castle Cary to Wincanton, through Bratton Seymour, is hard to beat, yet I confess I prefer the way from Bruton through Stoney Stoke by Charlton Musgrove, for it gives you, if you will, both Stavordale Priory and Penselwood.

Stavordale Priory, like Keynsham Abbey and Worspring Priory, was a house of Canons Regular of St. Austin following the Rule of St. Victor. The founder is unknown, but it probably owed everything to the Lovells of Castle Cary—perhaps its birth to that Ralph Lovell who died in 1159, and something certainly, if not its foundation, to that Henry Lovell who died in 1199.

Of late years the little ruined chapel we know so well as a dilapidated farm has been changed into a fine house with gardens and drive. In its great days, however, Stavordale must have been a delicious place. The fourteenth century was probably its most fortunate moment. It then appropriated the great tithes of Wincanton, and in 1374 won permission to serve the parish church. At the Spoliation Stavordale was not suppressed all at once, it was annexed first to the Priory of Taunton of the same Order but not the same Rule. Nevertheless, it was only respited, and in 1538 it fell—never, alas! to rise again. Stavordale, however, in its ruin has this interest for us, that it is almost the only church of religious in Somerset which has come down to us more or less intact. This beautiful church is a building of the time of Henry VI, and until a few years ago the nave was used as a barn, the chancel as a dwelling-house. Some of the conventual buildings—Stavordale was but a small house—remain to the north of the church, and were till lately used for barns and pigstyes.

> Since brass nor stone nor earth nor boundless sea,
> But sad mortality o'ersways their power,
> How with this rage shall beauty hold a plea
> Whose action is no stronger than a flower?

Above Stavordale to the east the great escarpment of Wiltshire with its mighty woods, all that is left perhaps of Selwood, comes to an end. Just there is set the village of Penselwood, where it is thought Alfred gathered the men of the south and west before he marched upon the Danes at Aethandune. This great battle, which as we know saved England for Christendom, was, according to some authorities, fought at Edington upon the Polden's; according to others, and I think with a better show of reason, at Edington in Wiltshire, where upon the Downs the White Horse might seem to mark some great event. In either case Penselwood would have made a good meeting place, and certainly there are signs there of encampment far earlier perhaps than Alfred. Nevertheless the theory which saw in the Pen pits early British habitations might seem to be disposed of, for they would appear, indeed, to be nothing more than old quarries.

Penselwood church is a small and spoilt building, with a Norman door on the south and a Norman font. For the rest it was rebuilt in 1805.

The road, a byway, to Wincanton from Penselwood, runs through Southmarsh and Charlton Musgrove.

CHAPTER XII

WINCANTON AND THE ROAD THROUGH CAMELOT TO ILCHESTER

WINCANTON is not itself of much interest, but it is the key to much fine country and to many interesting places. Set upon the river Cale, for the most part above it upon the hill that looks southward into the Blackmoor Vale, it is a place of high antiquity, certainly known to the Romans and occupied by the Saxons, while Norman William granted its manor, with some thirty-three others in Somerset, to Walter de Douai. In time, however, it came to the lords of Castle Cary, the Lovells, and from them passed by marriage to the Seymours and the Zouches. This last family lived at Marsh Court at the very head of the true Blackmoor Vale some three miles to the south of Wincanton. The place is now a farmhouse, and as we see it it is a building of the Restoration (1661). It is still in part surrounded by a moat. It is now in the seventeenth century that whatever of romance we can connect with Wincanton is to be found. It had played a small part as meeting place in the Civil War, but in the Revolution it was the scene of a fight between some troops of the Prince of Orange and some Irish Dragoons of James I—the first skirmish of that despicable business. Macaulay, the Whig historian, gives the following account of it: "Mackay's regiment, composed of British soldiers, lay near a body of the King's Irish troops commanded by their countryman the gallant Sarsfield. Mackay sent out a small party under a lieutenant named Campbell to procure horses for the baggage. Campbell found what he wanted at Wincanton, and was just leaving that town on his return when a strong detachment of Sarsfield's troops approached. The Irish were four to one, but Campbell resolved to fight it out to the last. With a handful of resolute men he took his stand in the road. The rest of his soldiers lined the hedges which overhung the highway on the right and on the left. The enemy came up. 'Stand,' cried Campbell, 'for whom are you?' 'I am for King James,' answered the leader of the other party. 'And I am for the Prince of Orange,' cried Campbell. 'We will prince you,' answered the Irishman with a curse. 'Fire,' exclaimed Campbell; and a sharp fire was instantly poured in from both the hedges. The King's troops received their well-aimed volleys before they could make any return. At length they succeeded in carrying one of the hedges, and would have overpowered the little band which was opposed to them had not the country people, who mortally hated the Irish, given a false alarm that more of the Prince's troops were coming up. Sarsfield recalled his men and fell back, and Campbell proceeded on his march unmolested with the baggage horses. This affair, creditable undoubtedly to the valour and discipline of the Prince's army, was magnified by report into a victory won against great odds by British Protestants over Popish barbarians who had been brought from Connaught to oppress our island."

Later on his march, the Prince passed through Wincanton and slept in a house in South Street, where a room is still known as the Orange room.

The town suffered greatly not only in 1553 from plague but in 1747 from fire. The church is in fact entirely modern. And so, as I say, little is to be seen in Wincanton; this little is fully made up to us by the richness of its villages—and first Cucklington.

Cucklington, some three miles to the south-east upon a great ridge which here runs out from the escarpment of hills along the Dorset border, has a church dedicated to St. Laurence, in which there is a piece of ancient glass. The building itself is of an ordinary type, common hereabout, with a reconstructed tower to the south of the nave, a Norman font and some charming reminders of the thirteenth century. The south chapel by the tower, however, has some late Perpendicular windows, and one of them contains a piece of old glass showing the head of St. Barbara, who has a well in the village.

Another journey to be made from Wincanton will take us first by train to Templecombe Junction. Here is the village of Abbas or Temple Combe. The church, which has been restored, still keeps its old waggon roof and a square Norman font of Purbeck marble—the pillars of which are modern. And on a little hill to the south of the village stands the Manor Farm, where there are still some remains of an ancient establishment, the only one in Somerset, of the Knights Templars who owned the place. On the suppression of that Order in England it was conferred upon the Knights Hospitallers.

A little to the south of Templecombe, scarcely a mile away, is the village of Horsington, which boasts of perhaps the most curious village Cross in all Somerset: it stands upon a circular platform some eight feet high and is approached by four rows of steps—a calvary. The Cross itself is a monolith of nine feet in height on a square base of three feet. On the south of the shaft is the sculptured figure, perhaps of a friar, under a strange canopy, on a bracket which is carved apparently with a ram's head.

But by far the most charming spectacle to be had from Wincanton is Milborne Port. This can be reached by train from Templecombe to Milborne Port station, under the great earthwork of Milborne Camp, whence the village lies about a mile and a half to the south.

Milborne Port is an ancient borough, though now it consists of but a few cottages. In Domesday Book we find that there were then six mills within the town, and in 1307 it already returned two members to Parliament. It soon lost its franchise on its own petition on the ground of expense, and it was not till Charles I restored its privilege in 1640 that it returned two members again, but it continued to do so till the Reform Bill. The old Guildhall, still with a Norman doorway, remains in the village street. Such being the history of the place we are not surprised to see the noble church it still has. This is of high antiquity, a considerable part of the building being early Norman. The nave, however, has been rebuilt, but the southern doorway, the lower part of the tower with its stair turret, the south side of the chancel, the windows in the vestry, are Norman. The mighty arches of the tower are wonderfully impressive, and the arches into the transepts have never, it would seem, been tampered with. The chancel, apart from the southern wall, dates as we see it from the fifteenth century, but the south transept was rebuilt in 1842, and the north about 1867.

From Milborne Port it is a walk of from four to five miles, in which we pass in and out of Dorset, to Henstridge. Just before we come into it at the cross roads we pass the Virginia Inn, where it is said Sir Walter Raleigh smoked his first pipe of tobacco, and, being discovered by his servant, was drenched with a bucket of water.

Henstridge church is to be noted chiefly for its fine canopied, fifteenth century altar tomb, with effigies of Sir William Carent, high sheriff of Somerset and Dorset, who died in 1476, and of his wife Margaret Stourton. Sir William built this tomb in his lifetime to the memory of his wife, for he was a widower. For some reason or other Bishop Beckington of Wells granted forty days' indulgence "to all true penitents who should go to the tomb of that worthy man, William Carent, armiger, erected in the prebendal church of Henstridge, and should devoutly say a *Paternoster* and an *Ave* for the welfare of the said William Carent, and of the venerable Nicholas Carent and John Carent his brothers, and also John Carent his son, during their lives, and for the soul of Margaret, late wife of the said William Carent, and the souls of the aforesaid after their deaths."

From Henstridge one may take the train back to Wincanton and thence early one morning set out upon the great road for Ilchester on the Fosse Way.

By this road we come first some two miles out of Wincanton to Holton, where in the little church is a Norman font and a fine stone pulpit, perhaps of the fifteenth century. And then through very pretty country, and, after leaving Blackford, taking a byway to the left through Compton Pauncefoot among the woods, we come to South Cadbury, under the dark height of Cadbury Castle, a great ruined earthwork that I like to believe is, alas! all that remains to us of Camelot. For here we are on the verge of the marsh again, and the isolated hill upon which Cadbury Castle stands was probably once an island. Here it was that Arthur first saw his sword Excalibur. For, when Uther Pendragon was dead, reigned Arthur his son, and on a day, "Well," said the king, "let make a cry, that all the lords, knights, and gentlemen of arms shall draw unto the castle called Camelot"; and there the king let make a Council General and a great jousts.

"So when the king was come thither with all his baronage and lodged as they seemed best, there was come a damosel the which was sent on a message from the great lady Lile of Avelion. And when she came before King Arthur she told from whom she came and how she was sent on message unto him for these causes. Then she let her mantle fall that was richly furred; and then was she girt with a noble sword, whereof the king had marvel, and said: 'Damosel, for what cause are ye girt with that sword? It beseemeth you not.' 'Now shall I tell you,' said the damosel; 'this sword that I am girt withal doth me great sorrow and cumbrance, for I may not be delivered of this sword but by a knight; but he must be a passing good man of his hands and of his deeds, and without villainy or treachery and without treason. And if I may find such a knight that hath all these virtues, he may draw out this sword out of the sheath. . . .' 'This is a great marvel,' said Arthur, 'if this be sooth; I will myself essay to draw out the sword.' . . . Then Arthur took the sword by the sheath and by the girdle and pulled at it eagerly, but the sword would not out.

"'Sir,' said the damosel, 'you need not pull half so hard, for he that shall pull it out shall do it with little might.' 'Ye say well,' said Arthur; 'now essay ye all my barons. . . .'"

Well, we know how Balin, arrayed like a poor knight, pulled out the sword which after was the cause of his death; how Merlin by his subtlety put the sword into a marble stone standing upright, as great as a millstone, and how this stone by adventure swam over to the city of Camelot, and how at last Arthur got him the sword Excalibur whose light was as the light of thirty candles.

Now, whether indeed Cadbury Castle was Camelot, who shall say? The life-long enthusiasm and study of the Rev. J. A. Bennett were enough to convince anyone, it is true; but even if they be put on one side the traditions of the people which he has recorded are sufficiently interesting. For it seems that the country people here have always believed this hill to be hollow; that the plain upon the top has, within memory, greatly sunk; and that "one year the crop was barley, which was stacked just within the northern earthwork where the ground dips towards the eastern entry gate. When the mow was built it was visible from the fields below, near Chapel, but it had disappeared, sunk down out of sight, by threshing time."

Again: "there is a well with a stone cover high up upon the hill's eastern face called King Arthur's Well. There is another spring, opposite, low down, upon the western face, the whole mass of the hill lying between them; let anyone listen carefully beside the western spring while his friend claps down a cover upon the well with a good rattle and he will hear the noise. 'Now this, sir, could not be unless the hill were hollow.'"

Yes, in the opinion of all the people about Cadbury the hill is hollow; and it is full of gold put there by the Fairies when they were obliged to leave Old England when the bells were put into the churches—all but Puck, as we know, he stayed with us.

And at least there is this; the name of Arthur clings to the hill. As I have said, the well upon the east bears his name, and there is his "Hunting Causeway" running, it is said, all the way to Glaston, but certainly visible here, where any Christmas Eve you may hear him ride by with his knights, and, perhaps, if you be lucky, see the flash of his silver horse-shoes as he goes from Camelot to the spring by Sutton Montis church.

And last but not least there is Leland. "At the very South Ende of the Church of South-Cadbyri standithe Camalatte, sumtyme a famose Town or Castelle. . . Much Gold, Sylver, and Coper of the *Romaine* Coynes hath be found ther yn plowing; and lykewise in the Feldes in the Rootes of this Hille, with many other antique Thinges and especial by Este. Ther was found *in hominum memoria* a Horse Shoe of Sylver at Camallate. The People can tell nothing ther, but they have hard say that *Arture* much resortid to Camalat."

In any case the amazing earthworks we see lack any certain explanation. The excavations that have been made would seem to prove that they belong to very various periods, and that though certainly not in their origin the work of the Romans or even of a Romanised people, they were probably used by them as they would have been by a later and barbarian defender. Indeed, what has been discovered would seem to support rather than to overthrow the very ancient traditional claim of Cadbury Castle to be:—

"Arthur's ancient seat
Which made the Britons' name thro' all the world so great.
Like Camelot, what place was ever yet renowned?
Where, as at Caerleon oft, he kept the table round

> Most famous for the sports at Pentecost, so long
> From whence all knightly deeds and brave achievements sprung.
> As some soft-sliding rill, from which a lesser head
> (Yet in his going forth by many a mountain fed)
> Extends itself at length unto a goodly stream,
> So, almost thro' the world his fame flew from this realm.
> That justly I may charge those ancient bards of wrong,
> So idly to neglect his glory in their song;
> For some abundant brain, oh, there had been a story
> Beyond the blind man's might, to have enhanc'd our glory."

There is little or nothing to be seen in the village of South Cadbury except the church, which is so crouched under the dark hill as to seem to seek its protection. What is left of old therein is of the fourteenth century, to which the south arcade belongs; the whole building has been thoroughly restored.

Upon the hill, on the other side of this valley, in which the Cam rises, stands North Cadbury, with its noble manor house and fine fifteenth century church, dedicated, as is thought, to St. Michael.

This church was collegiate, and the college, which was for seven secular chaplains and four clerks, was founded in 1417, in the time of Henry V, by Dame Elizabeth Botreaux, widow of Sir William Botreaux the elder. As we see it, the church would appear to be of much about this time; for though the piers and capitals of the nave arcades have Decorated mouldings they have Perpendicular bases. That a fourteenth century church was standing here before 1417 is, I think, certain, and it probably consisted of nave, chancel, and south aisle and chapel. Of the new church, built about that time by Dame Botreaux, the tower would seem to have been the earliest part, and two heads over the western door might seem to represent Elizabeth Botreaux and her husband. This tower is very plain, but the church itself is a noble piece of work of fine, and curiously symmetrical proportions. The chancel is of a great size because the church was collegiate; it was, of course, filled once with stalls, which have disappeared. The finely carved tabernacles on either side of the modern reredos still retain traces of their ancient colouring. The benches, which are of oak and very curious, are dated 1538, and the roof would seem to belong to the same date.

In the tower is the fine altar tomb of Sir William Botreaux and his wife, Elizabeth, the founder of the college and the rebuilder of the church. He died in 1392, but this tomb is of the fifteenth century, and was in all probability not erected until after Dame Elizabeth's death, which does not seem to have happened till after 1420. Sir William Botreaux is seen in full plate armour with the Lancastrian collar about his neck. Dame Elizabeth wears a tall mitre-like head-dress. Near by are two other tombs of the seventeenth century, but it is unknown who lie therein.

Some fragments in the west window are all that remain in the church of that storied glass which we might hope to find in such a church as this. But in Cadbury House, the noble manor-house close by—a gabled Elizabethan building dating from about 1551, with a modern south porch—there are said to be "some panels of stained glass of late date" which we may fairly assume once ornamented the windows of the church; just as in the vicarage garden there are some remains of a fine pulpit of the fifteenth century. Here Whichcot, Provost of King's College, Cambridge, was rector from 1643 to 1650. It was his aim in a miserable age "to turn men's minds away from polemical argumentation to the great moral and spiritual realities lying at the root of all religion, from the 'form of words' to 'the inwards of things,' and 'the reason of them.'" In or about 1650 he resigned his living, and was succeeded by another remarkable man, Ralph Cudworth, the author of "The True Intellectual System of the Universe wherein all the Reason and Philosophy of Atheism is Confuted and its Impossibility Demonstrated." This was all very well, but it did not save Cudworth from writing an heretical tract, "A Discourse concerning the True Notion of the Lord's Supper," in which he, with some learning, set out to prove that the "Lord's Supper" was not properly a sacrifice but "a feast upon a sacrifice." Cudworth was born at Aller in the marsh in 1617, and became a leader, as we might expect, among the Cambridge Platonists. He had a fine knowledge of Hebrew, and a great admiration for Oliver Cromwell, to whom he dedicated a treatise on the book of Daniel; certainly an appropriate offering.

From North Cadbury we return to the high road and follow the way to Sparkford, a mile to the south of which lies Queen's Camel, a large and charming village with a fine church a mile away boasting a good tower. This church was originally a building of the thirteenth century, when it was given by Hubert de Burgh, Earl of Kent, to the Cistercians of Cleeve Abbey. As we see it, its earliest parts are of the fourteenth century, to which time the low arcade belongs with its octagonal piers. The rest of the church is Perpendicular, and consists of nave, clerestory, and chancel tower. The south porch is of the eighteenth century. Within, the fine roofs and fine Perpendicular screen and pulpit should be noted, as well as the piscina and sedilia, and the font with its late niches and statues.

In the neighbouring village of West Camel the church is cruciform, with a tower and small spire over the south transept. The font here is Norman, and the chancel and north transept are of the fourteenth century. The nave is Perpendicular and has a fine roof.

But I had little time to see West Camel, for I had spent so much of the day at Camelot that night was now drawing in, and it was under the falling darkness that, very weary at last, I pushed my way across the old marsh through the level fields for some four miles till I struck the Fosse Way where it entered Ilchester.

CHAPTER XIII

ILCHESTER, LYTE'S CARY, LIMINGTON, ASHINGTON, CHELTON CANTELO, MARSTON MAGNA, AND RIMPTON TO YEOVIL

ILCHESTER, as I found next morning, is an ancient decayed town with very little to interest the traveller. It stands on the marsh, which is still liable to flood, upon the river Yeo, or as some call it the Ivel, whence it gets its name, and upon the great Roman road that runs clean across Somerset, the Fosse Way, just where a branch of it departs south and east for Yeovil and Dorchester. That it had some importance in mediaeval times is certain, and this was probably due to its situation upon this great road, to its central position in the marsh, and to its command of the river crossing. It is this real importance in the Middle Ages which has lent it a fictitious greatness in the Roman period—a greatness that never belonged to it. In all probability what Ilchester is to-day—and anyone who cares to visit it may know what that is—it was in the Roman time; a poor and unimportant village.

Even its Roman name is lost to us. The old archaeologists and topographers invented the name of Ischalis for it; but it has no foundation in antiquity, and is first heard of in the sixteenth century. Florence of Worcester called it Givelcester, others Ivelchester, which is correct, for it was the Chester on the Ivel, but what has that to do with Ischalis, or, better, Iscalis?

Nevertheless, though Leland was, like all other topographers, his contemporaries and successors down to our own day, mistaken as to the Roman importance of the place, let us hear him if only for the pleasure he invariably gives us :—

"I enterid by South West into *Ilchester* over a great Stone Bridge of vii Arches, yn the midle wherof were ii litle Houses of Stone; one of the right Hond, wher the commune gaiol is for Prisoners yn *Somersetshir*. The other House on the lift Hond. The lesser of booth semid to me to have bene a Chapelle.

"The Toune of *Ilchester* hath beene a very large thyng, and is of the auncientest Townes yn al that Quarter. At this tyme it is yn wonderful decay, as a thing in a maner rasid with men of Warre.

"Ther hath beene *in hominum memoria* 4 Paroche Chirchis yn the Toune, wherof one is yet occupied. The tokens of other 2 yet stond, and the 4 is clene yn Ruine. Ther is a fre Chapelle in the Toune, the bakside wherof cummith to the Ryver side even hard bynethe the Bridge and ther joynith a right praty Mansion House to this Chapelle. I have hard say That many yeres syns ther was a Nunry wher this Chapelle ys. Ther was also a late House of Freres yn this Toune. The greatest Token of auncient Building that I saw yn al the Toune ys a Stone Gate archid and voltid and a Chapelle or Chirch of *S. Michael*, as I remember, over it."

That bridge over the Ivel by which Leland came into Ilchester may possibly be Roman in its origin, but is more likely to mark the site of a paved ford, and it is certain that pavements, tiles, and coins of the Roman time have been found here; enough in fact to prove that a Romano-British village occupied the site of Ilchester, but no more. Yet even as Leland saw it Ilchester must have been eminently worth a visit; alas! nearly every fragment of antiquity, whether Roman or mediaeval, has vanished to-day. The Roman walls, if they ever existed, have vanished with the fortifications of the Civil War. Of the four parish churches Leland talks of but one remains, that of St. Mary Major; the great gate of stone, "archid and voltid," has been destroyed, as have its three fellows. Of the Dominican Priory near the West Gate not a stone remains. Of the Hospital of the Blessed Trinity, later a House of Augustinian Nuns under the rule of a Prioress—the Nunnery of which Leland speaks, which was called White Hall—not a trace remains; it stood by the North Gate close to the church of St. Mary Minor. Nor is anything at all to be found of the Hospital of St. Margaret founded in 1212, or of the Almshouse founded by Richard Venele in 1426. Of the gaol nothing is left, it was destroyed in 1843; of the Guildhall not a stone, and indeed nothing but the lines of a town, the church of St. Mary Major and the Market Cross remain to us in Ilchester to remind us of those Middle Ages of which the town was once so full.

Can it have been of Ilchester and its Dominican House that

the old peasant speaks to the Puritan fellow in the Somerset ballad?

PURITANUS: God speed you, ancient father,
  And give you a good daye;
What is the cause, I praye you,
  So sadly here you staye
And that you keep such gazing
  On this decayed place,
The which for superstition
  Good princes down did raze?

RUSTICUS: Chill tell thee by my vazen
  That sometimes che have known
A vair and goodly abbey
  Stand here of bricke and stone,
And many a goodly vrier
  As ich may say to thee
Within these goodly cloysters
  Che did full often zee.

PURITANUS: Then I must tell thee, father,
  In truth and veritie,
A sort of greater hypocrites
  Thou couldst not likely see;
Deceiving of the simple
  With false and feigned lies;
But such an Order truly
  Christ never could devise.

RUSTICUS: Ah! ah! che zmell thee now, man,
  Che know well what thou art;
A vellowe of mean learning,
  Thee was not worth a vart.
Vor when we had the old lawe,
  A merry world was then,
And everything was plenty
  Among all zorts of men.

. . . .

Chill tell thee what, good vellowe,
  Before the vriers went hence,
A bushell of the best wheate
  Was zold vor vourteen pence;
And vorty egges a penny
  That were both good and newe;
And this che zay myzelf have zeene,
  And yet ich am no Jewe.

. . . .

Chill tell thee my opinion plaine,
  And choul'd that well ye knewe,
Ich care not for the bible booke,
  'Tis too big to be true.

Our blessed Laydyes Psalter
  Zhall for my money goe,
Zuch pretty prayers as there bee,
  The bible cannot zhowe.

. . . .

Cham zure they were not voolishe
  That made the Masse, che trowe;
Why, man, 'tis all in Latine,
  And vools no Latine knowe.
Were not our fathers wise men?
  And they did like it well,
Who very much rejoyced
  To heare the zacring bell.

. . . .

Yea, yea, it is no matter,
  Dispraise them how you wille,
But zure they did much goodnesse,
  Would they were with us still!
We had our holy water
  And holy bread likewise,
And many holy reliques
  We saw before our eyes.

. . . .

Ay, hold thy peace, che pray thee,
  The noise was passing trim
To hear the vriers singing
  As we did enter in.
And then to zee the Rood-loft
  Zo bravely zet with zaints;—
And now to see them wand'ring,
  My heart with zorrow vaints.

Of what does remain in Ilchester what are we to say? The church of St. Mary Major is small and contains little to attract us save part of a thirteenth century arcade, a pretty east window, a fine and curious octagonal tower. And the village Cross is merely a fine and lofty pillar crowned by a sundial. No, the true glory of Ilchester cannot reside in such ghosts as these, but rather is to be sought in the memory of that great son of hers—the "Doctor Admirabilis," Roger Bacon the Franciscan Friar, who was born here in 1214, and who is said to have invented the magnifying glass, but whose great claim upon our reverence is that he was perhaps the greatest of all those forerunners of the modern world who gave up their lives to arrive at a systematic knowledge of Nature.

But if the material remains of even a near antiquity are lacking in Ilchester we know something of its record. It was for many ages the county town of Somerset, possessed of a Corporation whose thirteenth century mace remains in the present Town Hall. It was during this time and until the Reform Bill the only place of polling in the county, and its gaol, now so unfortunately destroyed, was the prison for the whole of Somerset. It had the honour of sending Sheridan to represent it in the House of Commons in the eighteenth century, when it was of course as rotten a pocket borough as was to be found in England.

Disappointing as Ilchester is, it has for the traveller afoot this compensation, that though it be nothing in itself, yet it is the key to many interesting places. Among these the beautiful manor house of Lyte's Cary some four miles to the north, and just to the west of the Fosse Way, is not the least.

Lyte's Cary is the ancient home of the old Somerset family of Lyte which has apparently been settled here since the middle of the thirteenth century.[1] The manor house as we see it however dates from the fifteenth century and has attached to it a fourteenth century chapel. These buildings which of old surrounded a small court upon all its four sides, now stand upon but three. On the east is the Great Hall with the chapel to the south of it; to the south is the old part of the dwelling house, the north wing of which has been much altered and has served as a farm-house. The whole of the buildings upon the west have perished. Perhaps the best view of the place is to be had from the north-east, where we see the beautiful porch with its oriel, the Great Hall also with its oriel and chimney stack, and the sanctuary of the chapel with its fine traceried windows—three gables projecting from the low roof and body of the house.

The oldest of these buildings as I have said is the chapel, which was built in 1340 in the style of that time which we call Decorated, of which it is a late sort. This is reached from the south by a fine doorway and consists of a simple nave once divided by a fine screen, with an open roof of wood. The windows are three, of which those upon the north and south are square-headed, while that at the east has triple

[1] See an interesting paper upon this family by Sir Maxwell Lyte, C.B., in *Som. Arch. Soc. Proc.*, xxxviii (ii), pp. 1-100.

lights and is pointed. A fine bit of thirteenth century tracery is to be seen to the south of the altar which may, perhaps, be evidence of the existence of an earlier chapel. It is said that originally, indeed all through the fourteenth century, the chapel stood detached and alone, but that in the fifteenth century the house was enlarged and joined to it. It was repaired in 1631 by Thomas Lyte, to whom the coats, and blazonry generally, are due.

But delightful as Lyte's Cary is, it is by no means the only treasure lying about forsaken Ilchester. About a mile to the east of the old county-town stands Limington. This was the first living held by Cardinal Wolsey. Born at Ipswich, "an honest poor man's son," the greatest of all English Ecclesiastics had been sent early to Oxford where he graduated at fifteen and was known as the "boy bachelor." In 1497, when not much more than twenty, he was elected fellow of Magdalen, and in 1499 he became senior bursar, but was forced to resign because he applied funds without authority to complete the great tower we all love so well. He had had, however, the sons of the Marquis of Dorset under his care and when this trouble came upon him their father presented him to the Rectory of Limington, to which he was instituted on October 10, 1500. But his troubles were not over. As Cavendish tells us, "One Sir Amyas Paulet, knight, dwelling in the country thereabout,[1] took an occasion of displeasure against him, upon what ground I know not; but, sir, by your leave, he was so bold to set him (Wolsey) by the feet during his pleasure." In other words, he put Wolsey in the stocks: "the which was afterwards neither forgotten nor forgiven; for when Wolsey mounted the dignity of Chancellor of England he was not oblivious of the old displeasure ministered unto him by Master Paulet, but sent for him and after many sharp and heinous words enjoined him to attend upon the council until he were by them dismissed and not to depart without licence upon an urgent pain and forfeiture; so that he continued within the Middle Temple the space of five or six years or more. . . . Now this may be a good example and precedent to men in authority, which will sometimes work their will without wit to remember in their authority how authority may

[1] Sir Amyas Paulet of Hinton St. George, connected with the Paulets of Nunney Castle.

decay. . . . Who would have thought when that Sir Amyas Paulet punished this poor scholar that ever he should have attained to be Chancellor of England, considering his baseness in every condition. These be wonderful works of God and fortune."

The church which Wolsey served consists of nave, chancel, north chapel and plain tower at the west end, and is interesting to us chiefly for its north chapel, a chantry founded by Sir Richard de Gyverney, lord of this manor in 1329. He lies there with his wife beside him, a knight in full armour, his legs crossed, in a fine Decorated recess. The chapel is most fortunately almost untouched, save that the roof in the east has been repaired and the north wall strengthened.

Under the arch which divides this chapel from the nave, on a great tomb, lie two other figures, the man cross-legged but not in armour. These probably represent Sir Gilbert Gyverney and his wife. There are also in the nave two ancient pews with bearings of the houses of York and Lancaster. The font is of the sixteenth century. The doorway of the church is of good antiquity and seems to be Transitional.

A mile to the east of Limington stands Ashington, with a small church with a fine bell-cote over the western gable, supported by great buttresses. It is dedicated to St. Vincent, who appears between two other figures at the eastern end of the church in a niche above the roof of the chancel. The two figures on either side St. Vincent represent, in my opinion, St. Catherine of Alexandria and St. Nicholas, with whom (notably in Antoniazzo's panel at S. Francesco in Montefalco) he appears so often. The little building consists of a Perpendicular nave with good windows and a decorated chancel with very small pointed windows.

The manor house has been spoilt. It was a fine Elizabethan building, of which a good illustration before its mutilation appears in the *Gentleman's Magazine* for 1820.[1]

From Ashington I went on my way to Mudford, where there is a good Perpendicular church which once belonged to the Priory of Montacute. Here I crossed the Ivel and proceeded north towards Marston Magna, taking Chilton Cantelo on my way, where, it is true, the church has been entirely rebuilt, but where in the rebuilding were discovered some wall

[1] This was reproduced in *Som. Arch. Soc. Proc.*, vol. xxxii.

paintings, of what the parson who lectured upon them to the Somersetshire Archaeological Society, in the year 1874, insisted upon calling "The beautiful legend of the Assumption of the Virgin." "The whole of the history is of course legendary," says this sometime Provost of Eton. These paintings were discovered under the Protestant whitewash in the north transept of the church, and the Rev. lecturer tells us that "the legend appears to be carefully followed"; but as in the year 1864 the rev. gentleman pulled down the church and rebuilt it, nothing at all remains of these paintings to-day.

Marston Magna has an interesting if not a beautiful church that in the reign of Richard I was appropriated to the Priory of Benedictine Nuns at Polshoe, in Dorset. It consists of nave with north chapel, north porch and western tower and chancel. That a church stood here in Norman times is proved not only by the font, which is Norman, but also by the two small pre-Norman window heads of stone, rebuilt in the fourteenth century into the east wall of the nave over the chancel ceiling,[1] and on the north wall of the chancel itself will be found some herring-bone masonry which is probably of the end of the twelfth, but may be thirteenth century work. The east window is a triple lancet of Early English style, erected in 1828. The church, however, was apparently entirely rebuilt in the middle of the fourteenth century, and thus for the most part what we see is a church in the Decorated style with a few early works built into it with many later additions. The chief of these later works is the north chapel adjoining the porch and divided from it by a screen surmounted by a gallery built in the fifteenth century, with the archway between it and the nave. The chapel is of great interest, and perhaps unique. To the south-west of the church is an old manor house of the time of Elizabeth, and to the south-east is a moated field or paddock, known as Court Garden, which is said to have been the site of an episcopal palace, but which may well have been that of a grange of the house of Polshoe.

A mile south-east of Marston upon the Dorset border stands Rimpton, which before the Conquest was a manor of the See of Winchester, as it remains, and for this reason it is

[1] See C. E. Ponting, F.S.A., "The Church of S. Mary, Marston Magna, Somerset" (*Som. Arch. Soc. Proc.*, xlvi (ii), p. 296 *et seq.*).

annexed to the hundred of Taunton, though so far away, for the tenants of the Bishop were bound to do their suit at his court there. The church is very charming, being cruciform with a very early fourteenth century chancel, having an eastern triplet and a single lancet in each wall north and south. The nave is later and keeps its original sixteenth century bench ends, some of which bear the Tudor rose, and the pulpit is a fine one of the Jacobean time.

Now, when I had seen all this and all these places I was very weary and evening was drawing in, so that in spite of the loveliness of the world hereabout I gladly made my way back to Marston Magna and then made the six miles or so into Yeovil by train.

CHAPTER XIV

YEOVIL AND ITS NEIGHBOURHOOD

YEOVIL, I think, is the most disappointing town in Somerset, for apart from its church and a couple of old inns it has practically nothing of antiquity to offer us. This is generally said to be due to the disastrous fire which devastated the town in 1449, when "one hundred and seventeen houses were destroyed by fire, among which were fifteen houses belonging to the chantry of the Holy Trinity, founded in the parish church here, eleven belonging to the chantry of the Blessed Virgin Mary without the church, nineteen belonging to another chantry of the Blessed Virgin Mary within the church, and two belonging to the almshouse. Forty days of Indulgence were granted to charitable contributors on this occasion." So says the excellent Collinson; but this fire cannot explain the absence of Tudor and Jacobean buildings in Yeovil, of which indeed one might expect the town to consist. This is probably due to the "progressive spirit" of Yeovil and to its long acquaintance with industrialism, for it is an old seat of the manufacture of leather and kid gloves. Yet the town conserved its ancient government till our own day, being ruled by a portreeve and eleven burgesses, out of whom the portreeve, who was a magistrate for the time being, was annually chosen. But this only makes it the more astonishing and disappointing that Yeovil is to-day a town materially more uninteresting than any in the county. The traveller must console himself with the knowledge that Yeovil is the key to that district of Somerset, which is perhaps richest in beautiful and ancient villages; and as for the town itself he must make the best of the church and the two old houses I have named.

The church of St. John Baptist, though it has suffered from restoration, is a very fine and noble building, for the most part of the fourteenth century, standing over a crypt of about the same time. The manor of Yeovil had for many years been vested in the successive rectors of the church of St. John Baptist when, in the end of the fourteenth century, the then rector resigned the parsonage with the town and lordship to King Henry V, and the King granted the manor and lordship, "with its appurtenances, such as views of frank-pledge, leets and law-days, together with the stocks, pillory, and tumbril, and all fines and amerciaments, and all prosecutions, imprisonments, and attachments, and also the appropriate rectory of the church of Yeovil" to the Abbot and convent of the Blessed Virgin Mary and St. Bridget which he had founded at Sion in Middlesex. This house, the only one in England of the Order, had been founded by the King in 1414. The Order, which is reckoned among the Benedictine congregations, because though the founder, St. Bridget of Sweden (1344), gave a Rule yet she ordained that "whatever was wanting to it" should be supplied by the Rule of St. Benedict, was a double one for men and women, and the men were subject to the nuns of the related House. It has been generally supposed that it was this Order which built the church of St. John Baptist in Yeovil. But if, as we may be sure, that church was for the most part built in the fourteenth century, this might seem impossible, since it was only in 1414 that the Order was established in England. This doubt is confirmed, too, by the absence of any evidence in the accounts of the Nuns of Sion having contributed anything to the work; and altogether it might seem that they had nothing at all to do with it, for in the will of Robert de Samborne, Canon of Wells, lord and rector (not vicar) of Yeovil, a considerable legacy is bequeathed "towards the work of the church begun by me until it be finished." This in 1382. Thus we may probably look upon Robert de Samborne as the builder of the beautiful church we see, which Freeman was used to declare was "as truly the work of genius as Cologne itself."[1]

As we see it the church consists of a wide and lofty nave, with aisles and tower at the western end, transepts, and large

[1] This is not to say that the church of Yeovil can compare in beauty with, for instance, Bruton church.

chancel. It is a building, as we have seen, of the late fourteenth century in the early Perpendicular style, and wonderfully light and harmonious, light by reason of its great and glorious windows, harmonious because it is at one with itself and all in the same style. The crypt under the eastern part of the church, entered by a vaulted passage, and itself vaulted from a central pillar, is perhaps earlier than the rest of the church, but not much earlier. It is now used as a vestry. The font is a good piece of Perpendicular work, and the magnificent brass lectern, with its undecipherable Latin inscription, should be noted.

Collinson, as I have shown, speaks of several chantries with their houses which were destroyed in the fire of 1449. It is impossible to say to which of these the old chantry house in Middle Street, now the Castle Inn, belonged. The George Inn, once the Three Cups, nearly opposite, is also a good specimen of a half-timbered house and an ancient hostelry.

No visitor to Yeovil should fail to climb Summerhouse Hill, a walk of half a mile whence one looks over Newton House, a magnificent Elizabethan mansion, the seat of the Harbins, and across its woods to the uplands of Dorset. Nor should a visit be omitted to the sources of the Ivel, whence Yeovil, or Gefel as it was anciently called, gets its name ; but the true pleasure of Yeovil, as I have said, lies in its villages.

The first of these is Preston Plucknett, and it lies upon the road to Montacute not much more than a mile from Yeovil. Preston of old was divided into two tithings, of which one bore the name by which it is still known, the other from its connection with the mighty Cluniac Abbey by the Thames was known as Preston Bermondsey. It is, however, in Preston Plucknett, "so called from its early lord Alan de Plugenet," that the beautiful mediaeval manor house with its fine octagonal double-storeyed openwork chimney, now closed with brick, and the barn for which Preston is famous, stand. They have nothing to do with Bermondsey Abbey, but are lay buildings and have always been in lay hands. When the Plucknetts died out, somewhere about Edward II's time, they were succeeded by the family of Stourton, and it was probably Jenkin Stourton who built what we see in the time of Richard II. At that time he owned not only Preston but also Brympton and Pendomer, and his three daughters by his three wives each inherited an estate; to Joan, who married John Sydenham, went Brympton, to Alice, who married William Daubeney, went Pendomer, while Cicely took Preston to John Hill. Jenkin Stourton himself was buried in Stavordale Priory, whither he was borne "in his best waggon drawn by his best team of oxen," which remained as his bequest to the Priory that he had rebuilt and endowed.

That Brympton which Joan Stourton brought to John Sydenham in the time of Richard II is perhaps the loveliest

Abbey Farm, Preston Plucknett.

of all the noble and lovely country houses for which Somersetshire, beyond any other county whatsoever, is famous; at any rate with its chantry house or old manor and its church it makes a quite incomparable group.

Brympton, Brympton d'Evercy as it is called, from the family who, according to Collinson, were seated here in very early times, at the Conquest got for lord the great Roger de Courcelle who held also the manor of Ashington hard by. But before the time of Edward I the d'Evercy family held Brympton, and in that king's reign Sir John d'Evercy gave it to Peter d'Evercy and his heirs. Peter died in the reign of Edward II leaving an only daughter Anne, the wife of Sir John Glamorgan, who held the manor in her right, but he left no son and soon we find Dame Isabel d'Evercy in possession of Brympton, and after her death her grandson by her daughter Amice, one Piers Glamorgan, got Brympton. The Glamorgans seem to have held Brympton till Jenkin Stourton got it and gave it to his daughter Joan, who brought it to John Sydenham in

Brympton d'Evercy. The Garden Front.

Richard II's time; according to Leland it was the first manor the Sydenhams had. Joan's heir was that John who was the son of Walter Sydenham, and his heirs held Brympton till the family became extinct in 1739, or rather until the last Sydenham, a few years before his death, sold it to a man of the same name, who in his turn sold it to a Mr. Penny who became bankrupt. Brympton was then sold to Francis Fane for the sum of twelve thousand pounds in the year 1730, in whose family it still remains.

The beautiful manor house dates from the time of Henry VIII, when the Sydenhams began to build it, its oldest part being a wing on the north. The house has largely been hidden by later additions. The garden front, for instance, Mr. Bligh Bond tells us, is characteristic of the work of Inigo Jones, to whom Walpole assigned it; it recalls the Banqueting Hall in Westminster. But is this the true representative of the manor house of the d'Evercy? It seems doubtful. The enigmatical building between the present Manor House and the church is thought by some to be the original manor house,[1] while others speak of a Chantry House occupied by the priest who served the Chantry, founded in 1309 by Sir Peter d'Evercy; another suggestion is that it may have been the stables of the manor. Whatever it was, it is a building of the fifteenth century.

The church which stands beyond this building is an extremely charming little example of a Somersetshire church before the rage for rebuilding set in in the fifteenth century. It never had a tower, but always since Elizabeth's time, at any rate, the great bell-cote we see over the western gable, and was perhaps originally cruciform, consisting of nave, chancel, and transepts. The style of this building is that of the early fourteenth century, the chapel on the north side of the chancel being later work. Within, the church is lovely, with a fine stone rood screen of the fifteenth century, with stone benches upon both sides. Upon this screen are three coats, of which the first is that of Jenkin Stourton. The arch to the south transept is especially beautiful, as is the window in the north wall. The monuments are very rich; in the north transept, beneath a fine canopy, lies the figure of an ecclesiastic, which has been tampered with, the carving upon the canopy being original; beneath another canopy, which has also been tampered with, is the figure of a lady, which has not been touched. In the chapel are two more figures, a knight and his lady, of the fourteenth century, perhaps John Sydenham and Joan Stourton, his wife. Between chancel and chapel is the strange tomb of Sir John Sydenham, who died in

[1] Mr. J. J. Hopper thinks it to be the original Manor House (*Som. Arch. Soc. Proc.*, xvii, 86). Mr. Chisholm Batten thinks it a Chantry House [xxxii (i), 34]. Mr. J. Batten says it is stables (*Hist. Notes on S. Somerset*, p. 57).

1626, on which, amid all sorts of Heraldry, is the following inscription :—

> My founder Sydenham, matcht to Hobye's Heyr,
> Badde me inform thee (Gentle Passenger)
> That what he hath donne in mee is onlie meant
> To memorize his father's and 's discent
> Without vayne glorie, but he doth intreat
> That, if thou comst his legende to reapeate,
> Thou speake him truly as he was, and then
> Report it (Sr) he dyed an honest man.

A walk westward, through the fields from Brympton, brings one to Odcombe with its lofty church, where Tom Coryate,

The Tudor Front and Church. Brympton d'Evercy.

the famous traveller, hung up his shoes when he returned from his first great journey through Europe.

Tom Coryate—Il Signor Thomaso Odcombiano, *Furcifer*, the Hierosolymitan, Syrian, Mesopotamian, Armenian, Median, Parthian, Persian, Indian Legge-Stretcher, was born at Odcombe in 1577, the son of the then rector there. He seems to have begun life as a "comic attendant," or Fool to Prince Henry, the elder brother of Charles I, and all his life he continued to play the fool, to be that is the best sort of

Englishman and the most typical, the very best of good fellows. Beside his enormous humour and his excellent good spirits Tom was most typical of us, in this also, that he was always restless. His ambition presently was to be the greatest of travellers and as he says on his return, in a letter to his "right worshipful neighbour Sir Edward Phelips" (of Montacute): "I doubt not but that your Honour will congratulate the felicity of our Somersetshire that in breeding me hath produced such a traveller as doth, for the diversity of the countries he hath seen and the multiplicity of his observations, far outstrip any other whatever that hath been bred therein since the Incarnation of our Saviour." His first journey resulted in 1611 in the publication of his book, "Coryate's Crudities hastily gobbled up in five months Travells in France, Savoy, Italy, Helvetia, *alias* Switzerland, some parts of High Germany and the Netherlands; newly digested in the hungry aire of Odcumbe, in ye County of Somerset, and now dispersed to the nourishment of the travelling members of this kingdome."

Tom had set out from Dover, as we might do, at ten o'clock on the morning of May 14, in the year 1608. He got to Calais at five in the evening, having "varnished the exterior of the ship with the excremental ebullitions of his tumultuous stomach." From Calais he set out through France and Italy, in the first part of his journey, taking advantage of any wheeled thing he could get, but on his return he "walked afoote with only one pair of shoes from Venice to Flushing," a distance of a thousand miles: and on coming home hung these shoes up in Odcombe Church, a thankoffering of his safe return.

> Tom Coryates shoes hang by the bells
> At Odcombe, where that beldam dwells
> Who first produced this monster.

On his journey he had seen many remarkable things, and indeed all that was worth seeing in the world, and it is curious to note how in his merry account of all he had seen he continually remembers Somerset and his home. In Savoy, for instance, he speaks of a lake with waters so swift that the fish were dashed to pieces against its stones, and many of these he tells us were even greater than the "great stone upon Hamdon Hill, in Somersetshire [destroyed in 1824], so famous for the quarre, which is within a mile of Odcumbe, my dear natalitiall place." In Venice the city, which of all he saw in his travells he most wondered at and adored, where, too, he was nearly killed by the Jews, for Tom was a learned fellow, and enjoyed a robustious disputation, he found it a fault that the noble Piazza was only paved with brick; it should have been paved with "diamond paviour of free stone" as was the hall of "Sir Edward Phelips in his magnificent house at Montague, in the County of Somerset, within a mile of Odcumbe, my sweet native soil." Nevertheless, he loved Venice so well that he declares had he been offered the four richest manors in Somerset and not to see Venice again, he would choose to see Venice his dear darling.

I say Tom was a learned fellow and like all men with a robust sense of humour he was a very sensible one. His knowledge of Latin was considerable and of great use to him; yet he found his English pronunciation (which still persists) a huge handicap, as I have done, and, thinking it over, concluded that the English way was wrong and foolish, as undoubtedly it is.

In Cologne, on the way to which he found neither Latin nor Greek of use with an angry German farmer, he asserts that the Archbishop's Palace is a poor affair: "superior to it there is in mine own county of Somerset, even the magnificent house of my most worthy and right worshipful neighbour, Sir Edward Phelips, Master of the Rolles" Coryate's book indeed long remained the only handbook for Continental travel for an Englishman, and it is certainly the best and most amusing ever written.

But Tom's ambition grew by what it fed upon. He could not remain in the "hungry air of Odcumbe." So in 1612 he set out again, this time for a tremendous journey through Palestine and India. He fell sick of dysentery at Surat, and his last words are curiously and pathetically characteristic of him; for hearing by chance, as he thought the English word sack; "Sack, sack," he cries, "is there such a thing as sack? I pray you give me some sack." And so saying he died.

Dear Tom—there be none like thee in this our day; here in Odcombe we will remember thee: "Rest thou in peace within thy foreign urn."

Perhaps Coryate's most famous achievement was the introduction of the fork into England, and for this his friend Laurence Whitaker of Yeovil calls him *Furcifer*.

"I observed," says Tom, "a custom in all these Italian cities and towns through which I passed that is not used in any other country that I saw in my travels; neither do I think that any other nation of Christendom doth use it, but only Italy. The Italians do always at their meals use a little fork when they cut their meat. For while with their knife which they hold in one hand, they cut out the meat of the dish, they fasten their fork, which they hold in their other hand, upon the same dish, so that whatsoever he be that sitting in the company of any other at meat should inadvisedly touch the dish of meat with his fingers from which all at the table do cut, he will give occasion of offence unto the company as having transgressed the laws of good manners, in so much that for his error he shall be at the least brow-beaten if not reprehended in words. . . . The reason of this their curiosity is because the Italian cannot by any means endure to have his dish touched with fingers, seeing all men's fingers are not alike clean."

From Odcombe I went over the high land, up and down, by as pretty a road as there is in the world; till suddenly I found myself looking over a deep and narrow valley to the isolated hill of St. Michael, not too unlike Glastonbury Tor, and beyond over all the marsh as far as Glaston itself there in the distance, with the great mountain of Hamdon close on my left.

Presently when I was full of all this glory I made my way down to that Montacute which Coryate praises so much, and indeed it is worth all he says of it, for besides its own natural beauty there at the foot of St. Michael's Hill, it can boast of perhaps the greatest mansion and the noblest in Somerset, the ruin of a Cluniac monastery and a fine church; and besides all this Montacute is full of legends, and its hill is famous and sacred in our history.

"After the Hill of Senlac and the vanished choir of Waltham," says Freeman in his affected way, "we may fairly place the wooded hill of Montacute." And why? For this reason. In the days of Cnut the king, was miraculously discovered upon this hill the great Rood which founded Waltham Holy Cross and gave their battle cry to the English at what in spite of Freeman I shall still call the Battle of Hastings. Now in those days, the days of Cnut, Tofig, the standard-bearer, a Dane, was lord of Montacute which was then known as Leodgaresburgh (for it got its name Mons Acutus from the Normans) and also he held vast lands in Essex. And it befell while this lord was absent, a certain smith of this village of Leodgaresburgh, who is said at the time to have been sexton, dreamed three separate times that Christ appeared to him and bade him go to the priest, and taking men, to go to the top of St. Michael's Hill and dig.

Montacute House from the South-west.

Twice the smith disregarded his dream, but the third time he dared not for our Lord was angered with him. Therefore he sought out the priest and told him all, and together, taking men with them, they climbed the hill and dug and came upon a great stone which was suddenly cleft in twain and in the cleft they saw a great Crucifix of glistening black flint and beneath it another, smaller, of wood, with a bell very old, and an old book. Now when Tofig heard of it he came with all speed, yet he knew not what to do, but, counselled by the priest, who argued that He who discovered this Cross was not without His intention regarding it, he placed the greater Crucifix of flint, with bell and book, upon a wain and harnessed thereto twelve red oxen and twelve white cows, and let be, waiting to see whither they would go. And lo, by and by, they began to move, nor could any man prevent them till they came right across England to Waltham in Essex and halted before a cottage Tofig had there for use in hunting. There they stopped, and there Tofig built a church and an abbey, and over the high altar he set up the Holy Cross of Leodgaresburgh and there Harold knelt before it upon the eve of Hastings, and it bowed to him so that the English in the battle cried ever "Holy Cross!" "Holy Cross!" and there as it is said Harold was buried, for he had built a great Minster there in honour of the Rood.

So it was of old; but when Norman William came Leodgaresburgh was called Montacute and was granted to the Conqueror's "insatiable brother," Robert, Earl of Mortain, who here built a castle "looking down like a vulture's nest on the surrounding hills and rich valleys at its foot." Against this castle went out the men of Somerset and Dorset in one of their isolated rebellions against the Norman power which nowhere had much success. This was the last of them, and it was ruthlessly crushed by Geoffrey Bishop of Coutances. The Castle has gone, every stone of it, and nothing that Robert did is to be remembered here any more; but his son William succeeded him, and to him is due the foundation of that Cluniac monastery at the foot of the hill something of which, out of all the evil 'twixt now and then, remains to us.

The Priory of Montacute was perhaps in truth the successor, albeit a new and Norman foundation, of the college of priests which had been established in Leodgaresburgh in honour of the invention of the Holy Cross.[1] It was founded in 1102

[1] Tofig had handed it to the church, and it was known as Bishopstown; later it was in the hands of the abbot of Athelney. See *V. C. H.* (*Somerset*), ii, 111.

and was one of the few Cluniac monasteries in England, for that noble great Order never took root among us and was indeed—Burgundian as it was—always regarded as a foreign thing. For such was the Rule that the monks had to journey to great Cluny itself to be professed, and whether for this cause or another the Order took no root here. It was in truth in English eyes a Norman thing, for the first English house had been founded at Lewes by a companion of the

The Priory, Montacute.

Conqueror in 1077. Moreover, this first great reform of the Benedictine Rule remained by reason of its very nature eternally foreign. The ideal of Cluny was the establishment of a great central monastery upon which all its daughters through the world were always dependent. Of all the Orders, that of Cluny was the most perfectly and completely feudal. The superior of each daughter house, howsoever large and important that house might become, was but the nominee of the Abbot of Cluny. It was this dependance which caused several of the lesser houses of this Order to be suppressed as "alien priories" during the French wars at the end of the fourteenth century; and possibly to escape this fate, in 1407, we find the Priory of Montacute renouncing its allegiance to Cluny and acknowledging as the head of the Order in England the Prior of Lewes, and from this time to the Spoliation, Montacute was reckoned an English house. The last Prior was Robert Shirborne; he surrendered the house to the king's commissioner Petre in 1539. Petre was granted the site and soon sold to Robert Freke, who, in his turn, sold to the Phelipses who at the time had acquired other parts of the Manor. They hold the place still.

So passed Montacute with the rest, and all that remains of it to-day is the beautiful fifteenth century gateway with its oriels and staircase turrets. In the village, which has a very old-world air, and where almost every house is built of stone from the Hamdon Hill quarries, there is a pretty house near the gates of Montacute House bearing the initials between two figures of the last Prior, Robert Shirborne.

As for Montacute House, that glorious great house that has taken the place of the Priory, and bears witness, if anything ever did, to that great change which befell in the sixteenth century in which we lost so much; it was built, Walpole says, by John Thorpe, to whom he also assigns Longleat and Burleigh, and for Sir Edward Phelips, the friend and neighbour of Tom Coryate, between 1580 and 1601. It is perhaps the finest specimen of Elizabethan architecture to be found in Somerset; but the stone screen of the west front did not originally belong to it; it came from the great manor house of Clifton Maybank, south of Yeovil, in 1787, but it is itself a design of 1589. Upon the garden front of the house, the supposed Thorpe design, are set nine statues, called the Nine Worthies. It is of these that Caxton speaks in his apology for his Life and Death of King Arthur:—

"It is notoriously known," he says, "through the universal world that there be nine worthy and best that ever were, that is, to wit, three Panims, three Jews, and three Christian men. As for the Panims, they were before the Incarnation of Christ, which were named: the first, Hector of Troy, of whom the history is common both in ballad and in prose; the second, Alexander the Great; and the third, Julius Cæsar, Emperor of Rome, of which the histories be well known and had. And as for the three Jews, which were also before the Incarnation of our Lord, of whom the first was Duke Joshua, which brought the children of Israel into the land of behest; the second was David, king of Jerusalem; and the third, Judas Maccabæus. And since the said Incarnation have been three noble Christian men, called and admitted through the universal world into the number of the nine best and worthy, of whom was first the noble King Arthur; the second was Charlemagne or Charles the Great, of whom the history is had in many places both in French and in English; and the third and last was Godfrey of Bulloigne."

Within Montacute House the best room is generally considered to be the Library, with its splendid heraldic glass of

Montacute House. Garden Front and Gazebos.

1599, with some later additions. The great Gallery upon the top floor, which extends the whole length of the house, is sixty yards long, and the great Hall is very fine indeed, with its screen at one end and at the other a quaint relief of "Riding the Skimmetty," as described at length in Hudibras.[1] To ride the Skimmington, or Skimmetty, was the fate of a man who

[1] *Hudibras*, pt. ii, cap. 2.

was henpecked. The man rode horseback behind his wife with his face to the horse's tail. He held the distaff, and she beat him with a ladle.

Montacute church is dedicated to St. Catherine; it is a building of various dates, and is the parish church of Montacute; it has nothing to do with the Priory. The earliest work in it is to be seen in the chancel arch, which is Early Norman. The transepts are charming Early English work with an early and interesting Decorated window in the south transept. The

Montacute House and Formal Garden.

rest is Perpendicular, the nave being very much restored. The tower is a very noble one, and should be especially noted. The monuments are chiefly those of the Phelips family.

No one who visits Montacute will fail, I should hope, to climb Hamdon Hill, and he is wise who goes by the beautiful lane up from the Priory with its overarching trees and hanging woods. The great entrenchments upon the top are worthy of every notice,[1] but what will strike the traveller most, will be the very noble great view that he has from there. To the north one may see as far as the line of the Mendips with all the moor between; to the south lie the Dorset highlands; eastward one sees the great escarpment of Wiltshire over Selwood Forest, with Alfred's tower conspicuous on the highest point; while westward one can descry the Quantocks, and more easily the Blackdowns to the south.

Close under the northern steep of Hamdon lie the villages

Typanum of Norman Doorway. Stoke sub Hamdon Church.

and hamlets of Stoke, all together known as Stoke sub Hamdon.

Stoke sub Hamdon, small as it seems, is full of interesting things, and surely not the least pleasant of these is the inn itself—the Fleur de Lis—of whose history we know nothing, but it is certainly charming to look at, and, with its arched doors with carved spandrils, might seem almost to have been part of some Priory or religious house. But after all the

[1] One of these is known as the Frying Pan. It is said that the Guild of Stonemasons used, upon Shrove Tuesday, to hold their feast here—hence the name.

finest thing in Stoke is its noble little church, cruciform now, but originally a simple Norman building of which very much remains. To begin with, what can be more satisfying than the Norman nave and chancel, the two little windows one with its relief of St. Michael and the Devil, and the Norman doorway with its fine relief in the tympanum of the Zodiacal signs Sagittarius and Leo[1] on either side of a tree, on which are three birds, while to the right is the lamb bearing the cross on its uplifted foot? To this building, in the twelfth century, was added the north transept, Transitional work, with its tower, and in the early fourteenth, the south transept. At this time, too, the lancets in the nave and chancel were inserted, a fine window made at the west end, and another placed in the tower over the north porch. The Perpendicular windows were, of course, introductions of a later time. Within, the church is very lovely and impressive, with its great recessed chancel arch, magnificent with splendid carving, and its font. The tombs, too, should be noticed in chancel and south transept, and the good Jacobean pulpit.

When Leland came to Stoke from Montacute, he says:

> "I saw at *Stoke* in a Botom hard by the Village very notable Ruines of a great Maner Place or Castelle, and yn this Maner Place remaynith a very auncient Chapelle, wheryn be diverse Tumbes of Noble Men and Wimen. . . . Ther is a Provost longging to this Collegiate Chapelle now in Decay where sumtyne was good Service, and now but a Messe said a 3 Tymes yn the Weeke. The Provost hath a large House yn the Village of *Stoke* therby."

The chapel with its tombs has long since disappeared, but the Provost's house remains in some sort and is still in occupation. The outer gateway in fact remains as it always was but the rest is hardly to be explained. Within the gate on the left is a small building with a bell-cote, probably an oratory; but the hall is utterly decayed and the present dwelling house has been so completely rebuilt and altered from time to time that it has little interest, save that one room has some Elizabethan panelling with the date 1585 and several initials, referring to the Strode family, who got the place when

[1] Mr. Monk [*Som. Arch. Soc. Proc.*, lvi (i), 55] would give this a political meaning: Sagittarius was the badge of King Stephen, the Lion that of Geoffrey of Anjou, husband of the Empress Matilda; but this seems too late for the character of the work.

the Chantries were suppressed by the King. The circular dove-cote should be noticed.

About a mile south of Stoke, under the southern escarpment of Hamdon, lies Norton-sub-Hamdon, to which the couplet refers:

> When Ham Stone hears the Norton chimes at midnight clack,
> It rolls down-hill to drink at Jack o' Beard's, and back.

Here there is another and finer circular dove-cote, but the church has been restored too thoroughly.

Stoke stands only just east of the Fosse Way and we cross this adventurous road on our way—and it is a pleasant way—across the old marsh to Martock, which is a pretty place with a fine great church with a very glorious nave, perhaps the finest of any parish church in Somerset. For the most part the church with its double windowed tower, which is a little later, is of the fifteenth century and in the Perpendicular style, but the east wall of the chancel with its lovely window is of the thirteenth, and is as fine an early English work as is to be found anywhere in the county. As for the nave, it is glorious with its clustered piers, decorated arcade, lofty clerestory, noble roof and aisles. The chancel arch after all this wealth is curiously plain, but it once held a noble screen and rood which have been destroyed.

Close to the church is a perfect specimen, so far as the stone-work is concerned, of a fourteenth century manor house which Parker describes as "one of the most remarkable buildings in England." Not far away is an old barn, now and for long a meeting house, once belonging to the non-jurors.

Martock is in every way a delightful spot, and one may easily spend a week there, as indeed one may in any of these wonderful villages between Yeovil and the marsh. There is Tintinhull, for instance, with its beautiful thirteenth century church—note the lovely double piscina in the chancel—added to in the fifteenth century, and certainly with a wholly delightful result so far as the south porch is concerned and the Jacobean pulpit. Here, too, the village stocks remain. And there is Chilthorne Domer, where the church has a square bell-cote over its west gable, similar to those at Brympton and Ashington.

But full of delight as are all these places which lie to the west of Yeovil, there are others only less lovely and full of interest to the south of the old town like roses on the way to Crewkerne. Of these the first, Barwick, lies a little to the south of the highway. Here is a church, dedicated to St. Mary Magdalen, dating from the Norman time, to which its font belongs; but unhappily it has suffered a considerable restoration, the chancel having been entirely rebuilt. The tower stands in the angle between the north aisle and the

Martock. Fourteenth Century Manor House.

chancel, so that it represents something earlier than the fifteenth century, as does the nave, whose piers may be of the twelfth century, altered later. The north aisle was added with its fine roof in the fifteenth century, and the south aisle, which is at a lower level, is possibly representative of something, perhaps a chapel, as old or older than anything we have here, though as we see it its masonry is of the fifteenth century. In the south porch is absurdly placed the heating apparatus. Perhaps the best thing left to us in the church are the bench ends, which date from the sixteenth century, and in the chancel bear

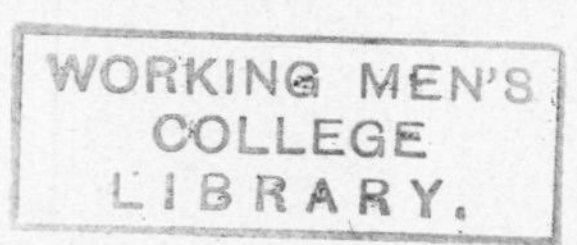

heraldic shields, in the nave are carved with birds and animals. The pulpit is Jacobean.

Close to Barwick lies among its trees East Coker, as pretty a place as there is, with church and Court well grouped together, and a row of almshouses on the way to them. The Court, however, a fifteenth century house, perhaps modernised, is not the old manor house. That, known as Nash House we passed as we came out of North Coker into the village over the Bridge.

Here, where the fine old windows still wink at you in the sun, Dampier was born in 1652. This man was a buccaneer of the real old school. He gained his experience of the sea, and none knew it better, if it is to be known at all, in adventures to Newfoundland, Bantam, Jamaica, and Campeachy Bay. He spent two years among the lawless woodcutters of Yucatan, and then in 1679 he joined a band of buccaneers, crossed Darien with them, and ravaged all that coast. In 1683, on another expedition, he seized a Danish ship at Sierra Leone, then set out for Chili, crossed the Pacific, and after a tremendous voyage was marooned on Nicobar Island. But he was not beaten even then. He made his way in a native canoe to Acheen, and, returning to England in 1691, wrote and published his *Voyage round the World*. Soon he was off to the South Seas again, where he has left his name in the Dampier Archipelago and Strait. He was wrecked at Ascension on his way home, and for over two months in this desert island lived with his crew on turtles and goats. And after all this and more, much more, that will never be known, he died in his bed in London in 1715. All that came out of East Coker. It seems out of proportion with the place.

Just south of East Coker on the Dorset border is the village of Sutton Bingham, partly situated on a long ridge. There is a church, originally Norman, consisting of nave and chancel, which still retains a small and narrow Norman chancel arch; but its most interesting feature is its Early English chancel with its small lancets. Here are some very curious wall paintings of the Coronation of the Blessed Virgin with saints and angels, which should not be missed. They may be thirteenth, but look more like fourteenth, century work.

Close to Sutton Bingham is Pendomer, with a church con-

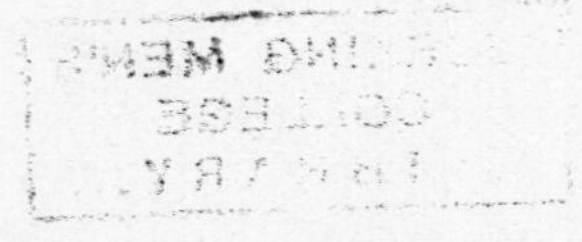

spicuous from the railway, small and not very interesting save that it holds a fine monument in an arched recess in its north wall, surmounted by a canopy, of a recumbent figure of a knight clad in complete ring mail. An embattled cornice runs across the point of the arch of the recess, and is supported by two pinnacled and panelled piers, which stand upon plain corbels projecting from the wall. Against these piers, and upholding the cornice, standing upon the corbels, are two small figures, one of which might be St. Roch, for he shows a wound on his thigh. The cornice once bore prickets for lights, five remain. This is the tomb of Sir John de Dummer of Penne Dummer, who lived in the times of Edward I and Edward II, and brought to this village its second name. It should be compared with the earlier tomb of a member of the same family at Chilthorne Domer. Close to the church is a fine old farm house.

From Pendomer it is easy to return to the railway at Sutton Bingham and so to come by train into Crewkerne.

Montacute House. Detail of Garden Ornament.

CHAPTER XV

CREWKERNE, CHARD, AND THEIR VILLAGES

CREWKERNE is a pleasing but not a very picturesque town in a curious valley, or rather in the crux where four valleys meet, and is everywhere surrounded by hills. It has its centre in its market place, but its chief attractions are its noble and finely situated church, a cruciform building with a central tower, and its ancient Grammar School, founded in 1499, the old buildings of which remain near the church, though the school itself has taken to itself new buildings outside the town upon the road to Yeovil.

At first sight, certainly, the great parish church of Crewkerne might seem to be a building wholly or almost wholly in the Perpendicular style of the fifteenth century, but the fact of its central tower certainly gives us pause, and a little examination will presently convince us that in this noble building we have many remains of an earlier church. The font is Norman, all that is left of a Norman or Saxon building, but the church as we see it was originally a cruciform building of the thirteenth century, and of this many fragments are left to us, such as the eastern wall of the south transept, with its arch still faintly stained with ancient colour, where, as it might seem, once opened a chantry or chapel. Here, too, is a piscina, certainly of the fourteenth century, as there is in the chancel. For the rest we have here a fifteenth century church, of which the earliest part is the chancel and the south transept with its interesting figure of St. George upon a mullion of the east window. In the east wall of the chancel two doors appear, which, as at North Petherton, might seem once to have led to an eastern sacristy[1]; over one of them appears, supporting a disfigured shield, the boars of the Courtenays, the old lords of Crewkerne. The other shield, also disfigured, is supported by angels, and these seem to bear witness to the fact that this church was appropriated to the monastery of St. Stephen, at Caen,[2] by the Conqueror.

The chancel and south transept are the first works of the fifteenth century in the church; they are followed by the nave, the aisles, the porch, and the tower. The nave and aisles are very spacious, the arches of the arcade being very wide, only three upon either side, and the aisle windows are really enormous. The five clerestory windows over the wide arcade are, however, not satisfactory, though they doubtless help to fill the church with light, as does the beautiful west window; the church is, in fact, a "lantern," and deserves the title as much as the "Abbey" of Bath. The last work anciently done in building the church was the addition of the north transept with its chapels. Looked at from the outside the church appears finer than it does within, and has many interesting features, of which not the least is the extraordinary series of sham gargoyles upon the porch. Here a crowd of curious figures are playing upon all sorts of instruments, and are no doubt engaged in a hymn of praise—perhaps the "Te Deum." A similar feature is to be found at Curry Rivel. Originally the west front must have been splendid, its niches filled with figures; even as it is, it is a fine composition.

Outside the south transept we see a curious work of the same date as the nave and aisles. It is thought that this was a "Friar's Pulpit," or, as others say, a shrine. The tower, which has always been in its present position, bears witness to the fact that the thirteenth century church was without aisles, for the buttresses at three of its corners are now within the church. What we see, however, is a tower of the fifteenth century of the same date as the nave.

To the north of the churchyard stand the old buildings of the Grammar School. This was founded about 1499 by John Combe, a Canon of Exeter, who from 1472 to 1496 was

[1] But this may have been a chantry of the Blessed Virgin which was in the churchyard here.

[2] This suggestion was put forward by Mr. Buckle at the Som. Arch. Soc. meeting in Crewkerne in 1891.

vicar of Crewkerne. The endowment given by him was for a free Grammar School and one schoolmaster. In 1538 a certain John Byrde was schoolmaster, "a man of honest conversacyon, well lerned and of goodly judgment; he dothe much good in the countrie in vertuouse bringing uppe and teaching of children, having at present six or seven score scolers." There is little else that is old to be seen in Crewkerne, but no one should fail to visit the old house, partly of the fourteenth century and partly Tudor, in the Market Place.

Leland describes Crewkerne, or Crokehorn as he calls it, as "a Mene Market Town," and says, "There I saw nothing very notable." He went on to Haselbury Plucknett, as we do, and notes that "at this place lyvid the Holy Hermite and Prophete Wulfrik yn King Henry the I Dayes."

St. Wulfric, as we have seen, was born at Compton Martin on the northern slope of Mendip. He seems, after a wandering life, to have become a priest, and to have served at Deverell in Wiltshire. It was there, as it is said, he first became a recluse, but later he came to Haselbury, where, clad in chain mail, he lived in a small cell near the church. He was visited by Henry I and by Stephen, to whom he prophesied that he would be king. He died more than ninety years old in 1154, and was buried by Bishop Robert of Wells —who was with him on his death-bed, it is said—in his cell, where his tomb was much visited by pilgrims. Later the monks of Montacute petitioned that his body might be removed to their church, but the chaplain of Haselbury opposed them and succeeded in removing the relics of the saint to the aisle or chapel of the church of St. Michael, which is still known as Wulfric's aisle. The church of Haselbury Plucknett, however, has in the main been so much restored that it is scarcely worth a visit save for the sake of St. Wulfric.

From Haselbury it is a cross-country walk of some two miles to Merriott, where the church is a curious and interesting building of many different ages. The chief attractions are perhaps the old gargoyles all round the building, the pretty niche over the doorway, the curious relief over the vestry door, called the "Fighting cocks," and a very crude and ancient crucifix.

A mile to the west of Merriott upon the hills stands Hinton

St. George, the home of the Paulett family, which should on no account be missed, both on account of the fine house and the notable tombs in the church there.

The Pauletts do not spring from this part of the country at all, but from the rich pastures between Bridgwater and the sea. Hither, in the time of Henry I, came Hercules, lord of Tournou, in Picardy, and the family takes its name from the place. When we come to the reign of the sixth Henry we find William Paulett still there, a gallant soldier knighted for his work in the French Wars. He it was who married Elizabeth Denebaud, the last of that family which had been lords in Hinton since the time of Henry III. Elizabeth's father probably lies in Hinton church in the tomb on the north side of the nave, and it is his effigy we see there, a knight in armour of the latter part of the fifteenth century. Their eldest son was that Amyas Paulett, who was knighted for his work at the battle of Newark-upon-Trent in 1487. He it was as High Sheriff of Somerset who put Wolsey in the stocks, and had so many years of repentance. He also, in all probability, built the tower and other parts of Hinton church, and lies buried there in a tomb bearing his effigy in cross-plate armour. His eldest son (by his second wife) was that Sir Hugh, who was supervisor of the rents of the surrendered abbey of Glaston for Henry VIII, and as a supporter of the Protestant cause was charged with the "good order of the shires near unto them in the west." His tomb is on the north side of the church, and bears two effigies, of a knight in armour and a lady, and the inscription: *Hic jacet Hugo Poulet miles qui obiit* 6 *die Dec. An. Dom.* . . .

Sir Hugh's son was another Amyas. He was a convinced Puritan, very eager in his suppression of the Catholic religion, and became keeper of Mary Queen of Scots for Elizabeth, a post that Lord St. John had refused. Mary protested against his selection, fearing his puritanism, and in fact he told Walsingham that he was prepared to kill her rather than give her up alive. Indeed his bitterness against the poor lady is extraordinary. When she was condemned, he considered her execution unduly delayed, and he not only treated her without ceremony but bombarded Walsingham and Burghley with letters concerning the need of executing her without delay. He boggled, however, at murdering her himself, "an act which God and the law forbiddeth." He died in London in 1585, and was buried in St. Martin's Church in-the-Fields. His remains, however, when this church was rebuilt, were removed with the monument to Hinton; this in 1728. He was succeeded by his second son Sir Anthony, an extraordinary autocrat, Captain of the Guard to Elizabeth, and, like his father, Governor of Jersey. He died in 1600 and lies, as they all do, in Hinton Church in a great tomb with his wife and ten children, under a canopy, between the north aisle and the nave. Other and later monuments of the same family will be found there.

Hinton House is a fine mansion, parts of which date from the time of that Sir Amyas Paulett who put Wolsey in the stocks.

There are two other things in Hinton that, in my opinion, are more attractive than either the church or the mansion; I mean the very noble village cross, now spoiled, but still retaining a figure of St. John Baptist, and the old thatched house known as the Priory which is quite charming. Another fine old house, a manor house of the time of Elizabeth, is to be seen at Wigborough, two miles north-east of Hinton. But perhaps the best specimen of a small Elizabethan manor in this neighbourhood is to be found at Wayford, just north of the railway line between Crewkerne and Chard. This was originally the home of the Daubeneys, and came to them by marriage from the Pauncefoots.

Beyond Wayford is Winsham with an interesting church, originally Norman, with a central tower, but rebuilt in the fourteenth and fifteenth centuries. But what is most remarkable and interesting is the fact that here and here alone, perhaps in England, and certainly in Somerset, the Rood remains. This consists of a remarkable painting upon a wooden screen of our Lord crucified between the two thieves with the Blessed Virgin and St. Mary Magdalen on either side of our Saviour. This screen is said to have been placed in the eastern arch of the tower and to have been there covered with whitewash and so preserved from harm.

Close to Winsham, though not strictly in Somerset, is Ford Abbey, once a house of Cistercian monks, founded first at Brightley, in Oxfordshire, by Baldwin de Briau, Sheriff of Devon, in 1133, and for various reasons removed here in 1141.

What remains to us after the spoliation of Henry, the disasters since, and the work of Inigo Jones, is, I suppose, the most perfect specimen we have of what a Cistercian house was like. It is, of course, now a private house, and very naturally it is not lightly to be visited at all. I mention it here in order that, when we come to speak in detail of poor murdered Cleeve, we may remember it.

To the north of Winsham, and quite among the hills, stands Cricket St. Thomas with Cricket St. Thomas house, the seat of Lord Bridport, in its glorious gardens far below the road in the little valley or glen which opens into the valley of the Axe. Here, in the little church, the first Lord Bridport, Alexander Hood, who fought at the "glorious first of June," lies buried. Cricket might, indeed, seem to breed great sailors, for it was of old the seat of the Prestons, and it was here the brave and gallant Sir Amyas Preston, Lieutenant of the *Ark* in the actions against the Spanish Armada, was born. It will be remembered that it was he who commanded the boats in the attack upon the great galleons lying before Calais on July 29th, 1588, when he was dangerously wounded. He lived not only to plunder the Spanish west, and to command the *Ark* in the Cadiz expedition, when he was knighted by Howard, but to send a challenge to Sir Walter Raleigh, then Privy Councillor. Raleigh refused to fight because, while he had a wife and children and a fine estate, "Sir Amyas was a private single person though of good quality." They were reconciled before Sir Amyas died about 1617.

Above Cricket St. Thomas rise Windwhistle Hill and St. Rayn Hill, bearing the high road from Crewkerne, which we now join, and in two miles or less come into the ancient town of Chard.

Yeovil disappointed us, in Crewkerne we came short; but a man may get his fill in Chard and not exhaust its interest, I think, in a whole month. And to begin with the whole situation of Chard, or Old Chard as it is called, on its hillside is noble and generous; it commands, perhaps, the most ancient entry into Somerset, that, namely, of the valley of the southern Axe, and it is said that the water which runs through its streets flows both north and south into the English Channel and the Severn Sea. The town consists for the most part of one great street which climbs the hills from east to west, and it has, until the year 1801, save for a short interval in the sixteenth century, when it appertained for a moment to the Duke of Somerset, always belonged to the Bishops of the diocese whom we find holding it in the Domesday Inquest. In 1206, Bishop Jocelyn of Wells incorporated it as a borough. Edward I confirmed its charter and gave it the right of sending two members to Parliament. This privilege, however, Chard only held for some thirty years. Its government, time out of mind, has been exercised by a Port Reeve and Burgesses; but Charles II, who granted the town a new charter, changed them for a mayor and council. Queen Anne, however, who gave another charter to Chard, restored the old institution, which lasted until, in 1835, a mayor and council were again set up.

Chard has, too, borne its part in the great affairs of England, and this especially in the Civil War, though no doubt it already had its part in the Roman occupation, for the Fosse Way passed clean through it, and it was, in spite of its Saxon name, which would seem to connect it with the mysterious Cerdic, known and used at any rate in the later years of that wonderful time. In the seventeenth century it is particularly prominent, however, for it lay directly upon the route of Charles I, when in high spirits he set out for the west, as it did again when, a broken and hopeless man, he returned two months later with some 10,000 horse and foot and 17 guns. On that disastrous return, as it happens, the King was detained for a full week in Chard, waiting for the provisions Somerset had promised him, and at the last moment had failed to provide. That delay cost him dear, for otherwise he might have reached Oxford before the enemy was strong enough to stop him; but as Clarendon tells us that "stay could not be prevented except he would have left the money and cloaths (which the Commissioners of Somersetshire had provided and did deliver there at last) behind him; which would not have been grateful to the Army." He marched out of Chard upon the 30th September, 1644, leaving Exeter under Sir John Berkley, but the west as a whole in anarchy. What misery must have been there in the heart of that narrow and pure soul, as he went on that last September morning along the Somersetshire roads to dine at Hinton St. George, where Prince Rupert and Lord Digby joined him from Bridgwater. He slept that night—did he sleep?—at South

Perrott manor house, and next day was in Sherborne. It was his last look at the west he had taken in that early autumn day.

Another tragic and unfortunate figure was some forty years later, in 1685, to march through Chard on his way to disaster. This was Monmouth—dearly the town paid for his visit. For the Bloody Jeffreys a little later found there twelve victims, whom he hanged upon a great oak in the lower part of the town, which remained till our day and was known as the Hangcross Tree.

But let us turn from such wretched memories as these to Chard itself, the town as it remains to us to-day. The church, which is a low cruciform building in the Perpendicular style, the tall porches forming transepts, was, as we see it, built in the years 1400 to 1440. The most interesting feature outside the church is the series of gargoyles which are very fine. Within, the roofs of the north transept and the chancel are fine, and the carved seat ends curious, but perhaps the most interesting thing here is the monument, now in the north transept, of "William Brewer of Chard, phisitian, and Deanes, his wife, who living forty years in happy wedlock, in full age departed this life; shee dying 8th November, 1614, and hee 24th July, 1618, having issue only six sons and five daughters, all men and women growne and all comforts to them." The monument which is very elaborate, of porphyry and marble, is ornamented with angels and various figures. Corinthian columns support a cornice, beneath which in arched recesses are the effigies of William Brewer and Deanes, his wife, kneeling at a prie-Dieu facing one another, with the six sons, two by two, behind their father, and the daughters behind their mother; a charming if expensive thing.

Through the oldest part of the town we come to the Grammar School, founded in 1671 by William Symes of Poundsford, and well worth a visit, and then to what is the true splendour of Chard, I mean "Waterloo House" and its neighbour. These are supposed to have been the Court House of the Manor; they date from about the end of the sixteenth contury, and are perhaps the finest examples of their kind left to us in Somerset. In fact, the noble front with its porches and mullioned windows is only less charming and delightful than the rear, which is reached under the arched porch. Here on the first floor is a noble room lighted by two twenty-light mullioned windows, with a fine plaster covered ceiling and a notable fireplace, above which is a phœnix with

Doorway of old Manor House, Chard.

two grotesque half figures at the sides. Above this is a wonderful design of birds and animals. At the other end of the room are three panels; in the midst the Three Children in the Fiery Furnace, on the left the Judgment of Solomon, on the right, Daniel in the Lions' Den. Between the panels we see figures of Justice and Law; a fine frieze runs down the whole room. Who can have been the author of such work as this? One hears suggestions of "strolling Italians," but the work has nothing Italian about it; it is English, and colloquial English too, I think.

In the same great street of Chard is another notable house; this is the Chough's Inn, which is better within than without.

But fascinating as Chard is, or at least as I found it, there is

Whitestaunton.

more than one sight in the country about it which must on no account be missed. Of these the chief is undoubtedly Whitestaunton, a village some two miles to the west among the hills. On the way thither he is wise who seeks and finds, at about a mile from Chard, the old sixteenth century house, now a farm, of Weston, which was of old the home of the Monner family, when it seems to have been known as Watson. Here again are two fine plaster ceilings.

At Whitestaunton which lies high on the Blackdown Hills, upon the border of Devon, there is a spring in a sheltered nook, known as St. Agnes' well. The church, of course, stands close beside this well which is supplied by a warm spring and

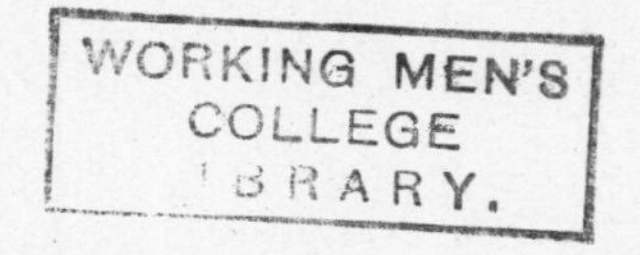

possesses certain healing qualities. Here, in 1845, were discovered the remains of a Roman villa, and these in 1882–3 were excavated by the late Mr. Charles Elton, Q.C., M.P., the owner. The whole plan of the villa was not made out, but enough was shown to assure one that here an elaborate house with baths, hypocausts, mosaic floors, and frescoed walls had stood, and something of all this may still be seen.[1]

As one comes down into the shelter of Whitestaunton one notices at once the charming group of church and manor house, which might indeed, seen from the hills, appear to be one. The church, dedicated to St. Andrew, the successor of a Norman building to which its font still bears witness, is a Perpendicular building of the end of the fifteenth century. It has two chancel chapels, of which that upon the south would seem originally to have been the mortuary chapel of the Bretts to whom long ago Whitestaunton belonged, but it is now a later and poorer building than that upon the north, which was the Chapel of the Guild of Our Lady. Within, in the south chapel, lies Simon Brett, who married Johanna Hugyn in 1513. The small screen of the same date as the church is a good one and should be noted, as should that of stone which divides the chancel from the north chapel.

As for the manor house, when we first hear of it at the end of the fifteenth century it was in the possession of the Hugyns. Part of the present house may be of that time, but most of what is ancient there dates from the time of John Brett, a hundred years later.

Another village that should be visited from Chard before one leaves it for Ilminster, is South Chard beyond Tatworth on the Fosse Way. Here is an old chapel, a thatched building occupied now by the Baptists, I think, and still known as St. Margaret's Chapel.

[1] *V. C. H.* (*Somerset*), vol. i, p. 334.

CHAPTER XVI

ILMINSTER, THE VALLEY OF THE ISLE AND THE ROAD TO LANGPORT

ILMINSTER—ILEMINSTER—for it is lowly situated upon the river Isle within sight of the Castle Neroche, that great prehistoric camp on the Blackdowns, which frowns at it across the meads, lies in a rich and beautiful country and is to be loved as all such old-world towns are more and more as they fall away from us. It is set upon the cross roads from Crewkerne to Taunton and from Chard to Langport, and just to the west of the Fosse Way where it began to take the southern hills. It is a very old place—its market, which it still holds on Saturday, dates from the Conquest—and it possesses one supremely lovely thing in the triple-windowed central tower of its church which rises there like some Magnificat by Marenzio or Byrd—the church is dedicated to our Lady—over the sound and sight of many waters. A man born within sight of such a thing may reckon himself fortunate if in his last hours he may see it again; and he who has spent all his youth within its influence shall never forget it or come under the influence of lesser and foreign things.

Always the Church held Ilminster, and for many centuries, until the Spoliation, the Abbey of Muchelney far away in the marsh possessed it, and indeed the last Abbot of that dear and holy place was an Ilminster man. Then, when Henry VIII flung down the Religious Houses and destroyed the Church, the Manor of Ilminster came with so much else to the Duke of Somerset and remained in the Seymour family, for Elizabeth restored it to the Duke's son Edward Seymour, till in 1684 it was sold to Sir John Speke and two others

But of this enough. Ilminster to-day in sight of the hills lies in the meadows in the shadow of its beautiful church remembering none of these things.

That church, with the exception of its nave—a building of

Ilminster Church.

1824—is as noble and glorious a building as is to be found in Somerset. It is, of course, but the latest of a series of churches built upon this site, being itself a noble work of the fifteenth century which has suffered certain restorations, though none, with the exception of the complete rebuilding of the nave, of a very serious nature. The church is cruciform, its glorious tower being a central one about which the church is grouped, this tower, the transepts, and the porch having been built in the time of Henry VII by Sir William Wadham of Merefield or Marsfield, half a mile to the west of Ilton in the marsh.[1] The church is very spacious with a fine groined stone roof, and the chancel is large though not so rich as the rest, especially the north transept. Behind the chancel is a vestry. In the north transept is a fine brass to the founder and his lady, of the middle of the fifteenth century, and here too are the tombs with brasses of Nicholas Wadham and his wife Dorothy who founded Wadham College in Oxford. She was the daughter of that Sir William Petre who was introduced to the Court by Anne Boleyn. He succeeded in extirpating the Gilbertines, the only religious Order of English origin, and acquired an enormous estate at the Spoliation. Sir Nicholas, however, was not a politician, he lived quietly at Merefield, saved 14,000 pounds out of his income, and having no children determined to spend it on charitable purposes. In 1606 he founded an almshouse at Ilton and is said to have contemplated the founding of a college at Venice for English Catholics, to which Faith at one time he had leanings, as his wife, curiously enough, had always, as had her family; but when he founded Wadham College his statutes were wholly Anglican. He died at Merefield in 1609. In the south transept is a monument to Humphrey Walrond, who in 1586 founded the Free Grammar School of Ilminster, the building of which still stands and is now a girls' school.

Some more fine monuments are to be found in the otherwise dull church of Dowlish Wake a mile to the south-east of Ilminster. Here in the chapel on the north side of the chancel is a whole series of monuments, the oldest of which would seem to be that in the arched recess of the north wall where we see the figure of a woman in a headdress of the fourteenth century. Between the chapel and the church stands an altar tomb on which are the figures of a man and woman, the man in full plate armour, while the panels about the tomb show us other male and female figures and a coat-

[1] Nothing remains of his house there.

of-arms. This shield is that of John Speke (d. 1442) and Joan, great-great-granddaughter of Isabel Wake, from whose family Dowlish got its second name. The Wakes came to an end with Isabel and her two sisters. Their father was, it seems, murdered by his wife Joan, who was at any rate burnt to death for her crime. On the floor of the chapel is a brass of a man in full armour of the Tudor time, and an inscription showing that here is the tomb of George Speke and his wife Elizabeth. He rebuilt this part of the church and died in 1528. On the north wall is the monument and bust of Captain John Speke the African explorer, who discovered the sources of the Nile and died in 1864, having after all his adventures accidentally shot himself while partridge shooting.

Some more Speke monuments will be found in the church of Whitelackington, about a mile out of Ilminster upon the Ilchester road. This church is cruciform of the thirteenth century, with nave and aisles as we see them of the fifteenth, and all under one roof; a curious thing to see. Here in the north transept is the monument, of the end of the sixteenth century, of that Speke who married a Luttrell. On the monument are two swords and two helmets. In the south transept are two effigies of the end of the fourteenth or beginning of the fifteenth century, of which nothing seems to be known.

We now come through a beautiful country to South Petherton, passing on the way the two Seavingtons—Seavington St. Mary to the south, with what looks like a plain Early English church, and Seavington St. Michael with a cruciform church and legend of a lady who was buried in a trance and wakened by the sexton who would have stolen her rings.

South Petherton church is a fine one, with a strange central eight-sided tower, Decorated windows in the chancel and south transept, but for the most part it is a Perpendicular building that has been restored. The fifteenth century monument to Sir Giles Daubeney with a fine brass should be noted. It was while Daubeney held Calais for England that the Sieur des Querdes Governour of Picardy, declared, according to Bacon, "that he would be content to lie in hell seven years, so he might win Calais from the English." Daubeney saved him from that. But the best thing to be seen in South Petherton is the noble old house, now rather spoilt by restoration, known as King Ine's Palace, "the many palaced Ine," a very beautiful manor house, of the fifteenth century with its exquisite great double window. No one should on any account miss seeing this fine old place or omit to glance at more than one old house in the charming little town.

From South Petherton one makes one's way through the byways, delightful as they are, to Shepton Beauchamp and Barrington.

Shepton Beauchamp has nothing to show, but who would not go a long way through such lanes as these hereabout to see the wreck of stately Barrington? It beckons as you come, and you are in love with it while still far off. On nearer approach you see, however, what has been lost. Barrington Court is now a farmhouse going to ruin—the great Hall, a cider cellar, and all spoilt. It was one of the noblest efforts of a great age, that of Henry VII, and is said to have been built by the Daubeney of that time. Later it came to the Phelips and then to the Strodes, and here Colonel Strode entertained the Duke of Monmouth some years before his Rebellion. It is a pity that so noble a house as this is not, in lieu of better, a public and a national care.

One could linger about Barrington all day for the village is delightful, the inn an old and tried house, and the church beautiful and quiet; a cruciform building with a central eight-sided tower, where the Strodes are buried, and I suppose the Daubeneys and the Phelipses before them.

In love with the byways and the meads from Barrington I made my way up the water meadows of the Isle to Isle Abbots, like Ilminster time out of mind a possession of the Abbey of Muchelney. In doing this I missed Ilton which I knew of old with its pretty Decorated church and its tombs of the Wadhams—one of Joan but not the murderess. Isle Abbots I could not miss, for its beautiful double-windowed church tower, though small, is one of the finest in Somerset, and with Ilminster still in my heart I desired to be reminded of such things as these. The beauty of the tower among the trees is extraordinary; its details are exquisite and then it has this major advantage that nearly all its niches retain their figures, and these are numerous. On the west you may see first the Blessed Virgin Mary and a curious representation of the

Resurrection of our Lord, and then, above, St. Peter and St. Paul; on the east you have St. John the Baptist and that Pope Clement who, Tertullian tells us, was the first successor of St. Peter. On the south stand St. Margaret and St. Catherine with St. George on horseback, and on the north St. Michael.

Nor is the church less charming within; the chancel, which is large is delightful, a good piece of Early English work, and though the east window is poor, the side windows are lovely; and here too is some fine Early English carving with piscina and sedilia. The body of the church is less lovely with a late roof and only the lower part of its screen, but the Jacobean screen in the tower is fine. The font with its ancient carvings is Early Norman.

In Isle Abbots, because I loved it, I slept, being weary too, and very early next morning I went on to Fivehead, not forgetting to visit the house that John Walsh built in 1559—I mean Cathanger manor house with its great gatehouse and his tomb in the church where there is, too, a Norman font.

So I went in the early morning over the meadows, but now under the hills, to Swell, where there is so small a church which is not at all swell but rather broken down and out at elbows; but I liked it well enough with its Norman doorway and font and its rude benches, and its Beauchamp shield in the eastern window, and its Jacobean chancel furniture. Here, too, is a fine old house known as the Court House. And here I climbed the ridge and went into Curry Rivel.

Curry Rivel, or Revel, was probably always a part of the demesne of the Wessex king, for it never paid geld but formed with North and South Petherton "a ferm of one night," being a fifth of the whole. The manor remained with the Crown till, in the time of Henry II, it was granted with Langport to Sir Richard Revel, later sheriff of Devon and Cornwall, from whom it gets its second name. His heir was Sabina, wife of Henry de l'Orti, and from her Curry passed to her son, also Henry. A hundred years later, however, in 1391, we find that the church of Curry was appropriated to the Canons of Bysham in the diocese of Sarum by Bishop Ralph of Wells.

The lord of the Manor of Curry possessed the right of driving, or "preying," West Sedgemoor, which lies below the village in the west, West Moor beyond it towards the sea,

Barrington Court

Week Moor and the Forest of Neroche. In Curry to-day, however, really the only thing of interest lies in the church, which is a fairly fine specimen of the Somersetshire Perpendicular style, with a tower that has been rebuilt. Within the Perpendicular building, however, there is one corner left of some beauty from the older church which once stood here before the time of Henry VII. This is the north chapel, which is a work of the thirteenth century, and was probably built by one of the L'Orti. Even this chapel has not escaped alteration, some of the arches have been refashioned and the windows have been tampered with, perhaps at the time when the rebuilding of the church was begun. The tomb of one of the Jennings, of later date than the chapel, stands within it, and another between the chapel and the chancel bears effigies of Marmaduke and Robert Jennings with little figures of mourners. In the north aisle there is some fine old glass in the good Perpendicular windows, and the roofs, both here and in the south aisle, are to be noted, as are the bench ends. The fifteenth century screens across the aisle are all that remain of the great screen that crossed the whole church.

Burton Steeple, the column on the hills west of Curry, was erected by William Pitt, Earl of Chatham, to the memory of Sir William Pynsent, who, the last of an old Somerset family, bequeathed his fine estate and mansion of Burton to the national hero, with whom he had no personal acquaintance, "in veneration of a great character of exemplary virtue and unrivalled ability," and also be it added on account of Pitt's having opposed the tax on cider! Pitt does not seem to have cared much for the place.

As we go down hill off this long and isolated ridge into the valley of the Parrett on the northern bank of which river Langport stands, there is a little village upon our right called Drayton that is perhaps worth a visit, for there is a fine cross in the churchyard on the shaft of which we may see St. Michael battling with the devil, always an uplifting spectacle.

CHAPTER XVII

LANGPORT, MUCHELNEY ABBEY, SOMERTON AND THEIR VILLAGES

LANGPORT, "formerly more celebrious than now,"—an assertion of Collinson's confirmed to us by the position of the place, its obvious strategical importance, of which the remnants of its old fortifications remind us, as well as by the fact that it was here Henry I intended to establish the great Benedictine community that was later set up at Reading, and here Sir Richard Revel had his castle—stands upon a hill on the right bank of the Parrett, just below the spot where that sluggish river is joined in the marsh by the Ivel and the Isle. It is not to-day perhaps a place of much interest or beauty, but it possesses one or two buildings which one would not willingly miss, and it witnessed what I suppose to have been the most ignominious defeat that the Royalists sustained in the Civil War; moreover, there lies in its churchyard one whom I think all modern Englishmen must hold in respect. Let us take these things in order.

As a matter of fact, Langport—which holds all the marshes, but is itself isolated, and therefore can never have been what Bridgwater was, the true capital of all the marsh country—is not best entered from the west. A man bent on making the best of Langport should come up to it from Muchelney by Huish Episcopi, and then enter by the great gate with its Hanging Chapel that happily still remains—perhaps the most pleasing, as it certainly is the most astonishing, thing the town can boast of. It is obviously a very old building, and though it has been strenuously denied that it ever was a gate, chiefly because no sign of a portcullis remains to it—all things are

On the Moors between Langport and Huish Episcopi.

denied—what else can it have been? The chapel above is, or rather was, dedicated to our Lady. It might seem that it got its present name from its position, but it has been asserted that three persons were hanged here by Judge Jeffreys in 1685 for complicity in the Monmouth Rebellion, their names being Humphrey Pierce, Nicholas Venting and John Sellwood. However this may be, since the change of religion the chapel has been desecrated. At one time it was used as a school, then as a museum, and now it is become a Freemasons' lodge-room.

Just above this great gate with its spoiled chapel stands the church of All Saints, looking far across the marshes of the valley of the Parrett. The tower, which is a good example of a triple-windowed tower of the third class, is of the time of Henry VII, and the church as we see it is—the nave somewhat earlier, the chancel and chapel somewhat later—of the Perpendicular time. The best and most interesting part of it is the chancel, which is a very fine and spacious one, as is the beautiful "Heron chapel" to the south of it. To the east of the chancel there is a vestry as at Ilminster and Crewkerne and elsewhere.

But if the chancel is the finest thing in the church, the finest thing in the chancel—though I do not forget the two beautiful windows on the south—is the glass in the east window, which is all, or nearly all, old and very beautiful. The window is a large one of ten lights with traceried transoms, and has replaced that now in the east wall of the north transept.

Above, under two crests and coats-of-arms of the Pauletts and the Herons are four small figures of Saints, perhaps the two Saints James, St. Bartholomew, and St. John, with eight others below. In the window itself are large figures collected here, it is said, from the two beautiful side windows on the south. Beginning on the left we have St. Cecilia, St. Gabriel Archangel, the Blessed Virgin—these two probably once formed an Annunciation—St. Elizabeth, St. Lawrence, St. Anthony with his pig, St. Clement, St. Peter, St. Gregory, and a figure now labelled St. Joseph. Of this last it may be said that he bears two cruets in his hand and is in Oriental dress and has been thought to represent one of the Magi.

Turning now to the nave we find the west window filled with modern glass in memory of Walter Bagehot, the economist and essayist, who was born in Langport in 1826. We shall find his grave in the churchyard overlooking the far stretched melancholy marsh. Bagehot's life, properly understood, is bound up with Langport to a remarkable degree. In this sober little town with its "Portreeve," where so long ago as the time of Edward I they begged to be relieved of the duty and privilege of sending burgesses to the House of Commons, he grew up, yes, imbued with these curiously provincial and particularist traditions, boasting of them indeed, as examples of "true political sobriety." In the eighteenth century, Samuel Stuckey had founded his Bank at Langport, and it was with this Bank that Bagehot early became connected, for his father had married a niece of Stuckey's and was vice-chairman of the business; in which post Bagehot succeeded him. I suppose the book by which he will chiefly be remembered is that upon the "English Constitution," which makes such salutary reading for us to-day, when what we had all thought indestructible has been broken before our eyes by men not of our traditions, and for the most part not of our race; but I shall always think of him as the author of those literary studies—those, for instance, upon the "First Edinburgh Reviewers," "Hartley Coleridge," and "Bishop Butler," which not only display his peculiar and detached habit of mind, but so much of that strange vivacity mixed with caution which was so charming and amusing in him.

The author of the "English Constitution," that wise and peaceful book which may now be put on one side, I suppose, and is certainly forgotten in the avalanche of modern rhetoric, looks down from his high grave, across the marsh upon a battlefield which certainly helped to make that constitution and the government of this country.

In that miserable Great Rebellion which did so much to fix upon us the oligarchy which has governed us ever since, Langport had been continually held for the King, and in the Somersetshire campaign of 1645, Langport, of course, had its part. Upon the 10th of July in that year, Goring for the king was broken by Fairfax under Somerton Hill, in a defeat that "was rather a flight than a fight," and as Fuller goes on to say "henceforward the sun of the king's cause declined, verging more and more westward till at last it set in Cornwall."

If we would visit this forgotten spot, we must pass down out of Langport under the great gate with its "Hanging Chapel," and pass on to Huish Episcopi, where we shall forget all about such misery in the glory of the church tower there, a thing really to stop the breath with a joyful astonishment.

We know nothing of Huish till the thirteenth century, but it is probable that it always had been, as it was then, parcel of the revenues of the bishopric of the diocese, and thus it gets its name, Bishop's Huish. Certainly, in Norman times a church stood here, of which in fact the doorway upon the south

Huish Episcopi. Church Tower.

remains, while the outer doorway of the south porch, too, bears witness to the thirteenth century, and the church in part would seem to be a rebuilding of the late fourteenth century; certainly some Decorated windows remain in the chancel, but the church as a whole, and, of course, the very noble double-windowed tower, are Perpendicular. The Jacobean pulpit dates from 1625, and in the east window of the south aisle is some glass by Burne-Jones. However, it is the tower that really attracts us here, and nothing anywhere can be more glorious, crowned as it is with pinnacles, graceful, and excellent.

But glorious as this tower is, it cannot keep us long from what is, when all is said, the great spectacle of this part of Somerset, I mean the lonely Abbey of Muchelney there in the marsh to the south. I do not know what it is in these old Somerset religious houses, of none of which more than the ruin remains, that attracts me so profoundly and so sweetly, unless it be that even in their stillness and their ruin they whisper, as no modern thing has known how to do, of that Faith beside which nothing in the world is of any account, is worth a single thought or a single tear. Man has done all but his worst at Glaston, at Hinton, at Witham, at Stavordale, at Cleeve, and, indeed, here too at Muchelney, yet there is in all these places in the very stones of them, though they be hacked out of all recognition, in the broken arches, yes, in their very silence, as of something spellbound, a divinity, a sense of beatitude that you will miss altogether in Wells Cathedral or Bath "Abbey," or in even the loveliest of these lovely churches, which are the pride and the joy of this county. About these places, where no alien creed has ever raised an altar, there is a charm, an exquisite air of grace, pathetic and beautiful, which it seems can never pass away. For in truth they are really unapproachable by us, these lonely and broken sanctuaries of an England that is dead. Though we cannot look upon them without love, though we cannot linger among their stones without tears, or trace with our finger some undecipherable inscription, some figure of a saint or the Cross of our Lord; yet we know them not, what they are, what they mean—refuges from a world that was always "too much with us"; for the world is our all. For us there is no curtain that shall presently be drawn aside; for us there is no abiding here or there in the blue sky; for us all that is gone for ever, between us and such a place as Muchelney a great gulf is fixed, and no man can over pass it. What, then, is it that we feel—for indeed we feel something, and that very keenly—in such a place as Muchelney? It is, I think, a nostalgia, a true home-sickness, that we suffer there, for we are homeless, and all that was ours has been taken away from us, and this not only in spiritual but in material things. We have lost both our Faith and our property, and men without the Faith and without land are but a little removed from slaves. Perhaps one day Muchelney, after so many years of oblivion, shall rearise. After all, the most characteristic article of the Christian Faith lies in just that doctrine, that magnificent and heroic statement: Exspecto resurrectionem mortuorum et vitam venturi saeculi. Amen.

Of the history of such a place as the Benedictine Abbey of St. Peter and St. Paul at Muchelney, there is little to say since all that is involved in happiness has but little that can be recorded. Its founder is said by some to have been King Athelstan, who built it and endowed it as a thankoffering for his victory of Brunanburgh in 937, when as we know:

> We, the West Saxons,
> Long as the daylight
> Lasted, in companies
> Troubled the track of the host that we hated;
> Grimly with swords that were sharp from the grindstone,
> Fiercely we hack'd at the flyers before us.

Others, however, and among them were the monks themselves, claim Ine as the founder. However that may be, when the Domesday Inquest was made the Abbey of Muchelney held Chipstable, Ilminster which in 1201 passed to the Church of Wells, Isle Abbots, Cathanger in Fivehead, Drayton, West Camel, and the three islands of Muchelney, Middleney, and Thorney. Muchelney was always a little monastery of about the same size as the later foundation, Athelney, and both it and Athelney were wont to seek the protection of their great neighbour, Glastonbury. This, however, could not save Muchelney from Savaric, that wily and rapacious Bishop, who seized Glaston itself. He induced Abbot Richard of Muchelney to give the church of Ilminster to the cathedral church of Wells in 1201, and since he was Abbot of Glaston as well as Bishop, Muchelney could not save himself. Savaric immediately, to make all secure, created a prebend out of the church of Ilminster, and made the Abbot of Muchelney prebendary, and thus a member of his chapter, so that henceforth the Bishop of the diocese might claim his obedience. In the fourteenth century at one time we hear that the discipline at Muchelney was lax and no doubt it suffered in the great pestilence. Of its history in the fifteenth century we know next to nothing, but that it then maintained about thirteen monks. This number had decreased a hundred years later, for at the Spoliation there were but eight or ten monks beside the Abbot and Prior at Muchelney. On January 3rd, 1538, Thomas Legh, the King's commissioner, came to Muchelney and reported that "he found the abbot negligent and of doubtful character, and ten brethren which all war ignorant and unlernyd and in the manor no servauntes

Muchelney Abbey.

maynteyned or hospitalite kept." It never seems to have occurred to Thomas Legh that if the brethren were "ignorant and unlernyd" so was Christ their Master, and that if they "maynteynd no servauntes," neither did He.

The Surrender was signed at this time, and by the spring the Abbey and its manors had been granted to Seymour, Earl of Hertford. The manor of Muchelney is now the property of Mr. Walter Long, M.P.

William of Worcester tells us that the Abbey was a large

and fine structure, the church being one hundred and fifty-six feet long and forty-five feet broad, the cloister eighty-one feet by fifty-one, with a chapel in it dedicated to the Blessed Virgin Mary.

Nothing of the Abbey church was until recently known to exist, but largely owing to the exertions of the Rev. S. O. Baker, the foundations have been traced to the south of the parish church and a certain amount of the ruins laid bare.

Muchelney. Fifteenth Century Priest's House.

The design of the church would seem to have been Norman, but this was altered and the church rebuilt in the fifteenth century. But though nothing really remains of the church, much does remain of the Abbot's House, now a farm house, and something of the cloister, which is now used as a cider cellar. The house, to which it is perhaps not reasonable to expect to gain admission at all times, is a very fine example of the work of the fifteenth century. The south front which is easily seen is, to a large extent, as it always has been, and the stone panelling of another room to the east is extremely

U

beautiful. Within, the house is even more interesting, for one of the rooms appears to be still practically unaltered since Henry VIII's time.

But the ruins of Muchelney Abbey, lovely as they are, are by no means all there is to be seen in the beautiful island of Muchelney. The church is interesting, though its double windowed tower is not very splendid. It has both north and south porches with chambers, and within both piscina and sedilia with beautiful canopies. The roof, too, of the nave is still fine with curious paintings. The lovely tiles in the chancel and at the west end were found in the ruined abbey church.

Perhaps more interesting than the church is the dear little vicarage house upon the north side of it, across the road, dating perhaps from the fourteenth century; and there is a good though restored village cross.

From Muchelney, when I could drag myself away on that September morning, I went on through Thorney, across the golden marsh to Kingsbury Episcopi, a charming old village with a fine but locked church. The double windowed tower is, indeed, almost as fine as that of Huish Episcopi, but not so harmonious, I think, for if you find the crown of Huish too much for its tower, what will you say of Kingsbury's crown? All the same, Kingsbury tower has this advantage that to a large extent it retains its statues, though what these are I have never been able to make up my mind. The church, too, is a fine one, with clerestory and north transept with fine windows of that noble Perpendicular style which we know so well and love so much in Somerset. Here, too, is a vestry at the east end as at Langport and a good screen which Langport cannot boast.

Kingsbury vicarage, too, should be noticed, for it has some ancient fragments built into it, notably a good Perpendicular window; but the whole village is ancient and charming.

The name of Kingsbury and Kingsbury Episcopi—Bishop's Kingsbury—the place was an ancient possession of the Bishopric—might seem to be answerable for the local legend that there was a whole line of Bishops of Kingsbury. Kingsbury belonged to the Bishop of the diocese, and in an ecclesiastical sense, too, he was her Bishop, but she shared him with the rest of Somerset.

All these beauties lie to the south of Langport in the marsh, but there are things nearly as fine to the north; Aller for instance, where Alfred brought Guthrum for his baptism. "After seven weeks," says Asser, "Guthrum the Pagan king with thirty of the principal men of his army redeemed their promise and came to Alfred at the place called Alre and King Alfred adopting him as his son stood sponsor for him at the sacred font of Baptism." I suppose none of us to-day can really understand just what that meant. At least one has seen the most fantastic explanation, as that Alfred hoped that the word of a Christian man might be trusted better than that of a heathen. The truth is, of course, that the only thing that really mattered was the conversion of the Danes. Consider what it must have meant when these heathen, rude and devilish savages without any sort of civilisation—for in Europe civilisation and Christianity were synonymous terms—swept into England. Even Alfred could not turn them out or save us altogether: but after breaking them at Æthandune he achieved at one blow all that was possible and doubtless more than he had hoped when he brought Guthrum to the font at Aller. By that act he had rid England of the pagans and all that paganism stood for—murder, rape, lawlessness, and all we mean by the term barbarism.

Aller lies at the western foot of Ham Hill on the edge of Sedgemoor. Its little church stands firmly upon a rising ground well out of the marsh, and, wonderful to relate, within is the very font in which Guthrum was made a Christian more than a thousand years ago. At least, I like to think so; it is certainly very old, almost certainly Saxon, and considering the enormous number of Norman fonts up and down the county, it would not be so wonderful after all if this very famous and most glorious relic of the Christian victory of Alfred had been preserved by the Church in Alfred's own Somerset through all these ages. Surely here within sight of Athelney across the marshes this might well be.

High Ham on the other side of the hill, to be reached by a byway over it through the woods, was the southernmost manor of the great central territory of Glastonbury. The church was, however, rebuilt anew from the foundation in the year 1476 by Abbot Selwood, Paulett, and others, as we learn from the history of this parish left by its Protestant rector, Adrian Schael (good old English name that) who presided here from 1570–1599. It was finished in the space of one year, all but the tower, which is older than the church, and of Ham Hill stone, while the church is of Doulting. The benches, too, are of the fifteenth century, earlier than the present church; the noble rood-screen and lectern are, however, works of the first years of the sixteenth century. In the east window we may still see Abbot Selwood in the glass with his mitre upon his head and his great crosier in his hand. The font is Norman and we may well ask again, if High Ham has conserved its Norman font which was never famous, why should not Aller have conserved its Saxon font which was known through Christendom.

Not far from High Ham lies Low Ham, where there is a very notable little seventeenth century church, but in the old fashion, and with clerestoried nave; a curious and rare example of imitation at that period. The original church here seems to have been the domestic chapel of a manor house now destroyed; but it was endowed by Sir Edward Hext in 1662. His effigy and that of his wife are to be seen upon their tomb in the north aisle. One George Stawell rebuilt the church as we see it in 1668. He lies in the south aisle. The screen comes from the Mayor's chapel at Bristol, having been brought here by Sir Charles Wathen, who at one time was owner of this manor.

When I had had my fill of Langport, I set out one morning for Somerton, and instead of going over the hill, I went by the southern road through Long Sutton. Here I found another fine church, with a very lofty but plain triple-windowed tower, and here the best thing was the woodwork. This is not to say the church is uninteresting, on the contrary, it is notable, for it is one of those churches like High Ham, which we can date. We know that the church, as we see it for the most part, was built in 1490, and on examination we can see that the tower, the porches, and the chancel chapels are later work, practically nothing remains of an earlier church. Here, again, the roof is very good, its embattled tie-beams ornamented with angels, and the screen and the pulpit, though restored in 1868, retain something of their ancient beauty.

Traditionally, the capital of old Somerset, a walled town

with a castle, Somerton though it has lost not only its old renown but its walls and its castle too, strikes the traveller as a picturesque and quaint place enough with two redoubtable inns, the Red Lion and the White Hart, with still more redoubtable signs. King Ine is said here to have had his capital, and I must say he was a wise man to choose so quiet and old world a place. For I refuse to believe that Somerton was ever different, in temperament at any rate, from what it still is. Well did that wise man, Sir Edward Hext, whose motto is mistakenly supposed to be written up in Low Ham church:

Somerton Market Cross.

"My son, fear the Lord, and meddle not with them that are given to change," found here his almshouses, and indeed, as he says, "his benevolence remaineth for ever." Somerton, I think, can never have loved those who were given to change, least of all at the time of the Civil War, when she must have been seething with them, strenuous ill-mannered troopers, Colonel Strode and Colonel Bovett, and the rest of the quarrelsome gang. To-day, however, they are gone, and Somerton remains to sleep, if not to dream. And so we find her and very dear she is.

Let a man who would see her at her best stand in the

market square, with the town hall to his left in the foreground, the seventeenth century market cross before him, and the beautiful octagonal church tower beyond rising over the roofs of the old houses, and if that does not win him nothing can.

But after all, the best thing in Somerton, and a very good thing it is, is the church. This is an Early English building with later rebuildings and additions. The nave, at any rate, in its eastern part, is Early English, as are the arches leading into the transepts, and indeed the transepts themselves. Then in the fourteenth century the aisles were added, the nave was raised, the clerestory was built, and the noble roof "made in the carpenter's shop at Muchelney Abbey" was erected. This roof is nearly as fine as that at Martock. In the fifteenth century the upper part of the tower was rebuilt, the fine octagon being added, and later still the chancel was rebuilt. The pulpit is a fine work of the early seventeenth century; it is dated 1615, and the altar, which is carved, bears the date 1625, and in the north transept there is a seventeenth century brass.

From Somerton it is easy to visit several places of interest; Kingsdon, for instance, where in the church there is, in the north transept, the effigy of an armed knight, perhaps a crusader; Charlton Mackrell, in which parish is Lyte's Cary, and in whose church so many of the Lytes lie buried; Charlton Adam, too, where in the south chapel of the church there is the fine canopied tomb of one Baker, and a Norman font and Jacobean pulpit; and Keinton Mandeville, with its church in a field, the birthplace of Henry Irving.

Having seen these things, I left Somerton with regret, and set out along the ridge of the Polden Hills for Bridgwater, for before I examined Sedgemoor and its many wonders I wished to see it all, as it were, in a glance, all through a summer's day, and I wished to see its old capital, Bridgwater. Therefore I went by the long way over Polden, because by this road I should be always above the marsh, and I should have Glaston in view too, and the Mendips and perhaps the sea. For though the Polden ridge is not very high, nowhere three hundred feet as I was to take it, yet upon it one seemed on a mountain ridge with all the marshes north and south, the vale of Avalon as well as Sedgemoor at one's feet.

All that way is beautiful and fair, among the fairest in the crooked shire, and that is as much as to say among the fairest in all this great world of ours. I set out by Littleton and came to Dundon, two round hills in the marsh behind which, at the foot of Polden, pretty Compton lies with its manor house under the camp on Dundon Beacon. So I went on up past Redlands and then along the ridge down Walton Hill, by Pipers Inn that pass of the Poldens, and so on up again through Ashcott on to the height above Moorlynch, where, before I came to Loxley Wood, I was a good two hundred and fifty feet or more over the world of the moors with their great church towers, Othery, Middlezoy, Weston Zoyland, their colour, their mystery, and their enormous age, and I had them all (though they be always in my heart), better than they are to be had from Mendip or Quantock or any of the great heights.

And on I marched happy as the wind that went so white across the long grass of the moors, leaving Catcott with its funny little old church, and Edington that falsely claims the great victory, and the sham priory of dear Chilton, and Cossington that is to be loved—for these are the names of those villages—upon my right, with Puriton out of sight over the hill, the only manor in England which Norman William bestowed upon the church of St. Peter in Rome. So I went down Cock Hill, that is so fine, and past Bawdrip where they found some old tiles, and thought of Rome forgetting the old Chantry that was there; turning at last beyond Knowle into the great straight way that brought me at last into the notable town of Bridgwater, and through all the shouting and hurly-burly and dangers of market day there, across the Parrett full of great ships to the Clarence Hotel by the Town Hall, before which Admiral Blake stands frowning at the place of his nativity.

CHAPTER XVIII

BRIDGWATER AND SEDGEMOOR

BRIDGWATER astride the Parrett the true division, as no range of hills so low or so easy as the Polden could be, of Somerset proper, of Somerset, that is, between the Mendips and the Quantock Hills, is not only the capital of the moors, of all those great marshes with their old towns and dear villages; but, situated upon the most notable river in the county, very much as Exeter is upon the Exe, that is to say just above the estuary, but not, like the western city, out of reach of the tide, Bridgwater is also, rightly understood, the port of Somerset, the sea-gate, and for this cause, if for no other, it is a very considerable place.

No one, I think, can come out of the moors, where those lovely, lonely, church towers speak far off, the one to another, and there is so wide a silence, into the town of Bridgwater, without being impressed by its size and ancient importance. Its church, for instance, one of the largest in the county, an ancient building capable of seating some thirteen hundred persons, brings this home to you at once, as in another way does its notable spire, surely the loftiest building in all this county, thrust up there out of the marsh a unique thing as though in a county of towers to stand separate and gather them about her.

And the history of this ancient borough fully bears out one's first impression. It was never a walled town, but it had its four gates, north, south, east, and west, and Leland tells us that the "Waulles of the Stone Houses of the Toune be yn steed of the Towne waulles." It gets its name not as was long supposed from its position astride the river, Bridgwater, Aquae

Pons, but from that Walter de Douai, who held it after the Conquest, whose Burgh it was, and it no doubt played no inconsiderable part in the subjugation of Somerset. Walter's son had for heir a daughter, Julia, who brought Bridgwater with other manors to her husband William de Paganel, whose son in the time of Henry II granted it to William de Briwere. It was this William who built a new Castle, to be so famous, upon the west side of the Parrett by leave of King John, and to the south of it he began, if he did not complete the bridge of three or four arches over the river, which was finished by a certain Triveth of Devon, and which, perhaps, Leland saw. William de Briwere, too, obtained for the town a charter erecting it into a free borough; all of which was confirmed by Edward I. He also founded before 1213 a Hospital in honour of St. John the Baptist served by a Prior and Brethren, of the Order of St. Augustine, to maintain thirteen poor persons and assist pilgrims through the town. This Hospital stood in the east part of the town partly without the East Gate where Leland saw it "a thing notable." It was apparently then served by a College of Priests who wore the dress of Seculars "with a Cross on their breast." In 1412, however, the Parish Church of St. Mary the Virgin was appropriated to the Canons of St. Austin who served the hospital. They were, of course, able to serve the church themselves and they did so with the assistance of a secular chaplain. The hospital had considerable property in Bridgwater and, besides the parish church of Bridgwater, those of Wembdon, Northover, and Isle Brewers were appropriated to it, beside others in Cornwall. At the Suppression the site was granted to Humphrey Colles. Nothing at all remains of this Hospital whose site is occupied by the modern church of St. John, and of the Castle so famous in the seventeenth century only a great stone archway on the western quay, part of the old watergate, remains. The Castle, however, was in the Great Rebellion in excellent condition. It mounted some forty guns and was with the town held for the king by Colonel Windham till, when the battle of Langport was lost, it was taken after a defence of less than a week in which it sustained a cannonade of three days' duration. Over one thousand officers and men, with other gentlemen and clergy, were taken prisoners and goods of over £100,000 value.

The moors had thought the place impregnable and had poured all their wealth into it for safety. The King had thought so too, and always considered the surrender inexcusable, as I suppose it was. Certainly the fall of Bridgwater was the crown of Fairfax's work, it cut off the loyal west from the rest of England and seemed so important to Cromwell that, fearing the town might be lost again, he determined to burn it, but in this the rebels were only partially successful. Eastover, however, had been fired by the red-hot shot of the garrison. That was in 1645. Forty years later the rebel Duke of Monmouth was proclaimed King in Bridgwater by the Mayor and Corporation, and it was, as we shall see, from Bridgwater Castle that he set out by War Lane upon July 6 to meet his fate at Sedgemoor in the last battle fought upon English soil.

The castle of Bridgwater, thus so famous, is no more; the Hospital of St. John has been destroyed and scarce a stone is left of the Grey Friars,[1] the only Franciscan House in Somerset, which was founded about 1230 by William de Briwere's son. Leland, who saw all these, gives the following account of the place in his Itinerary: "These thinges I markid yn the Weste Parte of the Towne; one large Paroch church. A goodly house wher sumtyme a college was of Gray Freres. *William Bruer*, sunne to *William Bruer* the first buildid the House. One of the Lordes *Botreaux* and his wife were especial Benefactors to this House. Thereupon his Hert and his Wifes Body were buryed there. The Accustumer of *Bridgwater* hath translatid this Place to a right goodly and pleasant dwelling House."

Indeed Bridgwater as we see it has suffered almost as much change as Ilchester has, and of all its most notable buildings of old only the "large Paroche chirch" remains to us. This is a notable and even beautiful thing, in its foundation an Early English building standing doubtless upon the site of a Norman church, though not a stone that we may consider Norman is left to it. But the church, as we see it, would seem, large and especially wide as it is, to stand upon thirteenth century foundations, though it has been carried further east and the two side chapels have been added since then.

[1] An arched doorway in Silver Street may have belonged to this house.

The church as we see it is extraordinarily spacious and bears indisputable witness to the early importance of Bridgwater. It is a building of all sorts of dates, but in the main Perpendicular, with a curiously irregular arcade in that style and a clerestory whose windows stand over the pillars instead of over the arches. And yet in spite of this and the variety of style and date of the windows throughout the church, it is a fairly harmonious building, with some claim, chiefly, after all, on account of its spaciousness, to be considered beautiful as well as curious. Its best feature is its furniture, the fine screens that abound in it, the panels in the chancel, the pulpit. The old rood-screen, perhaps of the fifteenth century, is now broken, and used as sidechoir screens. In the seventeenth century before the rood-screen there stood another. This, which is of that time, is now placed on the south before the Corporation pew.

Of old there were at least seven altars in the church and three chantries, of Our Lady, of St. George, and of the Blessed Trinity; of these nothing at all remains. Apart from the woodwork, the finest thing in the church to-day is the great picture of the Deposition over the altar. This was presented to the church by the Hon. Anne Paulet, a godson of Queen Anne. It is said to have been taken from a privateer at that time, but what a privateer could be doing with a great picture such as this, and how it came by it, no one has yet explained. The picture is certainly of one of the North Italian Schools, probably by some Bolognese master, and it is a very fine piece of work.

Without, the church is chiefly notable for its tall spire upon a short tower—not a beautiful arrangement. The scurrilous pamphleteer, John Oldmixon, born in 1673—whom Pope represents in his *Dunciad* as climbing the side of a lighter so that he may plunge further into the mud of the Fleet Ditch—is buried in the churchyard. Two old houses, at least, remain in Bridgwater which must be seen. One of these stands to the east of the churchyard, and has a very fine ceiling. The other is the house in which Admiral Blake was born, where also there is a fine ceiling and fireplace. Blake was born here in Bridgwater in August, 1599, the eldest of twelve sons. He was educated at the Bridgwater Grammar School till he went up to Oxford, where he remained for ten years from 1615 to

1625. In 1640, after many a voyage, he returned to his native town and threw in his lot with the Rebels, and in 1645 became a member of the Long Parliament. He was, in fact, an ardent Republican, a soldier as well as a sailor, for after serving in the attack on Bristol and defending Lyme, he held Taunton for a year against Prince Maurice. In 1643 he was put in command of the Fleet by the Commonwealth as Admiral and General at sea, and his encounters with Van Tromp, the Dey of Algiers, and the enemies of his country wherever they could be found, are a part of our glory. He died on his way home at last, just as his ship was entering Plymouth Harbour, and Cromwell buried him in Westminster Abbey, but his body was exhumed at the Restoration and buried in a grave with a score of others on the north side of the church. The town of Bridgwater has very rightly erected a monument to her most famous son, who if he did fight "for whoreson Cromwell's sake," was a great and heroic seaman. There is, however, no reason why in placing lines written by another great Englishman, Spenser, upon the monument, it should misspell the poet's name.

Bridgwater is, as I have said, the capital of the moors; but before crossing the Parrett to lose ourselves in their vastness in searching out those little lonely villages—each indeed a garden of Eden that grew in the marsh—it will perhaps be better to explore the country which lies between the river and the Quantock Hills. For, in fact, Bridgwater is an excellent centre from which to explore at least the northern part of that famous range, and though it is not such a business I would now suggest to the traveller, there are several villages of the foothills, as it were, that must be spoken of here.

Setting out, then, upon the road for Enmore, we come in little more than a mile of pleasant country, every step of which brings us nearer to the great hills, to Durleigh. Here is an old towered manor house, very picturesque and beautiful, and once of some size, too, of which a part remains. This is called —in Somerset we may be sure of a beautiful name—West Bower, and is locally reputed to have been the birthplace of Lady Jane Seymour, though it seems without a shadow of reason. The place boasts of a curious, and, I think, unique *columbarium*, circular in form and built of mud, in which there are nests for some nine hundred birds.

Beyond Durleigh the road breaks into three ways, one to Enmore, one to Goathurst, and one to North Petherton. We take the last, which is charming, and in a little over a mile find ourselves in the shadow of quite the finest double-windowed church tower in this district; the only one that can compete with it is the triple-windowed tower at Weston Zoyland, but that is on the other side of the Parrett, and it must give way to North Petherton, which is more beautiful and elaborate, crowned, too, with an exquisite coronal, and still retains the figures in its niches. The church and manor here belonged to the Priory and Preceptory of Mynchin Buckland, or Buckland Sororum, near Durston, a House of Sisters, as the name implies, of the Order of St. John of Jerusalem, and the only Priory of Women which the Order possessed in England. The church itself is a fine Perpendicular building with two porches, the southern with a gallery open to the church. At the eastern end, as at Langport and Ilminster, there is a vestry.

North Petherton, which is even now a charming and quiet place under the spell of the great hills (the walk to King's Cliff and its woods should not be missed), was of old the centre of the Forest and Park of North Petherton, in the former of which were situated the monastery of Athelney, founded by King Alfred in memory of his great defence and the Priory and Preceptory of Mynchin Buckland.

Not more than half a mile south of North Petherton, and within the forest, lies North Newton, where the church tower might indeed seem to be the oldest in Somerset, and to date, perhaps, from King Alfred's time. The church, which is a modern rebuilding, and without interest in itself, contains a very lovely screen, with four figures in good relief, viz., Faith, Hope, Charity, and, I think, Obedience, a door nobly carved, with figures of the Wise and Foolish Virgins, leading into the vestry, and a fairly good seventeenth century pulpit (1637). It was in this parish, in 1693, was found the famous "Alfred Jewel," now in the Ashmolean Museum at Oxford. What exactly this "jewel" was, what it was used for, and what it was meant to commemorate, have never been discovered or decided. It remains a complete mystery, bearing as it does merely the inscription :—AELFRED MEE HEHT GEWYRCAN —Alfred caused me to be made.

After returning to North Petherton, we proceed thence over

the foothills of the Quantocks to Goathurst, with Halswell House, built originally in the Tudor time, but rebuilt in 1639 by Sir Halswell Tynte, in as beautiful a situation as may be found anywhere in Somerset. The neighbouring church contains the seventeenth century monument of Sir Nicholas Halswell, with effigies of his wife and nine children kneeling as mourners (c. 1633): this in the chapel on the north. In the south chapel the Tyntes lie buried. Their strange name was, according to a tradition recorded by Burke, won for the family by a young knight at the battle of Ascalon. "In 1192, at the famous battle of Ascalon, a young knight of the noble house of Arundel, clad all in white, with his horse's trimmings of the same colour, so gallantly distinguished himself that Richard Lionheart declared publicly, after the victory, that the maiden knight had borne himself as a lion, and done deeds equal to those of any six crusaders; whereupon he conferred on him for arms a Lion Argent on a Field Gules between six Crosslets of the First, and for Motto, *Tinctus cruore Saraceno.*"

West of Goathurst, and still among the foothills of Quantock, stands Enmore, with its hideous eighteenth century "castle" and great modern house. The church, however, close by, and outside the village, has a fine tower, an angel supporting a niche upon its southern face, a good Norman doorway upon the south, and a restored Early English chancel.

From Enmore it is a delightful walk in the shadow of the hills and the woods by the byways to Spaxton, a place entirely lovely and delicious. Here the church is wholly Perpendicular save for the fine east window, which is in the earliest Geometrical style, and to about the same time belongs the little window in the north wall. But it is here certainly that we begin to notice a difference both in construction and in decoration from the great series of churches which glorify the moors and the southern and eastern parts of the county. Here we find the usual and beautiful freestone replaced by the local sandstone of the Quantocks, and for this reason among others a ruder and more primitive style of work. In the chancel arcade, indeed, we get frank Devonshire work. But Spaxton church is chiefly interesting, like so many of its western neighbours, by reason of its woodwork and furniture. It has a great deal of fine oak carving; the various panels in the pulpit, for instance, and the equally various bench ends so Flemish in character, and certainly for the most part of the sixteenth century, on one of which we see the figure of a fuller at work with a mallet with two handles. The alms box, too, with its three old locks is to be noted. But our interest in this fine old carpentry must not make us forget the fourteenth century monument in the church, with its effigies of a knight and his lady, as some say, of the Hill family, which held the manor at that time; nor the fine churchyard cross with its two representations of the Rood, with two figures.

Spaxton was once notable for its Agapemone—the Abode of Love, founded in 1859 by Brother Prince, who, born at Bath in 1811, founded here a strange community of "religious visionaries." Brother Prince began as a doctor of medicine, and later took Orders in the Anglican Church. His community, which did not lack funds, whatever else it came short of, at one time numbered two hundred persons, of whom five were parsons. The Abode of Love was surrounded by walls about fifteen feet high enclosing a delicious domain of about five acres. In those early days a flag bearing a "holy" lamb used to fly over the towered gateway when Brother Prince was at home, and I have heard my grandfather say that this fellow would come into Bridgwater in state with outriders and heralds crying out "Blessed is he who cometh in the name of the Lord." For it seems that Brother Prince claimed in some sort to be the Messiah. His heresy was not new, but it was certainly both sinister and corrupt, and it is not easy to see how anyone was really deceived. We are told that his chapel, which was quite without any aspect of religious observance, was "covered with a blue Turkey carpet, and contained blue velvet armchairs and sofas and other drawing-room furniture; the place of the altar being occupied by a billiard table." The place soon got a bad name, and it seems wonderful that it was not suppressed as a disorderly house.

Charlinch, in which parish rather than at Spaxton the Agapemone was founded, has an interesting church with Norman font and south doorway, an Early English chancel arch, fourteenth century east window, and Perpendicular chapel and tower. But the best thing to be had hereabout, save the country itself with its noble views of hill and wood and sea, is the old towered manor house known as Gothelney

House, with its spoiled great hall and a minstrel gallery upon the first floor. The house is still full of old portraits.

Gothelney House lies to the east of Charlinch by Gothelney Green; but another old manor house is to be seen to the north at Blackmoor Manor Farm, with its desecrated chapel and stone staircase. Beautiful old places; they are part of that great heritage of beauty which is so fast passing away.

From Blackmoor he is wise who returns to Bridgwater by way of Cannington, where there is a very venerable church in some ways unique in Somerset, and there, too, at Brymore House, that celebrated rebel John Pym was born.

From outside, the church at Cannington would seem to consist merely of one large undivided chamber of some height, for the roof is unbroken from east to west, and covers nave, chancel, aisles and all. Something like this we have seen before, it is true, in the church at Norton-sub-Hamdon, far away in the south of the county; but at Norton, certainly, there is a chancel arch which divides the church into two parts; here at Cannington there is nothing but the screen. Nevertheless, the church within is very impressive and dignified, and this by reason of its height. Most Somersetshire churches are inclined to be low and unadventurous; here at Cannington we feel the height. It is a church of the Late Perpendicular style, with two fine windows in the chancel, the better of course being the eastern, which is very fine and spacious, and another on the south. The church stands curiously with regard to its tower, which is an earlier building, and to explain this we must take into account, what is after all the most interesting fact about Cannington, namely, that of old it was the home of a community of Benedictine Nuns. This Nunnery, of which nothing remains but the low wall of the enclosure, stood where now the great house with mullioned windows stands, close to the church. This was built long after the Spoliation and—for here, at least, time has brought about its revenge—was in 1807 occupied by a community of French Benedictine Nuns, and is now a Catholic Industrial School.

The Benedictine Nunnery of Cannington was founded in the year 1138 by Robert de Courci, of Stoke Courci, and was situated "hard adnexid to the est of the parish church." The nuns, we are told, were drawn largely from the county families—at Combe Florey there still remains a thirteenth century tombstone of one of them, Dame Maud de Merriete of Hestercombe—and the house was no doubt largely used as a place of retreat. It consisted of a Prioress and about twelve nuns, and at the Spoliation its site was granted to Edward Rogers, in whose family it continued till, about 1670, it was escheated to the Crown, and was granted by Charles II to Thomas Lord Clifford, of Chudleigh, who possibly built the great house, now a school, as I have said, near the church. The legend that Rosamond Clifford, the fair mistress of Henry II, was born here rests upon no secure foundation.

Brymore House, where Pym was born in 1584, lies to the west of Cannington. It was an ancient seat of the Pyms, who had lived here since the time of Edward I.

To the east stands Street Farm, an old manor house which still retains its ancient chapel, a very small one but complete, with carved roof, above which is the priests' chamber reached by a staircase of solid oak. Behind is a panelled room with a window looking into the chapel; altogether an interesting place.

When these few places are done with, we shall eagerly turn to the great moor of which Bridgwater is the true captain and head.

Sedgemoor, Sedge-mere, the sea-lake, I suppose, is not, as we see it, what it was in its most famous days, the days of Alfred, for it is his name which comes first into the mind when we think of the marshes, or even what it was in the Duke of Monmouth's time. But anyone who has spent a wet winter in the lonely and desolate country between Bridgwater and Langport and Taunton, when, not the whole, perhaps, but certainly many thousand acres, even to-day become a great lake, will begin to understand what was the ancient condition of this country, how extraordinary must have been its mystery and, yes, its melancholy beauty; and what sort of a refuge it provided for the great Christian king. Even a wet winter, however, will not show the traveller a really true picture of Sedgemoor, or explain to him the fundamental nature of the country. The study of the Ordnance map, however, will reveal it. It will there be seen that Bridgwater, with the land between it and the sea, though it seems to lie low enough, yet stands higher than the land behind it, which is itself scattered with islands and ridges which rise out of the marsh. In the old days, when the only means of draining all this country was the Parrett, this country behind Bridgwater was always, save perhaps in the height of a very dry summer, a salt-mere, a sea-lake out of which these low ridges rose. There was a small island at Chedzoy, a long curved ridge of good land ran from Weston Zoyland through Middlezoy to Othery, Athelney was a small island, and a long neck of good land was thrust into the mere at East Lyng, another appeared also at North Curry, but apart from these the whole of the country between Langport and Bridgwater, the Poldens and the foothills of the Quantocks, was a vast salt-mere full of mystery and silence. It may be said that, changed as this country has been by drainage and cultivation, there is even now no considerable community established within it save upon those islands and ridges of which I have spoken. And certainly in the seventeenth century, though I suspect the country has changed but little in the interval 'twixt now and then, it was, even upon that Sunday night in July, 1685, when the Rebel Duke went slowly out of Bridgwater to be beaten there, a country of fog, of uncertain and winding ways, of mystery and the little sound, in the vast silence, of running water.

Now the first of those pieces of good land, of those islands and ridges of which I have spoken, is Chedzoy, the second south of Chedzoy is Zoyland, on the western end of which Weston Zoyland stands; it was in the triangle formed by these two villages with Bridgwater that the last battle was fought upon English ground which is known to us all as the battle of Sedgemoor.

It had been noted by an officer of the Horse Guards on the night before, the night of July 5th, that though it was midsummer and the moon was at the full, "the marsh fog lay so thick on Sedgemoor that no object could be discerned there at the distance of fifty paces." In Bridgwater, doubtless on that Sunday night, everyone was in the streets, but outside the town over all that strange country there had fallen with night the accustomed silence, and when the Duke with his guard rode out of the Castle as the clock struck eleven, it was a man already beaten that the children greeted, as, at the head of the Foot, he passed by the lane still called War Lane into the vast emptiness of fog. That silence which was so much a part of the marsh seems to have fallen upon the army too; no man sang, no drum throbbed through the night, no gun was fired. So marched all that host in the darkness and the fog for two hours, till about one o'clock they found themselves upon the open moor, knowing that before them lay the enemy, though exactly where it must have been impossible to say.

They crossed, horse and foot in a narrow column, the great drain of the Black Ditch, they expected it and found the causeway, all in good order. They found the Langmoor Rhine, they expected it, but their guide missed the causeway and they went over, after a delay, in some confusion, in which a pistol went off. That pistol shot in the immense silence, the emptiness, and the fog was enough; it was heard by a patrol of Horse Guards on the watch, who gave the alarm, both to the Cavalry at Weston Zoyland and to the infantry. Nevertheless the rebels were ready; they had but to march on to find the enemy in the confusion of that sudden alarm in the fog. Monmouth bade Grey lead with the Cavalry, and he followed, as before, with the Foot. Grey rode on expecting every minute to get into touch; but before him lay an obstacle of which he knew nothing. What he found was not the enemy, but suddenly, blindly in the fog, another great drain—the Bussex Rhine—and on the other side of this the English army. There is said to have passed between the armies a challenge in the night. "For whom are you?" "For the King." "For what King?" "For King Monmouth." And then we are told there came the old rebel war cry from the Parliament Wars—too good for them or for this—"God with us." Then came a volley of musketry and the rebel horse were off whither they knew not. Came Monmouth and his Foot. They too were ignorant of the Rhine which lay before them, but the men were peasants and they were not to be easily turned back. The musketry duel endured without ceasing for near an hour. Then when the Life Guards and the Blues had come up and scattered what remained of Grey's Horse, who in their flight spread panic among their comrades who drove the ammunition waggons, the battle was decided. Day was dawning; Monmouth mounted and rode from the field.

"Yet," says Macaulay, "his Foot, though deserted, made a gallant stand. The Life Guards attacked them on the right;

the Blues on the left; but the Somersetshire clowns with their scythes and the butt ends of their muskets faced the Royal Horse like old soldiers." When at last they broke, more than a thousand of them lay dead upon the field. So says Macaulay, but in a manuscript account of the battle, preserved in Weston Zoyland church, it is stated that but three hundred perished in the fight, though many more died of their wounds. Those who fell were buried under a great heap of sand that has long since disappeared, though even now bones and skulls are turned up from under the green grass of "The Grave Ground." They were happy who perished in fair fight, and knew not the cruelty of Colonel Kirke and the devilish barbarity of Jeffreys, who, in Somerset alone, is said to have sentenced more people to death than she who is hardly known as Bloody Mary, saw-led to the scaffold or the stake.

It is said that the approach of the Royal army was discovered first, in the affair which ended there on Sedgemoor, from the tower of Chedzoy church, and that through a telescope, which is still preserved in the Museum at Taunton. That tower, though not very high, is of a good and noble sort of the famous Somersetshire kind, double-windowed, of freestone too, for we are on the northern side of the Parrett. The church itself, dedicated to St. Mary, is an Early English building, the nave arcades being very charming examples of that style, as is the south aisle, and the chancel, which originally had a chapel. Chedzoy was a Royal Manor, and why the porch of the church, sometime Early English in style, should bear the initials of Richard Beere, last Abbot but one of Glaston, I do not know. A stone here bears the date 1579, probably the date when the church was rebuilt. The aisle upon the south is very wide and, as I have said, Early English in style. That upon the North is very narrow and in style Perpendicular. But there is no doubt that an Early English aisle formerly stood there, and it does not seem to have been any wider than the present one. In the fifteenth century, the clerestory was added to the nave, probably when the north aisle was rebuilt, and the tower at the west. The holy water stoup, double piscina, and sedilia are also worth notice. But the woodwork in the church should attract us too, the bench ends are dated 1559, bearing Queen Mary's cypher. The pulpit with its linen pattern carving, the lectern dated 1618, and even the roodscreen, which though modern, contains some of the old work. There is, too, by the south door, a good military brass (1490); and the altar frontals here have been made out of a fine old cope discovered under the pulpit. Without, on a stone—a sandstone—in one of the southern buttresses, you may still see where swords were sharpened before Sedgemoor.

Dr. Raleigh (1586–1646), the nephew of Sir Walter and a staunch Royalist, was rector of Chedzoy from 1620. While he was attending the king his rectory-house was plundered by the rebels, his property stolen, and his wife and children driven away. He returned, only to be compelled to fly after the battle of Langport. And when Bridgwater fell he was taken and sent to Chedzoy, a prisoner in his own house. Then some rascal, Henry James was his name, a "nonconformist divine," anxious for the rectory of Chedzoy, carried him off to Ilchester and threw him into gaol. Thence he was taken to Banwell and thence to Wells, where he had held the Deanery since 1641. There he was murdered by the infamous shoemaker, David Barrett, to whose care he had been entrusted, "while attempting to screen from Barrett's impudent curiosity the letter he had written to his wife."

It is a devious way across the marsh from Chedzoy to Weston Zoyland, where the lofty and beautiful triple-windowed Perpendicular church tower stands over the battlefield, from which, indeed, the best idea of the field may be had. Weston Zoyland was a manor of Glaston, and therefore we are not surprised to see Abbot Beere's initials on a buttress of the south chapel, as well as on one of the windows and on a bench end. If Chedzoy church is Early English, Weston Zoyland is in its chancel Decorated, and in the rest Perpendicular in style. It is a fine and spacious building with two large transepts. The north transept is extremely lofty and the nave not only spacious but very long, the clerestory very lovely and graceful. In the north aisle is a fourteenth century monument under a fifteeenth century arch, bearing the effigy of an ecclesiastic.

It was in Weston Zoyland that in 1685 the Royal cavalry were quartered, and here in the church many of the rebel prisoners were temporarily confined. The church has a fine memorial of those times: "Ann account of the ffight that was in Langmore the six of July 1685 between the King's Army and the D. of M.," in which we read: "The Ingagement began between one and two of the clock in the morning. It continued nearly one hour and a halfe. There was killed upon the spott of the King's souldiers sixteen; ffive of them buried in the church, the rest in the churchyard, and they had all of them Christian buriall. One hundred or more of the King's souldiers wounded; of which wounds many died, of which wee have no certaine account. There was killed of the rebels upon the spott aboute 300; hanged with us 22 of which 4 weare hanged in gemmasses [*i.e.* in chains]. About 500 prisoners brought into our church, of which there was 79 wounded and 5 of them died of their wounds in our church.

"The D. of M. beheaded July 15, A.D. 1685."

From Weston Zoyland the road, for we are upon the ridge of the island of Zoyland, goes direct to Middlezoy. Here too, there is a fine and interesting church dedicated to the Holy Ghost. The tower, a storey lower than that at Weston Zoyland, and double-windowed, is still a fine one. The church is chiefly remarkable for the beauty of its Geometrical tracery which is especially delicate in the eastern window. But the woodwork here too is very good and the roof, the pulpit (1606), the Perpendicular screen, the bench ends, the spoilt *miserere* in the chancel, and the old chest with its three locks should be noted. No one will pass quite unmoved the brass in the floor to Louis, Chevalier de Misiers, a Frenchman, who fell in the Royal cause at Sedgemoor:

"Here lyes the body of Louis Chevalier de Misiers, a French gentleman who behaved himself with great courage and gallantry 18 years in the English services, and was unfortunately slaine on ye 6th of July, 1685, at the battle of Weston, where he behaved himself with all the courage imaginable against the king's enemies commanded by ye rebel Duke of Munmouth."

Othery, which lies almost at the southern end of the island of Zoyland, a little to the east of it, is in some way the most interesting of these marsh villages. Its church, which is a very remarkable building, cruciform in plan, with a central octagonal tower, Perpendicular in style, with figures of the Virgin and Child, and St. Michael and the Dragon, is a thirteenth century building altered and in part rebuilt in the two following centuries. It has, however, suffered a good deal from restoration. Its most curious feature, however, is the low side-window, with a squint through the buttress but not looking to the high altar. These low side-windows which occur in several Somersetshire churches, as Middlezoy, are a puzzle, but there is not one in England so great a puzzle as this at Othery, for, in connection with its squint, it is unique of its kind.

From Othery we follow the causeway westward to the most famous spot in all the moor: the island of Athelney and its famous Abbey which Alfred founded in honour of Our Blessed Saviour, St. Peter, St. Paul, and St. Athelwine, to commemorate his safe-keeping and his victory planned there in 879. Nothing remains of that Isle of Nobles, nothing of that glorious Abbey, for the one has been swept out of existence by the better draining of the marsh and the other without a thought, as though it had been but another wife, was swept away by Henry VIII. Yet no one can come to the lonely spot by Boroughbridge, lonely as a battlefield, without recalling those hard and dreadful days in which Alfred plotted to save the west, to save it for Christ, and succeeded. Asser, who came here in Alfred's life-time, thus speaks of it:—"Alfred," says he, "built a monastery for monks in a place called Aethelinga-aeg which is surrounded on all sides by water and by vast and impassable peat bogs. Access can be had to it only by causeways or by a single bridge built and lengthened out with great labour between two elevated forts. Towards the western extremity of the bridge a fort of very great strength and most beautiful construction had been raised by the king."

And William of Malmesbury, writing in the twelfth century, three hundred years after Alfred's day, thus speaks of it:

"Aedalinga-ag is an island surrounded not by the sea but by fens and overwhelming marshes, inaccessible altogether except by boat. On this island there is a forest of Alders of vast extent, where stags and buck and other game find shelter. Of dry land there is barely two acres; a small monastery with houses for the monks stands there. Its founder was King Alfred, who, being driven over the country by the Danes, spent some time here in secure privacy. Here in a dream St. Cuthbert appearing to him and giving him assurance of his restoration, he vowed he would build a monastery to God. Accordingly he erected a church, moderate indeed in size, but as to method of construction singular and novel: for four piers driven into the ground support the whole fabric, four circular chancels being drawn round it. The monks are few in number and indigent; but they are sufficiently compensated for their poverty by the tranquillity of their lives and their delight in solitude."

The Abbey was a Benedictine House, and those buildings which William of Malmesbury described were certainly magnificently replaced later, in 1321, but not a vestige remains here of anything. Robert Hamlyn, the last abbot, with his eight monks surrendered the house to Henry in February 1539, and the site was granted to John Clayton. A stone pillar commemorates Alfred and his foundation: as though we who have utterly destroyed his tomb and his work should want to be reminded of him.

Close by, the village of Boroughbridge lies in the shadow of its conspicuous Mump, upon which is a ruined church dedicated to St. Michael, a rebuilding of the eighteenth century, for it had been garrisoned, held, and spoiled in the Civil War.

From Athelney, or rather Boroughbridge, I made my way to Taunton, spending a long day on the beautiful road. Lyng I saw with its fine double-windowed Perpendicular church tower and its old benches, a pretty church that has been less spoilt than most; and from Lyng I went a little out of my way to see both North Curry and Stoke St. Gregory. Both have fine cruciform churches with central octagonal towers. At Curry, the north door is Norman, and indeed the church is in many ways a very beautiful one that is worth almost any trouble to see ~~; it is called~~ "The Cathedral of the Moors." There are two notable monuments; that in the chancel is of the end of the fourteenth century, and represents a layman of that time; that in the north aisle is more curious, it represents an emaciated figure, perhaps a monk, with a figure I think in the Benedictine habit telling beads below. It may have come from Athelney.

Close by is Slough Farm, a good example of an Elizabethan manor, and probably the successor to the house in which the person represented on the monument in the chancel of the parish church passed his life, for his name appears to have been John of Slough.

What chiefly interested me at Stoke St. Gregory was the notable pulpit with its figures in relief of the Blessed Virgin and Child, and Faith, Hope, Charity, and Time; and the stocks in the churchyard; but the church indeed is fine, though not so fine as that at North Curry.

Having seen these two notable places, I returned to the high road and made my way to Durston. Durston church is not worth a visit; nor, I suppose, will the traveller think it worth his while to note, even in passing, the site of the utterly vanished Priory and Preceptory of Mynchin Buckland, of the Order of St. John of Jerusalem, the only Priory of women that the Order possessed in England. Alas! it is true:

> "Owls do shriek where the sweetest hymns
> Lately were song;
> Toads and serpents hold their dens
> Where the Palmers did throng. . . ."

And no more is the white Christ there now to receive our salutation and love as we trudge into Taunton; and no Ave bell at morning, at noon, and at evening, sounds across the Old Rhine and the lonely moors to Athelney. For summer is gone, and the Garden of Eden makes ready for the Second Spring. And so with these thoughts in my head, I went on through the falling twilight towards the silent towers of Taunton.

CHAPTER XIX

THE VALE OF TAUNTON DEANE

IF Bath is the gate of Somerset, the eastern gate, Taunton is equally the western, and indeed it would be difficult, if not impossible, to enter the county at all, by any western road, without passing through Taunton, which is on the whole, I think, the most characteristic of Somersetshire towns, and in many ways is still, as Clarendon called it, "the fairest, largest, and richest town," in the county.

Well set, upon a rising ground, amid all the wealth and beauty of the delicious country known as Taunton Deane, between the Quantock Hills, the Brendons, the Blackdowns, and the marsh, Taunton is of considerable antiquity, and has played perhaps the first *rôle* in the history of the county. It was founded by King Ine, apparently as a mere fortress, about 720, at once defending and marking the limit of his conquest in the west; but doubtless long before Ine's day, the site that Ine chose upon the Tone, within reach of the great hills and the moors, had been occupied by the British, but it seems altogether unlikely that it ever formed a Roman station. It is a Saxon town, its true founder was Ine. The castle, however, which he founded there was not destined to endure. For it was lost almost at once to the rebel Albriht, and when retaken by the Queen Ethelburga it was, as happened again in the seventeenth century, and for like reasons, dismantled and evacuated, and it is not till nearly two centuries later we learn that it had been granted to the Bishop of Winchester, in whose hands it was to continue until the Civil War. It was the Bishop of Winchester, William Giffard, who, in the time of Henry I, is thought to have founded the great castle which in some sort we still see, about which the town was to grow up, and it was the same great ecclesiastic who about the year 1115 founded a Priory of Austin Canons, the successor to that settlement of clergy, perhaps a monastery, which had existed here certainly since the beginning of the tenth century. It was these two foundations, the one military and the other ecclesiastic, which may be said to have established the prosperity and secured the future of Taunton, and to them doubtless she owes almost everything.

What part, what notable part, Taunton played in the Norman

Taunton and the River Tone.

Conquest, if indeed she played any part at all, is unknown to us, nor does she appear very prominently in the history of England till that pathetic impostor, Perkin Warbeck, who claimed to be Richard Duke of York, the second son of Edward IV, landed in Cornwall.

> And all the path for "the rose" to walk
> Was strewn with flowers and posies. . . .
> I was the milk-white rose of York,
> The rose of all the roses.

At the head of some six thousand men, Perkin Warbeck laid siege to Exeter, and, failing to take it, fell back upon Taunton, which he held till he heard that Lord Daubeney was at Glaston and in full march against him. At midnight, upon September 21st, 1497, he stole out of the Castle with some sixty horsemen, but, soon leaving them behind, he rode on with three companions to Beaulieu, in Hampshire, where he took sanctuary.

> "And after that, what brooks it to say
> Whither I rode, or why?
> I was as loath to leave my play
> And fight, as now to die.
>
> "For I was not made for wars or strife
> And blood and slaughtering;
> I was only a boy that loved his life,
> And I had not the heart of a king."

Perhaps Warbeck was not of the stuff to break the impudent rascality of the Tudors, who had no more right to the throne of England than you and I—no, nor as much. But

> The white rose of fair England
> Turned red on Bosworth field. . . .

and there is not one of us that has lived in England since but has lived to regret it.

Taunton was to see many a misery follow upon that swift and sudden nightmare of 1497. In 1545 she saw her priory suppressed and its site and possessions granted to that land-jobber, Matthew Colthurst, and soon thereafter she was deprived of her religion. Then, indeed, begun the troublous days in which Taunton bore no inconsiderable part here in the west. For Taunton was taken and retaken by both sides in the great Rebellion, and in 1645 she was the scene of perhaps the most spirited sieges in all that long disaster, I mean the fine defences of Taunton made by Blake in 1645, when, though ten thousand came against him, he would not think of surrender, and when all his ammunition had gone, and he and all in the place were starving, declared he "would eat his boots before he yielded." Temporary relief was brought to the heroic garrison by a small company of men, under Colonel Weldon, upon Sunday, May 11th, 1645, and for many years we are told the anniversary of that day was kept as a festival in

Taunton, a sermon being preached in St. Mary Magdalen to commemorate the "great deliverance." Finally, on July 3rd, the approach of Fairfax dispersed the besiegers, to be defeated at Langport on July 10th.

Almost exactly forty years later, on June 18, 1685, the rebel Duke of Monmouth rode into Taunton from Chard and was accorded an amazing welcome. On the 20th of that month, he was proclaimed King in the market place. Upon the 10th of the following month Colonel Kirke and his "lambs" drove in some two hundred prisoners from Sedgemoor and whilst he ate his supper at the "White Hart" thirty of them were hanged for his delight upon the sign-post. But this was by no means all. The Bloody Assize had yet to come and the infamous Jeffreys, who presided in the Great Hall of the Castle, condemned to be hanged, drawn, and quartered some two hundred persons, so that Bishop Ken remonstrated with the King that Somerset "smelt of death." Worse still was the vast sale of over eight hundred English folk into slavery in the West Indies and the public floggings of women and the sale of Justice by the Court of England. No wonder that even such a King as Dutch William was welcomed in the West; the devil himself would not have lacked cheers after Kirke and Jeffreys and the rest had passed by.

So much for the story of Taunton. Of the town itself what remains? Unfortunately very little that is old. Of the Castle—now happily in the possession of the Somersetshire Archaeological Society, who have established there a museum—something remains, but hardly more than a shell, including an outer gate, a square block of building, dating perhaps from the time of Edward I, and the great Hall dating from 1577. All, however, has suffered from restoration, inevitable, I suppose, but none the less unfortunate. You cannot restore a building any more than you can restore a flower or a tree, you can only conserve it or destroy it.

Nevertheless, the Castle is very well worth a visit, and the more so as it contains a fine museum which, however, is far too ready to accept all sorts of curiosities. It should properly confine itself to those things which belong to Somerset, and even so only a limited number of specimens should be on exhibition at one time, for such things grow enormously in beauty and interest by the art with which they are shown. I suppose we shall never understand this in England; the British Museum is itself as great a sinner as any. The art of exhibition is not yet appreciated in England.

Something then of real interest may be said to remain of the old Castle of Taunton. Of its contemporary foundation, the Priory of Austin Canons of SS. Peter and Paul, practically nothing is left—a dilapidated but still beautiful Barn, not far from St. James's Church.

This Priory was the religious head of Taunton and the noble parish church of St. Mary Magdalen was, as it were, but a chapel which it served, for Bishop Gifford granted to his Priory "all the churches of Taunton together with their chapels and all appurtenances." It is reasonable then to suppose that already in the twelfth century a church stood where now St. Mary Magdalen's stands and the fact that in 1244 the Archdeacon held his court in this church would suggest that it was of some size and importance. The church we see, however, is a Perpendicular building of the fifteenth and sixteenth centuries, while the admired double-windowed tower is, as we see it, a work of our own day, an "accurate copy," as it is said, of the noble tower it has replaced. The church is a very spacious, if cold, building with double aisles, lofty clerestoried nave, and very lofty chancel. The piers in the south aisle would seem to be Early English work, but the most notable thing in the church is the font, splendidly carved with figures of the apostles and others. The oak roof over the nave is also fine, and the pulpit dates from 1633.

The church of St. James would seem, in its foundation, to be as old as St. Mary Magdalen's. Certainly a church stood on its site in 1180 and fragments of this Norman building have been found. The present church is of the early fifteenth century so far as the nave and the north aisle go, but even these have suffered from restoration and the rest of the church has been rebuilt; even the double-windowed tower which is a fine one, and rather like, though a long way off, the masterpiece we shall find later at Bishop's Lydeard, has been rebuilt and that in 1871–3.

But if the Churches of Taunton are disappointing, there are in the town, always so cheerful a place and full of good-will, more than one old building which deserves notice, as the old

Grammar School in Corporation Street, now part of the Municipal Buildings, the two fine half-timbered houses in the Market Place, and the two almshouses in West Street.

Taunton, too, of old boasted a Leper Hospital, dating certainly from the thirteenth century. It was dedicated in honour of the Holy Ghost and St. Margaret. This happily survived the change of religion, and we may still see it at the present time, for it is now an almshouse in the eastern part of the town called East Reach. The old thatched houses seem, after all, the most appealing things in the place, and still bear Abbot Beere's monogram and arms, though why, I cannot tell. Of the Carmelite convent not a stone remains.

One always thinks of Taunton as a town of towers, for whether you come in by train, or march in by road, it is the tall towers you see and wonder at and yet not one of them is really, as we see it, a hundred years old. The true towers of this part of the county we shall see later at Bishop's Lydeard and Kingston and Staple Fitzpaine, things one cannot forget, and as fine in their way as the noble series that glorifies the county on the other side of the Parrett.

Meanwhile, there lie about Taunton many fair villages which no one should miss. The first I explored was Ruishton, to the east. Here I found a great, but unfinished tower with double belfry windows, not, I think, a pleasing example, and the church, too, was disappointing. I fared better at Creech St. Michael, perhaps a mile further, set right upon the Tone, and at the head of one of the long arms of the great marsh. Here the church looked at first sight like a Perpendicular building, though parts of the tower seemed to be Norman. On examination I found that the church was once a cruciform building with central tower, and that the noble nave, and indeed all the walls of the building, were of the twelfth century, two of the arches of the tower being Early English, though the western arch was Perpendicular. The arch of the south porch was, I found, also Early English, but the rest of the church proved to be what I had first taken it all to be, and very good of its kind. The north chapel, where there is a monument to a member of the Cuffe family (1597) is curious with its gallery in the thickness of the wall, but not pleasing. The roof, however, is a very fine piece of work as is what remains of the rood screen. Without, over the western window, is a representation of the Blessed Trinity, and in the churchyard are two great yews under one of which the village stocks remain. Close by the church is what remains of a fine old house, now a farm.

From Creech, the day being young, I came in the early sunshine of a perfect summer morning to Thornfalcon, where I hoped for much because of its beautiful name, forgetting for the moment that in Somerset are so many beautiful names that they are no help to the traveller; and truly, at Thornfalcon I found nothing, or next to nothing. But a little further, going south at Ash Cross, I came upon one of those rare wayside Crosses which are now so blind and dumb. In France it would have borne, for certain, the invariable salutation—

Ave Crux Spes Unica.

but here, as invariably, there is nothing.

So I went on to Thurlbear which is all in a garden and there I found a church, small as I hoped, with fine Norman nave and arcades, a rare and admirable thing if you think of it, hereabout, and always wherever met with to be worshipped, because such a thing stays to remind us of a double salvation; that which concerns the soul which we share with all Christendom and that which concerns England which is particular to us. For the Normans came in when we were like wood and lathe, and saving us from our heaviness and stupidity, made possible all that very glorious history down whose shining avenues we look with such pride . . . and with such regret.

Now at Thurlbear the hills called me, even the long ridge of the Blackdowns, and I went on to Staple Fitzpaine, and there I found that very noble and beautiful double-windowed tower which I have mentioned already. No man can desire a better, I think, for though it is not very high, it is very nobly formed and its decoration is worthy of it, crowned as it is with a cluster of tufted spears, brave and graceful. And here too I found the Normans, for they built the south door of Staple Fitzpaine church, and no doubt at all they built a church too to which it led, and I wish the fifteenth century had left it so: and if that could not be, I wish our fathers had left whatever they found alone, for they have certainly spoiled whatever it was. Almost the only thing to care for at Staple Fitzpaine was the screen, not the spoiled screen before the chancel, which is not the original rood-screen at all, but comes from Bickenhall church, another "*small Norman structure demolished by a late incumbent*," but that which parts the vestry from the chancel, and which would appear to be all that is left of the rood-screen of this church.

I did not linger in Staple Fitzpaine, for the hills called me, as I say, and I was for the Blackdowns and Castle Neroche, from which I hoped to see all Somerset between the Mendips and Exmoor, as indeed I did. The Castle is an earthwork of very great strength and possibly held, though this no longer seems probable, an old trackway along the Blackdowns. It was mainly used and perhaps constructed, as recent excavations have proved, by the Normans, and no doubt was one of their strong places by which they held Somerset and the road to the West—to Exeter, and it probably saw its last fight in the days of Stephen.

When I had had my fill of Neroche I went on over Staple Hill above the woods and so to Widcombe where the Culm rises, a Devon stream, and down to Pitminster with its octagonal tower with a spire over it—a large and beautiful place—and so towards evening I came to Trull and was satisfied.

Trull church in itself is interesting, yet nothing to boast of, but it has perhaps the finest old oak fittings of any church in West Somerset. It is for the most part a fifteenth century building, with an arch and window at the tower end, of the thirteenth century. But the glory of the church is its woodwork, its great screen, its bench ends and its beautiful pulpit. And yet there is one other thing I have no intention of forgetting—the fine glass in the chancel; in the east window our Lord, the Blessed Virgin, and St. John; in the south window St. Michael, St. Margaret, and St. George. For this alone the church would be worth a visit; but we have beside the notable woodwork of which I have spoken. Undoubtedly the chief glory of the church is its rood-screen with the wings north and south of it. This is of the Devonshire type, but it has, alas! lost its tracery. It crosses the nave in three very wide bays, which of old, of course, were divided by a great central mullion in each. The screen, however, still keeps its elaborate fan vaulting, its ornaments and its four cornices. No doubt, as at

Winsford, a painted rood stood over this screen upon the great beam above it, which still shows a tympanum under the roof. On both sides of this rood-screen is an aisle-screen of most rare design and beauty of tracery; all alike are a joy to look upon.

As for the pulpit, I know not where to look for its like, for

Trull Church, near Taunton. Fifteenth Century Pulpit.

it is not only a noble thing in itself, but it boasts five statuettes, representing St. John with chalice and dove, and the Four Doctors of the Latin Church—St. Gregory the Great, a Pope St. Jerome in his Cardinal's robes, St. Ambrose of Milan, and St. Austin of Hippo; and all around are little

figures of saints and angels—alas! spoiled in the time of Edward VI, when the larger figures were saved by being removed and buried. The number of saints represented in the church may possibly be explained by its dedication to All Saints.

The bench-ends, too, which are said when in their proper order to represent "a mediaeval procession," are worthy of notice; they date from 1510. Here, too, in the churchyard the stocks remain. And the following pretty memorial verse should be noted over a child's tomb, dated 1658.

> "A spotless child lies here within
> Whom fate allowed not time to sin.
> But after death had given it rest,
> Christ took into His arms and blest;
> Where now among that choir on high
> It sings its own sweet lullabie.
> The mother to its earthlie bed
> Bequeathed this stonie coverlet."

Fine things though there be, and in a fine country, too, to the south and west of Taunton, neither they nor the country may compare, of course, with what we have to the west.

> "What ear so empty is that hath not heard the sound
> Of Taunton's fruitful dean? not match'd by any ground. . . ."

and it is certainly at its best and its most fruitful "where seaward Quantock stands," and the Brendon hills close towards Exmoor; the days I have spent in these dear places can never be forgotten. And first upon that road stands Norton Fitzwarren, under its dark hill crowned with that vast British camp. Here at Norton, unfortunately, the church has been largely rebuilt, but the tower is still notable, and seems, standing here at the very gateway, to welcome us to West Somerset. The best thing within the church is the screen work of the three screens, the chancel screen, that across the north aisle, and that on the north side of the chancel. The first two are fan-vaulted on the western side, and doubtless are in their original place, but have lost their eastern vaulting, and have otherwise been tampered with. Their tracery, however, is strange and beautiful, as are the canopies between the uprights and the very rich cornices, the lowest being carved with the legend of St. George and the Dragon. The Rood over the very beautiful doorway is modern.

Leaving Norton I went, in the divine morning sunshine, through the fairest of countries to Bishop's Lydeard, which gets its name from the fact that Edward the Elder bestowed it upon the biographer of Alfred, Asser of Sherborne, in 904. Its noble blood-red, double-windowed tower is the finest in all this country, a thing to delight one in the memory of having seen it. It was, perhaps, the first of such towers to rise in all this rich vale of Taunton Deane. This as I say, rejoiced me, for I was full of the morning; so that I saluted the beautiful churchyard cross, a fourteenth century work, still with its calvary and east and west our Lord in Majesty, and the Resurrection, and in the lateral niches a figure of a Bishop, perhaps Asser, and a figure of a monk; upon the shaft is St. John the Baptist.

The church too is fine, and especially rich in its carved work. The screen is rich and noble, beautiful with fan vaulting and lovely cornices; all along it is carved, and this in the sacred Latin tongue, *Credo in Deum Patrem omnipotentem factorem coeli et terrae*—the Apostles' Creed. The bench ends too are fine, and should be examined, for there are to be found scenes of hunting and venery, as well as a carpenter, a miller and his windmill, a sailor and his ship. The pulpit, too, is beautiful and old. There is a brass in the south transept of the end of the sixteenth century. The village cross should also be noted for it has three decorated niches and in each figures of the Blessed Virgin and her little Son.

From Bishop's Lydeard, which is so fair I was loathe to be gone, I made my way by Halse and Fitzhead to Milverton. Halse, which lies always in view of the Quantocks, which, I think, nowhere appear so lovely as here, has a very curious and interesting if a small church, with a Norman or Transitional font and an east window full of Flemish glass, which is dated 1548 and bears the arms of the Van Hoynfen family of Bruges. This comes from Florence to Halse as the gift of Mr. John Sanford of Nynehead Court. We see there, among other subjects: St. Catherine with her wheel, the Mass of St. Gregory, St. Peter turned back by our Lord when he would have fled away, Susanna and the Elders, Tobit and the Archangel, and St. Anne with the Virgin and Child. The most notable thing in the church, however, is the rood-screen, a very beautiful and rich example of early sixteenth century work. In the vestry is a rough hewn Peter's Pence chest.

Another fine rood-screen will be found at Fitzhead, about a mile west of Halse, as well as an old manor house, Fitzhead Court.

And so I came to Milverton. Milverton may say what it likes, it is a village, with—Norton had prophesied truly—as thoroughly West Somerset a church tower as I could hope for. It stands very well, upon a hill, and for all its rude Exmoor air is good enough. The church is very fine, with a curious plan and is worth some trouble to see. The north wall of the church is obviously longer than the south wall, apparently because of the angle at which the tower stands with regard to it; and yet church and tower seem to be of the same date. The fact that the north side of the church is longer than the south has, apparently, set all the piers of the nave at variance, no two being opposite one to the other. The most interesting things in the church, however, are the bench ends and the choir stalls, which seem to be Flemish work of the earlier part of the sixteenth century. It is suggested that a "a band of Flemish carvers went through Somerset about 1540, stopping for a time and working at different places."

But perhaps the most interesting thing in Milverton is the vicarage house, a perfect example of a small house of about 1500. It is a popular belief that this beautiful little place was built by Cardinal Wolsey. No evidence has ever been found to support this pious belief.

In good hopes I went on to Wiveliscombe; but of Wiveliscombe I have nothing to say; it is not, perhaps, worth a visit save that it is the key to three fine things; the church of Huish Champflower, the country in which Chipstable lies, and the screen at Raddington; these are worth some trouble to see, as indeed are the neglected hills among which they lie; but of these more when we get to Dulverton.

So from Wiveliscombe I made my way at last southward over the hills to Langford Budville, where they have for centuries been endeavouring to frighten the devil away to the neighbouring village of Thorne St. Margaret. It seems that this charitable custom, however, is not peculiar to Langford, but was practised also at Wellington, but there upon Midsummer day, while here it was done on the Feast of St. Peter and St. Paul. Professor Boyd Dawkins thus describes the ritual: "Once every year the people met in the churchyard and formed a ring round the church. They advanced towards the church, and on the side opposite the door the ring broke, and the two leaders—something in the style of the dance 'Sir Roger de Coverley'—went straight to the wall and were followed by the others. Then they made their way back to the entrance to the churchyard, and when they got there they gave three shouts." This was known as "clipping the tower," and would seem to be of pagan origin.

Langford church is nothing to boast of, all its interest lying rather in what is curious, as that old custom, than in what is beautiful. Thus, the one thing you must not miss in the church is the needle and thread, the needle a foot long, on the bottom of one of the capitals in the south arcade. You may debate over the meaning of this for hours, and yet not find a solution. The local solution is that the church must have been built by a woman.

From Langford it is better to go on to Wellington by Chipley with its avenues of limes, where Locke wrote part of his "Essay on the Human Understanding," and to use that not unpleasing place where they manufacture "woollens" as a centre from which to explore the neighbouring villages, which are full of good things. The only thing in Wellington that should delay you is the parish church, with its noble great freestone double-windowed tower. Within, the church is lofty and spacious, but the chancel and north aisle are rebuildings of 1848; the Early English window in the former, however, is preserved, and it is worthy of our best attention as an early example of tracery. The tomb with recumbent effigy, now at the east end of the north aisle, is also early, probably of the first years of the fourteenth century. But the church as a whole is of the fifteenth century. The fine Elizabethan tomb with canopy and effigies of Lord Justice Popham and his wife should be noticed, for it is a fine example of its kind, though the paint is all modern.

It is curious, and, I think, has never been explained, why the Iron Duke chose to take his title from this little Somersetshire town, but so it was, and the Somersetshire people in acknowledgment of the compliment raised the great obelisk we see upon the highest point on the Blackdown Hills. As originally proposed, this tower was to have been crowned with a bronze equestrian statue of the Duke; but probably the subscriptions did not run to this; at any rate, it remains without its figure.

I said there were many interesting things to see in the country around Wellington. One of the best of these is the glorious old manor house of Cotehay, some four miles south-west of the town. Cotehay, Cothay, locally known as Cothay Abbey, is one of the best examples of an Early Tudor manor house in this part of Somerset. It is largely unaltered, and the door, the great Hall with its gallery and screen, its fireplaces and daïs, and withdrawing room beyond, are all perfect; the gatehouse is partly destroyed, but retains its picturesque bell-turret. It was of old the home of the Bluetts.

Two miles beyond Cothay is Greenham Barton, another house of the Bluett family, dating in part from the fourteenth century, but for the most part a building of the time of Henry VIII. The windows to the right of the porch are beautiful, as is the great fireplace in the Hall. Behind across the court is another building that may well have formed part of the great house. Another beautiful but Jacobean house lies by West Buckland to the east of Wellington, Gerbestone manor house; it should not be missed.

Before finally leaving Wellington, every traveller must go to Nynehead church, where there is a fine screen and some fine old (?) glass in the east window. But the main attraction is the collection of Italian sculpture of the fifteenth century, Robbia terra-cottas, and a relief of the Blessed Trinity, said to be by Mino da Fiesole. Certainly these are strange things to find in a Somersetshire village.

CHAPTER XX

THE QUANTOCKS AND THEIR VILLAGES

THE Quantock Hills, those romantic and beautiful mountains some twelve miles long, I suppose, from Hestercombe above Taunton Deane to East Quantockshead, where they fall slowly into the sea—nowhere more than four miles wide, though often more than a thousand feet high (at Will's Neck, indeed, more than twelve hundred)—are best explored from two main centres upon the railway, Bridgwater on the north and east and Taunton on the south, with the help of two minor centres based upon these, Nether Stowey upon the Bridgwater side, and Crowcombe, or better perhaps Bicknoller, upon the west. At Nether Stowey the Inn is excellent, and though neither Crowcombe nor Bicknoller has anything so good to offer, the Inns in both are comfortable if rather primitive.

Though the escarpment of the Quantocks is upon all sides sudden and steep, it is much steeper upon the west than upon the Bridgwater side, but any loss of beauty that this might seem to involve is more than made up by the fact that here to the north and east the range is everywhere broken by innumerable and thickly-wooded combes, from King's Cliff by North Petherton to Hodder's Combe beyond Holford towards the sea. These beautiful valleys that come so reluctantly down from the high hills are nowhere to be found upon the steeper escarpment of Quantock to the west, but there, from Cothelstone to Crowcombe and beyond, the hills are so often glorified with hanging woods, and their form is so noble, that we by no means regret the gentler beauty of the eastern slope. In fact, wherever you may be upon Quantock, of pleasure and of beauty you may always take your fill. If anything is lovelier than the great road, for instance, from Kingston to Enmore on the way from Taunton to Bridgwater, it is the corniche road over the sea by St. Audries and up into the Holford Woods past Alfoxden. And then, every byway is a path in paradise.

With so great an embarrassment of riches to choose from, it is always a little difficult to know where to begin; but if the traveller is established in Bridgwater, he will do best to begin with Nether Stowey and to explore all that part of Quantock which is beautiful with combes and woods—Cockercombe, Quantock Combe, Seven Wells, Rams Combe, Bin Combe, Holford, and Hodders Combe. And all this country is sacred to poetry, too, for here Coleridge and Wordsworth stayed in 1797. On the other hand, if the traveller is established at Taunton he will have a line of railway to help him, and he will find that there is nothing lovelier to be found in the world than Cothelstone, Crowcombe, Halsway, and Bicknoller; and from here, too, the Brendons to the west are his, with all their villages — Combe Florey, Lydeard St. Lawrence, Tolland, Elworthy, and Stogumber—pleasant places where one may be at peace and the summer is long and loathe to go.

For myself I began my exploration by making my way from Bridgwater in that motor omnibus of theirs to Nether Stowey under the blackness of Great Bear and loftier Dowsborough.

Nether Stowey, a stronghold, it would seem, in prehistoric times, for its great earthworks, where the Normans built a Castle, are still to be discerned, is mainly interesting to us because Father Parsons the Jesuit was born there in 1546, and in 1796 Coleridge and Wordsworth came to live there, and upon these hills were composed both "The Ancient Mariner" and "Peter Bell." These memories and the fifteenth century Manor House known as Stowey Court are all that the little place can boast of, the church being mediocre, and containing nothing at all remarkable.

Robert Parsons was the son of the Nether Stowey blacksmith. He was born in 1546, and the parson seeing his quickness and promise, helped to pay the expenses of his education, sending him first to school at Stogursey, and later, for three years to Taunton. When he was eighteen the boy went up to Oxford, and was elected a fellow of Balliol in 1568, becoming for a time bursar and dean of his college. He took, twice over, it is said, the oath of royal supremacy, but left Oxford for some unexplained reason connected with the religious controversy of the day in 1574. He went to study medicine in Padua, fully persuaded of one thing, namely, that he would never be a papist. But he had got no further than Louvain, when it appears he was received into the Church, so that he had no sooner arrived in Padua than he set out for Rome, where he offered himself to that great Company of Jesus, those soldiers who had before all else determined to hurl back the Reformation. In this business Parsons, who was ordained in 1578, was heartily ready to take his part, and in 1580 he left Rome with Edmund Campion and several others on a forlorn adventure, the conversion of England. He entered this country at Dover disguised as a soldier—which he was—"in a suit of buff laid with gold lace with hat and feather suited to the same," and the whole of the rest of his life, till his death in Rome in 1610, was perilously devoted to the restoration of England by persuasion or by force to the Catholic Faith. To this end he urged with all his powers and influence the Spanish attack upon England, and his very great intellectual powers were all bent to the same end, and, as we know, altogether without success. The road which began at Nether Stowey led him a long way and a dangerous way to the grave; surely he must often have thought with longing of these great and peaceful hills.

But in Nether Stowey the blacksmith's son is wholly forgotten, and I am not convinced that Coleridge, who lived here during the years 1796–98 in the last house on the left going west, or Wordsworth, who to be near him came to Alfoxden close by, are any better remembered.

Coleridge, who had been living at Bristol, where indeed his first volume of poems was published in April, 1796, in the January of that year had been travelling in the north to gain subscribers for his new venture "The Watchman." He had also become an occasional preacher in Unitarian chapels—at his first performance in Bath appearing in "blue coat and white waistcoat"—when a friend found him this cottage at Nether Stowey for seven pounds a year and in the winter of 1796 he settled there with Lloyd.

The friend who had found him this place was Poole the local tanner, who proved to be one of Coleridge's staunchest allies, and who lies in the parish church, where there is a mural tablet to his memory, on which he is described as the friend of "Wordsworth, and Davy, Southey and Coleridge."

Coleridge himself describes his "house." "Our house is better than we expected. There is a comfortable bedroom and sitting room for C. Lloyd and another for us, a room for Nanny, a kitchen and outhouse. Before our door a clear brook runs of very soft water; and in the background there is a nice well of fine spring water. We have a very pretty garden and large enough to find us vegetables and employment, and I am already an expert gardener and both my hands exhibit a callum as testimonials of their industry. We have likewise a sweet orchard, and at the end of it T. Poole has made a gate which leads into his garden."

Wordsworth came to Alfoxden, not far away to the west of Stowey, in a lovely situation, "the principal inducement being Coleridge's society." And here he tells us,

> "That summer, under whose indulgent skies
> Upon smooth Quantocks airy ridge we roved
> Unchecked, or loitered mid her sylvan courts;
> Thou, in bewitching words with happy heart,
> Didst chaunt the vision of the Ancient Man,
> The bright-eyed Mariner, and rueful woes
> Didst utter of the Lady Christabel."

Nor is Coleridge behind his friend in praise of the place,

> "And now, beloved Stowey, I behold
> Thy church tower and, methinks, the four huge elms
> Clustering, which mark the mansion of my friend;
> And close beside them, hidden from my view,
> Is my own lowly cottage, where my babe
> And my babe's mother dwell in peace."

And here the two poets contrived and wrote that famous volume called *Lyrical Ballads*, published in September, 1798, which the *Ancient Mariner*, according to Wordsworth, wrecked.

Alfoxden Manor, which Wordsworth took—the rent, says De Quincey, consisted in "keeping the house in repair"[1]—lies some three miles west of Stowey, and to reach it we pass

[1] As a fact, however, Wordsworth paid £23 a year for the place. See agreement printed in *T. Poole and His Friends*, i, 125.

the old inn, now a boarding house, the Castle of Comfort, and, a little south of the road, the pretty village of Dodington, with its beautiful old Elizabethan manor house, and the still prettier village of Holford with its picturesque church, and all the way is glorious with views of the channel, and, on a clear day, of the Mendip Hills.

At Alfoxden, in the beginning of 1798, Hazlitt found Wordsworth there, and describes him as "a gaunt, quaintly dressed being," not unlike his own "Peter Bell." Here, however, and in the great hills he composed "We are Seven," "The Idiot Boy," and indeed most of those poems which appeared in *Lyrical Ballads*, and he always regarded this as "a very pleasant and productive time of my life." His sister, too, bears witness to the natural beauty in which they found themselves. "Wherever we turn we have woods, smooth downs, and valleys with small brooks running down them, through green meadows hardly ever intersected with hedgerows, but scattered over with trees. The hills that cradle these villages are either covered with fern or bilberries, or oak-woods—walks extend for miles over the hill tops, the great beauty of which is their wild simplicity."

And indeed, these "walks over the hill tops" are perhaps the greatest delight to be had in this beautiful country. Any one of these famous and lovely combes will lead one to the broad back of Quantock, smooth turf, or heather-clad moorland, with here and there a great wood of oak or beech, as above Holford. The road I love most, though it is not perhaps finer than any other, is that which runs up just to the east of the Castle of Comfort, and brings you in a mile or so on to the great empty upland; but better are the roadless combes, and perhaps best of all is Cockercombe.

No matter by what hill you come, when you have reached the upland you will find a great track running roughly the whole length of the hills from Beacon Hill over the sea, to Cothelstone Hill above Taunton Deane. Here a man may have pleasure any day in the year unless, indeed, a gale of wind be blowing, when he would find it hard to keep his feet; but wet or fine, sun or shadow, morning or evening, here is liberty, and if anywhere in the world "day and night, brother, both sweet things and likewise a wind on the heath." And when the traveller—if indeed he be a traveller and not a mere slave of the train--would leave the northern side of Quantock, with its delicious combes and fair far views of the green fields, the round hills, the sea and the Welsh mountains, for the southern side which looks ever upon dark Exmoor, let him choose one of these paths for his road. Let him cross Quantock afoot and find the great trackway under Thorncombe Barrow between Holford and Bicknoller, and then choosing his time for pleasure and making sure if he can of fine weather, let him travel along it on foot or on horseback, a whole delicious day by Thorncombe Barrow and Hurley Beacon and the great hill over Crowcombe by Will's Neck, which is the loftiest of all, and Lydeard Hill, till he can descend, and by a good road, through the great hanging woods to Cothelstone. Or, if he be not spent, let him continue along the road round to the south of Cothelstone Hill with its column, and crossing the Bridgwater road by Broomfield Hill, let him go on to Broomfield, a famous place, and find the valley, and a bed too, at Kingston in the vale.

But this is counsel of perfection which only the young can profit by. For those who must fear fatigue, the hills from this side naturally divide themselves into two parts, one upon either side of the Taunton Bridgwater road across them. That part which lies east of this road is best visited from Taunton; that which lies to the west from Crowcombe or Bicknoller.

Coming into the hills from Taunton a man will go by Kingston, and so quickly into the high places.

At Kingston there is a church set upon the first rising ground of the hills, with a very fine double-windowed western tower, almost exactly like that at Staple Fitzpaine, save that it is quite different in colour, for this is red, while that is grey. The oldest part of the church here is the nave and the aisles, which are in the Early English style of the thirteenth century. The chancel, which is fine and spacious, dates, like the tower, from the end of the fifteenth century, as does the noble south porch, with its fan tracery and its niche for a figure, probably of the Blessed Virgin, in whose honour the church is dedicated. To this period, too, is due the fine parapet without, and the font and beautiful carved benches within. At the east end of the south aisle is a fine altar tomb, certainly of about the end of the fourteenth century. It is supposed to be that of John de la Warre, who at the battle of Poitiers in 1356 helped to capture the king of France. The Warres were in old times the great family in this neighbourhood. Their home was at Hestercombe, a little to the south-east of Kingston, now belonging to the Portmans.

From Kingston the road takes to the hills, and is beautiful all the way because of them. A lane upon the right, steep but not too bad, brings one in half a mile to Broomfield church, where in the churchyard is a fine old cross of the early fifteenth century, happily unrestored. The church as we see it dates from the fifteenth century, and is to be especially noticed for its fine bench ends, very like those at Kingston. In the old glass in the chancel you may still read: *In principio erat verbum et verbum erat apud Deum*—the first words of the last Gospel at Mass; and again, as though the last four hundred years had been but a dream: *Orate pro bono statu Alicie Reskemer.*

Over beyond Broomfield, westward past Ducks Pool, stands the curious triangular Camp of Ruborough, not a Roman but a barbarian entrenchment.

From Broomfield that is a good way which brings you almost to Timbercombe across the valley, and then, where the ways meet, down, down, all the way, through the hanging woods to the marvel of Cothelstone.

Cothelstone is unique. There is no old manor house in all Somerset more charming or more beautiful than Cothelstone Old Manor, and I know not where I am to find a tomb nobler or lovelier than that one finds in the little church there behind the house; and I am very sure there is not in all England a finer tree than the famous walnut here, unless it be the great elm in the churchyard.

Cothelstone is to be loved for so many things; to begin with, I like so much the great gateway at the end of the avenue, where Jeffreys hanged two of Monmouth's fellows because Lord Stawell, whose home this was, protested against his devilish cruelty. One is reminded of another barbarian—Bismarck—wiping his boots all over the carpets at Versailles. Then I cannot say how much I like the arched gateway, through which one gets so fair a glimpse of the beautiful house across the court with its two green lawns within. And best of all I like the house which stands about that fair court, and in spite of Blake, who partially destroyed it in the Civil War, still offers so fair and so fine a face to the beautiful world about it.

And then there is the church, dedicated to St. John Baptist. This for the most part is in the Perpendicular style, but it is full of wonderful things, a noble font, good bench ends, and some old glass in which we see St. Cuthbert of Durham, St. Thomas Cantelupe, St. Dunstan with the famous tongs, St. Thomas à Becket, and St. Aldehelm, and, best of all, by the

Cothelstone. Manor House and Church.

Norman pier which bears two arches opening into the south chapel, two tombs, one of the fourteenth and one of the seventeenth century. The latter is probably that of Sir John Stawell, who died in 1603, and his wife, the daughter of Sir Thomas Dyer. The other—and it is beyond compare, an altar tomb with effigies, lovely and exquisite without boast or pretentiousness, fragments of colour still upon it—is probably that of Sir Matthew Stawell and his wife. He died in 1379.

I can never leave Cothelstone, though it be for Crowcombe, without regret, it is so exactly one's ideal of what an English home should be, and yet Crowcombe is fair enough under its hanging woods, gathered about its very noble church and its exquisite fourteenth century cross upon its calvary, the most graceful, I think, of all Somerset crosses, like a lily towering there, bearing its white immaculate bloom.

The church is interesting; for the most part as we see it a building of the fifteenth century, with a fine fourteenth century font carved with the following subjects: God the Father in benediction; a man praying; the vision of Zachariah; St. Anne teaching the Blessed Virgin; a Bishop; the Blessed Virgin enthroned; a Bishop; a Knight praying. The north aisle is later, having been built by Thomas Carew in 1655, probably to take the place of an aisle or chapel earlier than the rest of the church; while the south aisle is exquisite, the best thing in the church. The bench ends are remarkable and the fine vaulting in the south porch should be noted; there is a chamber above it. The tower has been restored. It once carried a stone spire some eighty feet high, but this fell in December 1725 when it was struck by lightning, and never was rebuilt. In the churchyard is a fine cross with three figures upon the shaft, to wit, St. John Baptist, a bishop, and a nun.

Close to the church, on the opposite side of the road, is a remarkable building recently restored. This is the church house, and it dates from long before the change in religion. Crowcombe Court is the home of the Carews, and you may lie awake all night in the inn hard by listening to the shrieking of the peacocks there.

From Crowcombe two places should be visited; a mile beyond the village, and just off the high road, stands Halsway manor house, under Hurley Beacon, a beautiful place, partly ancient still, which is said to have been in the possession of Cardinal Beaufort. This seems curious, for from the time of Edward III, certainly from 1346, it was in the hands of the Stradlings till the time of James I, when it passed to the Cades, one of whom lies in Stogumber Church. There seems to be no doubt, however, that it was at one time in Beaufort's hands, though why and wherefore I do not know.

Perhaps two miles down the valley beyond Halsway and still further from the highway, indeed from Halsway it should be reached by the beautiful byway above the road, lies Bicknoller, with a little church consisting of a nave, chancel, north aisle, tower, and south porch with a chamber over it. Within, here too, are some very remarkable bench ends, indeed some of the best hereabout.

These few notes upon the villages on this side of Quantock by no means do more than point the way for the traveller, who here at any rate may be left to his own devices; to find in hill and valley, in moor and wood, all the delight that is in his heart. To describe, nay, even to name, the innumerable walks and rambles to be had on these splendid and companionable hills would be impossible even in a professed guide book, and here altogether out of place; but no one who has once felt the Quantock heather and turf under his feet will need a book to guide or to encumber his pleasure with useless directions.

From Crowcombe, leaving the Quantocks, there is a way across the valley, and a pretty way it is, over Doniford Brook, to the village of Stogumber, among the foothills of the Brendon Hills—those hills which upon their further side, and indeed in the greater part of their extent, are so strangely neglected.

Stogumber, where they make a famous ale with water from a medicinal spring near by, is not a very interesting place; nor is its church, though spacious and fine enough, very attractive. In the main it is a Perpendicular building with a south-western tower, two porches, and two chapels, that upon the north having been built, as it is said, by Cardinal Beaufort. I suppose the best thing here is the sixteenth century brass to Margery Windham, and the monument to Sir George Sydenham, a Cavalier who lived to see the king get back his own again. His ghost is said to ride down Sydenham Combe, where the Sydenhams had long before made their home. Indeed, it was Elizabeth Sydenham of Combe Sydenham that Sir Francis Drake married as his second wife.

Following the way to Combe Sydenham just before it turns up to the house, and this is a fine Elizabethan structure, with farm buildings dating from the fifteenth century, a noble and a curious house, we take the way to the right, and a quarter of a mile further come to the village of Monksilver, still under the woods, where the church has a very beautiful south aisle, some curious gargoyles, and a fair screen and pulpit. Continuing on our way through Monksilver, at Woodford we turn into Nettlecombe Park and make our way up the lovely combe to the most interesting little church and the fine manor house, Nettlecombe Court, the home of the Trevelyans. In the time of the Confessor, Earl Godwin held Nettlecombe, but in Henry II's day it had been granted to Hugh de Ralegh, of Ralegh in Devon. The last Ralegh, Simon, fought at Agincourt and as we shall see is buried here in the church. He left Nettlecombe to his niece, who in 1453 married John Trevelyan, of Trevelyan in Cornwall, and it is a happiness to know that a Trevelyan holds it still.

Nettlecombe Court was built in the end of the sixteenth century by that Trevelyan who married Urith (note the name), a Chichester of Ralegh, in Devon. And it is consoling to know that the good wishes he received from his cousin in London—"I do heartily leave you with happy end of your buildings, a long continuance in enjoying the same to your own desired comforts,"[1] have been fulfilled for his descendants, as they were indeed for himself. The house, however, has seen some stirring times. When the Civil War broke all England in twain it found the Trevelyans strongly Royalist, and while the King's "trusty and well beloved George Trevelyan" was at the wars, the rector of the parish church, as strongly Parliamentarian, appeared one morning before the house with a band of ruffians and proceeded to burn it down, in which, so far as the out-buildings were concerned, he was successful. At the Restoration, George Trevelyan, the son of the Cavalier, who had had friends on both sides, got a baronetcy. It was his son, John Trevelyan, who built the south wing of the house in 1733.

As for Nettlecombe church, it has suffered somewhat from restoration; but is an interesting building. The south aisle dedicated in honour of St. John Baptist—the church is dedicated in honour of the Blessed Virgin—is the Ralegh chantry, and there old Sir Simon who fought for England and Henry V at Agincourt, lies, his effigy stretched beneath his shield. Among other interesting things in the church should be noted the font with its representations of the Seven Sacraments of Holy Church, elaborate sculptures still with colour upon them;

[1] *Som. Arch. Soc. Proc.*, liv (i), 18.

and the windows in the aisle north of the chancel, where we see, in the old glass, the figures of St. Lawrence, St. Margaret, St. Urith, St. John, St. George as Bishop, St. Catherine with sword and shield, and St. Peter. But the really marvellous and priceless possessions of Nettlecombe church are the pre-Reformation chalice and paten, said to be the earliest left in England; they date from 1479.

From Nettlecombe we return to Monksilver, and then make our way by Combe Sydenham to Elworthy, where we shall find a small Perpendicular Jacobean screen and pulpit. From Elworthy by a very splendid and lofty road which gives us the most glorious views all the way over Taunton Deane and the marsh beyond, and always upon the north the great woods and barrows of Quantock, we come to the inn at Handy Cross, and turn down to the left there for Lydeard St. Lawrence on its hillside, where Southey's grandfather was a farmer. The church tower here is fine and lofty, but plain. The church of St. Lawrence is, in the nave and chancel at any rate, a building of the fourteenth century, the chancel especially being, it is said, untouched from that time. It still possesses curious sedilia and piscina. The nave is finer; but the aisle is of the fifteenth century, as is the arcade which divides it from the nave. The capitals of this arcade, also of the fifteenth century, are curiously carved with a fox and goose, four angels, foliage and interlaced pattern work. The screen is apparently unfinished and has been restored; the pulpit is Jacobean, and has been much tampered with. The font is a most curious one which I cannot explain. It seems like two fonts, the one on the other, and must surely be a modern erection of old material, a Norman font under a very old holy water stoup perhaps.

From Lydeard St. Lawrence, I went to Combe Florey, and all the way was beautiful in the evening, and Combe Florey itself seemed to me perhaps the loveliest village I had seen. Here, Sydney Smith was rector from 1829 until his death in 1845. We read of his pleasure in the place, of his bringing his old servants with him, and his delight in gathering his books about him and of his beginning at once "to rebuild his parsonage" where he welcomed his old friend Jeffrey of the "Edinburgh." In the autumn of 1844 he was taken to London to be under the care of his son-in-law, Dr. Holland,

and there he died in February, 1845. He was, as a parson, a good Whig who considered the Church of England to be a branch of the Civil Service, and was very suspicious of any enthusiasm or success. As a man he was full of drollery rather than of wit, but he was neither vulgar nor malicious, and it is said that he had the confidence of his parishioners. If this be true it is, I think, the best tribute ever paid him.

The church which Sydney Smith served is chiefly interesting on account of its monuments. There is to begin with the little stone slab in the north aisle where we read in thirteenth century character, "LE QUER : DAME : MAUD : DE MERRIETE: NONAYNE : DE : CANNYNTUNE," that is to say, "the heart of Dame Maud de Merriete, nun of Cannington. Then there are the three thirteenth century effigies here, supposed to be Merriets, for they had the manor on a time as had Nicholas Francis after them, to whom there is a brass in the floor of this aisle. That is all. Only, as I passed on my way I noted an old house in the village, and then with the sun setting behind me I set out on the six miles and a-half into Taunton.

CHAPTER XXI

EXMOOR

WHEN a man, wandering along the broad back of Quantock, or lying perhaps among the bracken over the Crowcombe woods, turns his gaze westward he sees before him a country different from anything else to be found within the confines of the county of Somerset. Those vast uplifted headlands, Elworthy Barrows and the nobler Dunkery, are the outliers of Exmoor, a strange and, always upon its confines, a very beautiful country, but one that has little or nothing in common with Somerset proper, that is, in fact, a place apart with a peculiar interest all its own. This, I think, is generally realised, so that many books have rightly been devoted to Exmoor, more perhaps than have been written about the whole of the rest of the county, for it is a country peculiarly its own. It is, then, not without a sense of unfairness that in this book I have confined what I have to say of Exmoor to a single short chapter. But after all Exmoor is but a small and very sparsely peopled quarter of the county of Somerset, and it is with Somerset I set out to deal; so that from the point of view of my book I have been right to confine what I have to say of this great tract of free moorland to so small a space.

And first, as to the extent of this great moorland country, in which of old the Royal Forest of Exmoor was situated. According to Sir Henry de la Beche, Exmoor extends, "from the valley of Stogumber and Crowcombe, separating it from the Quantock Hills on the east, to the Hangman Hills on the Bristol Channel, near Combemartin in the west. Near the latter place this high land forms a point whence it sweeps to the south-east by a curved line passing to Parracombe, Chapman Barrows, Span Head, and the North Molton Ridge. Its southern boundary ranges from thence by Molland Down, Dulverton Common and Haddon Down, to Heydon Down, and Main Down, near Wiveliscombe, whence the high land trends away to the Stogumber and Crowcombe Valley above mentioned." That is a most excellent definition of all that we mean by Exmoor, but no moorsman would for one moment endorse it; he would never allow that the great Brendon range which lies between the Wheddon Cross watershed and its valleys north and south and the Stogumber valley was a part of the moor. And, in fact, he is right, those neglected and monotonous hills do stand apart, and to-day more than ever, from the moorland to the west of them, divided from them by the long pass at the two ends of which stand Dulverton and Dunster.

But if we would set down thus the boundaries of the moor, how are we to define its character? I have said that it is utterly different from any other part of Somerset, that it is a place apart; but the moor in fact is very deceptive, or rather we easily deceive ourselves about it. The true capital Simonsbath is hard to get at and is consequently but little visited, yet Simonsbath would give us the truth about it. But wherever Exmoor is easily accessible, as at Dunster, or Porlock, or Lynton, or Dulverton, it presents to us so enchanting and so delicious an aspect that we always think of it as perhaps the most beautiful thing in all southern England, with nothing of the monotony of the Downs or the dreariness of Dartmoor. As a fact, however, the moor proper which comparatively few of us ever see, is more monotonous than that "noble chain of mountains" the Downs, even at their worst, know how to be, and unbroken by any Tor and unenlivened by any human interest, the heart of Exmoor is drearier than Dartmoor can conceive. Happily the traveller seldom gets so far; the melancholy sources of the Exe by Pinkerry Pond, the monotony of the Deer Park are unknown to him; he sees only the fringe and confines of the moor, the glorious country at the foot of purple Dunkery, the Hawkcombe and the Horner woods—valleys of Paradise—the fair and lovely vale of Porlock, the noble uplifted road over the moor above the sea between Porlock and Lynton, the delight of the valley of Watersmeet, of the nobler

Badgery; or the fine Dulverton country, the valleys of the Barle and the Haddeo, and the valley of the Exe between Exton and Dulverton. These and more than these deceive him with their loveliness till in his heart the moor is only a part of Paradise, the fairest upland in the garden of Eden, a glory of heather, of valleys filled with woods through which innumerable waters half hidden sing in the sun and the shade, of all pleasure and of all joy. And this sure enough is true of the confines of the moor everywhere; of the moor itself it is ludicrously untrue.

If a man would know what Exmoor is, let him not waste his breath by climbing Dunkery, seventeen hundred feet and more over the sea. Dunkery stands upon the seaward confines of the moor and will tell him little beyond the lie of the land. Let him march afoot from Porlock to Simonsbath and on to Moles Chamber, and then back by Exe Head and Pinkerry Pond to Badgery Water; not till he has done this will he have seen the moor, that bare rolling waste very like the sea, with its long heaving monotony of grey water, without a voice, without life, and without human habitation; for there is only the sound of wind and of running water, only the life of a rare black cock or curlew, a rarer pony or herd of deer, only far off, lost in the rolling bald downs, a shepherd's hut for dwelling. That is the moor and its face is the face of eternity.

As for the history of this wild open country, it has none any more than has the sea. Only its loneliness has always been a refuge; Dunkery Beacon, Showlsborough Castle, Mounsey Castle, Hoar Oak Hill, Old Barrow, Span Head and the rest were known to us before history began, and they will remain when our works have passed into nothing. Yet I suppose Exmoor to have been always sparsely peopled; no stone circles and but two hut circles have been found there, and no evidence at all of Roman habitation, for the inscribed Longstone on Winsford Hill, upon which we read *Carataci Nepus*, would seem to be of Goidel origin. As long as history stretches, and that for Exmoor is but to Norman times, we hear of "Exmoor Forest," but until the time of Edward I we have no precise idea of what this meant, nor of how great a part of the moor was included within it. The Foresters—the first was a certain William de Wrotham, after him the De Peches, who sold the office in 1337 to Sir Richard D'Amori, who sold to Mortimer, Earl of March, with whose descendants it remained till it came back to the Crown in the time of Edward IV—were people of distinction, but we know very little about them and almost nothing about the moor, till in 1815 the Forest of Exmoor, which had once comprised, perhaps, some 80,000 acres, was disafforested. Its extent was then but 18,810 acres and this was allotted, a little more than half to the king, one-eighth to Sir Thomas Dyke Acland in lieu of the tithes of the whole forest, which he held, and the remainder to various other persons. The King's portion was at once put up to auction and sold for £50,000 to Mr. John Knight, whose descendants have since sold to the Fortescue family of Castle Hill.[1]

Like all other such high and waste places, Exmoor is the parent of many rivers and streams, the two greater being the Exe, which has a career so noble in Devon that it bears the great city and capital of the west upon it, and the Barle, loveliest of streams, which joins the Exe upon our border by Exebridge, some two miles or so below Dulverton. These streams like their valleys are the most considerable upon the moor, and the latter waters the most considerable of its towns, indeed the only place that may pass for a town upon it, Dulverton.

The Exmoor streams which flow north, and after a short but always beautiful course fall into the Severn Sea are many, but not one is of any size. True mountain streams they are, from the Lyn and its sisters in the Devonshire corner of the moor and Badgeworthy, which, for so great a part of its course, marks the county boundary on the west, to those delightful waters of Hawkcombe, Horner, and Avill, to name but three, which sing through the tall woods about Porlock, and the pleasant valley behind Dunster.

Now it is true that for many excellent reasons the great majority of tourists and travellers who have come to love Exmoor explore, and always will explore, it from Dunster, Minehead, Porlock, or Lynmouth, all upon the northern extremity of the moor where it falls so magnificently to the sea. With these places I shall deal, however, in this book in

[1] *V. C. H.* (*Somerset*), ii, p. 566.

the next chapter, for they are in truth as much or more of the coast than of the moorland. And so here I propose to enter Exmoor by its great southern gate, Dulverton; and without more ado or reason why.

Dulverton station is two miles from the town, but close to Brushford, where in the Early Perpendicular church there is a fine thirteenth century font of Purbeck marble, and an early fifteenth century screen much spoiled and defaced. In the churchyard there is one of the finest oaks to be seen in the country; reported to be six hundred years old, and has been in a decaying state for over a hundred years. Three feet from the ground it measures sixteen feet in circumference.

Just beyond Brushford stands Combe with an interesting sixteenth century house; the old home of a branch of the Sydenham family.

It is a pleasant road between high wooded hills that takes us to Dulverton and the Carnarvon Arms. The town itself is without interest, but the hills about it offer glorious views of the two wooded valleys, of the Barle and of the Exe, and a mile north of the town in the Exe valley we find the meagre ruins of Barlynch Priory; all that is left of a house of Augustinian Canons, founded in the twelfth century by William de Say, lord of the manor of Brompton Regis. It was the only religious house in this moorland district except the Benedictine cell of Bath, at Dunster. It never had more than nine religious, and documents concerning it are few; we do not even know when it was dissolved.

Brompton Regis is a village of the Brendons, behind Storridge Hill over the wooded valley, through which runs the Haddeo water. Sir Henry de la Beche includes all this in Exmoor, but for us it lies upon the wrong side of the great pass between Exmoor and the Brendon Hills, which may be said to end at Dulverton. Up this pass, down which for many miles the Exe flows, there goes a great road up to Wheddon Cross on the watershed and down to Dunster.

To-day, however, this is not our way. We are for Exmoor, and so we take the road opposite the Red Lion Hotel, up the valley of the Barle, splendid all the way with woods, by Mounsey Castle, the first of a line of strongholds, Hawkridge Castle, Brewer's Castle and Ring Castle, called Cow Castle on the Ordnance map, which hold the way up the valley.

Following the road, up and down, some five miles from Dulverton, we come to the finest prehistoric monument upon Exmoor, and the most notable of its kind in all England, I mean Tarr Steps, the beautiful bridge of stones across the Barle.

"Tarr, or Torr Steps," says Mr. Page in that best of books[1] upon Exmoor, "consists of large slabs of stone laid on mighty piled piers projecting about a yard on either side of the roadway. The average length of a slab is perhaps seven feet, the width three feet six inches, the longest being five feet wide. In the centre they are laid singly; towards the ends the stones, being narrower, are placed side by side. The piers facing the current are protected by sloping stones about four feet in length. There are no less than seventeen openings. The total length of the bridge, including the paved approaches, is one hundred and eighty feet, and its height above the water, except in flood time, when it is submerged, is about three feet. There is not an atom of cement in the structure."

All sorts of tales are told of this wonderful structure. It has, it seems, been ascribed by a rector of Hawkridge to "a man named Tarr"; on the other hand, a former rector, presumably of the same place, had very good reason to ascribe it to the Devil. For it seems it was built in a single night by the ancient enemy of man, exclusively for his own use. Indeed, when one day a cat ventured to cross, it was instantly torn in pieces. This was too much for the rector of Hawkridge, who, besides seeing his parishioners in peril, had had enough and to spare of the devil's nonsense. Therefore, gathering up his cassock he set out to cross, and did so in safety, stopping and turning now and then while he exchanged compliments "more forcible than polite," says Mr. Page, with Master Devil on the bank. It seems the devil called the parson "a black crow"; to which the parson replied that he was not "blacker than the devil." It would have delighted me to have seen and heard this; alas, now-a-days, how rare such encounters have become.

Nothing can be lovelier than the valley at Tarr Steps under the bleak moorland of Winsford Hill, two miles to the north, along which the road lies to Withypool and Exford. Here on Winsford Hill, the first outpost of the moor, we find beside an old trackway that notable Longstone which bears the

[1] *An Exploration of Exmoor and the Hill County of West Somerset*, by G. Ll. W. Page (Seeley, 1893).

inscription CARATACI [N]EPUS, which would appear to mean the kinsman of Caractacus. Possibly, therefore, we have here a memorial to a relative of that great British king who, after bravely defending his country, was betrayed to the Romans, who in A.D. 51 carried him to Rome; but his bearing was so noble and his speech so became him that Claudius gave him back his liberty.

From this high ridge some fourteen hundred feet above the

Winsford. Royal Oak Inn.

sea it is possible to see far away to the south the height of Dartmoor, while to the west lies the wild moorland, to the east the woods over Dulverton, and to the north Dunkery, and if you be lucky the Severn Sea.

Upon the northern side of the great hill, in the valley of the Exe, lies the beautiful village of Winsford, where the church has this interest at least, that nave and chancel are under a single roof, reminding us of the churches at Cannington and Norton-sub-Hamdon. The tower, too, is to be noted as a fine example of the church towers in this moorland corner of Somerset. The font is Norman, as are those at Hawkridge and Withypool.

Withypool, some two miles west of the high ridge of Winsford Hill, is a pretty spot much frequented by fly-fishers, as indeed are all the villages upon the Barle and the Exe. It is here for all the meadows by the stream that we really come on to the moorland. And here a man has a choice of ways; he may either go north, perhaps three miles to Exford, and so by the good road to Simonsbath, or he may stick as close as he can to the Barle—and this is far the lovelier way—at any rate to the five-arched Bridge at Landacre, where the moor comes right at him and he has no choice but to lose himself in its vastness and silence.

Exford is the headquarters of the Devon and Somerset staghounds, for here are the kennels, and it is, after all, to the stag-hunters that Exmoor may be said primarily to belong; it is largely the ancient glory of their sport which lures so many to this great wild, and it is the pleasure and excitement of the "meets" and of following the hunt afoot that fill the days of so many summer visitors.

Exford, however, is nothing to these people: they come from Minehead, Dunster, Porlock, Lynton, Dulverton, South Molton, and half a score of villages round about, to witness and to enjoy the finest sport on earth. Exford knows them not, it is too far in the moor. Its position, indeed, is the most central that can be found in the Exmoor country, and it was for this reason, I suppose, that the late Mr. Bisset built the kennels and stables here twenty years ago.

To Mr. Bisset the "Devon and Somerset," and stag hunting, too, as a true sport, owe everything; at any rate, he established stag-hunting as *the* sport of the west.

With his name must be linked in the heart of every true west countryman that of Parson Jack Russell, who kept hounds when he was at Blundell's, and continued to follow the staghounds until he was over eighty years old; indeed, in 1880, when he was eighty-five, he was appointed to the rectory of Torrington, reluctantly leaving his beloved Swymbridge, where he is buried; his first act was to start a pack of harriers. Of course, his popularity was enormous, and for all his love of sport, he won the following tribute from one of his parishioners, which the Rev. S. Baring Gould records: "as for old Jack Russell, up and down his back-bone, he's as good a Christian, as worthy a pastor, and as true a gentleman as I ever seen." Happy is he who can win such an epitaph from his fellows.

Exford church is chiefly interesting on account of the fact that its dedication seems to have been changed with the change of religion. St. Peter, in whose honour the church was dedicated in Catholic times, was in disgrace, as given to Popery at the Reformation, and so the church was re-dedicated in honour of St. Mary Magdalen, a very appropriate choice, we may think, considering the record of the new "Supreme Governour" of the Church of England.

The road from Exford to Simonsbath is monotonously wild enough, but it is nothing to the so strangely desolate glen of the Barle water between Landacre Bridge and the capital. Yet, by the road you pass the bog called Cloven Rocks, where it will be remembered Carver Doone and John Ridd met at last, and the Doone sank down to death in the treacherous ground.

Simonsbath itself, however, is quite an oasis in the barrenness of the moor. It lies in a cup of the hills beside the Barle, and is chiefly notable as the capital of the moor, intended to be the residence of the owner, that Mr. Knight who bought the moor from the King in the hope of reclaiming it and bringing it under cultivation. To him the church is due, and the great ruined house that was never finished. Simonsbath can boast at least of the presence of two outlaws —that *Symon* who it is said used to take a *bath* in the pool above the bridge, and the famous Tom Faggus, who here escaped from his captors when they thought they had him safely in the Inn, the same, I think, as that we now see, the "William Rufus"—ominous forest sign.

From Simonsbath, he who would know something of the moor must make his way to the old bog, the worst upon the moor called the Chains, where the Exe rises and where that desolate "tarn" Pinkerry Pond remains as a witness to the hopelessness of all that man can contrive against the moor.

Exe-head is a desolate lonely place with nothing to relieve the mind in thinking of it. This lovely river, surely one of our loveliest and for all who have known it in their boyhood for ever sacred, rises in a spot as melancholy and silent as is to be found in England. The springs of all rivers are sacred, and though some have been spoiled and desecrated, as the springs of the Thames, others, as the rising-place of the Seine out of that cavern in the Côte d'Or, have been honoured with statues. Here there is nothing; only the ancient moor and the Hoar Oak Hill and the Hoar Oak Tree.

Pinkerry Pond by the Chains is not a natural tarn, as I have suggested. It was formed by the late Mr. Knight, who had some projects for a canal in his head, though where this canal was to go and what purpose it was to serve no one has ever been able to say. It was a part of his great scheme for reclaiming the moor, and fortunately for all those of us who love the moor as it is, it all came to nothing.

Out of the desolation of the Chains let a man climb the Hoar Oak Hill, whence he may have all Exmoor and Dunkery its glory, at a glance. Thence let him push on his way past Hoar Oak Tree to Brendon Two Gates and so into the Doone Valley.

The Doone Valley under the Deer Park is, I suppose, the most visited spot on the moor, and no one who has read Blackmore's fine romance can avoid a great disappointment. What! This miserable bare combe, just like a thousand others, the Doone Valley; it is impossible to believe it! Yet so it is; and we must all make the best of it, and of the "water-slide" that comes into Badgery water lower down, too. For the book is a work of art, and better than any real thing ever was. See how disgusted we are, it being in our hearts, with reality!

As for the Doones, what is the truth about them? Are they nothing but "art"—a tale that is told—too? That the Doones existed and here, that they were outlaws, who held the moorland villages in terror, that "girt Jan Ridd" was a real person, and that he was educated at Blundell's school in Tiverton; all this is true, sure enough. As for the rest it is as true as *Hamlet* is, or as a novel from the hand of Sir Walter. All this pother for reality is stupid; for has not Blackmore made Lorna, and her great lover and Carver Doone and Ensor Doone, and Tom Faggus and all the rest of the folks in the book, a good deal more real to us than most of the people we know and meet every day? So a fool, traversing Verona, might ask of his guide whether indeed Romeo and Juliet really once lived there, when in fact they are the only living people for him in the city to-day. A plague upon such nonsense say I. Why Augustus Cæsar, nay Napoleon and Nelson too, are not as real to us as Hamlet, as Lear or gaunt Macbeth, lonely with ambition, looking out of his castle windows at the grey day full of rain drifting across the moors about his home; and what would any English King be—and they were "real" enough—without Shakespeare and his Plays? "Dust to stop a hole withal." So it is with the Doones, and so it is sure enough with the moor; it lives in Blackmore's pages a wonderfully lonely, terrifying thing, looming out of the fog; but for you who come here in August and expect to see it while you picnic; bah! though you walk all over it, do you think it is real—what you see?

Now he is wise who takes a look at the ruins of the Doone houses and leaves the Doone valley for ever. Badgery Water awaits him and its noble valley, that will take him all the way to Malmsmead, a beautiful spot, and there he will cross the water by the stone bridge and go on to Oare.

Oare church, where Lorna was married, and where Carver Doone shot her as she stood before the altar, is a small plain building, with a short embattled square tower, very fitting for the moorland. According to Mr. Page, in Lorna's day the present chancel was not built. However that may be, no one who has read the great tale will ever forget that wedding, when, as Jan Ridd tells us, "the sound of a shot rang through the church, and those eyes were dim with death. Lorna fell across my knees, when I was going to kiss her, as the bridegroom is allowed to do, and encouraged, if he needs it; a flood of blood came out upon the yellow wood of the altar steps, and at my feet fell Lorna."

From Oare one may return to Malmsmead, and so into Devon, through Brendon to Lynmouth and Lynton, or going eastward through Oareford, he may climb up to Oare Post upon the coach road from Lynton to Minehead, and so by Culbone stables down Porlock Hill or the new road—and that is the finer way—to Porlock and the Ship Inn, where he may sleep.

Of Porlock and its very notable church of St. Dubricius I shall speak in the next chapter. Here I shall merely regard it as a resting place from which to explore the beautiful

Hawkcombe and Horner valleys, clothed in woods, among the loveliest in all this country of valleys; and as perhaps the best starting place for an ascent of Dunkery, or for the great August "meet" of the staghounds at Cloutsham.

I know not rightly what to say of these places which I love so well, and have known ever since I knew anything; for a man cannot describe what is become in long years so familiar as to be really taken for granted. They are what they are. Let a man come over the shoulder of Dunkery from Wheddon Cross, that desolate high place, by Dunkery Hill Gate, by the eastern road, and as he descends towards Cloutsham, when still a long way off, let him look down upon those woods; there is no fairer sight in the world. On a spring morning it is as though all the mysterious beauty of the wood in Fragonard's picture had suddenly fallen upon that valley in the tender sunshine. But these are places that should be known by heart; for they change not, but remain when all else that once seemed to be for ever has utterly fallen away.

Now from Porlock the way for Cloutsham lies up the Horner Water—which you must cross at last by the fifth clammer above Horner village, and climbing the steep woods make your way along the ridge to the farm. For sure enough in August the first meet of the staghounds will be there in the great meadow behind the old farm, and it is a sight not to be missed.

On the borders of the counties of Somerset and Devon, in this ancient Royal Forest of Exmoor, and here alone, linger the last of the wild red deer whose ancestors were hunted by the kings of England long before the Normans came to the land; and here, and here alone now in England, is the sport of hunting the wild deer still carried on, stripped of much of its pomp, it is true, but yet in all essentials the same as when William the Norman went forth to hunt in the New Forest.

Here upon Exmoor on the first Wednesday in August the Devon and Somerset staghounds meet at Sir Thomas Acland's farm of Cloutsham at eleven to open the staghunting season, and crowds of hunting people from all over the kingdom meet them there as they have done time out of mind.

But long before the crowd—and you with it—begin to think about leaving Porlock or Dunster or Minehead or Lynton or Dulverton, there is one member of the hunt staff who has been up and about in Horner Wood. Goss, the Harbourer, rode over from Dulverton the night before and at break of day he saddled his pony and rode up to Woodcocks Ley, and in the words of the old song:

> There he stooped and there he stood,
> And round the combe he made it good,
> And harboured in the lower wood
> A warrantable deer.

He is not, however, so discourteous as to try to see the stag he wishes to harbour, but he makes a tour of the woods, and

Dunkery Beacon from Cloutsham Farm.

having found the slot or footmark of a warrantable deer, that is to say, of one of upwards of five years old, going into the wood, he makes a tour, or as they say on Exmoor, a ring-walk round the wood, to be sure that the stag has not merely passed through and gone on his way. Then he goes back to Cloutsham Farm for breakfast and there he finds Tucker at the meet.

At eleven o'clock the pack is kennelled in the farm building, and a few couples of steady hounds, "tufters," are drawn to

tuft for, or to drive, the harboured stag into the open ; the field in the meantime stop at the meet. When the stag has been driven into the open, tufters are stopped and the pack is signalled for by the waving of a handkerchief, and is quickly brought up and laid on the line. If all goes well and he is heading for the moor we are in for a treat. On and on we go, past Hawkcombe Head, where there is a check due to our stag lying down and putting up a hind. But soon on we go again to Robber's Bridge, where he soiled, and so to Badgery Water where he stands to bay, after beating up and down the stream a few times.

Bawden, however, quickly throws the thong of his whip over his horns ; the huntsman slips in and drives his knife into his throat, and the big fellow sinks into the water, from which he is hauled a few minutes later, quite dead. He is laid on his back, the slots are separated at the joint, the tusks or eye teeth are cut out, the body is opened, the heart and liver given to the farmers and the entrails to the pack. The antlers, or in common talk, the horns, more properly "the head," are the property of the Master, and the carcase goes to the landowner on whose ground he was found.

Such is stag-hunting, and a very glorious sport it is; let the toast of the hunt: "Prosperity to Stag-hunting," be honoured wherever this book is read. But after all there are days when. . . .

Yonder is Dunkery, all glorious in purple; this is August sure enough, the hunt has passed far away beyond Hawkcombe. I am for the Beacon, seventeen hundred feet in the blue air. By that pile of stones I lie and look over this great world of moor channelled by many a deep combe, to the sea, where Severn lies dying or dead, to the solemnity of the Welsh mountains, to the sea beyond Lundy. At my feet is the moor, and, beyond the moor, half Devon, a flash of Cornwall, all the Somersetshire hills, and only the Dorset highlands hide the southern sea. Below in the great woods summer is sleeping through the long day; in heaven a lark towers in the eye of the sun pouring out its endless glory of song; and I here—my heart for it all—where my fathers signalled in the summer night the passing of the Legions, the Saxon onset, the Danish retreat, the Norman advance, the Armada, the sixty years of Queen Victoria.

CHAPTER XXII

THE COAST

THE long Somersetshire coast, something more than sixty miles in length, divides itself naturally into two unequal parts. From Glenthorne on the Devon border to Minehead it is both beautiful and very steep, for there the Exmoor highlands, clad in glorious woods, descend swiftly to the sea; but beyond Minehead, eastward to Avonmouth, it is, even under the Quantocks, flat and uninspiring, and, indeed, save where Brean Down thrusts out towards the island of the Steep Holm, or Worle Hill towers out of the flood behind Weston, it is without anything that rightly can be called a headland.

Now a man who would set out to explore this coast in its entirety, if he begin in the west, will do well to make Porlock his starting point. It is from this little place, as it were the postern gate of Somerset, that he should examine the noble bit of coast that still lies westward within the confines of the county, and this may be done in a long day afoot in the following fashion.

Setting out early from Porlock one makes one's way westward up the famous hill, or better by the new road, which is so full of beauty, commanding, as it does, all its winding way, glorious views of sea and towering wooded coast and solemn Welsh mountain; till just beyond County Gate, upon the noble great high road over the moor, where there is so lovely a glimpse of Glenthorne far below in the woods over the sea, one comes to Wingate Farm, and, turning in there, pushes downward many hundred feet till one finds a cliff path, and, following it eastward through the woods, comes to Glenthorne.

A A 2

Glenthorne is the residence of Mr. Halliday; it is an extraordinarily lovely place in a unique situation embowered in woods half way down the cliffs just over the sea. From Glenthorne, which stands upon the county boundary, it is possible to make one's way by the path through the woods on the steep cliff side, the sea shining through the trees, for some four miles to the tiny village of Culbone, with its tiny church, reported to be the smallest church in England. This very precious building, though so small, is perfect in all its parts, consisting of nave, chancel, and south porch, with a little slated spire over the west gable. The church is thirty-three feet long, the nave twelve feet eight inches wide, and the chancel under ten feet. The walls are said to be two feet six inches thick, and are certainly Norman, as is the font, but we have something even earlier in the small two-light window cut out of a single stone in the north wall of the chancel; this is certainly earlier than anything else in the church. As I have said, the church is complete in all its parts, and I might almost have said in all its fittings too. At any rate, the old chancel screen and benches remain, the screen being an early one; but the rood loft is gone.

The village of Culbone, which consists of about two houses, is named after a Glamorganshire saint, and to him the church is of course dedicated. He seems to have come from Wales with St. Dubricius, whom we shall meet at Porlock.

Leaving this wonderful little church we presently pass, still by this narrow way through the woods over the sea, Ashley Combe, the residence of Lady Lovelace, and a little later find ourselves at the little harbour of Porlock Weir, the most picturesque little port in Somerset.

Porlock Bay, which lies between Gore Point, under Ashley Combe and lofty Hurlstone eastward, is apart from this little harbour a great curved ridge of grey stones some three miles in length and some hundreds of yards wide, through which the Hawkcombe water and the Horner water filter into the sea. This "beach" is a miserable place without any sort of attraction, but Porlock Vale behind it and below it is one of the loveliest and noblest valleys in all the west country, as well as one of the richest, scattered with beautiful villages.

There is nothing to detain us at Porlock Weir beyond its

general quaintness, and the manor house of Worthy, the old manor house of Porlock, and so we push on past West Porlock to Porlock itself.

This is—or must I say was?—one of the most exquisite in this country of exquisite villages, enclosed on all sides save to seaward by great wooded hills under the northern escarpment of the moor where it first fails to reach the sea. The place, like all its fellows, is in spring and summer and autumn a

Porlock Weir. The Harbour.

bower of flowers, its picturesque little whitewashed houses with their tall and curious chimneys, as at the old Bank and the Ship Inn, are indeed half lost in towering fuschias, in creepers, and roses. But like all such places, Porlock, with its facilities for the staghunter and the tourist, is being quickly uglified, and it will not be long, I suppose, before all that we have so loved there is a tale that is told. To-day, however, much remains that is precious, and of this the church is best.

This is dedicated in honour of that St. Dubricius, in whose company St. Culbone came hither from Glamorgan, and it is very old and famous. For Porlock is none of your new places; she, too, has her place in history. As Collinson reminds us: "In the year 918 those turbulent visitors of England the Danes, having, under the command of the Earls *Ohtor* and *Rhoald*, entered the Severn and spread ruin and devastation along the opposite coasts of Wales, directed their course to Somersetshire and landed privately in the night at Porlock, for the sake of plunder; but the inhabitants, being timely alarmed, gave them so warm a reception that the greater part were cut to pieces; and those few who escaped alive were obliged to retire with great precipitation to their ships."

About this time Porlock had an extensive chase and it is said a palace of one of the Saxon kings. This latter, in all probability, was destroyed with the town not many years later on the following memorable occasion. Harold, as we know, sharing his father's disgrace, was fugitive and had gone to Ireland as it seems to raise troops, and sure enough he presently appeared off Porlock about midsummer, 1052, with nine ships full of a great company, where he secured a landing, seized everything that was valuable, and setting fire to the town after slaughtering many of the inhabitants, repaired to his ships with a great booty. He sailed round the Lands End and joined his father at Portland, and together they sailed up to London. They were, however, soon reconciled to the King, and at Easter in the following year were welcomed by him at Winchester.

It is quite possible that some of the stones in Porlock Church which bear marks of fire suffered in Harold's raid, but the earliest definite work we find there, the east window, the piscina in the chancel, and the tower window, is of the Early English period. The nave and south aisle—the Harington aisle, for the Haringtons were lords of the manor in the fifteenth century—are Perpendicular in style. A screen of that time separates this chapel from the church, and within we see the magnificent alabaster tomb of the founder, John Lord Harington, who died in France in 1418. His effigy, with that of his lady, lie upon the rich canopied tomb, which is a work of the last quarter of the fifteenth century.

The cross-legged effigy in the recess in the wall near the south door probably represents Sir Simon de Roger, who died about 1308.

In the chancel upon the north side is an altar tomb carved with the Five Wounds; this is said to be the base of the

Monument of John, Fourth Baron Harington of Aldringham, and Wife. Porlock Church.

Sepulchre for the Host reserved after Mass upon Maundy Thursday. As at Langport and North Petherton there is a vestry or sacristy under the east window, entered by a door

near the altar. The screen and rood-loft were taken down in 1768. In the porch is now an altar tomb, somewhat similar to that in the chancel, which is said to have held the Sepulchre in Holy Week; but this is thought once to have been the high altar of the church.

Without, the church does not appear so noble as it does within; the short truncated spire at the west end is curiously ugly. Close by the porch is the pathetic epitaph of Thomas and Prudence Rawle, who died within a day of one another.

He first departed; she for one day tried
To live without him, liked it not, and dy'd.

The "Ship Inn" at Porlock at the western end of the village is famous not alone for its picturesqueness, but also for the fact that Southey stayed there on August 9th, 1799, and in *The Morning Post* for August 26th of that year there appears the following sonnet:—

"Porlock, thy verdant vale so fair to sight,
Thy lofty hills which fern and furze embrown,
The waters that roll musically down
Thy woody glens, the traveller with delight
Recalls to memory, and the channel grey
Circling its surges in thy level bay.
Porlock, I also shall forget thee not
Here by the unwelcome summer rain confined
But often shall hereafter call to mind
How here, a patient prisoner, 'twas my lot
To view the lonely, lingering close of day
Making my sonnet by the ale-house fire
Whilst Idleness and Solitude inspire
Dull rhymes to pass the duller hours away."

This ancient inn stands, as I say, at the western end of Porlock; at the east end of the village is Dovery Court, a very small manor house of the fifteenth century, more like a cottage than a house, but a fine piece of work nevertheless, with its oak ceiling, stone fireplace, and beautiful window of four lights and fine tracery; altogether an interesting little place.

But the delight of Porlock lies as much in the lovely country and lovelier villages about it as in itself. There is Luccombe, for instance, a little place enshrouded in flowers, laburnum too, and white clematis all over the cottages; while about the church stand the dark tall cypresses as though verily

Luccombe were Lucca and in Italy. The church is very like that at Porlock, with a fine altar tomb under the tower, once in the south aisle, a double piscina in the chancel of the Early English time, and a good pulpit and reading desk. Note, too, the tomb of Dr. Byam, rector of Luccombe during the Civil War. He was a fine royalist and helped to raise a troop for the White King, in which four of his sons were captains. When the King's cause went down, his wife and daughter had to flee, but they were drowned in crossing to the continent, poor souls! Dr. Byam, however, lived to see the Restoration.

A way across Porlock Vale—for Luccombe lies under the eastern woods of Horner—brings us to Tivington, where there is a fine old fifteenth century chapel dedicated to St. Leonard, and from there we may return by the high road by Holnicote and Allerford to Porlock. I know nothing lovelier than Allerford under the woods with its old pack-horse bridge; England lives because such places remain to her.

It is quite possible, and indeed it is a splendid walk, to go out from Porlock across the Vale to Bossington with its famous walnut tree and its little fifteenth century chapel with the fine east window, up over the smooth grass to Hurlstone Point and so over Bossington Hill and Selworthy Beacon and North Hill, in sight of the sea all the way, to Minehead. A better plan, nevertheless, though at first it does not give you the sea, is to make your way through the woods—and one of them is a great *bosco* of sacred Ilex—to Selworthy, and then to seek the Beacon and so go over North Hill down into Minehead. Indeed, there is no fairer way in the world than this, and it gives you Selworthy.

Selworthy is only Luccombe *in excelsis*; it might be the perfect retreat of some religious Order that had repudiated the modern world—as a fact, it is a retreat for old people, contrived by Sir Thomas Acland. Here about a sunny green, all spread out with flowers, under the woods, is a number of old-world thatched cottages where any of us might be at peace. The view from the village is magnificent, and the church, much restored, is well worthy of a visit. For the most part it is of the Perpendicular time, the south aisle being dated 1527. The best things left to us in it are undoubtedly the roof and the windows in the south aisle; but of old this little church must have been a whole festival of colour and of beauty, for it was then covered with frescoes, fragments of which have been found from time to time. Over the porch there is a vestry, and there is a fine old oak chest to be seen. In the rectory grounds there is a fine old tithe barn with a little window upon which are some interesting emblematic carvings.

From Selworthy the traveller will proceed either by the nobler way over the hills by the sea, or by the high road into

Dunkery Beacon from Selworthy Churchyard.

Minehead. If you go by the hills you will pass the ruins of Burgundy Chapel, a very small sanctuary, measuring but thirty-five feet by sixteen. It is probable that Burgundy is but a corruption of Bircombe and in the Dunster Castle household accounts there is an entry for the year 1405 of a sum of money paid for the lord of Dunster going on pilgrimage to the chapel of Bircombe. Nothing really is known about the place. On the high road where it turns down to Minehead by Bratton stands upon the left Bratton

Court, a fine old manor house larger than most in these parts, but much restored. It is worth more than the glance in passing, that is all we can expect to be allowed to give it.

Minehead itself, like all the "watering places" upon this coast, Burnham, Weston-super-Mare, and the rest, is an unattractive place enough, beloved of the multitude. In the Plume of Feathers, however, it can boast of a fine old coaching inn; opposite the Assembly Rooms is an old building once a court house, and there are some seventeenth century

Minehead Harbour.

almshouses not far from the Market Hall, while the upper and older town under the North Hill is interesting and especially can boast of a very notable church.

The church of St. Michael—for it is on the hillside—has a good Late Perpendicular tower at its western end with an embattled parapet, and on the south side is a triple niche, a carving of the Blessed Trinity, on the east side we see St. Michael weighing the souls of the departed in his scales while the devil awaits his own. As a whole, however, the church may be said to belong to the Decorated period with additions from the Late Perpendicular time. It is approached

on the east by a lych gate, and on the south by a flight of steps. The nave and chancel strike one at once by their spaciousness. The doors on the south are perhaps the oldest part of the building; of the aisles to nave and chancel that upon the north was probably a Lady Chapel, and is, in fact, a fine piece of work. Without, on either side of the window we see an angel with a shield, and over it the following inscription:

> "We pray, Jesu and Marie,
> Send our neygboures safetie."

To the north of the chancel aisle there is a chantry chapel, now a vestry with a good waggon roof. The roofs, too, of both nave and chancel are fine, and, indeed, there is some remarkable wood-work in the church. The great screen which divides chancel and nave is very elaborate and beautiful, and in its general proportions is very like that we shall find at Dunster. The altar, too, is a fine piece of carved Tudor work, and the beautiful vestment chest should be noted.

In the chancel there is a notable tomb with an effigy under an elaborate and beautiful canopy in the Perpendicular style. The figure represents a priest in his Mass vestments holding the chalice in his hands. This seems to be a work of the early fourteenth century.

From Minehead to the shining cliffs of Blue Anchor it is flat marsh all the way; therefore, we take the road to Dunster, one of the most famous and one of the loveliest places in all this famous and lovely country.

Dunster has surely everything the heart of a traveller can desire; an aspect altogether quiet and pleasing, the noblest great castle in Somerset, a magnificent and monastic church, a fine old inn, a curious old market, what more can any man want? Yet Dunster adds to all these a neighbourhood overflowing with beauty and delight, and with what time and war, fool and vandal have left us of the noble work of our forefathers.

Whatever Dunster may have been before the Normans came to the land, its history begins, though that of its owners does not, with the Conquest, when it was granted to William de Mohun "one of a very eminent and ancient family in Normandy," who built here a castle, and no doubt helped to build the church, dedicated in honour of St. George, the advowson of which, together with a large estate, he presented to John de Villula and the monks of Bath.

The Castle thus built withstood King Stephen when he came against it to beat the Mohun of that day, who was busy laying waste the whole countryside from this fortress. It remained in the hands of the Mohuns till the fiftieth year of Edward III, in 1376, when it was sold absolutely by the widow of John Lord Mohun to Lady Elizabeth Luttrell, from whom it passed to Sir Hugh Luttrell, in whose family it still remains.

Dunster. The Priory Dovecote and Church.

It is, I suppose, needless to state that nothing of the Norman Castle remains to-day. The oldest part of the present very noble building (which is not open to the public—though the gardens may be seen upon Mondays and Fridays) is, I suppose, the old gateway of the time of Henry III, within the splendid fifteenth century Gate House, and the round towers to the right. Of the house, the part to the right of the entrance is Elizabethan, that to the left of the eighteenth century.

But the great days of Dunster were those of the Civil War, when the Luttrells were for the Parliament. In 1642 its lord held it for the rebels, and so well that the Marquis of Hertford failed to take it, and it was commonly reported to be impregnable. In the following year, however, it was surrendered and garrisoned for the King by Colonel Windham, who held it safe till in 1646, a year after the battle of Langport, he was forced to give it up; for that year it had been the only place held for the King in the whole county. It was during this period that Prince Charles, afterwards Charles II, came to Dunster and slept in the room still known as his, with a secret recess for a hiding place. It had been in November, 1645, that Blake and Sydenham began to lay siege to Dunster, which alone in all Somerset flew the Royal Standard. The besieged held out amid furious fighting until February, 1646, when Hopton relieved them, forcing Blake to retreat; but when Exeter, *Semper Fidelis*, had fallen, Fairfax reinforced him, and Windham surrendered the Castle after one hundred and sixty days siege.

Two years later, Dunster, which had not been dismantled as the Parliament desired, received a very distinguished prisoner, that Master Prynne whom Cromwell found such a nuisance —author it will be remembered of "The Unloveliness of Love-lockes," and other pestiferous Puritan pamphlets. He must have been a pretty spectacle by that time, for, poor wretch, he had not only lost both ears, but was branded on both cheeks with the two letters S.L. meaning "seditious libeller," which he undoubtedly was. He spent his time at Dunster in what I take to have been the only useful work of his life, for he there arranged the Luttrell family muniments as they appear to this day.

The castle on its hill, half embowered in trees, naturally attracts us first, but it is, as a matter of fact, not so interesting as the very noble church. This is cruciform, with a central tower, but no clerestory, and is, indeed, as we see it even, two churches, though no longer as it was in the fifteenth century, monastic and parochial.

It is impossible to say what William de Mohun found here after the Conquest, but he presently, as I have said, presented the church of St. George at Dunster with a considerable estate to John de Villula, the Bishop, and the monks of Bath. It seems certain that it was the Priory of Bath which built the church we see, as it did the monastic buildings beside it, all of which have disappeared except the Prior's lodging, the dovecot, and the great barn.

Dunster was then a cell of Bath, a Benedictine house; and

in the fourteenth century it consisted of a Prior and four monks. At the Spoliation its surrender was not demanded separately, but was included in that of Bath, and to that deed the Prior of Dunster affixed his signature.

Traces of the Norman building which the Priory of Bath raised here in the eleventh century remain; the west doorway, for instance, and the piers of the tower to the west. It is said[1] that at the late restoration of the church "a large portion of the Norman west wall was exposed to view, and

Castle and Park. Dunster.

also the jambs of the Norman west door. These jambs appeared to have been much injured by fire, as if in some early *émeute*—perhaps when King Stephen lay about the Castle, endeavouring in vain to reduce it—the church had been held by one side or the other, and an attempt was made by the besiegers to effect an entrance by fire."

The nave is Perpendicular, with north and south aisle, but the north aisle is two bays short because it abutted upon the monastic buildings, and this also explains the long windowless

[1] Prebendary Hancock in *Som. Arch. Soc. Proc.*, lii (i), 56.

wall here. The roofs are waggon roofs, well preserved except in the south aisle, where there is a rich panelled ceiling. The

Luttrell Monument, Dunster Church.

tower is not a very noble one, of rather poor design, and all the eastern part of the church has been much restored after the Early English style. The curiously beautiful Early English

arch at the entrance to the south aisle of the chancel, which is now filled with a very lovely fourteenth century screen, has been widened in Perpendicular times, possibly in 1498, when the church was divided, after a long quarrel in which the Abbot of Glaston was arbitrator, into two parts, one of which became the parish church and the other, the eastern part, the church of the monks. By this arrangement the monks held the whole of the chancel and transepts, the altar of the parish church standing just within the western arch of the tower. In order then to mark off a sanctuary for the parish church out of the old nave, the magnificent great screen was made. It stretched right across nave and aisles by the third pillar of the arcade upon the north side to where we see the rood-loft stairs; and of course it bore a rood. This magnificent screen has no fewer than fifteen compartments, and above the exquisite groining run most lovely cornices. The tracery heads and the panelling below the sill should be noted. It is probable that this beautiful thing was made by the monks, as were in all likelihood many of those in this neighbourhood.

In the old days the aisles north and south of the old chancel, that is to say of the Priory Church after 1498, were chapels respectively dedicated in honour of the Blessed Virgin, and the Blessed Trinity, while a small chantry of St. Lawrence opened out of the chancel to the east of the north aisle here, now used as a vestry, and here there is an ancient stone altar. According to Prebendary Hancock, the thirteenth century arched tomb beneath the doorway of the chapel is possibly that of Sir John de Mohun the third, who fought in Flanders and Scotland for Edward I, and did much for both village and Priory.

In the monastic choir is the effigy of a woman under a beautiful canopy of the Decorated period. This is commonly said to represent one of the Everards, but Sir H. Maxwell Lyte considers it rather to represent Lady Alice de Mohun, wife of Reginald de Mohun, Earl of Somerset (d. 1257). The south aisle here, once the chapel of the Blessed Trinity, is now as it were a mortuary chapel full of the ancient monuments, some of them very fine, of the Luttrells. In the north aisle are some fine old chests.

On leaving the church, the Prior's lodging, the dovecot with its ladder, and the barn should be seen to the north of the church. Here of old, beside the parochial church, the cloister

The Village Street, Castle, and Yarn Market.

court stood; but the Priory was always small, rather a farm than a complete monastery.

On leaving the church-yard the curious little house by the

gate should be noted. It was given by the Abbot of Glaston, in the arbitration of 1498, to the parish priest for a dwelling.

As we make our way down hill back to the Luttrell Arms, the old house upon the left at the corner—a three-storeyed building—should be noted. This is popularly known as the Nunnery; why, no one seems to know.

Before the Luttrell Arms Hotel stands the ancient Yarn Market, an octagonal building, in the middle of the wide place or street, built about 1600 by George Luttrell. The Luttrell Arms Hotel is also worth inspection. The porch is loop-holed for defence, and within, on the first floor, there is an old "oak" room with a good but restored roof; in fact, the whole room is very much made up. In another room on the same floor there is a remarkable and very ugly mantel-piece of plaster with a relief representing Actaeon being torn to pieces by dogs—the antlers upon his head.

Dunster, however, can boast of other things besides ancient buildings. As a centre for exploring the moor it is not so good as Porlock, but, on the other hand, it has gifts of its own which Porlock cannot rival. I know nothing, for instance, better in its way—it is unique—than the walk to Wootton Courtney under Grabbist Hill, beside the broad valley of the Avill, where Timberscombe lies so fair upon the further hills. This way should certainly be explored if there is no time for others, for it lies all under the woods, and the return may be made with great advantage over Grabbist Hill, climbing up by Wootton Courtney by a primeval track over which the hedges quite meet to Wootton Common, and following it homeward over the heights.

Wootton Courtney, if it has nothing else to show, and the church is interesting though restored, offers us one of the finest views of Dunkery to be had anywhere, and Timberscombe has, at any rate, a fine screen in its church, though badly recoloured, and a mile along the Dulverton road is the old manor house of Bickham, still very well worth seeing.

On leaving Dunster finally for the road and the coast, the old manor house on the way to the station, known as Lower Marsh, should be noted. The porch is still very well preserved, with what was once a little chapel above it.

We now follow the main road, really a causeway over the marsh between the hills and the sea, eastward to Carhampton.

The main thing here is the beautiful, but repainted, fan-vaulted screen in the church, with cornices consisting of no less than five rows of exquisite work, each row different from the others, and both above and below the crestings are perfect. The church is disappointing, having been very much restored and even rebuilt.

A far more interesting building is the church of St. Nicholas at Withycombe, not much more than a mile north-east of Carhampton, under Croydon Hill. Here, at any rate, the south doorway is a genuine piece of Early English work, with an interesting stoup beside it, and some of the windows are good work of the fourteenth century. The font is probably Norman, and the fifteenth century fan-vaulted screen with seventeenth century additions is a noble bit of work, as fine as that at Carhampton, and finer in that it has not been repainted. The tombs in the church are interesting, too. The monument on the north side represents a widow with a heart case in her hands. That upon the south side of the church represents a young man of the middle of the thirteenth century. Both would seem to represent heart interments. In the old days, if a man died abroad his heart was often removed for burial at home. These monuments would seem to speak of such instances. In the vestry is a brass to Joan Sandhill, who was born close by within this parish at Sandhill, a beautiful Elizabethan manor house dating certainly from 1588. She was a witch, at least so it was said, and she married three husbands, all of whom she murdered. She died in 1612 and was buried in Withycombe Church, but when her neighbours got back from the funeral they found her at home frying eggs and bacon.

From Carhampton we follow the road to Washford, and here, undoubtedly, we come upon the most beautiful and the most tragic spectacle upon all our way along the coast, the ruined and broken Cistercian Abbey of Our Lady of Cleeve.

The Abbey of Cleeve is the only Cistercian House in Somerset. It was founded by William de Roumara, third Earl of Lincoln, who gave all his lands here to God, St. Mary, and the monks of St. Lawrence of Revesby, a house of the same Order in Lincolnshire, which his grandfather had founded. All this befell towards the end of the twelfth century. At the same time that William de Roumara gave all his lands at Cleeve to the Cistercians ; he gave, and this first, the parish church of Cleeve to Bishop Reginald of Wells. This church and parish came to be known as Old Cleeve, and we shall visit it after we have seen the Abbey. The prebend of Cleeve was, however, held by the Abbots of Bec, who found it difficult to look after the parish church. Therefore they gave a perpetual lease of the church to the

Cleeve Abbey.

Cistercians of Cleeve, for which from the beginning of the thirteenth century the Abbey here was responsible.

We know very little of the history of Cleeve Abbey, only we know that as a Cistercian House it was less unpopular at the time of the Spoliation than the Benedictine houses were. In 1537 we read that Sir Thomas Arundell the King's receiver wrote to Cromwell: "Riding down to Cornwall and passing the monastery of Clyffe, hearing such lamentation for the dissolution thereof, and a bruit in the country that the King on your lordship's suit had pardoned it, I sent to Mr. Chancellor of the Augmentations to know whether to dissolve it as I had his letters for the dissolution of the residue of Somerset, and it seemed to be omitted by oversight, he being very busy. I beg in behalf of the honest gentlemen of that quarter that the house may stand. In it are seventeen priests of honest life who keep hospitality." Alas! neither the prayers of these "honest gentlemen" nor the "honest lives" of the monks availed to save Cleeve from a bloody, perjured, and adulterous king, urged on to Spoliation by his own greed and Cromwell's necessity. The house fell in that very spring, 1537, and in January of the following year Robert, Earl of Sussex, was granted the site of what had been the Abbey of St. Mary.

The beautiful Abbey whose ruins we now see was not a wealthy house. The Cistercians were an austere community consisting really of farmers, and their Abbey of Cleeve stood in what was anciently known as Vallis Florida—the Flowery Valley—and if it were so, it was they who had made it blossom like the rose. Sir Thomas Arundell speaks of the hospitality kept by the monks and one of the first things we notice is the legend over its hospitable door:—

Patens porta esto,
Nulli claudaris honesto.[1]

This great gate-house, which might seem from its size to have been both porter's lodge and hostelry, stands well in front of the monastic buildings proper, but within the gateway, of which only one jamb remains. Before it is a small open court, to which it stood at right angles, and behind it was the great court upon the eastern side of which stood, from north to south, the church, and the monastic buildings in two storeys about the cloister. Upon the south side of this court were the farm buildings, but upon the west there seems to have been only a wall, and upon the north only the gatehouse and the wall beyond it to the church.

The first building we come to is this gatehouse, on the

[1] "The gate is never closed to honest folk." In other words, the house was open to all; anyone, as to-day in Italy where a convent remains, might obtain food and shelter. A better system this than our blackguard workhouses. But we were Christians in those days, and did not consider poverty to be a criminal offence.

front of which over the inscription we see a Perpendicular window—though the lower part of the building would seem to be of the thirteenth century—and over it two niches, one of which still holds a figure of the Blessed Virgin with her little Son—for she was the true Abbot of the Cistercians, all their Abbeys were dedicated in her honour. On the southern face of this gatehouse we see another window, and above, between two empty niches, a Crucifix.

Crossing the Great Court, now a rough field, we come into the Cloister (after paying a shilling for the privilege). Standing in the midst of these, to the west we have what remains of the Refectory of the lay brothers, above which was once their Dormitory. On the eastern side of the Cloister, opposite, is, above in the upper storey, the beautiful Dormitory of the monks, with Early English windows, and beneath it, from north to south, the Sacristy with its broken rose, the Treasury, perhaps, and the magnificent vaulted Chapter House with its Early English doorway. Beyond this is another room called the Library, and the staircase to the Dormitory. Beyond this again was the Fratry or Common Room, under the southern part of the great Dormitory. To the south of the Cloister stands the most beautiful building left to us at Cleeve, the Refectory, with its great Perpendicular windows and splendid roof. It was surrounded on the west by the kitchen, and on the east by the buttery and garden of herbs.

The northern side not only of the cloister, but of the buildings upon its eastern side, was closed by the great church, a hundred and seventy feet long by seventy in the nave by over a hundred in the transepts, for it was a cruciform building, almost a tau cross, the square apse projecting but fifteen feet or so. The whole of this has now utterly disappeared; we shall never see it or know it in all its simplicity and beauty.

Yes, pay your visit to Cleeve and hurry away lest it remain too long in your heart and make you out of love with your own day. These old places which men built for God's delight and for love, and because there was something in the world which is no longer to be found, or not in any satisfying quantity, keep something about them which may easily drive us mad, fill us with misery and unavailing regret. It is not good to linger with them unless we are ready to turn upon this our time with a vain anger, contempt, and hatred, and to demand of it a perfection which it is too wretched even to desire, or to understand.

From Cleeve Abbey and Washford we return a little on our way and take the seaward road by Old Cleeve for Blue Anchor.

Old Cleeve in all its country beauty must not be missed for the church, though as we see it, a Perpendicular building of the fifteenth century is the mother church of Cleeve, and was before the Abbey was thought of. It was presented to Bishop Reginald by William de Roumara, and it is dedicated, as is the cathedral church, in honour of St. Andrew. Bishop Reginald, as we have seen, made it a prebend of his cathedral and annexed it to the Benedictine Abbey of Bec, which leased it perpetually to the Abbot of Cleeve.

But the earliest work remaining at Old Cleeve is that of the fourteenth century in the south porch and in the Cross there on its Calvary. There, too, but within the porch, stands a very material witness to the old religion, a huge Peter's Pence chest of the fifteenth century, when England yet was a loyal province of Rome.

In the north wall of the nave, within, is a recessed canopied tomb with the effigy of a man, his feet upon a cat whose paw rests upon a mouse with a long tail. This is, or seems to be, of the fourteenth or early fifteenth century.

Without, in the churchyard, is the grave of George Jones, Blacksmith, who died in 1808, with the following amusing epitaph:—

> My Sledge and Hammer lie reclined,
> My Billows too have lost their wind;
> My Fire's extinct, my Forge decay'd,
> And in the Dust my Body's laid;
> My Coal is burnt, my Iron's gone,
> My Nails are drove, my Work is done.

Beyond Old Cleeve on the road to Blue Anchor we have Chapel Cleeve. Here there are still remains (not open to the public) of an ancient chapel of Our Lady. This would seem to have been a shrine or wayside chapel in connection with the famous sanctuary of St. Mary *juxta mare*—Our Lady by the Sea, a celebrated place of pilgrimage on the shore near Blue Anchor which more than once it seems was spoiled by the sea or the fall of the cliff. The offerings at this shrine were doubtless an important source of income to the great Abbey, and even after the Spoliation we read that Anthony Bustard, who first leased the site of the Abbey, was willing to pay £20 a year for the chapel at Chapel Cleeve, which by that time may have taken the place of the destroyed shrine by the sea. It must have been to this place Leland referred; "*Clif* Chapelle, wher offering was to Our Lady, is set upon no very high Ground, but rokky. It is welle buildid; and on the south side of it is a goodly Ynne al of Stone of late usid for Pilgrimes. The Se is about half a Mile from *Clife*-Chapelle."

Blue Anchor under its alabaster cliffs upon the sea is quite charming; it is inevitably marked out as a successful seaside place, I fear, but it is not spoiled yet. Not far away upon the seaward road to Dunster stands Marshwood Farm, an old manor house with some curious plaster carvings in its porch.

From Blue Anchor we pass either by the low cliffs, or better, by the shore or by the road, a byway, to Watchet, of old so often raided by the Danes, as in 918, when, the Saxon Chronicle tells us, "the Port of Watchet was plundered," and a battle took place, in which the invaders were beaten, at Battle Gore in a valley towards Williton.

But the one really interesting thing about Watchet is the parish church of St. Decuman's, which is not in Watchet at all.

St. Decuman is said to have come hither from Wales with a hurdle for ship, or even a faggot, or as others say, his cloak, with a cow, which "of her own will accompanied him in all his wanderings, and fed him with her milk." When he was landed he sought the first hill he could see, and there established himself as a hermit, till he was found, when they who found him not liking the look of him, beheaded him; in vain, of course, for he took up his own head, and washing away the blood at a spring hard by, went away, recrossing the channel with his head under his arm.[1]

But St. Decuman's church is notable for other reasons; it is a tragic place; at Orchard in this parish was born and lived Robert Fitzurse, one of the murderers of St. Thomas à Becket;

[1] One of the statues upon the great front of Wells Cathedral is said to represent this saint; it shows us a man with part of his skull in his hands.

at Sampford Brett, also in this parish, lived another of them, Simon de Brett. Each did penance for his crime; the one gave the presentation of Williton to the vicar of St. Decuman's; the other gave St. Decuman's to found a prebend in Wells Cathedral. Fiction, too, adds to the tragedy; here Coleridge's Ancient Mariner set out, and hither he returned; and Blackmore says that Lorna's mother was buried in this churchyard.

As we see it, the church is a Perpendicular building, with many fragments from the older churches. Originally the church had a central tower, but that fell, and the present tower, a very fine one, with a figure of the saint, was built at the end of the fifteenth century. The most notable things now in the church are the Windham tombs and brasses in the chapel of St. Peter on the north. The Windhams' houses were at Orchard Windham, and at Kentisford, hard by, now a farm house. The most touching and splendid memorial to a member of this loyalist family will not, however, be found in marble or "brass eternal," but in the words of an epitaph upon a plain flagstone in the chancel which commemorates Sir Hugh Windham, the son of the brave governor of Bridgwater, who died in 1671. There we read:—

Heere lies beneath this ragged stone
One more his Princes then his owne,
And in his martered Father's warres
Lost Fortune, Blood; gained nought but scarres;
And for his sufferings as reward
Had neather countinance nor regard,
And Earth affording noe releafe,
Is gone to Heaven to ease his greefe.

In the churchyard will be found the following upon the grave of one Sully, who died in 1824:—

Tho' Borus blast and Neptune's waves
Have tossed me to and fro,
In spite of both, by God's decree,
I harbour here below;
Where I do now at anchor lay
With many of our fleet,
Yet once again I must set sail
Our Saviour Christ to meet.

Others, both curious and vain, abound in the church and churchyard.

From St. Decuman's we make our way to Williton, a

pleasing little town, a bower of flowers, and in the Spring, especially of laburnum. Williton was, as I have said, the home and the possession of Reginald Fitzurse, who with his fellow, Simon de Brett of Sampford Brett, claimed Somerset as their county. Where Reginald lies I know not—not in the chantry chapel he built at Williton, which is not now worth a visit; but Simon lies at Sampford Brett, where in the church you may see his recumbent effigy.

The most beautiful part of our journey is drawing to an end, but we have yet to make our way over the seaward headlands of Quantock, and the road from this little town of Williton to Stogursey is, in my view, not inferior to any other in the county. Indeed, I know none other that will give you such gracious views of hill and sea—the low hills leaning down to meet it—than will this way by St. Audries and West Quantoxhead, East Quantoxhead, through Stringston to Stogursey, on the last foothills, on the verge of the great marsh where all Bridgwater Bay, Brean Down, the Steep Holm and the Flat Holm, behind and beyond it, with all central Somerset, closed and guarded on the north by the Mendip Hills, lie before you.

And, to begin with, what is there lovelier than the road to St. Audries, or what is nobler than that great pleasaunce, a gracious English home, if ever there was one, amid its glorious trees and meadow and park, sloping to the sea in the solemn presence of the far mountains of Wales? It is true that the church of West Quantoxhead is modern, but it is one of our better efforts; and then not much further on there is East Quantoxhead to help you out, with a fine old church and a manor house that is still in the possession of the family that held it at the Conquest. "I saw," says Leland, "a fair Park and Manor Place of the Lutterelles caullid Quantock-Hedde bycause it standeth at the Heede of Quantock-Hilles towards the Se." And there it stands still, a great, strong English house, and in the church you will find an altar tomb of much the same date with this inscription:—"Here luyt hugh luttrell knyght wyhe departed 1522 the fyrst day of februarie, here lyt andro luttrell knyght his son wyhe departed the yere of our lord god MCCCCCXXX VIII the iiii day of may on whoys souly Jhu have mcy."

Beyond East Quantoxhead, stands "Kilve by the green

sea," as Southey called it, and it is Wordsworth himself who speaks of "Kilve's delightful shore," with its old decayed Court House close by, and a demolished chantry not far away towards the sea.

But we are for the red spire of Stringston, where in the south side of the church there is a very lovely Cross of the fourteenth century, canopied too, and with carvings of the Crucifixion, our Lady and her little Son, an armed Knight to guard them and a Bishop to bless all who pass by. And in a little over a mile we are at Stogursey.

Stogursey, more probably Stoke Courcy, like its neighbour on this side Quantock, Nether Stowey, can boast of a castle, and though there is nothing there now but a moat and a vaguely circular wall with the bases of certain towers, it has a long history. It was, so it is said, though this might seem unlikely from its size, the principal fortress of the Courcy house in the twelfth century. It is further asserted that it passed to the godless Fulke de Breauté, the meanest of the Normans, by his marriage with the heiress of the de Courcy house, Alice de Redvers, who took him for her second husband, and that he there established a "stronghold of robbers," till Hubert de Burgh, the justiciar, broke him and overthrew the castle. A little later the place passed to the Fitz-Paines, and from them to the Percies, but was finally ruined by Lord Bonville after the Battle of St. Albans. What remains is not the ruin of a Norman, but of a thirteenth century building.

The church is a much more interesting building, a really fine example of a Norman church with central tower. In the twelfth century it was given by William de Falaise to the Benedictine Abbey of Lonley, in Normandy, which founded an alien priory here, of which all that remains is a circular dovecot.

For the use of the monks the choir was enlarged by the addition of two aisles. These with the fine arcades which divide them from the chancel are very late Norman work. So far as can be seen, the church remained thus an example of two periods of Norman work till the fifteenth century, when a good deal was done, and, as we see, all the windows belong to this time, as does, indeed, the body of the church. The bench ends, some of which show a Flemish character, are of the sixteenth century. In the south aisle of the chancel, where once there was a chantry in honour of Our Lady of Pity, there are the tombs of Sir Ralph (d. 1352) and Sir John Verney (d. 1461).

Now at Stogursey let us say good-bye to those great and beautiful hills, the Quantocks, for the moor lies spread out before us, and more and more as we pass into its vastness those great hills will become just a vision behind us till they are lost in the mists of the levels, the width of the great sea plain. For West Somerset now lies all behind us with its glory in the golden sunset, and at Combwich we cross the broad and muddy estuary of the Parrett and find ourselves among the lowing herds on these fat Pawlett Hams banked so securely from the sea, where at Pawlett there is a cruciform church with a Norman doorway and at Huntspill—where "Master Guy was a gentleman"—a very fine church indeed (almost entirely rebuilt after a fire), and in the south wall of it, effigies of a knight and his lady.

I don't know, but I suppose this must be the richest grazing land in old England; but just here it is rather lacking in interest. Its capital, Highbridge, on the "marshy Brue," which a mile away loses itself in the mud of the Parrett, is utterly without any sort of delight for the traveller, who, indeed, is more used to curse than to bless it, for here is the junction of the Great Western Railway with the Somerset and Dorset line to Glastonbury, to say nothing of the Burnham Branch.

At Burnham we get back to the coast itself and the sea too, if you can call it a sea; for its colour is against it, and if you come upon it when the tide is out, the gold of its great sands will not impress you so much as the vast belt of mud which lies as far as the eye can reach along the great estuary of the Parrett upon which, and not upon the true sea, Burnham is set.

Burnham then, for all its wonderful sands, its sandhills and its golf course, is heavily handicapped as a pleasure resort; but for us who pass on it has this interest, that in its early Perpendicular church there is an altar-piece from the hand of Inigo Jones. This beautiful reredos of colured marbles Inigo Jones designed for the chapel of Whitehall. When that was burnt, the reredos was saved and Queen Anne gave it at the petition of the Dean and Chapter to Westminster Abbey and it was set up over the high altar, where it was wholly out of place.[1] Before the Coronation of George IV it was taken down with the whole of the wainscotting, seats, stalls, pulpit, and organ in the choir, by Wyatt, and Bishop King of Rochester, then canon of Westminster, obtained it for Burnham church where he had been vicar. Needless to say, it is almost as much out of place there as it was at Westminster.

From Burnham we may go on by the sea shore, but better by road to Berrow, where in the church there is a small pulpit and a gallery dating from 1637. From Burnham all the way the great Tor of Brent Knoll, a brother to Glastonbury Tor, is seen standing out of the marshes. This was, of course, an island of old, and upon its top there is an early encampment and thence one may get one of the really great views of Somerset; for Brent Knoll stands four hundred and fifty feet over the sea and the marsh. The camp is prehistoric and not as is popularly supposed Roman; the discovery of Roman coins within the camp is no evidence of Roman construction or occupation. Their presence here probably dates from the failure of the Roman administration, when they were still current, but when barbaric conditions were returning.

At the foot of Brent Knoll there are two villages: one to the south-west, commonly known as South Brent, and the other to the north-east, known as East Brent.

The church, of course of St. Michael, of South Brent stands well upon the side of the Knoll. It is an interesting building, but has been a good deal pulled about; the chancel, for instance, being entirely modern. The best thing in the church is the north aisle, which was built in the end of the fifteenth century. There is a noble roof which is of about the same time as are the carved bench ends. The church, however, has many interesting fragments from its predecessors. The south doorway, for instance, is late Norman, the south wall of the nave is all that remains of an Early English church, and the vestry was a chantry of the latter part of the fourteenth century; it is in the Decorated style of that time. The triple-windowed tower is plain but dignified.

[1] There is a good view of it *in situ* at Westminster, in Brayley's *History and Antiquities* (1823), vol. ii, p. 38.

East Brent church is remarkable for its tower and stone spire. On the west face of the tower we find carvings of the Blessed Virgin with her Son in her arms, the Blessed Trinity, and the Coronation of the Virgin. The two subjects which concern the Blessed Virgin are explained by the fact that the church was dedicated in her honour. The manors of East Brent, South Brent, and Lympsham all belonged to Glastonbury, and here at East Brent Abbot Selwood built a house with chapel which was destroyed utterly in 1718. But against the north wall of the church within are remains of a canopied seat which might have been his, for similar seats are found at South Brent and Lympsham. But here in East Brent church the best things are the woodwork, the glass, and the embossed roof of plaster, dating from 1637, in the nave, far better than the similar ceiling at Axbridge.

The gallery at the west end of old went across the chancel arch; it is a fine piece of work and dates from 1635, the pulpit being of 1634. The benches seem to have been made in the time of Abbot Selwood and probably to his order, for they bear his initials and the arms of Glaston.

The glass is very good, that in the east window being of the fourteenth century; the Crucifixion, however, is modern, as is the Ascension. In the north window are some old pieces, among them an exquisite head of the Blessed Virgin; while in the nave on the north there are three figures which are supposed to be of old German glass; they are certainly very fine.

All this is most easily seen from Burnham, and if the traveller will not put up with poor inns, it is the only way to see such lonely places. As for me, I returned from South Brent to Berrow, and then made my way along the road, by the shore, through Brean to Brean Down. And when I had seen all there was to see, I went over the difficult estuary of the Axe by ferry, and the ferryman was more like Charon than any other I am likely to meet before I see the great original and cross the Styx.

In Brean there is nothing to keep you, nor on Brean Down either for that matter, but I lingered about the old farm there for reasons of my own, and wondered again, as I had often done as a boy, to see Mendip come down thus stubbornly to the sea, protesting even half-way over in those melancholy and mysterious islands the Steep Holm and the Flat Holm, lonely there in the fog and the channel tide. The Steep Holm is so steep that only a bird one would think could find footing there, but there are still some remains of a Priory of Austin Canons upon it, of which I think nothing is known. The Flat Holm, some seven miles out and some two miles from the Steep Holm, boasts of a lighthouse and a farm; but neither it nor its neighbour carry guns, of which fact, and I think rightly, the good people of Bristol make complaint.

I had meant to sleep at Uphill, but when I saw it, for all its Roman memories and perhaps its Roman name Axium, its ruined Norman church on the hill, and its watch tower, I liked it little, so little that though I was very weary I went on to Hutton under its tall church tower, and from Hutton on the morrow I set out to explore the villages of Bleadon Hill, that great island hill of Mendip more than five hundred feet high, under which, to the south, the Axe passes into this mysterious sea.

These villages all together possess what is perhaps the most interesting group of churches in the county.

To begin with Hutton itself: this small and picturesque village at the northern foot of Bleadon Hill is well worth a visit, if only on account of its old manor house, Hutton Court, a too much restored and rebuilt mansion of the fifteenth century. The church here also has been much tampered with, the fine south porch of which we read having been utterly destroyed in 1849. Perhaps the best thing and certainly the rarest left to the church is the mediaeval pulpit in the Early Perpendicular style, a delicate and even exquisite work; but the brasses to the Payns, once lords of this manor, in the chancel are very well worth seeing, and at the west end of the south aisle is a fine Jacobean tablet dating from 1626. The tower is a simple but a noble one with a stair turret crowned with a charming spirelet; its ceiling in the lowest storey is of great beauty.

From Hutton I went round the eastern escarpment of Bleadon Hill to Bleadon. Here is a fine church tower (c. 1370) of the triple window type, and though not as fine a specimen of this class of tower as is to be found at Banwell, or better, at Winscombe, hard by, it has some characteristics all its own. The church is St. Peter's and St. Paul's,[1] and

[1] It is possible that the chapel which was on the north of the church was dedicated in honour of St. Paul.

consists of nave, chancel, and south porch. The oldest part of the church is the eastern part of the chancel, which is of the fourteenth century; but the east window is modern, and indeed, the chancel would appear to have once been longer than it now is. The nave and first bay of the chancel are of the Perpendicular time, and it has been suggested that a central tower once separated nave and chancel as at Christon. The font is Transitional and the pulpit a modern reconstruction, largely of old material. Upon the south side of the altar there would appear to be the base of an Easter Sepulchre, though it would seem out of place upon the south. Here, too, are two sepulchral effigies, which have no relation one with the other. We are told that for years they lay in the churchyard, but not side by side. They represent two male figures of the middle of the fourteenth century, and they once stood in all probability upon the north of the church. In the south porch there is a carving of the Blessed Virgin with her little Son and a spoilt Cross is in the churchyard, of which this possibly once formed a part.

If Bleadon church is interesting, that at Loxton under the south-eastern extremity of Bleadon Hill is much more so. Here we have a building which still retains much of its Norman and Early English characteristics. It consists of a curious and certainly early square battlemented tower of little height over the south porch; of nave, chancel, and north aisle. Before the porch stands a headless churchyard Cross upon a calvary. Within the porch is a small window which once commanded a view of the altar, and was probably used by the sacristan when he rang the church bell at the elevation. Within, the stone pulpit is a notable Perpendicular work; it rests upon a corbel in the form of a man. Of the same period is the font. Some old glass in the chancel is worth notice.

Not less interesting is Christon Church to the north of Loxton under the north-eastern height of Bleadon Hill. It consists of nave and chancel, with central tower with Norman arches. The south doorway, too, is Norman and richly decorated. But, perhaps, the finest of all these churches is that of Banwell. Banwell church was a peculiar under the jurisdiction of the Priory of Bruton, and this may account for its nobility. It consists of a very noble western tower of the second class, with triple windows in the top storey (the first tower of this type is that at Shepton Mallet), a clerestoried nave with north and south aisles, an aisleless chancel and south porch with parvise. The tower, as I say, is a fine one, and may be compared, though not perhaps to its advantage, I think, with that at Winscombe a couple of miles to the south, where the church is interesting, chiefly on account of its sixteenth century glass, but has been much restored. Upon the tower here at Banwell there are two fine panels representing the Annunciation. After the change in religion, or rather the death of all true religion, in the sixteenth century, these panels were said to represent Henry VI and his Queen. Therefore, it puzzled folks that the Queen had a lily before her, but the King none. About a century ago, still in sublime ignorance that the scene here carved represented the Nativity of the Word, the Salvation of the world, "Henry VI" was supplied with a lily.[1] Upon the eastern face of the tower is a figure of St. Andrew. The tower dates from about the end of the fourteenth century.

Within the church we are at once struck by its noble proportions, of the fifteenth century, and by its beautiful roof. The fourteenth century chancel, however, heightened when the nave was rebuilt, is small and disappointing, though I suppose its walls are the oldest part of the church, with the exception, of course, of such furniture as the font which though itself late Norman was carved in the fifteenth century, and the bases of the pillars on the north of the nave. The loveliest thing in the church, however, is perhaps the stone pulpit though it is spoilt by the modern staircase. At the same time the woodwork here is very glorious, the poppy-headed benches date from the fifteenth century, but the rood loft is a seventeenth century work and very fine and splendid it is. The Rood has of course gone, but the corbels still remain. Besides this there is the western gallery which about 1590 formed part of a pew built by Bishop Godwyn of Wells who was lord of the Manor of Banwell. This pew stood upon the south side of the nave just outside the rood-screen, and there it remained till, about fifty years ago, it was removed and its woodwork used as we see it. The font dates from 1621,

[1] See the interesting and learned article, Rev. C. S. Taylor, M.A., P.S.A., in *Som. Arch. Proc.*, vol. li (ii), 269-70.

and in the recess over the south porch there is a communion table, lectern, and credence of the same date. Mr. Taylor tells us that "the series is completed by a pulpit cover which still exists in the village." In the vestry in the chancel there is some fine old Flemish glass brought here from Belgium in 1855 by the then Vicar; here too is a brass to John Martock, Physician to Bishop King, who died in Banwell Manor House in 1503. John Martock was not only a physician, but a priest and prebendary of Haselbere; he is represented in his cope; he died two years after his Bishop.

Banwell Court, the manor house where Bishop King died, was built, not as we see it, by Bishop Beckington. Another old house, Tower Head House, was built in 1584 as a summer resort by Bishop Godwyn. Both are interesting and beautiful buildings.

Some four miles to the north-east of Banwell stands Churchill, under the great prehistoric camp of Dolebury upon Mendip. All this country and all these villages are beautiful, and all have lovely views of the great hills; but I think perhaps Churchill offers you most in the way of natural loveliness. The church here consists of a poor tower of the local stone, a nave with north and south aisles, and chancel. The arcades in the nave are of different times, the south being earlier, and perhaps of the fourteenth century, and the roof there is a good piece of Perpendicular work. But the best thing in the church is the roof of the north aisle. The chancel is poor with a modern east window. The bench ends in the nave remind one of those at Banwell. A remarkably vivid monument, originally of the seventeenth century, erected to the memory of one John Latch and his wife, stands upon the north side of the chancel; while on the floor of the south aisle is a brass of 1572 to Ralph Jenyns. Here, too, are some pieces of armour. In the porch are two fifteenth century effigies concerning which I could find no news.

Churchill Court is a fine old mansion; but its connection with the great Duke of Marlborough is very shadowy.

From Churchill I went down into the beautiful Wrington Vale by Langford House and the woods there under Burrington to Wrington over the Yeo.

Now the first thing that must strike any wayfarer on entering Wrington is the great double-windowed tower of its church, for it reminds one of St. Cuthbert's in Wells and of Evercreech, and is a very notable and noble thing in a lovely landscape. At the same time I cannot go all the way with Freeman, who described it as the finest square western tower of any parish church in this county. In my opinion it does not compare favourably with Evercreech, a tower absolutely of its own class; nor, to name other double-windowed towers, with such masterpieces as Bishop's Lydeard, North Petherton, Huish Episcopi, Chewton Mendip, St. Cuthbert's Wells or St. John's Glastonbury; and of course it is not so fine as the very best of the triple-window towers, Shepton Mallet, Winscombe, Bruton, Weston Zoyland, and Leigh-upon-Mendip. These towers in their two kinds are to my mind certainly the finest in the county, and I do not know in all broad England anything finer than these. Wrington is a noble double-windowed tower of the second class, and the second class in Somerset is as good or better than the first anywhere else. It may be, as Mr. Buckle once suggested, that the church dwarfs the tower, which was built for a much smaller building, "not much higher and not much wider than the (present) chancel; and with such a building as that no doubt the tower looked much better than at present." As it is, the nave is lofty with its triple-lighted clerestory windows, but too short. Yet it is the best thing in the church; the Early English chancel, with alas! Perpendicular additions, suffering very much in comparison with it.

As it happens, it is by chance that Wrington is able to boast itself the birthplace of that rather futile seventeenth century philosopher John Locke. His mother happened to be staying in Wrington when he decided to enter the world. The old thatched cottage in which he was born has long since been destroyed, and he is now commemorated by a tablet in the churchyard wall.

A nobler spirit and a more useful life is connected with Wrington in that Hannah More lies in its churchyard, with her four maiden sisters, and they have not destroyed her favourite house, Barley Wood, only enlarged and restored it! It was at Barley Wood that among other distinguished people the "prim" old lady received the young Macaulay whom we find in 1852 writing: "the valley of Wrington is as rich and as lovely as ever. The Mendip ridges, the church tower, the islands in the distance are still what they were forty years ago and more."

Lovely as that vale is, it is hard to pass on one's way—by light railway too, if you wish—to Congresbury and Yatton; and in fact I did not, for I visited these and other places from Wrington, always returning to it, for I could not drag myself away.

Congresbury has a very notable origin. It is said that St. Congar, a hermit, a son of the Emperor of the East, stole away from Byzantium in order that he might not be forced to marry, at least with the lady his parents had chosen for him. After wandering through Italy and France, he came to Britain, and here beside the Yeo in the marsh he built a little oratory of wattles to the Blessed Trinity. Finding him there, King Ine endowed this oratory with the land about it, and there St. Congar is said to have established a convent of twelve canons both Welsh and English as the King especially desired, for he wished above all things to reconcile us. But after a time, as it happened, St. Congar grew restless and went off again down the long, neglected roads for Jerusalem, where he died. It is said, however, that his body was brought back to England and was buried here at Congresbury where, by the way, he planted his staff as Joseph did at Glaston, only St. Congar's was not of thorn but of yew. So much for St. Congar; and I like to think of this wanderer from Byzantium in the marshes of Somerset; therefore I disregard the nonsense of the etymologists who would derive Congresbury from Koenig and by the way of Germany arrive at Kingston. And how, pray, are they going to explain the origin of that monastery here which Alfred gave to Asser if they banish St. Congar?

Congresbury is charming too. The church with a good spire is well worth seeing, for it has a lofty clerestoried nave with curious coloured figures between the windows, aisles north and south, chancel, and south porch with a parvise, now a gallery, over it. What strikes one at once as curious in the nave is the difference between the two arcades. That on the south is Early English with modern black shafts, which support nothing, about the pillars. The north arcade, later in date, has not been so ruined. The furniture of the church is good; the font Norman, the sedilia and double piscina elaborate and interesting. The rood-screen was carried upon a stone wall once richly ornamented but now ruined. The screen between aisle and chapel too is interesting. It is curious to note that the two square windows in the chancel and chapel are said to be

Yatton Church. Interior.

of the fourteenth century; they are surprising rather than beautiful.

Nothing I think can well be more different from Congresbury church than Yatton is; yet the two places are scarce two miles apart, but the Yeo, and therefore in old days the marshes, lie between.

Yatton Church is a noble cruciform building with a central tower, upon which stands a truncated spire. Over the fine west front, like but not so elaborate as Crewkerne, is a carving of the Blessed Trinity. Within, the clerestoried nave is lofty and beautiful, but the transepts are short and the chancel not only short but very low. The tower piers too, which are of the fourteenth century, are very massive, so that the chancel is scarcely seen from the nave. The church is indeed a fourteenth and fifteenth century building set upon a Norman plan, though the oldest work we see there is those tower piers, and the nearly contemporary transepts. In itself the chancel is good enough and even a charming piece of Early Perpendicular work, but it is lost in the church. The nave, clerestory and aisles are rich and Late Perpendicular work, and very glorious they are.

In the north transept is the alabaster monument of Sir Richard Newton and his wife; but this is wholly outstripped in interest by the tomb, under a foliated recess where are two effigies, figures of a man and a woman dating from the fourteenth century. The chapel out of this transept is the beautiful mortuary chapel of Sir John Newton, son of Sir Richard and his wife Isabel de Cheddar (d. 1487); a very noble monument commemorates them, against the north wall, over a fine relief of the Annunciation. But perhaps the loveliest thing in Yatton lies hidden in an epitaph:

> Here lies Merrily Joules,
> A beauty bright,
> Who left Isaac Joules her
> Heart's delight.

To the south-east of the church still stands the old fifteenth century vicarage house, and on the north are to be seen some old almshouses.

Not far from Yatton, a little more than a mile maybe, at the foot of the hills stands Brockley, a small and beautiful country village, with a small and quiet country church with no fundamental division between nave and chancel, save that the latter is not so high as the former. The church is really an Early English building with a roof of the late fifteenth century, and a very fine Norman font. If you have eyes to see, all England lies in such a little thing as Brockley Church.

Close by the church is an ancient court house, but this, which nevertheless has its interest, is not the main thing about Brockley. The best thing about Brockley is its quietness and its beauty, and perhaps the fact that from it you may pass up Brockley Combe, a place of wonderful woods and cliffs, to be seen and to be loved, as Coleridge knew:—

LINES COMPOSED WHILE CLIMBING THE LEFT ASCENT OF BROCKLEY COMBE, SOMERSET, MAY, 1795.

"With many a pause, and oft-reverted eye,
I climb the Combe's ascent; sweet songsters near
Warble in shade their wild-wood melody;
Far off the unvarying cuckoo soothes my ear.
Up scour the startling stragglers of the flock
That on green plots by precipices browse;
From the deep fissures of the naked rock
The yew-tree bursts! Beneath its dark green boughs
('Mid which the May-thorn blends its blossoms white),
Where broad smooth stones jut out in mossy seats,
I rest; and now have gained the topmost site.
Ah! what a luxury of landscape meets
My gaze! Proud towers, and cots more dear to me,
Elm-shadowed fields, and prospect-bounding sea!
Deep sighs my lonely heart; I drop the tear;
Enchanting spot! O, were my Sara here!"

But Brockley is not alone in its delight, the smaller village of Cleeve under Cleeve Hill and the old elms about Cleeve Court are worth a visit, nay, are worth indeed all the time you can give to such loveliness.

It was from Yatton that I set out for Weston; for there was no way of avoiding this place, since it offered me the best key to a tract of country I was determined to see.

I found Weston—Weston *super Mare* they say—much what I expected, but I was certainly delighted with one thing, namely, the walk that it offered me about Worle Hill over the sea, through the woods to Kewstoke, and I was delighted with the noble view from the prehistoric camp upon the summit at Worlebury.

Nevertheless, Weston is a very dreadful and popular place—dreadful as only a popular English place can be—and the traveller who has wandered through all the dear villages I have tried to describe in this volume, already too long, will not desire, any more than I did, to be bothered with it. Let him make use of it for sleeping, let it be a base of operations only, and it will be in its place and prove useful.

As for me, I went to the camp upon Worle Hill and enjoyed the view I got of the hills and the marsh, and the sea and the Welsh mountains, and then I went on by the road I have spoken of upon the seaward side of Worle through the woods to Kewstoke.

Kewstoke, a fair village, has a church after my own heart, for I love all such places; they are the very best symbols of England—the England that can surely never utterly pass away—and perhaps in this horrible age we live in they are all that is visibly left to us of her. At Kewstoke this is what I found, and this is why I loved it; I went in by the south door, which was Norman, I saw an Early English lancet in the chancel, and on the north I found lovely Decorated windows; the clerestory—there were no aisles—was Perpendicular, to which time, of course, the tower belonged. Of this glorious Somerset period, too, were the pulpit and the glass, perhaps, in the south chapel. You could not but love the place; like a thousand others—and thank God every day for all of them—it is an epitome of all that was best in us, and that I cannot but believe remains—remains to be expressed when we again awake.

Kewstoke was pure good luck—I had come not to see it, but to look upon what remained of Worspring by the sea. Here, too, I found more than I expected; a church, the church of the Blessed Trinity, St. Mary and St. Thomas the Martyr—our St. Thomas, a chantry, a court room, and a barn. These precious things, holy yet, in spite of every heathen and heretic desecration, with the prayers of more than three hundred years, I found used as farm buildings. And yet, why not? Was not our Lord born in a stable—had He where to lay His head—is not His very sepulchre still in the hands of the infidel? And then at least the degradation of these buildings from their high and holy office has saved them to serve in our hearts a memory—an uneasy memory—of the Garden of Eden, out of which we were led—I know not how—to minister to a mind diseased.

Worspring—not Woodspring—Priory was founded in the early years of the thirteenth century—the greatest of all centuries—by William de Courteney, a grandson of that murderer, Reginald Fitzurse of Williton, who, with his fellow assassins, struck St. Thomas that cruel blow and thus all unwillingly helped to establish a great new saint for England. Worspring was a house of Austin Canons, who followed the Rule of St. Victor, and it seems to have had some connection—though we do not know exactly how or what—with the great house of the Order in Bristol.

The house was a small one, and after flourishing for some three hundred and twenty years or so the Prior and seven canons surrendered it. The following letter shows how

Worspring Priory, near Kewstoke.

desirable it appeared to the greedy and godless men who broke the Church in England and later destroyed the throne.

"So if it pleasith it y^r m^{r}ship . . . my naturall ffather willed me to write to yor m^{r}ship and to none othere for to be good m^r unto me for a house of chanons yn somersett their called worspryng where my seyd ffather is ffounder thereof and as I do subpose of like value or thereaboutes. And if it wold please y^r m^{r}ship to be as god m^r unto me as to helpe me to worspryng Priorie I were and wylbe wylst I leve y^r bedeman and alweys redy to y^r m^{r}ship suche poore service and pleasure as shalbe come me to doo whillest I do leve god wylling who ever have y^r m^{r}ship yn his provysshion ffrom Bletherwere this present palme Sonday."

This blasphemous flunkey does not seem to have obtained his desire. For Worspring Priory was granted to Sir William St. Loe, who sold the same to William Carre.

I lingered at Worspring till evening fell and then got me back to Weston and the train and went on to Clevedon, better than Weston, less blatant and not without a certain quietness, but especially in this, that though it has forgotten Coleridge, yet in its old church "obscure and solitary" to the south of the town, on the hill, lies Henry Hallam, the historian, and he, too, in whose memory Tennyson built that monument more enduring than brass "In Memoriam." They lie in the south transept. Neither they nor the great poet who gave the younger that immortality in the memory of his countrymen he was too early called away himself to build, was of Somerset, and yet here they touch us; here the poet is ours. Was it not our strange Severn Sea he saw when he wrote:—

> "Break, break, break
> On thy cold gray stones, O Sea!
> And I would that my tongue could utter
> The thoughts that arise in me.
>
> "O well for the fisherman's boy
> That he shouts with his sister at play!
> O well for the sailor lad,
> That he sings in his boat on the bay!
>
> "And the stately ships go on
> To their haven under the hill:
> But, O for the touch of a vanish'd hand
> And the sound of a voice that is still!
>
> "Break, break, break
> At the foot of thy crags, O Sea!
> But the tender grace of a day that is dead
> Will never come back to me."

Doubtless it was of our sea that these words were written, and yet they are not to be taken too literally. Tennyson himself has told us, "I myself did not see Clevedon till years after the burial of A. H. H." He is, however, the author of this simple epitaph:

> "Here with his wife and children rests
> Henry Hallam the Historian."

which contrasts so with the long, long epitaph to Arthur Hallam written by his father.

There are two other things to see at Clevedon, beside the "obscure and solitary" church of St. Andrew's: Clevedon Court and Walton Castle.

Clevedon Court is one of those "stately homes of England," which we are all so proud of, though, unlike the monasteries, which they so often replaced, they are the private pleasaunce

Clevedon Court from the South.

of one man, and not for all of us. Clevedon Court, however, is so beautiful a home that it does seem to be a veritable part of England. It dates from the times of Edward II, but was greatly extended in Elizabethan times, and since then has been restored and changed and modernised; yet it retains much of its old delight. It is, of course, full of literary reminiscences of the Hallams—Arthur Hallam's mother was a daughter of the house—and of Thackeray, who is said to have written part of *Esmond* here; but surely Tennyson was not here till 1850, and it can have but few memories of him. Walton Castle, on the hilltop to the north of Clevedon, whence there is a great view, is a fine old place surrounded by round towers, and is well worth a visit.

From Clevedon it is easy and pleasant to visit Walton, Weston, Clapton—all in Gordano—as well as Portishead and Portbury, if you will.

Walton is a pretty place enough, but beyond its prettiness

Clevedon Court from the North.

nothing is to be had there. Weston in Gordano has something better to offer us in its charming little church with its curious Early English thirteenth century tower to the south of it, where there is a porch, too, with an unique gallery over it, perhaps for the *Gloria laus et honor* of Palm Sunday. The nave of the church is earlier than the chancel which has some elaborate windows. But the church as we see it is a rebuilding or a restoration by Sir Richard Percyvale, Lord of the Manor, who died in 1483, and whose tomb, with an epitaph in

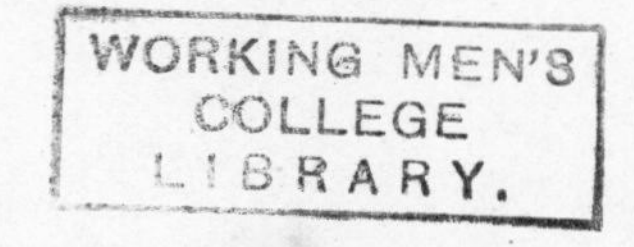

French, "*Gy gyste le corps de Rycharde Percyval le quel mourut l'an de boinet Jesus MCCCCLXXXIII Dieu ay pitie de son ame*," is to be seen upon the north side of the nave. The Norman font remains *in situ*, as does the high altar (the pillars in front are modern), while the ambo, in part at any rate, a work of the thirteenth century, is to be noticed. The bench ends and the stalls in the chancel are notable, though rough. The pulpit seems to be Jacobean, but the screen is a patchwork.

The chapel of St. Mary Magdalen on the south side of the choir was built in the sixteenth century; it, too, retains its altar. In the churchyard is an altar tomb to another Richard Percyvale, a crusader who died in 1190—for the Percyvales ruled here six hundred years; there we read "*Orate pro anima Ricardi Percyvale qui militavit in Terra Santa cum Rege Rycardo A.D. MCXC.*" Their old home has been destroyed *in hominum memoria*; it stood below the church where there is a farm.

From Weston in Gordano I went on to Portishead, quite a town this, running out to its green headland, with a church in the middle of the old village beyond which Portishead has grown. Beyond the fine tower there is little to see in the church; but close by is an old manor house that should not be missed. After returning quite through the town, I went on to Portbury where there is a very noble and spacious church, with ancient yews in the churchyard and with some Norman work within it: a fine south door, and something, at least in the chancel arch, which for the rest seems to be of the thirteenth century. The windows at the east end of the aisles are good—five lancets under an arch. The sedilia in the chancel and south aisle are also Early English. Just beyond the great squint in the north side of the chancel is a chapel with a stone barrel vault.

So I went on under the hills to Clapton in Gordano with its fine fourteenth century manor house, Clapton Court and a little Early English church, but with fifteenth century windows, with its equally early—at least equally early—tower. Under the arch leading into this tower, within, is a rough oak screen that has been brought here from Clapton Court.

From Clapton I crossed the hills, no light matter, for I was weary, and presently came into Wraxall lost in the woods.

The church here is for the most part modern save for an Early English porch, and, I suppose, the curious tower. In the modern chancel too in the north side is a tomb with two effigies.

It was already night when I came into Nailsea and found a bed. The best thing in Nailsea is not in Nailsea but a long way out of it to the south, the Elizabethan manor house Nailsea Court, a fine old building in a good state of preservation now a farmhouse. Close by is Chelvey where there is another fine old mansion and a church very like Brockley—dedicated to St. Bridget. Nailsea church is restored but retains its stone pulpit and a monument to one Richard Cole and his family.

My halt at Nailsea enabled me to visit Tickenham, a very interesting and charming place with a church dedicated to SS. Quiricus and Julietta, a curious dedication. Here the chancel arch is probably Norman and early Norman too. The two arcades are not much later and in the north aisle are three thirteenth century effigies, two knights in armour and a lady. Up and down the various windows I found a good deal of the old glass. The porch seemed to be of the thirteenth century; an interesting building.

From Tickenham I went through Nailsea again, a long straggling place, across the broad valley by very various roads to Backwell on the southern hills. This again is a delightful spot. The village has a prettily situated church with a very good Perpendicular double-windowed tower quite of the second class. Perhaps the most interesting part of the church is the chapel to the north of the chancel, where there is a tomb with effigy of a knight in armour. The chapel seems to have been the mortuary of the Rodneys and this tomb is probably that of one of them.

Under the hills and the woods I went into Flax Bourton where I found a small Perpendicular church full of Norman things; the south door, a very fine thing indeed, with a carving of St. Michael and the Devil, and the chancel arch with other carvings; a notable church.

A mile away from Flax Bourton in the hills is Barrow Gurney church, of which only the south aisle is old. But this south aisle is of great interest, for, near by, there once stood a Benedictine convent dedicated to the Blessed Virgin and St. Edward, King and Martyr, and this aisle was the nun's chapel. Little or nothing remains, however, even here, to remind us of those days. There were two Benedictine Nunneries in Somerset, one here and one as we have seen at Cannington. Close by is a fine old mansion, Barrow Court.

And now at last I turned, and with what growing reluctance I cannot truly express, to the last place in all my journey; Long Ashton already within the shadow of Bristol. Of Long Ashton, I have nothing to say but only this, that I was sorry to leave it for that resounding city whose sound is the sound of iron upon iron, the oldest port in old England, and I believe a county all to itself. As I came in to it I realised that my journey was over and done with, that I was back once more in the too well known torture of the great cities, and that to Somerset I had all unknowing bidden adieu.

Wells Cathedral.
The Apple Stealer

INDEX

B

H

I

M

N

THE END

Richard Clay and Sons, Limited,
BRUNSWICK STREET, STAMFORD STREET, S.E.,
AND BUNGAY, SUFFOLK.

Kent. By WALTER JERROLD. With Illustrations by HUGH THOMSON.

PALL MALL GAZETTE.—"A book over which it is a pleasure to pore, and which every man of Kent or Kentish man, or 'foreigner,' should promptly steal, purchase, or borrow. . . . The illustrations alone are worth twice the money charged for the book."

TRUTH.—"It will rank as one of the very best volumes in an admirable series."

Sussex. By E. V. LUCAS. With Illustrations by FREDERICK L. GRIGGS.

WESTMINSTER GAZETTE.—"A delightful addition to an excellent series. . . . Such beauty and character has the county, it requires of the writer who would do justice to Sussex a graceful and sprightly pen, as well as fulness of knowledge. Mr. Lucas is well endowed in these things. His knowledge of Sussex is shown in so many fields, with so abundant and yet so natural a flow, that one is kept entertained and charmed through every passage of his devious progress. . . . The drawings with which Mr. Frederick Griggs illustrates this charming book are equal in distinction to any work this admirable artist has given us."

Berkshire. By JAMES EDMUND VINCENT. With Illustrations by FREDERICK L. GRIGGS.

DAILY CHRONICLE.—"We consider this book one of the best in an admirable series, and one which should appeal to all who love this kind of literature."

DAILY TELEGRAPH.—"The author shows himself in this book to be possessed of a pretty touch in descriptive writing, a good eye for country, and a keen interest in literary and historical associations."

Oxford and the Cotswolds. By H. A. EVANS. With Illustrations by FREDERICK L. GRIGGS.

DAILY TELEGRAPH.—"The author is everywhere entertaining and fresh, never allowing his own interest to flag, and thereby retaining the close attention of the reader."

COUNTY GENTLEMAN.—"No better study of any well-marked division of the country has appeared."

Hampshire. By D. H. MOUTRAY READ. With Illustrations by ARTHUR B. CONNOR.

WORLD.—"Mr. Moutray Read has written a well-nigh perfect guide-book, and he has been thrice blessed in his illustrator, Mr. Arthur B. Connor."

STANDARD.—"In our judgment, as excellent and as lively a book as has yet appeared in the Highways and Byways Series."

MACMILLAN AND CO., LTD., LONDON.

Dorset. By Sir FREDERICK TREVES. With Illustrations by JOSEPH PENNELL.

STANDARD.—"Sir Frederick Treves is to be congratulated on a breezy, delightful book, full of sidelights on men and manners, and quick in the interpretation of all the half-inarticulate lore of the countryside."

FIELD.—"This volume, in literary style, and happy illustration by the artist, is one of the very best of the series."

Somerset. By EDWARD HUTTON. With Illustrations by NELLY ERICHSEN.

Devon and Cornwall. By ARTHUR H. NORWAY. With Illustrations by JOSEPH PENNELL and HUGH THOMSON.

DAILY CHRONICLE.—"So delightful that we would gladly fill columns with extracts were space as elastic as imagination. . . . The text is excellent; the illustrations of it are even better."

South Wales. By A. G. BRADLEY. With Illustrations by FREDERICK L. GRIGGS.

TIMES.—"A book which may be described honestly as one of the best of its kind which has ever been published."

SPECTATOR.—"Mr. Bradley has certainly exalted the writing of a combined archæological and descriptive guide-book into a species of literary art. The result is fascinating."

North Wales. By A. G. BRADLEY. With Illustrations by HUGH THOMSON and JOSEPH PENNELL.

PALL MALL GAZETTE.—"To read this fine book makes us eager to visit every hill and every valley that Mr. Bradley describes with such tantalising enthusiasm. It is a work of inspiration, vivid, sparkling, and eloquent—a deep well of pleasure to every lover of Wales."

Cambridge and Ely. By Rev. EDWARD CONYBEARE. With Illustrations by FREDERICK L. GRIGGS.

Also an ***Edition de Luxe.*** Limited to 250 copies. Royal 8vo, 21s. net.

ATHENÆUM.—"A volume which, light and easily read as it is, deserves to rank with the best literature about the county."

GUARDIAN.—"One of the most attractive volumes of the series that has yet appeared. . . . Artist and writer have combined to give us a book of singular charm."

MACMILLAN AND CO., LTD., LONDON

East Anglia. By WILLIAM A. DUTT. With Illustrations by JOSEPH PENNELL.

WORLD.—"Of all the fascinating volumes in the 'Highways and Byways' series, none is more pleasant to read. . . . Mr. Dutt, himself an East Anglian, writes most sympathetically and in picturesque style of the district."

Derbyshire. By J. B. FIRTH. With Illustrations by NELLY ERICHSEN.

STANDARD.—"One of the brightest contributions to the 'Highways and Byways' series. We have found Mr. Firth a careful guide, with a nice way of choosing from a great mass of material just such scenes and memories as appeal to the traveller of taste."

DAILY TELEGRAPH.—"The result is altogether delightful, for 'Derbyshire' is as attractive to the reader in his arm-chair as to the tourist wandering amid the scenes Mr. Firth describes so well."

Yorkshire. By ARTHUR H. NORWAY. With Illustrations by JOSEPH PENNELL and HUGH THOMSON.

PALL MALL GAZETTE.—"The wonderful story of Yorkshire's past provides Mr. Norway with a wealth of interesting material, which he has used judiciously and well; each grey ruin of castle and abbey he has re-erected and re-peopled in the most delightful way. A better guide and story-teller it would be hard to find."

Lake District. By A. G. BRADLEY. With Illustrations by JOSEPH PENNELL.

ST. JAMES'S GAZETTE.—"A notable edition—an engaging volume, packed with the best of all possible guidance for tourists. For the most part the artist's work is as exquisite as anything of the kind he has done."

DAILY TELEGRAPH.—"Mr. Bradley has done his work amazingly well. His heart has been in his subject. Mr. Joseph Pennell has found abundant scope for his graceful art."

Donegal and Antrim. By STEPHEN GWYNN. With Illustrations by HUGH THOMSON.

DAILY CHRONICLE.—"Charming. . . . Mr. Gwynn makes some of the old legends live again for us, he brings the peasants before us as they are, his descriptions have the 'tear and the smile' that so well suit the country, and with scarcely an exception he has brought his facts and his figures up to date."

DAILY TELEGRAPH.—"A perfect book of its kind, on which author, artist, and publisher have lavished of their best."

Normandy. By PERCY DEARMER, M.A. With Illustrations by JOSEPH PENNELL.

ST. JAMES'S GAZETTE.—"A charming book. . . . Mr. Dearmer is as arrestive in his way as Mr. Pennell. He has the true topographic eye. He handles legend and history in entertaining fashion."

MACMILLAN AND CO., LTD., LONDON.